BOOKS BY MARY COLUM

LIFE AND THE DREAM

FROM THESE ROOTS

Life and
the Dream

Life and the Dream

MARY COLUM

DOUBLEDAY & COMPANY, INC.
Garden City, N. Y. 1947

Copyright, 1928, 1931, 1945, 1946, by Mary Colum

To my grandmother
CATHERINE GUNNING
whose wake and funeral are described
in this book.

ACKNOWLEDGMENTS

Thanks are due the following publishers and authors for permission to include the selections listed below:

Alfred A. Knopf, Inc.—for the quotations by Elinor Wylie, from *Collected Poems of Elinor Wylie*, copyright, 1921, 1923, 1924, 1925, 1926, 1927, 1928, 1929, 1932, by Alfred A. Knopf, Inc.

Seumas MacManus—for the quotations by Ethna Carberry, from *The Four Winds*.

The Macmillan Company—for "Promise," from *Collected Poems of A.E.*; and for the quotations from the *Collected Poems of William Butler Yeats*.

Charles Scribner's Sons—for "Love in the Valley," by George Meredith.

CONTENTS

Life and
the Dream

ৡ⌇ CHAPTER I

Childhood

UNTIL THE DAY I DIE my first day at boarding school will stand out in my mind, my passing into a community of girls of all ages from small children to girls of seventeen and eighteen and a community of nuns, and to a life in which each hour of the day was divided into work and prayer with, at two intervals of the day, some time for recreation. It was a little like the change after death that one finds described by mediums in books on spiritualism. One felt a little as if one had died and passed into a new world which had some connection with the world one had left. But what made the day stand out was something more than even this. I had plenty of books in my preschool childhood, but in the west of Ireland there were few pictures and almost no music except some mediocre performances on a piano or a violin provided by friends or members of the family who had the common training in playing a musical instrument usual in those days. But my first day in school I came face to face with reproductions of great pictures, all naturally, in a convent, religious—Murillo virgins, Rubens's "Descent from the Cross," a photograph of Michelangelo's Pietà, reproductions of portraits of popes—all sorts of popes, old, young, handsome, and ugly. A sort of whirling ecstasy that was not all pleasure came over me as I encountered these creations of the spirit even in what were probably poor reproductions. On that first day, also, I was brought up against great music, and the effect of everything kept me awake at night wondering what sort of life these musicmakers and picturemakers had led and what they had cared about at all. A somewhat older girl—I was about thirteen—was deputed to attach herself to me for a few days to make me familiar with the routine, the rules and habits followed in the school, and in the evening she walked once or twice around the veranda that surrounded a large inner court and explained the hours of rising and of study. The door of the brightly lighted recreation hall was open, and from it there came the sounds of a piano played as I had never heard anybody play before, and a music that was so different from anything I had ever listened to that it, too, seemed out of another world. A nun, waiting for the girls to come in, was seated at a piano playing to herself.

"Sister Sebastian," said my companion. "She is the best musician in the convent. She was a great pianist when she was out in the world."

I suppose she was really one of those well-trained musicians who from time to time in every country give a public recital, but a great pianist I am sure she was not. To a schoolgirl's inexperience the rumor of her public recitals was glamorous. I tried to shed my companion with her explanations of rules and schedules and stepped inside the door to hear better the wonderful sounds that were coming forth. What she was playing I had no idea, but she was lost in her own music, bent over the piano so that I could not see her face, only the top of her black veil and her guimpe. Finally she raised her head and, seeing me standing inside the door, half clinging to the lintel, she said sharply, "My child, why are you not in your study hall?" Then, walking towards me with quick nervous steps, she said, "Oh, I see, you are one of the new girls. You should not be in the recreation hall for ten minutes yet." She was, I think, annoyed at being caught playing to herself, or maybe such self-indulgence was against the rule of the order. She was a tall young woman with very dark eyes, a slight stoop, and a face that still remains in my mind when more intimate ones have faded out. Her mouth was large and bulged a little, and as she stood talking to me she alternately fingered the huge rosary that hung from her leather belt and the black cross that hung on her white guimpe. She was full of charm and mystery. I was aching to ask her to go on playing, but my tongue was tied and I could not speak. She was nervous and high-strung in all her movements and in all her conversation, and I was equally so, so we made no progress at all.

Soon after the sound of a tolling bell the room filled with laughing, noisy girls, all dressed in the school uniform of black or dark blue with a little white collar, some wearing blue cordons and some red, draped round their shoulders. The girls with the blue cordons were the Children of Mary and those with the red cordons the Children of the Holy Angels. You served a sort of apprenticeship before you achieved either. I had been brought up very strictly in a discipline and obedience to elders that allowed for no abandon before them, and so I was astonished and thrilled at what happened next.

Sister Sebastian, who had been playing the wonder music to herself, was again seated at the piano and was beating out a waltz with great vigor. A tall girl with long fair hair—she seemed to me wonderfully beautiful—pulled off the long blue cordon that hung over her shoulder and danced up the middle of the hall, waving her sashlike cordon and singing, "I'll be all smiles, tonight, love, I'll be all smiles tonight, though my heart should break tomorrow, I'll be all smiles tonight." She was followed rapidly by a couple of other girls, who, pulling the ribbons off their long hair, let it float free, all joining in, "I'll be all smiles tonight, love, I'll be all smiles tonight."

Sister Sebastian stopped playing and rose to her feet; she clapped her hands and then pounded on the piano top with a little baton. "You must dance like ladies." She stood angrily by the piano stool, but was soon surrounded by the more daring of the girls, saying in their, to me, strange, soft Dublin accents, "Ah, Sister, Sister darling!"

She raised her pince-nez severely and waited until each girl stood in a line with her partner, the tall girls dancing the part of men, the short girls that of women, and soon the whole room was filled with waltzing girls. It all seemed wonderful to me, brought up, for the most part, by two old people and by men who were puzzled as to how to dress me for school or what to do at all with a young female person, except to keep her in careful ignorance and away from companionship that might prove to be what they thought harmful.

My clothing had been entrusted to a seamstress after much male frowning over the trousseau list sent by the school. One item, a bath dress, caused much bewilderment, and it was finally decided that a dressing gown filled all the requirements of that nature. But when the wardrobe sister went over my clothes and found the bath dress missing, she demanded, "Well, how are you going to take a bath? In a chemise, I suppose?" Nobody in the school took a bath naked, or ever looked at her own naked body. I was humiliated that my family had not been sufficiently advanced in culture to the stage where people were dressed for taking a bath, and I explained with some self-pity to the sister that I had no female relations to really inform me about such items, my available adult relatives at the moment being all male.

In the classroom I was also humiliated. I could read French well, but I could not write a simple sentence correctly. I had not been drilled in verbs or genders or subjunctive moods. I could with ease toss off from French into English fairly difficult works, but my French accent was not good; neither, looking back, was anybody else's except that of the few girls who had previously been in school in France or Belgium.

II

I could write English well, but I had not mastered properly the rules of punctuation. I had read enormously for my age—everything: poetry, novels, essays, history. Once, when a close female relative arrived on a visit and loudly professed her horror at the literature I had been immersing myself in, all the really thrilling books were put on high shelves out of my reach and a couple of schoolgirl tales, some Bible histories, and Maria Edgeworth's *Early Lessons* were left on a table for my perusal, beside some abstruse works that it was taken for granted no child would want to look at. But in desperation, after perusing the fare thought proper for me by this relative, I tried with the help of a dictionary to chew through Kant's *Critique of Pure Reason*, Burke on *The Sublime and Beautiful*, Locke on *The Human Understanding*. It may be assumed that no little girl of eleven or twelve could get anything out of these works, and my reason tells me she could not. But the truth of it was that I did, perhaps through some of those extrasensory powers that people now talk about, or perhaps somehow something seeped in through the pores, for though I have never looked at any of these works since, I still remember sentences from them. One of them ran like this: "All knowledge derives from experience, but does not begin with experience," and I pondered on it for years, not so much as to its meaning, but about the meaning of the word "derives," for in no language have I ever understood a word from the dictionary meaning, but only when some experience of life made it an emotional as well as an intellectual possession.

Not only did I get something from these books but they developed some critical part of my mind to a sharpened degree, to a sort of priggishness, so that I would listen to my elders to see if they contradicted themselves, or if they knew a great deal or understood the sort of words that were in these books. Whenever anybody used in his conversation a word that I had never heard before, I would be so enchanted that I used it myself at the first opportunity. Once, when an uncle was preparing to go to a race meeting, he asked a boy employed around the yard if he thought a certain horse would win the race. "Ah, no, sir; sure she's only an old bastard of a thing. Tommy"—that was the horse's owner—"doesn't know how to breed a horse." I waited for a chance to use the new word, and when the dressmaker came to fit me with a new dress, I fingered it with derision and said, "It is only an old bastard of a thing. She does not know how to make a dress." It was years before I had any understanding of the resulting horror that my words caused; to my bewilderment I was punished, and I could not comprehend why, for I had looked up the word in a dictionary and had found it meant "illegitimate; of inferior quality; born out of wedlock," and as a word to describe something inferior, such as an ugly-looking dress, it had sounded first-rate. On another occasion, when I had exhibited a new addition to my vocabulary before a visitor, he had burst into uncontrollable laughter and said with delight, "This is the best example of an *enfant terrible* in the whole country." I knew enough French to know what these words meant separately but not in combination. The punishment also on this occasion for my vocabulary was bewildering to me, but it increased my curiosity about words and my interest in them. The incident caused an uncle who came to the house infrequently to say with hostility, "Nobody ever ought to try to bring up another's child. She ought to be packed off to boarding school, the little wretch." I never forgot this, and with the intensity of memory that is perhaps peculiar to my race, I never now see him without remembering it, though he is a feeble and pathetic old man, disappointed and frustrated in life.

After the books had been put out of my reach I had no way of passing those long hours of childhood. I had not much outlet for my energies, for I had no playfellows, though occasionally a little girl would come to tea with me and we would try to make cakes together. Becoming baffled by the difficulty of the books that were within my reach, baffled by the hard ones and depressed by the silly ones, I took to roaming the field with a couple of dogs, red Irish setters. Horses or asses were often grazing in the fields, and I would mount them bareback, except for a piece of sacking instead of a saddle, and jog around. But once the horse I mounted was young and spirited, and besides his back was too wide for my knees to get any grip. He proceeded to race swiftly around the field and soon tossed me off, and though I suffered some internal injury that ever after came against me, I did not dare to tell my family, though for years and years it affected me and perhaps was responsible for numerous illnesses.

After that I thought up another diversion: there was a small, shallow brook that ran slowly near the house, and I conceived the idea of damming it up and making a large pool into which I could put some little fish. It was tedious work, for when I had built up a nice little construction, next morning the brook, though moving slowly, would have washed most of it away. However, once when the sun had dried out the water somewhat, I succeeded in achieving something that looked like a dam that might last, with great expense of labor dragging stones from neighboring fields and filling the interstices with mud. The labor messed up my dress and pinafore a great deal and of course made my shoes wet and muddy, but I proceeded home with a sense of satisfaction that the knowledge of difficult labor accomplished successfully gives one, and I was very happy. It was my intention somehow to get my dress and shoes changed before any too observant eyes beheld me. But when I got inside the door a scent of perfume in the air made my nerves shake; the relative who had caused the books to be placed out of my reach was there; she lived a distance away and had a habit of descending only at intervals, and I had thought I was free of her for a long time. But there she was, daintily dressed, her perfume like a breath in the air. She put up her hands in horror as I approached. "You little savage," she said, "how did you get yourself so dirty?" My uncle took his pipe out of his mouth and grasped his chin in bewilderment, an habitual gesture with him. From the distance I saw Bridgie waving a sponge and making signals for me to come out quickly.

My roamings as well as my readings were then curtailed, but not long afterwards, at the dressmaker's—she lived in a little house outside the church—I picked up a journal off the table called the *Family Herald*, and soon I was embarked on the sort of literature I had never found in our house. It was absolutely fascinating—about lords and dukes and beautiful poor young women who, wandering down a lane, met the earl's son, or it would be about an unknown young woman getting a job as wardrobe maid in a theater and who, through listening to rehearsals and performances, memorized the leading part so that when the star got a heart attack the maid was able at a moment's notice to take her place and play the role so magnificently that all the papers next morning greeted her as the greatest actress of the day. From that on, my ambition was to be an actress, varied with a desire to be an explorer, because about this epoch also there came into my possession some dazzling American literature called *Frank Read's Inventions*.

These were little books with pictures on the covers showing Frank Read's steam man, Frank Read's engine, and the contents were enthralling tales of all sorts of adventures engaged in by Frank Read, an inventor of a kind that was never seen on land or sea; he had two assistants, Barney, a redheaded Irishman, and Pomp, a Negro. I was as delighted with this sort of book as I had previously been with Scott's novels, Shakespeare's plays, or Jane Austen or the Brontës.

III

My life might have gone on all my days in this country by the sea, with its long range of mountains, its little lakes, its *raths*, its old ruins, its old customs and folk tales, but that a sudden death in the family changed my habitation and my future. I had had a peculiar relation with some of the old people around, whom I loved devotedly and with whom I used to go all alone to drink tea. A great many of them could not read or write, or if they ever knew how, they had forgotten, and they were in the habit of asking me to read the letters they received from their relatives in America and to write the answers for them. I was sworn to secrecy as to the contents of these letters, and nothing nor nobody could have pried out of me what was in the American letters or in the replies I wrote to them. The letters received would all contain money orders sent by some loving, hard-working son or daughter, and the replies would be very rambling, dictated to me by the old mother and father speaking in concert. I would seat myself at the kitchen table with a pen and ink and a twopenny packet of ruled writing paper, and first take down, more or less verbatim, what they wished said in these communications to America. These were always filled with bad news, though not of an especially startling kind, but always it would have to be stated that the mother or father was half dead with bronchitis, that the horse or cow had died or the newly ·hatched ducks strayed away, never to be seen again, and the horse or ass was growing too old to be driven any longer to the fair to do the marketing. When I had reduced all the miseries to paper the old father or mother would say, "Now, little colleen, let you English it better and I'll give you a nice blue duck egg."

Whatever money they got from America, they always told the neighbors that the amount was either double or only half as much. Though one family owed money to a relative of mine who was always being promised payment when the next money order from America arrived, I would never reveal that several money orders had come and had been cashed.

I enjoyed the chore of letter writing, and especially I delighted in the names of the strange, distant towns to which I addressed these missives—San Francisco, Chattanooga, Philadelphia, Nome. Even after I went to boarding school and, later, to college, the letters would often be kept until I came back on vacations and could indite the replies. My handwriting, however, got more illegible the more extensive became my education, and sometimes the loving son or daughter who received my screed complained that the letters were hard to read now that the nice round handwriting of my childhood became the scrawl of the university student. Once when the son of one old couple came home he gave me a brooch as a present for writing his mother's letters and reading his to her and never revealing the contents, and he said to me in a strong acquired American accent, "You have been a real gentleman to my ma." I treasured the compliment so seriously that ever since, when in a dilemma of any kind as to how to behave, I ask myself, not "How would a lady behave?" but "How would a gentleman behave?"

The death of my grandmother cut me off from this life except for a week or two on vacation. She had always been an invalid with chronic bronchitis, which few were free from in that rainy climate. She would spend a part, or the whole, of every day in bed, and though of all my family she was the one I loved the most, I some days saw but little of her, and she never had sufficient energy to pay a great deal of attention to what I was doing, though when she did she was, like all Irish people, very strict, with far stricter ideas of truth and honor than I ever found in anybody else. She was very beautiful, or to me she was; her face was like the face on the head of Dante which we had in the parlor. There was some tradition that she had Italian blood or was of Italian descent. She seemed to me a reservoir of knowledge, though the account she gave me of Dante was limited, I remember, to a tale of a romantic relation he had with a lady named Beatrice whom he loved all his life. It was long afterwards before I knew him as the author of the *Divine Comedy*. Though she was not well educated, she read a great deal in a scattered, half-attentive sort of way, mostly in bed, and one volume she had beside her, called *The Earthly Paradise*, I thought to be a book of pious meditation until after her death I picked it up and found it to be glamorous tales in verse by William Morris.

When, during one cold and stormy winter week, her bronchitis became first influenza and then pneumonia, nobody in that household of men noticed that she was any more ill than ordinary. Bridgie, who brought in her tea and toast, remarked that she had not eaten it. The doctor who came on his usual visit said vaguely that he thought her daughter, my aunt, should be telegraphed for. The morning after this, when her tea was brought to her bedside, she did not recognize Bridgie. As I came into her room I heard her say very solemnly, "Be sure that Eddie's confirmation suit and shoes are ready. Do you hear?" She repeated, "Get them ready."

"Saints in heaven," Bridgie exclaimed, "the poor woman is raving! Oh, she's done this time. After all she's been through, she's finished this time."

My grandmother turned her dark eyes on me unrecognizingly, strangely, her face flushed, her lips muttering something undistinguishable except for the name "Eddie" which kept coming at intervals.

I flung myself on her and sobbed, "Oh, Grannie, Uncle Eddie is long dead, but this is me, this is your grandchild." She gripped me a little weakly in her arms, but I do not think she ever again knew who I was.

Her bed was then made with the best sheets and coverlets; during this operation she was somehow placed sitting in an armchair; her brown death habit, long since ready, was laid on the pillow. The death habit had often been beside her during other illnesses, and there was nothing very unusual in its being placed there beside her. Various members of the family came on by train during the day, and a priest arrived to give her the last sacraments. He stayed with her long and came back in the evening when summoned once more. I still remember with pain the scene around her deathbed. Her money, what she had of it, was willed to me to be used only for my education, but her little trinkets and other treasures she tried to divide among the family in a brief moment or two of recovery from the delirium of her fever. As again she sank into delirium the whole family, led by the priest, knelt in prayer, and in her death agony, her struggles for breath, her head turning from side to side, she must have been disturbed by this rush of voices, praying louder and louder the more she struggled, as if they wished to storm the heavens.

In the middle of the Litany for the Dying, one among the kneeling figures arose and said solemnly and peremptorily, "The end is at hand. Will all the members of the family leave until her soul has passed?" We rose and left, not only the room, but the house, because it was an old superstition that none of the blood kin of a dying person should be in the house of death at the last moment. Everybody in that country always followed old customs at death or burial or christening, whether their reason gave allegiance to them or not. Hastily pulling on coats, we went outside to the yard in the chilling March midnight. We stayed a long time, for death, like birth, is sometimes delayed past its due. But at last, in the morning light, there appeared at the door one of the old women who, according to custom, attended houses of death and who laid out the corpse, and she beckoned to my grandfather. He came towards us as we sat crouched in a shed, and said softly and sobbingly, "You can all go in now; her soul has passed. May the Lord have mercy on her soul!"

When the old women had performed the death rite and garbed her in her brown habit, and brushed her straight black hair under a little cap, and closed her dark shining eyes with cold pennies, her face looked wonderful, more wonderful than in life, the wrinkles all smoothed out, the bones beautiful beneath the fine skin. One of the old women told me that she had certainly met God, and that her still face had on it the smile of those who had entered Paradise. But the smile seemed but a painful twist that wrenched her mouth out of place, and her face, beautiful as it was, looked very mournful and not the face of one who, departing this life, had seen Paradise opening before her. But I believed she had surely met God, for she had never harmed anyone and had spent her life thinking of the good she could do to others. If she gave away something she could not afford, she would cheerfully say, as if that explained everything, "It is for others." It was a quarter of a century afterwards, in France, before I heard again that insistent justification of anything that was difficult to do, or of possessions that were hard to give away, "It is for others!"

IV

My grandmother was waked two days and two nights, and the third day she was buried. At her wake people prayed for her soul all night in her room, and in the rest of the house they regaled themselves with refreshments. On the funeral day the tables were covered with baked meats, and people ate and drank as at a party. An uncle who lived, for the most part, on whisky had not come to life from the night she died until the morning of the burial, though at intervals somebody had tried to rouse him from his drunken stupor, but it was only on the funeral morning that he appeared dressed carefully in his stiff white shirt and black clothes with a crepe band on his arm.

The yard was black with people in funeral clothes, and the hearse and mourning coach drawn by black horses came from the nearby town. As her coffin was carried to the hearse by the men of her family, the old women who had prepared her body walked after them and were suddenly joined from out the crowd by two other crones in black shawls and white caps, and it was then, for the first time, I heard the traditional keen, the wail for the dead. It began on a very low tone, the four old women wailing in unison; then it rose higher and higher and louder and louder, as the prayers in her death chamber had grown louder, and finally the cry became words rhythmically chanted. I have often heard that the Irish keen makes the blood run cold, that it is like the wailing of lost souls. Eerie and unearthly it certainly was, but it seemed to be natural that she should be thus keened to her grave by four old wailing women. The words were in Gaelic, but we knew or were given the meaning of them, and I here write down what I remember of them. The words were ancient and were doubtless wailed for many corpses and at many burials, but I think that, maybe, these old women added a few lines that were meant especially for this dead woman. They were recited with ceremony, the old women, at one part, turning aside from the coffin and addressing the assembled people:

Tomorrow and every day the sun will bring delight and pleasure, but never more shall your breast beat at the return of his beams in the morning, generous and wellborn woman, cold is your rest! *Ochone agus Ochone O!*

Not of the blood of the Sassanach was she but of the high line of the Gael—O'Rourkes of Breffni, O'Donnels of Tyrconnell, O'Kellys of Hymany, and a hundred fighting princes of the Gael.

The reapers will reap and the young lambs play and bleat, but never again shall your eyes see the harvest or the spring returning, generous and wellborn woman, cold is your rest. *Ochone agus Ochone O!*

V

Not long afterwards I went to live, not of my own free will, with the relative who had got the books removed out of my reach and who had called me a little savage. Life then changed enormously, and I was not free for even five minutes of the day. I wore shining buttoned shoes and neat well-made clothes, and I practiced the piano and was made to learn by heart a book called the *Twenty-four Acts of Rudeness* to be avoided and the *Twenty-four Rules of Politeness* to be practiced. I also learned to embroider and made scalloped underwear for myself. I practiced hemstitching and crochet stitching and embroidery stitches, gradually being changed from a tomboy.

What stands out in my memory of this stitching, which was called fancywork, was the cushions I had to help her to make—and not so much the cushions, with their embroideries in colored silks, as the stuffing of these cushions with sea gulls' feathers. The sea gulls in winter would come up in droves to the houses on the coast looking for what food they could pick up, and they would be caught by boys in a sort of trap called a bird cradle and sold or given to the housewives for pillows and cushions. I had seen chickens killed without any emotions, but the first time I saw a sea gull's head chopped off I got a strange nervous shivering down the spine, and it lasted for days and disappeared after a secret bout of crying in the scullery. That same shivering has come back at intervals all my life whenever anything disagreeable has happened. A quite different emotion had affected me before, when I saw a fox killed and his brush handed to the first lady who had been in at the killing, who, I remember, was a plain, older woman in a very dingy-looking habit and a billycock hat with one piece of elastic around the roll of hair at the back of her head and another piece under her chin. I had been brought up to think foxes ought to be killed on account of all the chickens they had stolen and eaten, and for their peculiar wickedness, which I had read about in fables—Aesop's and La Fontaine's—so that the dogs and the hunters seemed to be doing a good deed.

This emotion took another coloring, however, when a few days later another fox was started, and at the bend of a road where a cliff overhung, he came suddenly face to face with myself and my uncle. Not knowing where to turn to escape from the dogs barking in the distance, before fleeing he stood for a moment looking at us with mystery and misery in his eyes, all his slender, swift, nervous body throwing out an awareness that his lease of life would be soon over, and that for this he was born, to be pursued by barking dogs and shouts of "Tallyho!" and men and women on horseback until he could run no more and would finally give in to the relentless chase. That a fox could know he was going to die, could show it in his eyes, made him seem a mysterious being, struck with a sadness that communicated itself and made me, who did not then know death, who never knew a person who had died, partly realize, which I had difficulty in realizing, that nothing lasted, that no life of man or beast was long. I have only twice since known people who, during a hunt, gazed into the frightened misery of a fox's eyes. The hunters, for the most, would see only his fleeing back and his brush, or his cunning head, but if they could see his strange, anxious eyes they might never hunt him to his death.

VI

My reading was thoroughly supervised and limited, for the most part, to works of piety. That life, however, did not last, for the pretty relative did not live long. I was terrified of her, but looking back now, I realize she was young and gay and feminine and dainty and high-spirited and flirtatious. She would talk gaily and wittily to men, and there would be laughter and banter whenever she was around. Her flirtations were numerous and, I am sure, harmless; her husband, anyway, never seemed to mind them. I was always stumbling on them. Once I came on her sitting on a bench by the sea with a very nice man with whom she was having a gay and mocking conversation, and he kissed her hand laughingly with his mustached lips, and I was quite thrilled and thought I should like him to do that to me. I walked over, and I shall never forget her look of anger and embarrassment as I stood before them. She misunderstood me as always, for I was envying her. In my grown-up days I have always thought the conventions that hemmed in men and women and kept them from these gay and whimsical and amusing friendships were perfectly savage. I was as happy as she was once, when a strange man called at the house about a horse. He did not know her, and taking her to be the daughter of the house instead of the wife of the man he had come to see, he remained cheerfully to drink tea with her. She slipped her wedding ring, as I had often seen her do, into the drawer of the tea table and engaged in happy and whimsical conversation, talking rapidly.

"You are beautiful," he said to her. "I never met anybody like you." I listened from a corner, entranced, to every word he said, and thought it was wonderful to have men talk like that to you. On this occasion she really wanted me around, because she could have sent me out of the room if she had wished. Like all Irish-women she did not want things to go beyond a certain point, past laughter and hand kissing. She seemed a little alarmed, I remember, when this horsy stranger, at parting, lifted a lock of hair at her neck and said, "It is spun gold." I wanted him badly to look at my hair, which I thought was prettier, but he barely even noticed me.

Not so long after, she died. The day she first became ill she sat quietly by the fire all day, hunched up. It was windy outside, and the waves, the wild Atlantic waves, were dashing up very high on the shore. Taking advantage of her quietude, I went out along the rocky seashore by myself for a long way, delighting in the sea spray, the waves and the wind, and at having escaped her supervision, jumping from rock to rock. Until I thought of going home I had not noticed that my frock was wet with sea spray, the leather of my kid shoes scraped by the rocks. In a minute there was slipping from me the carefulness and neatness she was trying to instill in me. What was worse, my new hair ribbon blew off into the sea, and the ringlets she had put in my hair were blown out by the wet sea wind.

Going home in fear, I found her still seated in an armchair by the fire. Tremblingly I waited to be scolded, but beyond asking me hoarsely to bring the tea tray closer to the fire she did not say anything or notice my appearance. She went to bed, haltingly climbing the stairs, and she never rose again. In a few days she was dead of pneumonia, the curse of that climate. Nobody was prepared for such an illness. The local doctors were poor, and before a good one could be got from the nearest large city, she was dead. The high wind that had started the sea to roar continued all through her illness, the waves dashing up on the rocks that were beneath her window. Her dog moaned all day and night, and on the cold early morning of her death I saw her husband standing on a rock looking out helplessly into the sea in the twilight of the morning and muttering and muttering to himself. She was young, about thirty, and I think she had been happy, and I knew happier without my living with her than with it, but she felt she had a duty to me. She had never been affectionate and had rarely kissed me, but when, without her, I was once more in the care of men, it was not the same as it had been before. I was growing out of childhood into adolescence, and though I had been happy only when left to my own devices and never bossed or interfered with, I was very unhappy after her death. The interval, though short, between her death and my being sent to school was a bewildered and miserable one. Mentally, in some ways, I was overdeveloped, as reading and an attempt to think will overdevelop a child. I had read too many books, too much poetry, and, difficult as was my adjustment to boarding-school life with its large community of girls and hard-working nuns, it saved me, perhaps, from becoming a problem child, or a neurotic, or whatever lonely and nervous beings become or are turned into during the bewildering part of life's journey that is childhood.

ॐ CHAPTER 2

Boarding-School Days

A CUBICLE in a cold dormitory, a narrow iron bed with a white counterpane, a combination prie-dieu and washstand, a religious picture, a little space for prayer books and meditation books, a hook for a dressing gown, a mug for a toothbrush—this was my new domain. Each of about twenty little girls, all of the same age or nearly the same age, had its replica, for this was the juniors' dormitory. There were also a middle and a senior dormitory equipped in a like way. I arrived at school a month after the term opened and so was the last of the new girls. The first night, once in bed in the dark, the last prayer said, the impression of the music and the dancing and singing faded, and there rushed over me, not exactly a homesickness, for I was glad to be at school, but the sense of loneliness that comes over one in unaccustomed surroundings, and a dread of the new life and the strange faces. I have at no time been adaptable, have never found it easy to accustom myself to change of any kind—changes in people, or places, or things. So I cried myself to sleep, not only that first night but many nights.

Sometimes waking early in the morning at that hour when physical life is at its lowest ebb and the nerves alone seem alive and at their sharpest intensity, I would wonder who or what I was and why I was alive at all, getting sometimes, I think, almost outside of myself in some strange way, and I would come to a frightened realization, without being able to put any name to it, that neither I nor any of my companions were completely conscious, and, my head covered with blankets, I would keep saying, "I—I—I—what am I?—I . . ." But the "I's" stopped somewhere, not far below, and I would know that the part of me that was familiar with that "I" was small, that I was incomprehensible to myself and to all others as they were to me.

I would be glad in those cold morning hours to hear the warm sound of bells as the convent awoke and started with every sort of sound except the sound of voices. Then, after many bells—the nuns' rising bell, the bell calling them to office, the Angelus bell —would come the school-rising bell, and soon after there would sound the voice of the dormitory sister giving the morning call. She would walk down between the rows of cubicles accompanied by a girl carrying a bucket of holy water and repeating at intervals, "*Benedicamus Domino*," and the girls would answer, "*Deo gratias.*" The sister would dip a large paintbrush into the bucket and sprinkle a little holy water on everyone. In spite of bell and voice and sprinkling, some sleepyheads always stayed slumbering, and the nun would arouse them, pulling the blankets off their heads. One or two would say determinedly, "I've a sleep today— Sister Vincent gave me a long sleep." This, I was to discover, meant that the infirmary sister, because of a headache or a cold, real or affected, had given them permission to stay in bed until the breakfast bell rang. But except for a few, the whole dormitory rose in the cold morning air, and, slipping on dressing gowns, washed and dressed rapidly in silence. The only sound was that of washing and brushing, the sound of water in vigorous movement in basins, and the swishing of brushes on hair and teeth. Tongues were silent, for it was the rule of the school that there should be no conversation except for needful remarks to the nun on duty from the end of night recreation until halfway through breakfast the next morning, when a gong struck by the refectory sister unloosed tongues in chatter for about ten minutes.

We rose early, at six or before in spring and summer; at half past six or seven in winter. Except in the depth of winter, when the morning light was dim and even dark, we started the day with study. But in winter we went straight down to the chapel after dressing, putting over our heads long black veils, thus obeying Saint Paul's instruction that female locks be covered in church. Even then some of our youthful minds were a little concerned as to whether Saint Paul's obsession with woman's hair could be quite set at rest by these flimsy net veils through which long, shining bronze or blue-black locks were very visible, for there were no short-cropped heads in those days.

In the loneliness and depression which always weighed on me, not only that first morning but on many mornings, a portion of which, I think, was brought on by the long morning fast, going into the little convent chapel, seeing the familiar pictures of the stations of the cross, and hearing the familiar opening of the Mass, "Introibo ad altare Dei. Ad Deum qui laetificat juventutem meam," did a great deal to dispel the gloom. Hearing the words, "God who giveth joy to my youth," I became certain, as undoubtedly did every other little girl kneeling before the altar, that whatever woes our childhood might bring on us, our youth later would be full of every joy, including those mysterious delights of love which novels and poems spoke of.

II

Not only the first days, but the first year was difficult, for convents, like courts and camps, have a traditional ritual handed down through centuries, and to get into the pattern was not easy. And, too, like courts and camps and totalitarian states, convents take no great stock in the individual: everything was for the general good and the general discipline. I spent most of the first day trying to familiarize myself with the rules. All the conventions and customs of a convent were both fascinating and difficult to get used to. Everything I did seemed to be wrong. I kept my seat when I should be standing up; I wore my house shoes when I should be wearing outdoor shoes; unwittingly I made myself audible so conspicuously during silences that for the rest of the year I hardly spoke at all. The schedule of the day's tasks was written out for me by a nun; even the time of private study was carefully mapped—fifteen minutes for this, ten minutes for that. I, who had done pretty well as I liked in the way I liked, found that at ten minutes to three I had to study French irregular verbs every day until I knew them and could repeat all the moods and participles without a mistake, and at half past one I had to practice embroidery stitches on a piece of cotton until I could do them well enough to embroider the blue velvet smoking cap which was given me as "work" to do. I never knew anybody in my life who wore a smoking cap, and if I had, this thing would not have fitted him, for it was too small for my own childish head. When I was sent to a music room to get my competency at the piano looked into, the sister invited me to play some scales, first straight and then in contrary motion. As I had accomplished the feat of being able to read French without knowing irregular verbs, so I had accomplished the feat of being able to play some piano pieces, some Irish airs with variations, something called "A Broken Melody," something described as a Mendelssohn fragment, without learning scales. Inexorably the sister took away all the "pieces" out of my music satchel and gave me a dreary collection called Czerny's "Five Finger Exercises" which I was to practice every day for twenty minutes after the rosary hour. I could not help but notice that the sister regarded music as exercises in fingering and time beats. She played something on the piano and asked me what time it was in. There was a metronome on the top of the piano, but I knew little about the instrument. At her insistence I said that what she was playing was a march, and in some temper she said, "Well, let me see you march to it." It was a miserable interview, and somehow I knew it had no relation whatever to music, to the art of music.

The unpacking of my trunk was another ordeal; it took place in the wardrobe room, where everybody had a locker with her number on it. On the first day there had been the humiliation of the bath-dress incident; now there came further humiliation. I was ashamed of my clothes, both inside and out, ashamed of what was called my school trousseau. It had been supervised by no woman, and some of it had been bought from an English mail-order house which advertised cheap school trousseaus. I had picked some garments out from pictures in the catalogue, and others were made by a seamstress. I did not have new sheets, for it was decided that, from the piles of linen that were then usual in every house, enough could be found for my needs. Consequently, instead of the nice, smooth cotton sheets the Dublin girls had, I had brought hand-woven linen sheets that were enormously heavy and rural-looking. The hemming on my table napkins—which were not new either and which were larger than anybody else's—had a ripped stitch here and there, and they had to be handed over to the sewing sister to mend. My bath towels were too small and my face towels too large. My pillowcases were square instead of the oblong usual ones. Worst of all was the collection of books I had brought. I was supposed to bring no books at all, as the convent supplied all schoolbooks, or the use of books, for fifteen shillings a quarter. But various members of my family had presented me, as parting gifts, with enough to fill a bookshelf. My writing uncle had given me Longfellow's translation of Dante, Maria Edgeworth's *Castle Rackrent*, and Charlotte Brontë's *Jane Eyre*. The uncle who had started life with the idea of being an opera singer in America, and had ended up by being an entertainer at mining camps and at salmon-packing stations in Alaska, gave me *East Lynne*, *The Mystery of a Hansom Cab*, *Lady Audley's Secret*, and *St. Elmo*. In addition, I had a prayer book and a Bible I had won as a prize at a small private day school run by an old Presbyterian lady who always gave prizes of Bibles to her little Papist pupils. The wardrobe sister seemed more astonished at my possession of the King James version of the Bible than at the other works, and she asked me severely who had given it to me. I explained it with some reservations. I had read the Old Testament with avidity, but I had a guilty feeling about it. I knew there was something naughty about certain of the stories, even though I did not quite understand what, and once a highly traveled male visitor, seeing me one evening immersed in the story of Lot, said acidly to my uncle and grandmother, "Why do you let the child read that putrid old book?" My feelings were confused about it all. I had read in many places that the Bible was the Holy Book, the most spiritual work in the world, inspired by God, yet I was almost certain it was not all holy. Still, I was unprepared for the disapproval of the wardrobe sister. "You cannot read that book without supervision," she told me. For years I pondered on all the remarks I had heard about the Bible and arrived at the conviction which has remained with me, that the Old Testament is not a book for the young or the unlearned. The nun confiscated all my books, and, instead, gave me the *Key of Heaven*, the *Introduction to a Devout Life*, and *The Imitation of Christ*.

After a day of humiliations I was delighted when the loud church bell rang, because I knew some convent ceremonial was at hand which would end this unpacking session and deliver me from this inquisitorial sister. It was the hour for the Rosary, and I joined the rest of the school. They were standing in procession. I followed the moving line with the companion assigned to me, and we walked in silence into the garden. I was made happy to see that the nun in charge was the sister who had played the music to herself in the recreation hall the night before. She walked beside the procession, her spirited face trying its best to put on a look of authority, and fingering nervously the long rosary that hung from her leather girdle. "The sorrowful mysteries," she announced. "First, the prayer of Our Lord in the garden. Our Father who art in heaven," she prayed. . . . "Forgive us our trespasses . . ." answered the voices in unison. "Hail Mary, full of grace, the Lord is with thee . . ." prayed the nun. "Holy Mary, mother of God, pray for us sinners . . ." answered the girls. "Second sorrowful mystery . . . Third . . . Fourth . . . Fifth," and so on, and on went the Our Fathers and Hail Marys and Glorias. Into the nuns' graveyard at the end of the garden the procession went, and we stood for a minute before a high cross with the figure of Christ strung on it, the thorn-crowned head turned sideways in pain, the same figure and the same sort of cross one sees at wayside shrines in Europe. But there are no wayside shrines in Ireland, and this was the first time I had seen a high crucifix in the open air. We stood before it to pray for the souls of all that were gone, the souls of all who had died in the world and of those who had died in the convent and were buried in this graveyard. There were rows and rows of graves, each grave with its slender black cross inscribed with the name in religion of the dead nun, the dates of her profession and of her death. In one spot there was the open grave ready for the next member of the community who would die—the little black cross, at the head, as yet nameless and dateless. Death, and making all life a preparation for death, filled the atmosphere, but when the procession left the garden and went on to the chapel, life began again. Sister Sebastian's fingers on the organ brought it back with a glow as she played the accompaniment for a hymn. After the girls sang in unison there was a pause; then a few bars, and a voice sang out alone. This voice, suddenly bursting out in a solo, had in it something so thrilling that I turned in my place to look at the singer in the organ loft, a breach of rule for which I was later reprimanded. It was the girl who had danced down the recreation hall the evening before singing, "I'll be all smiles tonight, love." After the restraint of the company of the dead in the cemetery, this singing lifted the mood of those who had any power of response. The swiftness of the change tore me rapidly away from the humiliations of the day and the gloom of the graves. The hymn the girl sang I heard for the first time:

> I arise from dreams of time,
> And an angel guides my feet
> To the sacred altar throne
> Where Jesus' heart doth beat.

It was a sort of parody of Shelley's "Indian Serenade" that some simple-minded and perhaps erotically inclined religious had turned into a hymn. The girl with the long, fair hair and the strange voice put some magic into the fatuous words and sang it as if it were some mystical love song, as if there was a great love in her heart, and as if she loved above all things to sing. The words were, no doubt, terrible, but then I did not know that, and I was completely carried away. She put some glamour into them, some gorgeous dream of time or of something that time would bring her before it brought her death. The hymn ended, we rose from our knees and genuflected two by two before the high altar, falling into procession, the girl who sang the solo coming last of all. I was trembling with excitement. Outside the dark chapel we kept our ordered ranks in silence until we passed a little gate that led into the grounds beyond. Here a babel of voices broke out with chatter and laughter. The girl who sang the solo hymn became the center of an admiring ring. Perhaps her voice was not so marvelous as we all thought it then, but it was a rare voice and had every quality to thrill adolescents for whom everything that happened, happened for the first time.

The mistress of schools, an agile little woman with darting eyes and a mundane manner, gave us a little allocution on the girl and her voice. "Finda," she told us, "may not have as much intelligence as some of you, but God gave her the gift of a voice. God, who sometimes devotes Himself to making a beautiful body or a beautiful brain or a beautiful tree, in Finda's case devoted Himself to making some wonderful thing in her throat. God has but lent it to her to use it in His praise." Finda, tall and lovely and long-haired, so haunting that the memory of her and her voice is vividly with me though she is dead for over thirty years, and though I knew her for only two years of my life. She gave to many of us then, in the morning of life, one of those thrills which, when received in impressionable adolescence, one never forgets. In fact there was very much in that first year of boarding school that I recall more vividly than the happenings of yesterday and which forever formed some part of my mind or of my temperament as the food one takes in youth forms the body. As the slight scar on my foot left by an accidental cut in playing hockey still remains, so there are also scars on my mind, some that healed something beneath, some that were but the ever aching remains of a wound.

III

Convents are really small, self-contained totalitarian states where life is lived according to a rigid schedule, with penalties for those who did not or could not keep to it. For me, however, the life became a happy, satisfying, if exacting one.

To try to act like everyone else became my constant preoccupation. We had everything in common. We rose, washed, and dressed on the same minute; said the same prayers in unison; wore the same uniform; did our hair in the prescribed way, plaited down our backs and tied with a black silk ribbon. "Form ranks" or "Get into ranks"—that was the order several times a day whenever we went anywhere in a body. We walked in step in ranks of two and two going to the refectory, going to the little chapel. We first genuflected in pairs before the altar, then we turned to our seats, the girls to the right entering the right seats and those to the left, the left seats, all with drilled and trained precision, for the procedure had been rehearsed many times. A couple of times a week we had actual military drill by a drill sergeant. Perhaps drilling and conformity and totalitarianism are not so alien to the ideals of the human race as we in democracies consider. The supervision was ceaseless; everything we did or even thought, it seemed to me, was known to the heads of the school. Our letters were read coming and going, and the letters we sent out were thoroughly censored— not always, of course, for subject matter, but for style and manner. How to write a ladylike letter was the matter of a half hour's instruction from time to time. No criticism of the school in letters home, as I recall, was ever permitted, criticizing the sisters being considered a very serious breach of conduct and manners.

There were many discomforts to be borne, but we did not then know that they were discomforts that could have been remedied, and they were common in European schools at the time. We had no central heating, and the cold of the dormitories and classrooms could be very numbing, and all winter we snuffled with colds, and our hands and feet, but especially our hands, became covered with chilblains. There was a point, I remember, where these broke or split and became very painful, but nobody thought of complaining much. Except for a few who had been at school on the Continent, or who had had a childhood in remote British possessions, none of us knew any other climate except the Irish one with its cold rainy winters, its early and sometimes enchanting springs, and its short, seldom warm summers, so we regarded colds and chilblains as a cross from heaven.

We washed every morning in cold water, winter and summer.

Bathing went on all day, as it had to if the bathrooms the school contained were to accommodate everybody. Each person had a bath hour, which was not oftener than once a week, and if you missed, for any reason, your bath hour, you had no bath till the following week, though there was, in addition, as I remember, another bathing ritual called foot bathing. One entered the bath clothed in a straight cotton garment with armholes, called a bath dress. It was reported that there were some daring and immodest spirits who eschewed this garment and took it off in the bathtub.

There were many punishments and penalties to be endured, though these were not excessive in spite of the rigidity of the discipline. Punishments were meted out if we did not know our lessons, if we were late for classes or meals or any ceremonial, if we broke the rule of silence or did not fold our chapel veils neatly and put them away in little lockers with our numbers on them. For we all had numbers and were often referred to by them instead of by our names, and during meals the refectory sister would make announcements, "Nineteen left her Latin grammar on the garden seat; Twenty-one left her walking shoes under her bed; a novel by Ouida [or other forbidden writer] was found under Fifty-six's mattress. Whoever smuggles in novels will please go and tell the mistress of schools." Sometimes the novel smuggling, like chocolate smuggling, was accomplished by the day pupils. It was not that we were forbidden to read novels, but we were allowed to read only on holidays or at recreation times, and then only what books were in the school library. This contained some rubbish and some masterpieces which we read indiscriminately and generally with equal enjoyment. The books were graded according to our ages, and I remember in my last school years reading many novels of Thomas Hardy that were not in the outside world considered suitable reading for the *jeune fille*. I also, while at this school, read through a whole encyclopedia, Chambers' Encyclopedia of English Literature, for it was left on the shelf for reference books and dictionaries, and before the crowded years dimmed my memory I could say by heart passages from all sorts of little-known poets that were quoted there—Elizabethans like Ford and Massinger, the Greene who wrote *A Groat's Worth of Wit*, Butler of "Hudibras," Shenstone, Robert Tannahill. My mind seemed to be like a blotting pad as far as soaking up poetry and the biographies of writers was concerned. At the same time I seemed to have no other talent of any kind. Some of my companions were very talented; they could play the piano, paint, draw, act, dance, write verses. I remember that the girl who came out highest at the yearly examinations could do almost anything well. She was not only best at Latin and English, but best at acting and writing verses, and could learn anything by heart. Only as the years went by, her mind never increased, though she had a good deal of artistry and her memory, as long as I knew her, remained extraordinary. Looking back at my girlhood friends, my school friends, it seems to me that the women who, in adolescence and young womanhood, have varied talents must be more numerous than men with like endowments. These girls often remain gifted amateurs all their lives, and some few of them spent years of adult life trying to recapture their schoolgirl reputation as writers, or actresses, or musicians. Some, however, settled down to happy domesticity, forgetful of all their accomplishments, and fingers that spent contented years making baby clothes lost their nimbleness in fluttering over piano keyboards or in fingering violin strings.

Class hours and study hours were long, and though we studied books and subjects assembled for us by an educational body called the Intermediate Education Board for Ireland, which at the start must have emanated from the head of some English bureaucrat, the whole way in which this school was conducted and the way we were taught was Continental. It was more French than anything else—so much so that the Abbé Dimnet, whose *My Old World* deals with the same type of training to which I was subjected, once wrote to me, "You and I have the same background, or had before I Anglicized myself." In fact my school was French in tradition, having been founded by a French religious order for the education of girls, and we had all sorts of French customs, since the school was not long enough in existence to have become completely Hibernicized. On feast days and birthdays we would kiss each other three times, once on each cheek and once on the lips, as is done in France; we had a French motto for our school and a French coat of arms on our exercise books. In spite of this and though we were turned into pretty good French scholars from the literary point of view, as we were turned into good German and Italian scholars, not much attention was given to the conversational side of languages, and it was only in my university days that I got to the point of speaking French and German with fair fluency. Some years' residence in France has made me a good enough French speaker, yet I am a better French literary scholar than I am a speaker. I speak what my French friends call a *très gentil français*, but it is with a marked foreign accent.

But the language and literature that really fascinated me at school was Latin. I can never forget the rapture with which, by the aid of a dictionary, I first poked a meaning out of the second book of Vergil; I still recall the English I tried to put on poems of Catullus and odes of Horace. I think some of the pleasure one gets out of making versions of poetry from difficult languages resembles the sort one gets out of solving crossword puzzles. I struggled to turn Latin poetry into sonorous English. From what I remember of the sentences, my efforts seem to have resulted in a rather fearful sort of poetic diction. "Horrible, O Queen, it is to relate the tale of Troy's last agony." But what a world of gods and heroes came to me out of Vergil! An entrancing world full of never-ending excitements. But, on the other hand, the world of Tasso's *Gerusalemme Liberata* was a very dull world, and as I remember, the language in which it was written was more perplexing than the language of the Aeneid, and to this day Italian literature and literary history evoke memories of intolerable boredom, of dull knights and fatuous damsels, and tedious moral tales in prose, and dramas that seemed to be a schoolmaster's rewriting of the French classical dramatists. I had a rage for translating into English, and through practice acquired a knack of being able to pick up a book in a foreign language and read it off into fluent English as if that were the language in which it was written. This accomplishment now remains with me only for French, though until the last few years I had it also for German and Italian. Some of my companions were wonderful little students. At eighteen several were, it seems to me, better scholars than many Ph.D.'s I have since known, thanks to the long hours of application and the devoted teaching.

While several of the best educated and accomplished people I have ever known were the result of the Irish intermediate and university systems, yet the teaching was far too literary, as perhaps it was everywhere in Europe before the war. A continuous abuse of the government and of government departments being in the routine of national patriotism, the type of education we received was bitterly criticized as an imposition of an alien government on a defenseless and overtaxed people. Such schools as the one I was at were private institutions, but they also were given a subsidy from the Intermediate Board of Education as a result of annual examinations, and the most brilliant pupils received prizes and exhibitions or scholarships. The funds for these came from the whisky tax, and the humor that a witty and ironic people could extract from this circumstance could always be exploited and used as a weapon against the government. Parents were told that whether their children got an education or not depended on the amount of whisky the country managed to imbibe every Saturday night, and that in any case the education in vogue was not suited to the needs of the country. I am convinced that this latter part was true. Even though the proportion of people who were subjected to secondary and university education at the time was not high, they formed an articulate and influential group. The education turned out a considerable number of trained and scholarly minds, but the country was too small to use as many of them as were turned out.

Goaded by criticism, the English Government decided to send a few Oxford and Cambridge dons to look into the Irish secondary schools. It never occurred to them to send anybody from the native universities or colleges—the natives were supposed never to understand their own affairs. There was a fantastic ferment amongst nuns and pupils when we heard that our school was to be examined by two English professors. These examiners were supposed to make a surprise descent, but as the day of their visitation approached, a polite letter from one of them announced that he and his colleague, Professor Stegall, would begin to inspect the school classes on a certain day. The letter was read out to the school in the refectory, and the name signed to it thrilled us. It was the very strange name of the classical scholar who figured on title pages of our textbooks as editor—Evelyn Shuckburgh. To us he seemed a high celebrity. His name was known to every boy and girl studying classics in the country, and when in due course he arrived, it was almost as if Vergil or Ovid, or even Homer himself, entered the room. "Professor Evelyn Shuckburgh," said our Latin teacher, introducing him and stumbling over the name, as often in Ireland one did not know how English names were pronounced or what sounds the syllables were turned into. The converse was also true, and the professor stumbled over the names of the class list he was handed, for as he read them down he would emphasize the wrong syllable and mispronounce the name in a way that made it quaint and fantastic. As he tried to be friendly and asked us what part of Ireland one or another of us came from, his innocence of Irish geography matched his innocence of pronunciation, and we became convinced that, in spite of his tremendous fame, he was a good example of that comic stupidity which English officialdom in Ireland was reputed to show. I was disinterestedly convinced of this myself when he pronounced me the best Latin scholar in the school, for, gazing into the dreamy eyes of this puzzled old savant who had lived his life in ancient Greece and Rome, I perceived how it was possible to fool him. Twisting the lion's tail was not the popular sport in Ireland; it was pulling the lion's leg. My practice at translating foreign languages into an English of my own stood by me, and when I translated for him an ode of Horace into words different from the shopworn language of the cribs and annotations, he accepted my Latin scholarship. His face and eyes shone with a delighted smile. Like a lot of my countrymen, I had fooled the Englishman with words. When another girl, actually the best Latin scholar of the class, showed him her version in Latin hexameters of the "Lake of the Dismal Swamp" and saw his pleased surprise, we knew that the battle for our school was won. This old scholar's idea of a good school was one where the classical languages were well taught, and when he parted from us he paid us graceful compliments and called us charming little learned girls—we were then around seventeen and did not care so much for the "little." When I told my writing uncle of Professor Shuckburgh's compliments, he, who regarded every manifestation of English control in Ireland with a sort of ironic fury, and scented patronage in every English compliment, quoted "Hudibras": "As learned as the wilde Yrisshe are." The English inspectors had indeed, with the best intentions in the world, behaved as if they were visiting the interior of some little-known British colony to look into the education of the natives.

ॐ CHAPTER 3

An Old-World Training

BUT IF WE WERE WELL TAUGHT we were badly fed; almost no attention was paid to purely physical needs. As we walked in to breakfast from the little chapel, often exhausted before the day began through too early rising, we sat down to a meal composed of tea and bread and butter only. Dinner in the middle of the day was always insufficient and often so unpalatable that we envied reverend mother's niece who had the privilege of eating no dinner but instead had tea for a midday meal. In the afternoon we had tea or milk and the inevitable bread and butter, and a similar meal in the evening. I do not think anybody, either nuns or pupils, thought much of the importance of food. We filled up on bread and butter. It is surprising that so many of us grew to healthy maturity in such an unhygienic mode of life, with so little open air and exercise. But youthful bodies seem to be able, often, to adapt themselves to most things. Too many, however, died of tuberculosis in their youth, or suffered all their lives from some ailment or another. Kneeling at early Mass in the mornings, I would be overcome sometimes by a violent pain; later in life I discovered that from childhood I had had chronic appendicitis, but the doctor who visited the school diagnosed it partly as indigestion and partly as a desire to evade early rising. Whenever I talked to the infirmarian about that pain or about the frequent headache—a migraine headache that began in my early teens and lasted until a New York doctor cured me of it not so long ago—she would be moderately sympathetic and tell me that when I had these aches I must meditate on the sufferings of Our Lord on the Cross, and I would not be tempted to overestimate my own puny pains. I grew up into a delicate girl, my physical energy drowned in the anemia I could never really rid myself of and which I was solemnly told was part of the penalty of having red hair, red-haired people being always supposed to be anemic.

Yet, despite everything, the life at school was a happy one—despite the food, the cold in winter, the long hours of class and of study, the fearful efforts to grow in piety and to eradicate faults, the perpetual meditations on life after death. Education was regarded as a means for fitting our souls for God rather than as a preparation for life. Life itself was looked on as a preparation for eternity, and the tribulations of life as designed by God to perfect our spirits and ennoble our souls by suffering. There was an inclination to believe that the more we suffered, the more pleasing we were to God and the better were our chances of eternal happiness. However, affection radiated on all sides. The nuns were affectionate; my school friends and I were very fond of one another. We had our intimate friendships, but these had to be in threes; the convent rule against what was called "particular friendships" made all friendships triangular, as it were. This rule was perhaps designed to guard against those schoolgirl crushes that I may say from my own considerable experience of boarding schools were so very harmless. Trios on vacation would write long epistles to one another and exchange novels and books of poetry; the return to school after the holidays was the happiest of reunions.

The nuns, on the whole, were very kind, though I recollect some petty tyrannizing from the younger and less disciplined ones and from the novices and postulants, for which I think they were reprimanded, for they were seldom twice guilty. The sum total of my impressions was of high-minded, devoted women who were often more than their own mothers to the little girls they trained and taught and brought up. If only their sense of responsibility towards us had included a greater concern for our health and physical welfare as well as for their own! Too many of the nuns died young, and too many overworked, overfasted, and overprayed.

The standards of unselfishness, magnanimity, devotion to others I rarely found in the world afterwards, and sometimes, in exchanging confidences with other women brought up in convents in the

Old World, we found ruefully that we all had had the same experience. Following the ideas and ideals instilled in our school days, we too often fell a cropper. We got along all right as long as we encountered people brought up in the same way, but step out of that little circle and that old European Catholic tradition, and little that we had been taught of life and behavior was of much use to us. It had been a narrow if delightful world, and any of us who stepped out into another sort of life got a good deal of our training rubbed off. The tradition of this school, as well as that of three or four others I was at, was an aristocratic one; the pupils and teachers might be as middle-class as they could be—in only one of the schools I was at were the pupils from the European aristocratic classes—but the tradition everywhere was the same. This sort of education before the war was almost identical all over Europe—the same discipline, the same ideals. Step from a convent school in Ireland to a convent school in France, or Germany, or Belgium, or Italy, and the difference was slight—same sort of discipline, same habits and customs, same uniform, same religious drill, same books of devotion, same stories about saints and martyrs, same notion inculcated that death, not life, was a thing to prepare for.

Religious instruction went on all the time as well as a more worldly instruction—in manners and general behavior. There were intervals of prayer during the day, and if one entered a room hastily or banged the lid of a desk, a small lecture on manners would be forthcoming. Piety was greatly stressed, but, being at a questioning age, we used to be puzzled as to why the most religious girl was not also the best in character and general ethics. Why was Anne, who dodged all religious exercises, a generous, courageous, and warmhearted person, and why was Eleanor, who would get out of bed early and go to two Masses on weekdays and who was always praying at shrines—why was she a fibber and a sneak, who never cared to take the blame on herself for any doings or breaking of rules? We would put such questions tactfully to the mistress of schools who gave us our Sunday lecture, and would get in reply a fluent explanation of the natural virtues and the supernatural virtues, the theological virtues and every other category of virtues, until our heads were bamboozled. But still the question remained: What about Anne and what about Eleanor? And then there was the question of what was meant by spirituality. This, according to the nuns, was a religious quality, but when a girl, after the holidays, brought back a book called *The Treasure of the Humble* by Maurice Maeterlinck, where there was a lot about spirituality of a kind which appealed to us a great deal more than the religious sort, there were more questioners. We cross-examined the mistress of schools on this new angle on spirituality. She, feeling we were getting out of hand at this stage, brought in a learned Jesuit to talk to us. He, on a blackboard, reduced Maeterlinck to major premise, minor premise, and conclusion, and showed that Maeterlinck had no logic and must therefore be ruled out. On the surface we did, in fact, accept a lot of what we were told without questioning. We were watched over carefully as far as our characters were concerned, and, at intervals, we would be taken aside, one by one, by the mistress of schools, who would point out our faults and try to correct them. We worked hard to improve ourselves a little every day and to discover our dominant passions and vices and try to get the better of them. Diligent efforts were made to cure us of vanity in any shape or form. If a girl thought she was pretty, and consequently curled her hair or dolled herself up—not much dolling was possible, as everybody was dressed in a uniform—she was seriously talked to. Occasionally, on a holiday, a daring soul would shake out her long heavy hair from the prescribed tight plait and boldly walk like that into the refectory. As a rule she was marched out again to put her locks into shape. A watchful nun came wrongly to the conclusion that I was vain of my long, light red hair and gave me a discourse on the evils of admiring myself and on the general undesirable nature of my appearance. I was sure she was right on the last point, as I had always wanted black hair and blue eyes. The net result of her scolding was to make me careless and untidy and to give me an indifference as to how I looked, which remained with me all the rest of my days. Soon after, a more vigilant nun looked into my character for other manifestations of vanity and came to the conclusion I was suffering from "vanity of mind." I had read many more books than the other girls in my class; I had acquired a lot of out-of-the-way knowledge for a youngster, mostly of a literary and historical nature, and I always had my head in a book of some sort. Though this made me by no means the best pupil in the class, it caused me from time to time to adopt a sniffy attitude about the style and content of some of the pious books we were expected to assimilate.

II

The school library was an odd mixture, composed of the classics, the lives of the saints, and some good novels of the period that had got there by legacy. There were the novels of Thomas Hardy and George Meredith wedged in between the books of Hall Caine and Marie Corelli, and romantic works by well-intentioned lady authors. On the rare school holidays we all read a great deal of rubbish with a great deal of delight. When it would be announced that a certain day, generally a church holiday, was free from all studies, we would line up early in the library for "storybooks" as we would call them, and spend the rest of the day lying on our beds reading and munching chocolates. Ever since I have been convinced that there is some real value in reading rubbish; it helps one to understand people's dreams, by which I mean that sort of mental life that goes on in us during the waking day, the common dream life which never lapses, and which is behind all we do and think.

The nun who discovered my "vanity of mind" recommended that it be not catered to in any way, so when prize day came I was not given the high-class works of literature the other girls received as prizes, but a couple of foolishly written and sentimentally pious works. I read them and laughed at them with some cronies who were also qualifying for vanity of mind even if they had not gone as far down the path of vice in that direction as I had. A little youthful nun would wag her finger at me and say to my companions, "That is a lovely book she is despising. Do not pay any attention to her. She talks like that to attract notice."

Some of the conversations I had heard at home did not exactly prepare my mind for simple piety, or for a literary standard in which good morals in a book made it a fine work. Perhaps because the order which ran the school had been originally French, or perhaps it was just the usual meaning in Ireland, but "morals" was used in the general sense of ethics and not in the sense of sex morals as the word is so often used in America. In fact most of us were innocent of the fact that sex existed, and so it never came up. We, however, critically discussed some of the things the saints did to mortify themselves, such as wearing hair shirts, or belts with nails in them, their mortifications of the flesh, sleeping little, fasting a great deal, humiliating themselves before others. Then there were male saints, we heard, who would never look into a woman's eyes, not even into their mothers'. We pondered especially on a female saint called, I think, Saint Rose of Lima, who put pepper in her eyes to make them smart with pain. Our leader in these discussions was a youthful psychologist, the daughter of a Dublin doctor, who had apparently heard a good deal about human behavior in her home, and who prefaced her explanations always with, "My father says." I do not suppose she understood her own explanations very well, but her father, like many Dublin doctors, had studied awhile in Vienna and, no doubt, had picked up something of the new psychology and the new interpretations of human actions that were coming into vogue. That self-mortification was not always due to goodness or saintliness, she convinced some of us easily enough while she horrified others. In due course she was censured by the mistress of schools, who somehow seemed to hear everything we said and did by some sort of grapevine method. These ideas were said to be temptations from the devil, and it was whispered around that the girl's father was an atheist and never went to Mass or followed any religious duties. In fact, even in the remoteness of the convent, whispering campaigns concerning well-known persons in the outside world were not unknown or ineffective.

I think we all got a lot of moral lectures both from our teachers and our families. Every letter I received contained some sort of objurgation or injunction. But the letters I liked best were from the French wife of an uncle, written in French, assuring me that the great guide to life was *le bon sens*. She had been a governess before marrying and had acquired habits of instructing the young. When a little girl, she had been at a convent school in France, and it seemed to be the very image of the one I was at, with the same habits and customs, with the same sort of grotto next the greenhouse, with the same sort of statue of Our Lady of Lourdes.

Bernadette's Well had cured her mother of something, and she would constantly enclose a little picture of Our Lady of Lourdes. But in addition to the piety this aunt had a witty intellectuality and would write amusingly about books, begging me to be sure to read the *Jocelyn* of Lamartine, and the Journal of Eugénie de Guérin, and the *Centaur* of her brother Maurice.

Books and religion were for her the great refuge from life which, she would reiterate, was *triste, triste.* The word *triste* was common in her vocabulary, and I do not wonder, for misfortune dogged her life. She had been pretty and gay and artistic, but in the life she lived in a remote part of the country, who could have appreciated her or even noticed her wonderful courage, her artistry?—for she married into the side of the family that had no artistry, and that did not care for books, or even for pleasure, for a great deal of Ulster Calvinism was in its bones. Though I saw her rarely enough, I remember her singing of French songs, and her reciting De Musset and Lamartine. She would write me warnings against ever reading Zola, though she thought that when I grew older I might read a few selections from Flaubert for his style, which she thought was the most wonderful that had ever been achieved. She made me so interested in French literature that my natural delight and interest in anything written in French grew and grew through her correspondence. I think her writing to me gave her an outlet and reminded her of the young girl at a convent school that she herself had been. I did not like it, however, when she would sometimes return the letters I wrote her with penciled lines through my wrong genders and tenses and moods. The memory of her remains strongly with me, though I saw so little of her. Her life must have been extremely lonely, pining for France, for the Riviera, for the red wine of Burgundy, for Lourdes, and for the mellow religion of France so different from the dourness of the Irish Catholicism she knew.

She would sometimes send me a scapular that she had made herself in her fine French stitching and had got blessed by some priest. Both at school and at home we all wore religious emblems round our necks or sewed into our corsets. There were Agnus Deis and brown scapulars and blue ones and white ones; sometimes a whole set would be sewed together. With wear these would get dirty, and as they were all blessed, to throw them away would seem a sacrilege. We would usually give the soiled ones to the dormitory sister who, I think, would burn them. A little girl once threw hers away; it was said she flushed them down the toilet bowl. For this she got a remorse that lasted for months. "I committed a sacrilege," she would say, with sad, rigid face. We thought she had a sensitivity of piety unknown to our grosser minds, but I think in a modern school she would have been treated to a little mental hygiene. As it was, she kept up her endless repetition of, "I have committed a sacrilege," and she would go to confession to every new priest who turned up to get forgiveness for her terrible sin. From what I remember of her and one or two others who worked up remorses, I imagine she and they were embryo manic-depressives and that the remorse that she thought was for destroying a scapular was really not remorse at all but some other sort of sentiment. A strong streak of cruelty in her puzzled us, too, as to piety making people good. She would proffer the littlest girls—there were several around six or seven who all slept in little beds in what was called the babies' dormitory—chocolates in an open box, and, as the little eager fingers approached to grasp one, she would snap the lid to and take the chocolates away. "You must learn to mortify yourselves," she would tell the babies.

III

The great excitements of the year were the reception of nuns into the order and the school plays and entertainments, and to these may be added the annual retreat. The taking of the white veil, where the novice after a period as a postulant was received into the order, was a great event for nuns and girls, but especially for the girls; the taking of the black veil, where the nun took her final vows of poverty, chastity, and obedience, was not so thrilling. But when the novice took the white veil she cast aside the dress of the world which she had continued to wear as postulant, the postulant's uniform being a plain black dress with a little lace veil over her head. In all three convents I was in, the reception ceremony was different. In one order the novice would be dressed as a bride in ivory satin, with orange blossoms and a bridal bouquet, and would walk up the aisle on her father's arm as at a wedding; then she knelt alone on the prie-dieu before the high altar to be received into the order by the bishop. This was very affecting when the novice was a fair young girl, as was often the case, but sometimes she was not young, but had already spent years in the world, in some work or profession. When the preliminary details of the ceremony were over, the novice was led in a stately way to the sacristy by the mistress of novices. There she shed her wedding robes and had her long hair cut off and was dressed in the black habit of the order. Kneeling once more before the bishop, she would receive the white veil; she had yet before her a couple of years as a novice before becoming a professed sister and taking her final vows and her black veil. The young novice, after her reception, would appear a little later smiling and happy—no bride ever appeared happier—before us girls in the recreation hall, and the senior Children of Mary would have the honor of kissing her three times, once on each cheek and once in the vicinity of the mouth. In the convent parlor—I should say in one of them, for there were several—there would be a reception breakfast for the nun's relatives and friends, and we girls would have raisin bread for tea and an extra period for recreation. That the newly received novice would, as a nun, lead a more contented, more placid, and perhaps a happier life than women in the world, I have very little doubt. She would never grow old-maidish or prim or dried up, as unmarried women, and even married women, in the world often do, for she would all her life have children and young girls around her to bring up and educate, and her rule of life would not allow her to spend much time thinking of herself. She would try to improve herself a little every day, in mind and in virtue—not, alas, in body, because of the poor fare of the order and the mostly indoor life. The practice of religion and self-sacrifice and of study would grow on her so that in middle life and early old age she would probably be very highly educated as well as finely molded in spirit.

When girls entered the order in their teens, as frequently was the case, they often, of course, grew more and more narrow-minded,

for the ignorance of life of the well-brought-up young girl in
Europe could be immense. A great friend of mine who entered
the order at eighteen was as ignorant of what was called the facts
of life as a newborn babe, as indeed I was myself. Long afterwards,
when I saw her, she had become a large-minded, generous woman
devoting her life to her school and her little girls, but she was
still very puzzled about many things, including what she called
"this love business." Why, in novels, were people supposed to be
in love with each other before they approached the holy sacrament
of matrimony? She believed she had never known anybody who
ever was in love. "Now, my own mother was never in love; my
uncle arranged her marriage with the canon's nephew, and she was
always contented. There were ten of us, and before I entered there
was always a baby in the cradle, that made her happy. But I would
like to know what really are the customs out in the world."

"Out in the world" was a common phrase in this, as indeed in all
convents. "Out in the world" was the usual phraseology to describe
all life outside our little totalitarian state. But, as if our life were
not sufficiently remote from the things of earth, we had each year
a "retreat" of three days given up to religious contemplation, religious practices, and meditation on life after death. During the
retreat we kept a silence that was practically complete; an odd
sentence might be spoken to a sister if one was in desperate straits,
but the bulk of the school kept an entire silence; anyway we were
conditioned to silences, both at meals and at periods during the
day. During these retreats we attended three or four sermons or
lectures and three or four church services a day, and in what time
was over we read religious books and pondered on the enormity of
our sins.

These meditations and sermons that take place at school retreats
are delineated memorably in Joyce's *Portrait of the Artist as a
Young Man*. Here the whole business has been put down with a
freshness, completeness, and integrity that any other writer can
only try to reproduce, so I shall skip what he has depicted and
confine myself to what was special to my school.

The ordinary school schedule stopped completely, and a new
general one for everybody was written out on a large blackboard
in the study hall which we all copied. I still, after all the years,

have a copy of a retreat schedule written into an old school prayer book which I have kept. Here it is. It represents a fifteen-hour day:

6:15   Rise at the sound of the bell. Wash and dress.
6:45   Meditation in the chapel.
7:15   Holy Mass.
8:00   Breakfast.
8:30   Make beds and tidy dormitories.
9:00   Reading devotional books.
9:30   Sermon in chapel.
10:30   Walk in silent meditation.
11:30   Study of Christian doctrine.
12:00   Lunch.
12:30   Walk in the garden.
1:00   Reading devotional books.
1:30   Rosary.
2:00   Needlework and mending.
3:00   Dinner.
3:30   Stations of the cross.
4:00   Sermon in the chapel.
5:00   Confessions.
7:00   Supper.
7:30   Confessions.
8:30   Sermon and Benediction.
9:30   Retire for the night.

SILENCE TO BE OBSERVED AT ALL TIMES AND IN ALL PLACES.

After three days' silence and meditation, if modern discoveries in psychology are true, we children or adolescent girls should have been nervous or hysterical after all the restraint we put on ourselves, after all the sermons we listened to, all the meditations on our sins, and the books that were read to us during meals—St. Teresa's *Vision of Hell*, the penances of the saints in the desert, the Martyrs of the Colosseum, and so on. But not at all. On the fourth morning after the visiting priest who gave the retreat said his last Mass and a bell rang to announce that the days of silence were over, we emerged high-spirited and happy and full of peace at the notion that we had been making satisfaction for our sins, whatever they were. There was a little gate at the end of a passage that separated the cloisters from the school: it was known as "The Wicket." But to most of the school it was spoken of as "The Wicked Gate." After silent periods were over, the signal for talking was the passage through that "Wicked Gate." As we came out of the chapel, two by two, after retreat was over, those behind would watch the first two of the procession as they passed through. On the other side they would joyously kiss each other three times and say "*Pax vobis*"; impatiently each pair in the long line would wait their turn to pass through and to say joyously to each other, "*Pax vobis.*" Then we would have a whole day's holiday, and we danced and played games, read novels, or storybooks as they were called, and were very happy. Once, however, in my last year at that school we had four days' retreat instead of three. This must have been too much for some of the pupils, and I remember one English girl, a convert, getting an attack of hysterics. The Jesuit father who gave the retreat thought himself, as he was later to tell me, that four days of silence and prayer was excessive for young girls in their teens. As relief from what he believed to be a strain, he asked us at the morning sermon on the third day to write him letters, unsigned, dealing with any religious difficulties we would like to have cleared up, and he would answer them from the rostrum in the chapel. I had long pondered on the meaning of the Old Testament and on those stories I had read as a child and was puzzled at the relation of that part of the Bible to the New Testament. Without knowing why, I did not think it would be ladylike to ask him about some of the stories or to bring up such matters as concubines and the children of handmaidens and the goings on of David with Bathsheba. But I wrote a note asking a sort of philosophic question: How was it that the God of the New Testament was a God of love, so different from the God of the Old Testament, Who was so hard and vengeful and jealous? Were both really the same God? The priest at the next sermon read out the letters he had received. For the most part, the questions took a simple answer: Could you go to Communion if you accidentally swallowed a drop of water while brushing your teeth, or would it be best not to brush your teeth on a Holy Communion morning? Could you marry your second cousin without dispensation? Was a marriage to a Protestant valid? Etc., etc. Could atheists go to heaven? He read out my note last of all, and when he said he wished to see the writer of it, I felt both frightened and important. I went to the sacristy to see him. He was an interesting, attractive man of middle age who before his entrance into a religious order had been an English violinist; though he did not answer my question, he talked very interestingly and for years kept up a correspondence with me, a humorous and paternal correspondence on his side, a schoolgirl's adoration on mine.

But what makes this priest stay in my mind was the fact that he was the very first person who talked to me in an interesting way about the new Irish literary movement. The mistress of schools had told him that I was of a literary turn as a way of accounting for my habit of asking disrupting questions. "Ireland is beginning to turn to literature," he told me, "though compared to us English you are not a literary people." I do not remember that this priest enlightened me much about God, but I snatched at all he said about literature and music. Long afterwards, when Joyce, who was some years my senior, would talk to me about our experiences in schools and college where we had both been educated the same way and had studied the same subjects, we found that this priest had made the same sort of impression on both of us. Joyce had known him at his school, where he had taught something or another, or maybe even had given that famous retreat described in *Portrait of the Artist*. He was not only less tightly bound in the minor conventionalities of formal religion than other priests, but a strain of artistry made him stand out from the bulk of the others. To Joyce he was pathetic because he was that lonely figure, an Englishman in a religious order in Ireland, a purely Saxon Englishman among Celts and Anglo-Celts, not understanding, in spite of all his efforts, this stubborn race with its refusal to accept English civilization, astonished and maybe hurt at the way we sometimes laughed at Englishmen. He was a Jesuit and had spent some time in the same house as Gerard Manley Hopkins. Joyce's memories of him were part of his admiration of the Jesuits to whom his own early memories were attached: he never forgot the justice with which the rector of Clongowes had treated him as a small boy, an incident related in *Portrait of the Artist*.

After the retreats and the interesting alienness of the priests who gave them—they were never Irishmen, as I remember, but English or Continental—and after the receptions of novices into the order, the next most delirious excitement was the school plays. These incursions into the dramatic art were often of a sufficiently surprising nature owing to the fact that what was called "a love play" was taboo, and all love scenes in our productions were altered by one of the nuns. Once, in a German playlet, the love scene was too long and too much involved in the play to be cut out entirely, so the scene was changed from an interchange of emotion between a young man and a woman to one between two young women. If all of us nuns and pupils had not been utterly innocent of what is called inversion in love, the passionate language of the two characters in the lovers' quarrel, played by girls of fifteen or so, would undoubtedly have paralyzed us. As it was, we felt a trifle uneasy; there still rings in my ears one of the final sentences spoken with grave emotion by a girl in a rich Munster voice, "*Alles ist mit uns vorbei. Ich werde dich nimmer sehen . . . nimmer mehr . . . nimmer mehr.*" And then the attitude of despair of my dear friend Mary who played the part with a schoolgirl's intensity!

A favorite drama in the schools was *Julius Caesar*, for there were no love scenes, and the references to any relations between men and women were so slight that they could be deleted. The play had several other advantages: the scenic effects were easy to produce, and the dressing demanded nothing out-of-the-way. Togas could be constructed from sheets or counterpanes or piano covers or similar haberdashery; the cast could be expanded to any extent, so that there was no reason why parents should be deprived of the sight of their offspring on the stage or of their names on the programme; any number of pupils could be put on as citizens listening to or interrupting Brutus or Mark Antony. I was first tried out as the Third Citizen, but failing to make myself heard in my one speech, the sister in charge invented a silent part for me. She made me a barbarian king visiting Rome, dressed up in the skins of animals, and muttering to myself on the outskirts of the crowd listening to Brutus. But the available animal skins fitted another girl better, and my muttering was ineffective, being rather like the bark of a strange dog, so I was demoted to the role of raising and lowering the curtain promptly on a signal, with my name on the programme.

We listened enraptured to every word of the play, and as a tall, fair-haired girl in a sheet bound with a purple ribbon postured around as Mark Antony and declaimed in a high girlish voice, "I would rather wrong the dead and wrong myself and you than wrong such honorable men," one could hear a primrose drop, so tense was the attention and so deep the emotion aroused. I have seen great actors in that play since, but never did I see one who could hold an audience as that convent school was held. It must have been partly the freshness of the audience, all at an age when everything in life is new; it was partly the poetry and partly that rare thing in literature, great oratory, the great oratory of Shakespeare, that triumphed through all the schoolgirlish elocution. I remember performances of *Fabiola*, a play current in convent schools all over Europe and which I saw four times in three languages, but it seemed to me a poor, sentimental, and irritating affair, with the chief part played in an affected voice by the school exhibitionist who always in adolescence exhibits something that seems talent for acting.

In a German school I was at for a while, the drama that fulfilled the same requirements as *Julius Caesar* was Schiller's *Joan of Arc*. With this the audience was even more entranced than were the Irish nuns and girls with *Julius Caesar*, for the play was more suited to girl performers. The one who took the part of Joan really gave the illusion of being Joan as a girl could never give the illusion of being Brutus or Mark Antony, and Schiller's poetry fascinated this audience as Shakespeare's the other, or anyhow, it fascinated those of the audience who could follow it, for to some of us German was a foreign language, and though we were made to study the play diligently beforehand, we could not follow every line.

I remember all the ingenuity put into the manufacture of armor for Joan and into the building of a large white horse on which Joan was mounted in one part of the play. Not only were the consolidated talents of the convent engaged, but those of the neighborhood: a carpenter made the outlines of the animal in wood, the village wood carver carved his head and hoofs, the nuns and pupils constructed his body of cotton and wool and upholstered the figure in white shiny material; mane and eyebrows and teeth were made for him. When completed he looked like a caparisoned charger. The armor for Joan was even more striking. Over a gray satin chemise was something like a pull-over in chain armor which, I think, was got from the neighboring *Schloss*. For the legs and arms the armor was made from cautiously coutured cardboard glued over with paper of the shiniest silver. I really think the part of Joan was as well played as any professional actress could have done it. The girl performer threw all her energies into it and was well coached by a teacher who not only knew how the part should be rendered, but who was a Schiller expert. Except for the finish of the performance, the whole affair might have taken place in the Irish school; there were the same excitement, the same overthrow of ordinary school discipline, the same desire to impress relatives, clergy, and important outsiders, the same humble admiration for the talent of the actress.

And except that many of the pupils were from all over the world and some from the European aristocracy, the resemblance of this German school to my Irish school was very great. It was more feminine in that it taught housewifery and cookery and general female accomplishments, while our education, as far as scholastic subjects were concerned, was exactly the same as in the boys' schools, and we went in for the same examinations. Music and singing in the German school were taught in a way I never knew them to be taught in Ireland, where people had almost no idea of the length of time and study necessary to play an instrument well or to sing well. In Ireland a girl was entitled to call herself a musician if she could play fantasias on Irish airs, *The Maiden's Prayer*, a little of Chopin or other classical composers. I have often found in America an attitude to languages not unlike the Irish attitude to music— a couple of years' study of a language, an ability to read it or talk it a little, was regarded as the height of linguistic accomplishment amongst some of my friends who had no idea of the years and years of drill and of study necessary for a fair grasp of a language.

In the German school the food was immensely better, and we would be given good German beer to drink at lunch and dinner. I acquired a taste for beer, and I remember drinking quite a lot of it. The American girls, however, were given a glass of wine, as beer drinking did not seem very refined. A good deal of attention was paid to our physical needs, and the girls were talked to about their health and bodily functions with a frankness disconcerting to the English, American, and Irish girls of the bourgeoisie who all had similar puritanical and genteel notions. That we were not as frank as she was, was very puzzling to the high-bred nun of old German princely stock whose business it was to supervise our health. The English-speaking groups would collect together at recreation times and discuss the difference between us and the Germans. The French nuns of the order who were arriving at intervals from Paris after the dissolution of the religious communities in France would groan for their beloved Paris with us Irish girls who were supposed to have the same temperament as the French; they would groan for a Paris of which they from their convent only saw the rooftops, but whose sounds they heard from their cloisters and walled gardens and whose gossip would be brought in to them by visiting ladies of the Faubourg. Rodin, later, got a bit of their convent for his studio in the Rue Saint Dominique.

One of the exiled nuns would read us a few pages of Bergson, then at the height of his fashion, and a few pages of Schopenhauer, both in French, and point out the difference between the French philosophic spirit and the German. The fact that I was eventually going to get a university degree and go in generally for higher studies separated me from the bulk of the others, who, when they left school, were going to come out in society of some kind, provincial or courtly, and marry early if they could. Only one of the German girls I was intimate with had any intention of going to a university, and she, as she explained to me, belong to a *bürgerlich* family, her father being an astronomer in Berlin, and her university training was to be, like mine, an insurance against the ills of fortune, an aid to earning a living. On vacations, she said, she was never invited to the houses of her school companions who belonged to *der Adel*—the nobility—and when she encountered them anywhere she was greeted remotely with distant courtesy, German and English snobbery and class distinctions being all of a piece in this prewar age.

There was at this school a number of girls with strange medieval-sounding titles like *Frei-Fräulein*, and one or two were *Durchlaucht*; at school, of course, everyone was on a footing of equality, and if one was a foreigner one did not really know who belonged to *der Adel* and who had or had not a title. One American girl from somewhere in the West delighted in mispronouncing and in stumbling

over names that were both Von and Zu, and in explaining to horrified groups that her mother, when first married, did her own washing, and she used to bring in with great effect that log cabin that
has done its picturesque duty so often in the history of Americans.
Once she was visited by a young man who had come to Germany
on a business trip, and she explained casually that he was her cousin
and a buyer for her father's store, and that when she returned home
she was looking forward to going to dances and parties with him. A
Frei-Fräulein expressed the utmost horror of a life where all the
men were businessmen who spent their days in offices and shops
and where one looked forward to a buyer as an admirer and dance
partner. "Who will your admirers be?" I asked her. "Whom will
you go to dances with?" "*Mit Offizieren,*" she said, sublimely, "*mit
Offizieren.*" The heroes of her dreams were all officers; she was looking forward to riding and dancing with young men in smart uniforms, to marrying one of them. The dreams of most of the other
German girls were the same—to marry an army officer or a diplomat.

A good many of the girls did marry into the army and diplomatic
services, but their marriages took place either a little before or a
little after the beginning of the war that was to change the world
and to change especially their world and the order they had been
born into. So that the only one at the school ever to become a full-
fledged ambassadress, as far as I know, was an American girl who
seemed to be out of that life altogether—Rose Fitzgerald of Boston,
later wife of the American ambassador to the Court of Saint James's.
She was one of the few pretty and chic girls who were in the school;
the Americans not only looked attractive and chic even in the plain
school uniform, but when they went into town with a chaperone to
do some shopping or to get the ends of their long hair cut and
singed—a ritual we all went in for once a month—they were allowed
to doff their school uniforms and wear their smart American clothes.
The bulk of the rest of us had no smart clothes at all, not even the
naturally chic French who, like almost all of us, had spent most of
their lives in convents, wearing dark blue or black uniforms, and
who had been lectured to so often on the dangers of vanity that the
usual young girl's interest in clothes and pretty appearance was considerably diminished, during school years anyhow. Besides this,
those who belonged to the European aristocracy led very sheltered,

not to say secluded, lives until they were married and did not do much dressing except for an occasional party. The Americans' clothes and wonderful feathery hats were looked at askance by some of these *jeunes filles*, and it was whispered that no well-brought-up European girl would wear such things, as they were of a style that had been put in fashion by Parisian cocottes. Most of us had only a dim idea of what a cocotte was.

We were, I think, all plain and dowdy in comparison with the Americans. Some girls of the Westphalian aristocracy, whom I was thrown among, were particularly plain, with oversized hands and feet, long, thick, fair hair, without any high spirits or vividness about them. The Americans were frankly regarded as different from the rest of us, belonging to a faraway country where people were not disciplined in youth as we were and had not studied so hard; their future seemed to promise a different destiny from ours, one in which almost everything might come about. The future for the rest of us seemed to be cut out and to hold no great surprises.

ࣷ CHAPTER 4

The Neighbors

THE HOLIDAYS were spent with various relatives in different parts of Ireland, a few weeks here, a week or two there. I was to spend only about a month of each year in the countryside where I was born, and that ended when I was eighteen. If it appears to me that the people I was born among, and everybody I knew around for miles and miles, were the most civilized, the most kindly that I have ever known, this may be personal bias. That this was only true of my birthplace, and not true of other parts of Ireland or of the cities, may indeed show that the whole idea is an illusion. In my child-hood I seemed to have been always receiving presents. Old men and women, especially those whose letters I wrote for them, would, out of their few pence, bring me home gifts from the fair. When out of a window I would see descending the hill in the distance, John

Shanley's ass and cart, he seated in front, his legs dangling neatly somewhere between the front board and the ass's tail, his wife seated with her back to him on a bag, I would run to meet them because I knew that John had an orange for me in his frieze coat pocket and Mary a bag of peppermints in her market basket. They would at the market have exchanged eggs and butter for the eatables they brought home, the most dismal sort of eatables generally, for they would sell their own good farm produce in exchange for tea, sugar, white flour, American bacon, and salt herrings. "The lovely white lamb," Mary would say of me to John in real or feigned admiration, "her hair like a gold sovereign! Sure she'll grow up to look like the Blessed Virgin, or maybe the blessed Magdalene."

There was a large oldish man called Bartley who seldom used any conveyance except his two legs to get him anywhere, and who, when I came home from boarding school, would bring me back silk hair ribbons or handkerchiefs from the fair, for I adored everything made of silk. Bartley lived in a mountain village which had never thought it necessary to change its mode of life or its dress from the eighteenth century. He wore knee breeches and buckled shoes, a half-high hat called a caubeen hat, and carried a large ashplant neatly trimmed into a walking stick. He and all his brothers—there were about seven of them—were tall, strong, red-haired men, fierce and gentle, lovable and generous. All of them except Bartley said they had been in love with my dead mother, that they had drawn lots as to which of them should have the daring to propose to her father for her, but at the end their courage failed. She had been reared too softly, though as wealth went in that countryside they were well off and had plenty of everything through trading in stock and farm produce with England. When four or five of these large red-haired men in their eighteenth-century garb would descend at a hotel in Dublin, where they went occasionally on business, they would order food and drink for everybody in sight. They were like semi-barbaric chieftains. Bartley, alone of the brothers, never went anywhere, but lived in a little house away from the others and their wives and children and had little contact with them unless he met them at a fair or market. He dealt in horses, which he sold to the North men. The reason he lived alone was that he had spent seven years in the convict prison of Spike Island for manslaughter. A man

had been killed in a brawl at a fair, and Bartley was tried and convicted of having caused his death. "If I did," Bartley would say, "I
never knew, for everybody was full of drink at the time. It might
have been me did it; it might have been the next one." After the
seven years were over, Bartley came home, having, it was said, grown
smaller than he had been and very silent in himself. He had grown
shy and was a trifle morose to the neighbors, but he never was
morose to me, and I used to go to see him often in the holidays,
accompanied by two red setter dogs, Joubert and Kruger, who would
walk solemnly beside me, generally one each side. For years after
the Boer War, we called our dogs after the Transvaal President
and his generals to keep their feats in our memory.

Bartley had, while in prison, somehow forgotten how to write, or
pretended to have forgotten, but he used to read everything he laid
his hands on, and I would bring him all the sixpenny reprints of
novels that my school friends and I exchanged with one another by
mail during the summer holidays. It was odd how many people in
that neighborhood used to say they had forgotten how to write, but
who were considerable readers. I have sometimes wondered if some
inherited fear of the Penal Laws was in their blood, and if it was a
convention of self-protection to say they could not write. Bartley
would give me short and not very interesting versions of the Irish
hero tales, of Finn Mac Cool and Cuchulainn, and he would listen
with eyes wide with excitement, his lighted pipe gripped in his
hand, while I would read him Yeats's Wanderings of Oisin, the
story of Oisin, who went off with the fairy Niav to the Land of the
Ever Living, and came back in a short time to find that he had really
been away three hundred years, and that he returned, not to the
Ireland of the Fianna, but a land covered with churches and bells
and crosses, for Patrick had been there and converted everyone.
Nothing, nobody was the same as he remembered, and Oisin
himself, the minute he touched the land of his youth, became
"shaken with coughing and broken with old age and without laughter, a show unto children, alone with remembrance and fear."

"It's my own story, surely," said Bartley, "for when I was rowed
from Spike Island and stepped on the soil of Ireland again, nothing was the same. The grass that used to be green was a sort of yellow, and the ships with their sails that used to be a sight for sore

eyes in Cove Harbour were not there, or there were a few only, quarter of the size. But there were these big American steamers with chimneys and never a sail, and the people in this country were not the same. Before I went to Spike I never saw an umbrella in anybody's hand. Now—wisha!—not only the dawny women with umbrellas, but the men, too, have got to be in dread of a drop of rain. You see them with their umbrellas all rolled up, looking like a walking stick." I think this was a reference to a rolled silk umbrella one of my family always carried, for Bartley was fond of having a satirical crack at my relatives and their pretensions. "I'll give in they have the learning," he would say with a nod, "and I've heard tell your uncle John knows the seven languages, but I'm of a better stock myself."

"But," said I, "Bartley, you could not have been like Oisin, because Oisin went away with a woman, with Niav of the Shee. But you just went away by yourself."

"Not by myself exactly, for there were two peelers, one on each side of me, and handcuffs on my hands, and the handcuffs were not taken off me when I was given the bit to eat—I had to eat like a beast of the field, the peeler holding the bread and the tea to my mouth. And if I did not go off with a woman, there was one in my mind. She was with me night and day for all the years I was in Spike, and I mad with lonesomeness for the sight of her face."

"Where is she now, Bartley?"

"She married a man in the far North, and I never saw her after."

"How wicked of her not to wait for you!" said I, in youthful sympathy. "Did she not write to you?"

"Och, why should she?" Bartley exclaimed, "'twas courting her in my own mind I always was. I never told her a word about it, or said anything to her except bid her the time of day, or sometimes to give a call at her house to pretend to give her father the present of a salmon—it was for her it was."

"Oh, Bartley," said I, stirred by the wonders of the romance, "didn't you bid her good-by before you went to Spike?"

"No, I tried to make the peelers who had me pinned to a sidecar drive around by her house so that I could see the trees or the haystacks around the place, but they drove me straight down to the gaol."

Bartley, unlike his brothers, dealt in horses, which he sold to the North men—that is, to the men from the far North of Ulster. They would come once or twice a year to buy horses from Bartley and others which they would ship to England, it was said. The North men, a whole tribe of them, would each buy a few horses and ride home with them; we would watch out for them, for it was one of the sights of the countryside to see the North men bringing home their horses, some of them I knew were Munster men, or Meath men, or even Dublin men, but they were all called the North men for simplicity. Sometimes they were late, and I would wait up at night to watch their passing. First a man would ride ahead on one horse, holding a couple by a rein, and then all the others would follow, each man mounted on one horse and holding a few by the reins. Sometimes the whole train would gallop past quickly, but now and again not so swiftly, for the horses would be troublesome and prance around and everybody would have to get out of the way. When they passed and rode up the hill and over the mountains, it always seemed to me that they were going off into some wonderful land, maybe like the one Oisin and Niav rode into on a white horse. As long as I remember, all the joy and wonder of the world have been connected with the sight and sound of galloping horses.

One year, before going back to boarding school, I went as usual to bid Bartley good-by. He took from a large wooden trunk a sovereign which he said was the color of my hair and made a long speech to overcome my unwillingness to take it, for in that country nobody ever took money from anybody unless one was a very small child or a very old woman in poverty. But he explained that the next time I came on vacation he would either not be there or that somebody would be living with him, for he was getting lonesome by himself, and, besides, he was not as good with the horses as he used to be.

II

That winter, business and farm produce having brought Bartley's brother, Brian, near my school, he called to see me. Strange visitors, as was usual, were first interviewed by the mistress of schools, and to this day I feel a profound disgust with myself at the twinge of schoolgirl snobbery and ill-at-easeness that rushed through me when I entered the convent parlor and beheld Brian in his knee breeches and leggings, his red hair on end, his frieze overcoat on the back of a chair, endeavoring to conduct a polite conversation with the smart little curious nun. As she rose and left us alone, she said to Brian, "She can only have fifteen minutes from her class." He was embarrassed, for he had never known me unwilling to sit down for hours to listen to everything he or his brothers had to say. His surroundings denatured his conversation, and, a little taken aback that I did not seem to be the same little girl in that parlor as the one who ran around wild through the countryside with dogs and a book of poetry, he did not stay even the fifteen minutes, but got up soon to leave after handing me about half a ton weight of chocolates. But he gave me one disquieting piece of information: Bartley had taken a strange man from America to live with him, somebody he had known in Spike Island, and neither one nor the other would speak to anybody.

The little mistress of schools rushed back to the hall to take the usual polite leave of callers.

"Good-by, madam," said Brian solemnly, not being used to addressing nuns. "This is appearingly a very grand school. But this young lady," designating me, "is a very grand, high-up young lady. You can't have many as grand here, if I may make so bold as to say so." I could see that at the back of Brian's mind there was some faint notion that his call had let me down socially in the eyes of the smart little nun, who, as he sensed, was a good deal of a snob, and he was making an effort to restore my prestige.

The following summer, as my youngest uncle had decided to get married, I had little time for my usual walks and calls on my friends. Marriages were all by arrangement in that part, as they were, in fact, in most parts of Ireland, and practically every day my uncle started off in a car accompanied by a friend and several bottles of whisky. He was handsome and well dressed, and though seldom sober, was to me a very interesting and attractive man; in fact, as some girls have father complexes, I had an uncle complex, with a mild inclination, later in life, to fall in love with any man who looked like my uncles. It seemed to me that these uncles of mine were not only the most distinguished and handsome of men, but also the most enter-

taining. Still I knew that this one would be far from making an
ideal husband. He was not young—no man married young in the
country places in Ireland—and there were rumors that he had led a
wild life in America, where he had spent a decade or so in an endeavor to become a singer. I remember that he had a list of mar-
riageable girls with a dot, and one by one he would drive up to
their houses. Their male relatives, knowing his errand, would receive him warmly or coldly as his attentions were welcome or not.
The errand was never openly broached but indirectly got round to.
One girl's mother had said, quite sharply I heard, "Well, sir, we
have other intentions for Kate; she can do better than you; you've
seen too much of the world." Something of this kind must have
happened a few times, for it was only towards the end of the summer that my uncle emerged from one of these voyages an engaged
man. I used to be quite humiliated when I would be asked in the
neighborhood, "Is your uncle not settled yet?" In the end he married a woman whom he had seen only a few times, and she loved
him dearly until the day he died, though he was not a good or
reliable husband, but he was, I think, a very attractive one. By
right he should have died an early death, for his diet was mainly
alcohol, but he contrived to live as long as anybody else.

When his marriage was arranged I set out at last to visit my old
friend Bartley, who had, of his own, made no effort to see me. Accompanied by Kruger and Joubert, I arrived at his house. I called
over the half door, "Bartley!" At first there was no answer. Then
there emerged a peculiar-looking dark-haired man wearing glasses
and holding a magazine in his hand—Bartley's new house companion, supposed to have been one of his convict comrades in Spike
Island. "If you give me your name I will ask Mr. Bartley if he desires to see you," said he in a tone of the utmost formality. "He is
not well, and I am not sure . . ." I felt, as I have sometimes felt
when calling on the newly married wife of a former bachelor friend,
I was being put in my place.

But in due course the voice of Bartley called to me from a room
off the kitchen, and I entered to find him lying in a large wooden
bed, turning the pages of an illustrated magazine. In some peculiar
way the strength was drained out of Bartley without his having, apparently, any actual illness, and the old life that was in his face and

in his voice was gone; so also was the old interest in me, his interest in my childhood, and then in seeing me grow into a tall girl. He was roused to see me, but not especially interested. His personality had undergone some sort of change, and the touch of melancholy that had been in him always had become a fixed sadness, a sort of melancholia. This was the first time I had ever seen that not unusual phenomenon, a change of personality after middle age, and being an impressionable girl, I was deeply disturbed. The companion, by name Darby, had been a prisoner in Spike Island with Bartley, supposedly a political prisoner, but on his release had gone to America, where he had spent some years in domestic service, there acquiring the style of speech in which he had addressed me on my entrance.

On leaving Bartley, who had seemed roused out of his lethargy by my visit, I paused in the kitchen for a moment and noted a remarkable meal that was being cooked by Darby. He was slicing slabs of cold Indian stirabout which he was putting in a frying pan with slices of fat American bacon. A teapot of tea was nestling on coals on the hearth, and a not inelegantly laid tray was on the kitchen table, evidently to be brought up to Bartley in bed. It had always been said in the neighborhood that Bartley and his brothers had never in their lives eaten anything except their own mountain mutton and their own pigs' bacon and their own garden cabbage and potatoes, and this newfangled diet introduced by the companion looked to me very dubious. The companion, on closer survey, looked as if he might be a man of unusual intelligence or imagination, but with some side of him undeveloped—he was, in fact, considered a little wanting by the neighbors. Later I knew him to be a man of fantastic imagination who read a great deal and who had even a published piece of writing in a Dublin journal about his life in America.

When Bartley died, as he did shortly afterwards, I felt as if a whole section of my life were gone. He had, in the end, sunk into a state of extreme sadness, and when he died he, who had been such a large man, had a body shrunken to the size of a boy's, or so the neighbors related. There were no horses left on Bartley's land, but the companion inherited the house and a few acres. The last summer I ever spent more than a few days in that country was the year before I went to Dublin to study, and I was then too grown up and subdued to roam around all day with dogs as I had been accustomed to do, and I remained more at home. One day there called to see me Darby in a new blue suit, accompanied by a girl who might have been his daughter, but who he told me was going to be his wedded wife, and they wished to invite me to the wedding. In due course I went to the girl's house, to which the wedded pair drove from the chapel after the marriage ceremony. Her father and mother seemed to be as pleased as if she were marrying a prince. "He's a traveled man," her mother said, "and he suffered for Grania Uaile; he'll give her as good a bit as anyone else, and he'll be a good head to her." After the wedding festivities the bride and groom rose from the table to depart to Bartley's house, now Darby's. The girl still wore her wedding outfit—a cream-colored dress of a material known as nun's veiling, and a wreath and veil on her head. The nearest way to Bartley's was straight across a lake, a gloomy, almost circular lake, with mountains on one side and a fairy fort on the other with a grassy mound known as the bed of Dermott and Grania, where that romantic pair had slept on their elopement from Finn Mac Cool. The wedding party walked down a path to where a boat was waiting to row Darby and his bride across the lake. One of the things that has remained in my memory is the girl in her white dress, her veil floating in the breeze, being rowed out in the twilight, corncrakes croaking, the reeds on the edge of the lake swaying in the wind, some of them broken and lying on the water. There was said to be in that lake a large prehistoric eel of enormous length and girth known as the master-eel, who lay at the bottom of the water, appearing at intervals on the surface and seen from time to time in each generation, foreboding some unusual happening in the district. "God grant he won't appear till the bride is safe across," said the bride's mother. Soon the music of the fiddles greeting the bridal couple on the far side of the lake let us know they had crossed safely.

ಀ CHAPTER 5

Strolling Musicians, Ballad Singers, Traveling Men

IT WAS ONLY AFTER I went to boarding school that I became consciously aware of the strolling musicians, fiddle players, ballad singers, tramps, and beggar women that were daily sights on our roads.
The rumors of the Irish literary revival had reached my school, and
it was reported that the new writers were making poems and plays
out of these characters. In my childhood they had formed such a
familiar part of the landscape, like the trees and the bushes, that I
took them for granted, but now on vacations I looked at them with
a fresh interest, a sort of literary interest. Some of them traveled all
over Ireland, on foot most of the time, but with an occasional lift
on a cart. When the strolling musicians and traveling men, as they
were called, returned regularly once or twice a year, they would receive a meal and a coin in our house, and sometimes a welcome,
for practically everyone was regarded as a friend in that country, and
all were familiar with one another, both gentle and simple, with
the exception of a few dour "planter" families. The best musician
was a rambling fiddler named Martin Fox, who used to play wonderful wailing Irish airs that, as it was declared, would draw tears
from a stone. I do not think he ever washed, and the chair on which
he sat and played was always scrubbed and put in the open air for
the breezes to blow on after he left. Similarly, the plate from which
he ate his food and the vessel from which he drank would be boiled
in soapy water and then put on a shelf in an outhouse. These were
always called "Martin Fox's dishes." I suppose he was exceedingly
dirty, but he was undoubtedly "a man of art," as he called himself,
a highly gifted musician, and his audience would listen entranced
to his fiddle playing. The whole household would sit around for an
hour or two listening to his tunes, the men drinking whisky punch,
the women drinking tea. The women never partook of strong drink

in company with the men, but they sometimes did in private with one another. One of my family who played the violin would try and catch from Martin the traditional Irish airs that were in his repertoire, but the old fiddler was foxy by nature as well as name and would try to prevent her getting down the notes correctly, suddenly changing his tune as soon as she caught some of the air. Many beautiful traditional airs may have been lost through the crassness of these strolling fiddle players, who had learnt them from other folk fiddlers.

The ballad singers were less entertaining to my family than the fiddle players, but were more popular, I think, round the rest of the countryside. The ballad singers were more of the tramp order than the fiddlers or the flute players, who often turned a good penny playing at dances. The ballad always told a story, but it was rendered in such a fearsome voice by the singer that it would have been better if he had simply recited the tale instead of decorating it with what he believed to be a musical setting. He would stand before the house, the verses held in front of him printed on a long galley strip of paper, and troll out in a voice that would rouse the dead from their graves some tale of Ireland's woes or glories. "Come all ye gallant Irishmen and listen to my tale." Because most of the ballads began with "come all ye," they were known as "come-all-yes," but often the ballad singer had beautiful or witty and humorous folk songs in Irish and English—"Breedyeeen Veasach," or "Mo vron er on fwarrage [My Grief on the Sea]," "The Croppy Boy"; then there was the satirical "Peeler and the Goat," "The Night before Larry Was Stretched," and an Irish-American ballad, "Finnegan's Wake." There were a couple of women ballad singers, but I remember only one woman fiddler: she had begun by rambling around with her father, a well-known fiddle player; then she had emigrated to America after his death, but the life on the Irish roads called her back. Her performance artistically was probably the worst of the lot, but it interested me especially. She seldom played the airs or the jigs and reels popular with the men players, but, instead, gave a performance personal to herself. She had a fair singing voice with a yearning note in it and would use her fiddle as a sort of accompaniment while she sang songs she had picked up during her American sojourn. She would troll out in a sad, haunting voice a song called "Belle Mahone," which had the lines, as I remember:

> Soon beyond the harbour bar
> Shall my barque be sailing far
>
> .   .   .   .   .
>
> Wait for me at heaven's gate
> Belle Mahone.

And also the song containing:

> The cottage walls at Bingen,
> Fair Bingen on the Rhine.

And there was a piece called "Spinning Wheel," as she informed us, which she sang in a heartbreaking voice and which contained lines which thrilled my teens:

> A year ago tonight, I mind,
> He sought me for his bride,
> But Mabel came among us
> And her face was fair to see.
> What wonder was it, Mother,
> That he thought no more of me?

But the traveling man with the most memorable personality was a well-dressed blind man; he had no companion, not even that traditional friend of the blind, a dog. Someone from one house would guide him to the next, and so on for his journey around Ireland. No matter how busy the members of a household were, somebody always went with him, for he was credited with the power of putting a curse on anybody who would refuse to companion him part of the way. He was always called "The Blind Priest," not that I think he had ever received even minor orders, but his clothes were cast-off clerical garments given him by priests, and he was a good Latin scholar. Of fine broadcloth, his suit was neat and well brushed, and he himself was clean and shaven; somebody every morning, it was said, man or woman, would take the razor out of his carpetbag and neatly shave him. Although he was blind, he was by far the cleanest of the men of the road. He generally came our way every July or August, led to our house by a boy from the last house he had called at. After he had rested, eaten, and talked for a while, I would, happily enough, escort him to the next house on the road that he chose to call at. He would not call at every house, and sometimes myself and the dogs, Kruger and Joubert, would have to accompany him a couple of miles of the road past several houses before he would release us by agreeing to call at some place. "Do not bring me to the Sneedys'," he would say. "They have little enough for themselves. Do not bring me to the MacGregors'—they're gloomy Scotch people. The Gallaghers are rude and uncultivated and have no learning. But bring me to a publican's or a strong farmer's, or to the first gentleman's place that would have a welcome for the like of me." He always referred to himself as a gentleman and a scholar; truly, I believe he was both. Nobody knew his history; one day, years before, dressed in his black clerical clothes, he had joined the procession of traveling men who begged their way on the roads, and had turned up at my grandfather's with a leather-bound Horace in his pocket. The tale that he was that superstitiously honored character in rural Ireland, a silenced priest, spread from mouth to mouth, but really no one knew where he came from or how he had started out. His accent was Irish, but belonged to no place-able province or county; he could repeat odes of Horace by heart, and he would make me repeat them after him, but he was horri-fied when he found that I had read Catullus at school, as he thought it unfit reading for a young female, and I think he re-garded it as a plot of the English Board of Education to corrupt the maidenhood of Ireland. Having been told by some gossip that I roamed around the countryside alone with dogs, calling at strange cottages, he warned me very earnestly not to let the roving life get too much of a hold on me, as, if one once got attached to the road, houses held no further interest. I think he feared I might grow up to be a tramp and was pleased to know that I was locked up inside a convent for nine months of the year. His convention-ality, apart from his mode of life, was deep-seated; he feared that I was allowed to do too much as I liked and was insufficiently dis-ciplined for a *jeune fille bien élevée.* His French, I think, was very good, and he would repeat poems of Béranger's which, he said, resembled Thomas Moore's. I remember he taught me one about an old soldier of Napoleon who after Waterloo became a tramp, begging his bread—"Like myself," the blind man would say. All I remember of the poem now is a refrain—"*Souviens-toi, souviens-*

toi." I think the fact that his French was so fluent probably told a good deal about him. He may have been a clerical student in some seminary in France or Belgium, where Irish students often went, and then had to abandon his studies on account of failing sight. This, however, is only a surmise, for nobody knew anything about him, not even his name; he was addressed as "Father" by everyone as if he were actually a priest. People were respectful to him, but he was not really liked as were the other traveling men, the fiddlers, the flute players, and the ballad singers; perhaps this was because he gave no return except his Latin recitations to the few who liked them. He could be arrogant and violent-tempered, particularly when he had something to drink, and always that curse he was supposed to have the power to put on people aroused fears in the bosoms of the superstitious, which included practically everybody in that country.

But I think this queer homeless man was fond of me; indeed, there has always existed between me and lone elderly men of all walks of life a great sympathy—men, as a Frenchman I knew once put it of the same type in his own country—"who have neither hearth nor home nor wife nor child, and who don't want them." As a child these men used to regard me paternally, as Bartley and the blind priest did; as I grew into a young woman they were sure I was sentimental about them; as I grew older still, even those who were much older than I regarded me in a sort of filial way and demanded a maternal sympathy. I was, and am, in fact, sentimental about them, for I have always been fascinated by "characters," and nobody has such a chance of developing a personality and becoming a "character" as a lone man without dependents or responsibilities.

Just before the last two times I ever saw the blind priest, my uncle's newly wedded bride, who had a distrust of all wanderers, warned me that he had called to see me to inquire when my holidays began, as he had a book to give me and an important communication to make. He was, she said, staying in the neighborhood until he could see me; the year before he had offered to give the secret of the curse he had to a cousin of hers, who, in terror, had declined it, and now my new aunt surmised that he might be wanting to pass it on to me. "If it was a cure, now, it would be all right to take it, but a curse can bring misfortune on the one who has it as well as on the one who is cursed."

In due course the blind man arrived, driven up on a sidecar by the coachman of the neighboring gentleman-farmer, himself a good Latin scholar and fond of listening to the blind man's recitation from Horace and Vergil. He was helped down grandly by the driver, gripping the carpetbag that he seldom let out of his hand. Me he greeted warmly as an elder might greet a youthful relative; then he sat down to his usual gossip, his meal and his bottle of stout. Then we both set out on the road together, I taking him by the arm to lead him to the next house he wanted to go to. I found he had been well informed as to my future movements. "I hear," he said, "that you are going up to the university and to the continent of Europe."

"I think so."

"After that," he continued, "it's best for you to enter a convent, some nice teaching order where you could use your brains and your education."

"I don't want to do that. I want to see the world and the people in it."

"The world is wicked, and life is full of trouble; the convent is the safest place for you; you've not been reared to face the world."

This idea of a convent as a safe retreat from the troubles of life had not struck me before, but it often did through life afterwards, when I had seen many countries and was weary of the struggles and anxieties of a writer's life. But at eighteen I thought I could never have my fill of life, and the blind man's words fell on deaf ears.

"A girl like you will never be happy; you are too nervous, and you feel too strongly." But I did not feel nervous then, and I thought strong feelings were a good thing to have, and I had an immense ignorance of life and a great notion of the enjoyments I would get from it. I was somewhat irritated at the old gentleman's desire to direct my future. "Now that there's a strange woman in the house and, maybe soon, a strange young family, this place will not be the same."

"There are other places in the world besides this, and people who will care about me."

"Childhood is the happiest time; you will never be as happy as you were here."

This was not true, but a platitude that elders hand out to young people, for my childhood was not happy, though I remember it with great interest and in great detail. After much further warning about the wickedness of life which he gave me in a mystical tone, he opened the carpetbag and produced the book which he had told my aunt he had for me. It was Saint Francis de Sales's *Introduction to a Devout Life.* As we proceeded along the road, arm in arm, he finally told me that he had in his keeping a curse which had been handed down to him and which had been used with success both by him and by his grandmother against one who had despoiled them of their property, and that he would like to pass it on to me, as he wanted someone to possess it before he died. I was the only one he knew whose native powers seemed to be fitting for the reception of such a gift. With difficulty I refrained from telling him that I had heard he had offered it to my new aunt's cousin, who was as unlike me as it was possible to imagine. My curiosity about the curse was intense. I imagined it to be a bundle of things such as was in the witch's caldron in Macbeth, and that it would be solemnly handed to me wrapped in the skin of a serpent, and that it would be taken out of the carpetbag he always carried. With a mixture of terror and expectancy I agreed to take it into my possession.

Then I found it was not a bundle, but simply something to be learned by heart. It was in Gaelic in separate lines or stanzas, and at the end of a set number of them was a Latin word, *"Fiat."* He would not repeat it all together and would not write it down, as he said it was dangerous to play with. There were three stanzas or sets of lines which I repeated after him until I knew them by heart. He would say slowly the Gaelic lines, and then in a thunderous voice at the end of each stanza or set of lines he would shout, *"Fiat!"* The malediction was not as long as I expected, and I must admit that I knew the meaning of only a few of the Gaelic words, but I went over it many times until it seemed to be in my memory. Before I left for Dublin and my new life he came back once again to make sure that I had the curse correctly. His instructions were that in my lifetime I was not to use it more than three times, and only against someone who treated me or mine with real wickedness. When putting the curse on any person I was to have a vessel of water on the left, a vessel of earth on the right, and to hold, in a tongs or on a fire shovel, a live coal. I was to use it only if the wickedness of the accursed was such that it put me in a high state of emotion, for the fire in my hand was to correspond to the fire in my mind, and only in such circumstances would the curse fall. I used it once, and I think it fell. However, now most of the formula is gone out of my mind, and only a half-remembered sentence or two stays in my mind:

No motion in your limbs, no wife or posterity to keen you, though fame was once yours. *Fiat!*

A blight on your brains, on your hearing, on your sight, on your voice. Want and tears on you. *Fiat!*

&v CHAPTER 6

The Land and the People

THE IRELAND I was born and brought up in has been described by some contemporary Irish writers as a feudal country, but I think that it really was a mixture of eighteenth-century and medieval. In the East, the Pale around Dublin was thoroughly eighteenth-century, but the part I knew, the Northwest, only at points touched anything as modern. For the rest, life had gone on pretty much in the same way for hundreds of years. My grandmother knew the time when the heads of native Irish families were still, in conversation among the people, referred to as princes—The MacDermott was called Prince of Coolavin, a MacSwiney was called the Prince of Donegal, the O'Haras were Princes of Annamore. Some of the families did their best to hold onto the chieftain's title of "The," and there were still titles like "The O'Donoughue of the Glens," "The O'Mahoney of Kerry," and "The MacGillicuddy of the Reeks." She had known a prince of the MacSwineys who was a musician and who would come on a visit on foot, with a servant boy walking three yards behind him carrying his violin in a green baize bag. Ireland was a poor country, as I had always heard, ground into poverty by the English, but later in life I was told by diplomats from other countries to the new Ireland that it was not as poor or as backward as countries of central and eastern Europe. And I heard M. Alphand, the French minister to Dublin, say it was a Celtic country mixed with Anglo-Saxon, whereas France was a Celtic country mixed with Latin. I have to admit that whereas London always appeared to me the capital of a foreign country, Paris seemed the capital of a country in which I was perfectly at home. A French friend of mine, a journalist, Simone Téry, always says that Ireland seems to her like a provincial France, and that everything that is bad in France is some degrees worse in Ireland, but of the same character, and that in Dublin she felt as if she were at home.

Though the country I grew up in had many of the marks of a conquered country and some of the habits and manners of an enslaved country, it was not oppressed as it had been in the past, and people, though poor, were as free as, in bad economic conditions, people can be. Some of the country people—the word "peasant" I never heard in my childhood—were very scraping and grasping about money, but in the main they were not, for they very rarely saw it or had it, as they lived by a sort of barter and exchange. Eggs, butter, and other farm produce were exchanged for groceries and shop articles, and what money came from the sale of farm animals or from relatives in America was used by the farmers to pay their rents. According to the fantastic land system, they not only bought and paid for the land they tilled, but continued paying rent for it to a head landlord who was usually, though not always, a man of English descent and associations who had been given a grant of the lands in some of the numerous wars between England and Ireland. Some of these landlords, as I remember, did not stay at home on their estates very much. On the surface they were shown a certain amount of deference by their tenants if they were popular, but locally they were generally referred to contemptuously as "Cromwell troopers" or "William troopers," for if they sometimes looked down on the natives, the natives had a fine contemptuous vocabulary for them in return. The English rule, though not really accepted, went on smoothly enough as I remember it. It was irresponsible but not really tyrannical in my childhood. Strange Englishmen would be sent over to occupy important official jobs, and, with the assistance of Irish underlings, they gave a sort of haphazard government to the country. The ones I knew or got to know as I grew up were slow-witted, well-intentioned men, bewildered by the Irish and sometimes fascinated by them; in fact, the convention was that we were a charming and witty people with an idolatrous Latin religion who could not govern ourselves. But while these people believed themselves as belonging to a governing race, they seemed sometimes far from sure that they belonged to a superior race. This state of mind has been common to the English, no matter where they have gone. In fact, what often happens to people transported from their own civilization and habits and customs happened to them; they often felt ill at ease and inferior in some things. Some of the petty English officials, such as those in the coast-guard and naval services and the officers of the army of occupation—or whatever the soldiers of the garrison were called—were not very bright and had boorish and awkward manners, though I remember the women as better housekeepers than Irish women. On the whole these people, all belonging to what is called the middle classes, had but little association with Irish people and kept very much to themselves. The really attractive English people whom I got to know long afterwards belonged either to the upper classes or the lower classes, the playing classes or the working classes, and these extremes both had a strong admixture of Irish blood.

The tradition in the Irish countryside was that in every generation there was a rising against English rule until the country would be freed of it. But the fight I heard most about as a child happened before I was born and was not a rising but a land war. Between the eighties and the rising of 1916 the land war was the shape the Irish rebellion against England took. The signs of it were still on the landscape, the remains of burnt houses, with roofless walls blackened and broken, showing where the landlords' bailiffs had battered down the cottages and set fire to them. The old and feeble, the sick and the infants had often been turned out to die in the open in the rainy climate. The neighbors looked after as many as they had room for; the others died or took refuge in workhouses or became vagrants on the road.

As remnants of the land war, too, there were here and there a number of hastily built cabins called Land League cabins which willing hands had built to shelter people who had been evicted. The evictions, apparently, had been terrible, and the people were not given the consideration due to the meanest animals. The insurrections of 1848 and of 1867 had failed; famine and evictions had done their destruction; the young and the vigorous emigrated; life sank to a low ebb in those who remained, and it was not until the beginning of the present century that the people began to recover spirit and vitality. Then they turned first to cultural and artistic matters, and once more to insurrection in 1916—this time with success. In my time, however, there was no overt oppression, and if the country was irresponsibly governed, I think that England was, too. England, like Ireland, was a small country, composed of a population, the majority of which was poor, less happy than the Irish in some ways because they were poor industrial workers in, often, uncertain employment, where the Irish were poor farmers and agriculturists who, at least, had always something to eat and a roof of some kind over their heads when they were not evicted. The English rule everywhere after the defeat of the Stuarts was a government of aristocracy for aristocracy, ultimately, of landlords for landlords.

I was brought up, like most Irish children, on the traditions and legends of Irish resistance to English rule, and on stories of the havoc wrought by Cromwell and his troopers and by William and his troopers, and of the help France had from time to time sent to Ireland, the last of which had been an army in 1798. This was talked about as if it had happened the day before, and old people would say, as if it were something very memorable, "My grandfather saw the French land at Killala." But in spite of everything, the tragedy of history, of famines, and frustrated insurrections, the people generally had a natural happiness and gaiety. I have heard of the Celtic melancholy, but I saw but little of it. Everybody known to us went to church on Sundays and believed that whatever limitations and unhappinesses were in this world would be compensated for in the next. I never in my day saw any great unhappiness or misfortune amongst the country people. Death was the great tragedy; the next, emigration of children to America; and, after that, foot-and-mouth disease amongst the cattle.

II

I remember still with emotion the emigration of the young people of the neighborhood to America. In those days the farmer's children were raised for export. There were times of the year—in spring or fall—when there would be a sort of group emigration; that is, a dozen or so would start off together once or twice a week for a few weeks to take the train to the boat at Queenstown or Derry. Generally each group was bound for the same town in America where they had friends or relatives who had paid their passage money beforehand or sent them their tickets. The night before their departure there would be a farewell gathering called an American wake in one of the houses of the emigrating boys or girls. There would be singing and dancing interlarded with tears and lamentations until the early hours of the morning, when, without sleep, the young people started for the train, the mothers sometimes keening as at a funeral or a wake for the dead, for the parting would often be forever and the parents might never again see the boy or girl who was crossing the ocean. There was, I remember, a steep hill on the road near our house, and when the emigrating party reached the bottom of it, it was their habit to descend from the sidecars and carts to ease the horses, and they would climb the height on foot. As they reached the top from which they could see the whole countryside, they would turn and weepingly bid farewell to the green fields, the little white houses, the sea, and the rambling roads they knew so well. The hill was called the Hill of Weeping in Gaelic, because of all those who had wept their farewells from the top of it. The bulk of the departing boys and girls were untrained and ill-educated, and so had to take unskilled jobs in their new country. But some of those who emigrated with education or some money became successful businessmen and lawyers, sometimes famous lawyers. However, I have known educated Irishmen and women in all sorts of work in America, a cousin of a peer a doorman, the son of a baronet a bartender, and others elevator men and waiters. In fact the educated Irishman often did not fit into American life at all. A few of those emigrating, especially the girls, would save enough money in the new country to come home for a visit. There were even a few who would save enough money for a dowry, and who would settle down contentedly enough as farmers' wives after spending seven or eight years in an American city, shedding the urban culture like a cloak except for a gold tooth or a deliberately cultivated nasal twang. Now and again there would arrive a young man or a young woman of the second generation to look up the homes and families their parents had come from. Some of these would be described as college students, but though bright and smart, they did not seem well educated. "There are only two universities in America," my writing uncle would say, "Harvard and Yale; the others are only prairie hedge schools. You had better stay in Ireland if you want to learn anything," he would inform these sojourners. And once in a way some of the young men would stay and study in Dublin, especially the students of medicine.

Emigration to America had often a sort of social stigma, and one would occasionally hear an old man or old woman declare haughtily, after eying the second-generation visitors, "None of my people ever had to go to America, thank God. We always had it," meaning money or material possessions. Though one of my uncles had been in America for a number of years, for some inscrutable reason he did not regard himself as an emigrant, but behaved as if he had gone there in pursuit of an artistic career as a singer. Yet he had been so down and out that he had to get money from home to take him back to Ireland—one of the few I ever heard of who got money from Ireland instead of sending it there. He would tell us at length about the great Irish lawyers in America, one or two of whom even had been born in the neighborhood; one, indeed, was a family connection.

The few native Americans I met come back to memory, the conversations rather than the people themselves on account of my sharp memory for words. Young men on bicycles, riding around in the summer months, looking up the homes and families their parents or ancestors had come from, being invited to tea in our house, sons of young men and women who had emigrated from the neighborhood when my uncles were children; friendly, talkative young men saying "I guess," "sure thing," "gotten"; saying "Toosday" and "noo," greeting one with a loud "hello," speaking with a nasal twang, wearing clothes with queer padded shoulders, easily recognizable a mile off as Americans, though their faces might seem Irish in America, gray-blue eyes, dark lashes, offhand manners; not at all like visiting English young men, very uninsular and strange to us, born and bred on an island, something of the citizen of the world about them, also something of a new civilization, passionately proud of America as if it were they who had made it, anti-English in an odd way different from our way, which was anti-English Government, not, I think, anti-English people; not well-educated young men—vulgar, some of the old people called them; American vulgarity on the top of emigrant vulgarity, my uncle John would say. Whatever it was, I had liked it and did not then understand my uncle's pathological snobbery, mostly picked up in England, where he had lived for years, having a faint English accent as my other uncle had a faint American accent. . . . We all spoke with different accents, even with differing pronunciations. I spoke with an Ulster accent; the American visitors noticed it. "My, but I like to hear you talk," said a young man. "People of education you all are. . . ." My uncle John, plunging into ill-humor, said later to me, "Why are Americans always talking about education?" And then we took to counting all the words that cropped up most in the Americans' conversation.

We in the country almost never saw any born American except the second-generation Irish. The returned emigrants were always referred to as returned Yanks. The first, I think, had nearly all worked with their hands, both gentle and simple, though some became lawyers. Peter, a sort of family connection, was a lawyer in Boston or near by. Well educated before he left, he got a law degree easily. He brought home on a honeymoon visit, in his forties, his New England bride—her family were in America before the Revolution, Peter told us, when he drove up in a new sidecar with silver things on the harnessings. . . . Had just bought it as a present for his mother, he said. In America before the Revolution . . . We quarreled about the Revolution date after Peter left, and finally found it in a preface to Burke's speeches. It did not seem a long time ago, some time before the rising of '98, before the French landed at Killala . . . the year before Peter's mother's house had been built. . . . The date was on the flagged hearthstone before the kitchen fireplace. "It all means," said my uncle, "that people who have a grandmother born in America are aristocrats over there. Peter wishes us to understand that he has married an American aristocrat." His mother had given us the Boston papers with the account of their wedding and with their photographs—curiously vulgar, as Boston papers are to this day, queerly written; a photograph of Peter in morning coat, silk hat in his hand, the bride in a long white dress and veil, her grandmother's wedding veil, the papers said. My uncle John had a silk hat in a leather case, but I had never seen him wear it. I think he wore it in England, in London probably.

Peter brought his American wife to tea. She wore a tweed coat and skirt, not like our tweed coats and skirts, but with funny shoulders in the coat and a lining of stiff silk, with a rustling to her skirt from her petticoat probably, high buttoned shoes, hat with a large veil. She looked a little withered, probably middle-aged like Peter. The best spoons were brought out, the small fashionable tea-cups. "We do not drink tea out of such small cups in America," said Peter, "but then we seldom drink tea at all." My uncle brought out the whisky and a sweetish wine. I got a little of it as we drank the health of the newly married couple. A little later Bridgie and I drained the whisky glasses in the kitchen. Peter was very amusing and told us how the Irish girls changed their names in America; Bridgets became Dellas, Annies became Annas, Noras became Honoras, Marias became Maries, which he pronounced "Murree."

I remember his wife as the first person I ever met who "made" conversation. She seemed to feel it a duty never to allow a moment's lull in the talk and to have a determination to put us at our ease. On her entrance she threw back the veil she had over her hat and stretched out her two hands with *empressement*, talking all the time in her Yankee voice. "You are the folks I most wanted to see in Europe." It had not occurred to any of us before, I think, that Ireland was Europe, as Europe to us was "the Continent," or France or Germany anyway. "I said to Peter," she gushed, "when ever are we going to see them? He has talked so much about you that I feel I know you all intimately." Now Peter hardly knew any of us except one uncle, and we got an uneasy feeling that whatever she knew about us she had got from local gossip since her arrival and not from her husband at all. She addressed my uncles as if they were small boys, looking at them with a studied eagerness. "Let me see. I bet I know who you are. You are the charmer and the musical one," addressing one uncle. And she turned to the other, "You are John, the tweedy one who has written a book." He always wore tweeds and had written several books, mostly biographical, but I had never met anybody who had read them. He was melancholy and snappish and grew more so under Anne's conversation. "You've traveled a lot, too, haven't you?" "No," said he determinedly. She got coquettish with my other uncle, the one who had been in America cultivating his voice. "You must come back and pay us a visit. We also have an old house—not as old as houses here," she said deprecatingly. "Of course we can't go into competition with you in old things." We all were silent, for we did not like old things at all unless they were ruined abbeys or carved crosses or things celebrated in history books or in Moore's melodies—"The round towers of other days" and all that, and if we had had the ready cash we would have flung out every old thing in the house, especially the wheezy spinet which she so admired and which she was told she could take with her to America if she liked. There were only a few notes on it that sounded, and we did not care for musical instruments that did not play. However, it did duty for holding books and photographs in frames. One was of our mayoral relative in his robes and chain of office. I lifted the lid of the instrument and showed Anne that it did not play, but her enthusiasm was not abated. "It's a broken old thing," said I. "Oh, you sweet little girl. I should love to have her spend a year or two with us," she said to my uncle. "Wouldn't you, Peter?" to her husband. He nodded. "We have such good schools, and she seems so intelligent."

"She is intelligent, but not sweet"; my uncle John was getting sourer and sourer, and I was mortified at his saying that I was not sweet, but Anne was equal to it, and I got up a liking for her that no later family criticism could wither.

"She looks both sweet and intelligent," she said. "She ought to have a good education surely, and we have splendid schools in Boston."

"She's overeducated already," said my uncle. "Overeducation in the middle classes is the curse of this country. The learned professions are crowded; too many doctors and briefless barristers and nobody able to mend a timepiece or make a good suit of clothes."

I had already heard him inform various callers at one time or another of the diverse curses the country was suffering under—the British Government, the Irish Parliamentary party, the number of people in government jobs with a pension, the publicans, priests having their photographs perpetually in the papers like the Dares (the Dares, Zena and Phyllis, were stage stars of the period).

"There must be worse things than that," Anne spoke in a mollifying tone.

"Well, there's too much horse racing and huntin'. Everybody who has a four-footed beast goes chasin' foxes." With a wave of the decanter he offered Anne the whisky, which, faintly horrified, she motioned aside and continued genteelly sipping the wine.

"What about whisky drinking?" she asked with an edge to her voice, but with a square wide smile that showed her large, nicely arranged American teeth.

Drinking always made my uncle John cross, because he did not drink steadily like my other uncle, but only convivially when hospitality demanded it, or else on bouts lengthily spaced to relieve his feelings. I never saw this uncle look happy, not even later when he married and had beautiful babies. He perhaps had the Celtic melancholy or something; he was good-tempered only when he was writing.

Anne and Peter did not remain long—a couple of weeks—but I remember everything they did, because in those days there was so little to remember. The local baronet's wife asked them to lunch. This was considered an honor, as she seldom entertained the local people to anything more than a garden party now and again, at which there was tea and strawberries, though her husband, Sir M., would invite a few of the men into the house to drink whisky. In her earlier years she was seldom seen out of a riding habit, but a fall off a horse had broken her arm, knocked out some of her teeth, and given her concussion of the brain, so now she was never seen on the back of a horse, though she drove a little and had even won first place in driving tandem at the Dublin Horse Show. Peter, who was

a hearty, happy person, had a good time at the luncheon and told
us all about it. Anne arrived, dressed in silk and her grandest hat.
Now, old Lady C. never wore silk except in the evenings, when it
was her custom to wear a low-necked watered silk evening bodice
over whatever skirt she wore in the daytime; thus her head and bust
above the dinner table was that of a lady in evening dress, while the
lower part of her was that of a lady who had been having a good
tramp with a walking stick on the roads with the dogs. She appeared
at the lunch in a tweed skirt and cardigan, and her husband, Sir M.,
in riding breeches. To Anne, a city person, this did not seem at all
comme il faut. "Very countrified," she called the C.'s afterwards;
not that this would have worried them, for Sir M.'s greatest term
of contempt for any man was to call him a "city jackeen." He was
more of an aristocrat than his wife, both by temperament and descent. Indeed, he was a good deal of a feudal personage and had
lived a life of extraordinary narrowness, maybe ignorance even,
though it was known that he made an effort to read the Latin poets
from time to time, his only known reading, and he could say in
conversation, "*Eheu fugaces,*" "*O tempora! O mores!*" "*Lacrimae
rerum,*" and "*Timere Argivos,*" by which it was said he meant the
English. Anne had made conversation steadily, we heard, and had
got Sir M. to talk. She told him about my uncle's notion of what
was the particular curse of the country and asked him if whisky was
not a worse curse.

"Not at all," said Sir M. "Whisky is one of the industries." Lady
C. belonged to a whisky-distilling family—"in the liquor business,"
as Anne would remark with horror. "No, whisky is an industry, a
fine business, though the Scotch are doing us out with that peaty
stuff they make up there. Ever taste it?" he asked Anne. "Not better than poteen. Indeed, better stuff is made in the mountain stills."

"That ought to be stopped," said Lady C., maybe thinking of the
family industry, and they spent the rest of luncheon quarreling as
to whether poteen making ought to be frowned on more than it
was. Sir M. was all for it. "The best poteen," he avowed, "goes
down your throat like cream. Beautiful drink!"

In the drawing room afterwards Lady C. had discommoded her,
Anne told us, by offering her some liqueur that the family had made
a hundred years or so before, drinking quite a lot of it herself, doing

a little fancy needlework the while, and asking questions about Red Indians and if she knew in America the boys and girls who had emigrated from the neighborhood, and if a gruesome story she had heard was true, that some of the girls were on the streets. Then she got to what my uncle later declared was the whole reason of her asking them to luncheon. A lot of her teeth had been knocked out by the fall off her horse, and more had been pulled on account of decay and toothache. She had had a set of false teeth made by a Dublin dentist, but they did not fit very well and jogged around in her mouth in a disagreeable way. She had heard that the Kaiser and the King of Italy had American dentists, that American dentistry was a miracle, and she was wondering, if she had a cast of her mouth made, if Anne would take it over and get a set of American teeth sent her by parcel post. Anne thereupon invited Lady C. over to America to get the teeth made, but the lady shook her head. She never intended to leave Ireland again and disliked travel anyway. How the matter of the teeth was settled, I never knew.

"I wouldn't call her a lady," said Anne thoughtfully as she assisted Peter in his account of the matter to an interested audience.

"Oh, she's a lady all right, or maybe even a gentleman."

"Well, not what we would call a lady. Not a woman of the world, really, not urbane." Down went the words "urbane" and "woman of the world" in the blistering little book my uncle was keeping of the words and language Americans were using.

The C.'s were the first people of title Anne had ever lunched with, and she was somehow disappointed. It was before the days of Hollywood, but I think that probably Anne had a sort of romantic, fairy-tale notion of the life of the titled classes. At the same time she was impressed by a kind of state surrounding the C.'s, the respectful menservants passing everything at luncheon, the French menu placed before Sir M.—he, assuming that she knew no French, courteously explaining "gigot rôti" and "pommes bonne femme," Anne tactfully listening, talking to him about his house, his portraits, the eighteenth-century furniture, trying to endure the chilliness of the dining room, the greater chilliness of the drawing room with the inadequate open fireplace and the windows all open, where women had always to wear shawls or scarves over their evening dresses at night and cardigans in the daytime. The sweater and skirt was a garb, I think, originally invented by or for these country house people.

ॐ CHAPTER 7

The Life of the Countryside

THE LIFE of my forebears on both sides must have been monotonous in the extreme except for a few of those who took service in the armies on the Continent as soldiers of fortune, and I would hear of the adventures of one who went to France to fight for "Boney" as if it had all happened the day before, as if the gentleman might walk in any day in his Napoleonic uniform. There were romantic tales of one who entered the British Navy, became an admiral, and wickedly left all his property to an illegitimate son, who didn't seem to have profited by it anyway, for it remained in Chancery as long as any of us could remember. There were vague lawsuits about it even in my time, and we still believed that through the mysterious dispensations of Chancery, the property would sometime reach us. There was another tale of a Conrad-like character, a sea captain who became governor of a small British West Indian island, got knighted as people of the kind do, and used to send home large photographs of himself seated in front of a long, low, white structure, magnificently called "Government House." He somehow begot little dark children. His negroid grandchildren or great-grandchildren are living in Boston, and one of them—a man of distinction—I am proud to know. But on the whole, the adventures of my family seem to have been tame.

Several of the families around us claimed high and ancient lineage, but their lands had been taken from them to reward English adventurers. Whether a moiety of the tales of high descent were true or not, numerous as were princes in Irish history, it could hardly be that all who claimed to be chieftains and princes of the Gael could have been such. Nevertheless many of the country people had every traditional aristocratic attribute—fearlessness, courtesy, a high sense of honor, ease of manner, pride and charm, delicate and beautifully formed bodies, fine silken hair, and long slim hands, though they walked or rode so much that they developed that muscularity of leg and ankle that one sees in the offspring of generations of horse riders.

Others, obviously, were of what is called peasant stock—small, thick-bodied, thick-limbed people, though I am not sure that any sort of lineage or class distinction has anything to do with such things, but maybe some interior or psychic quality. The farmers of English name and descent were not many—they were Protestant, and somewhat different in appearance from the others, having light, fair hair and sallow complexions, whereas those of old Irish name and stock had very fair skin, dark hair and blue eyes, or reddish hair and green-gray eyes. Of course the country must have been always of mixed race, and the names showed the various invasions— Danish, Norse, Norman, and English. There never had been a Roman conquest as there had been in Britain, and we had no Roman roads or Roman remains. There was almost as much English blood in Ireland as Irish blood in England. In the West, all along the coast by the Atlantic, there were people of pure Gaelic stock, but, for the most part, the most that one could say for those who claimed to be pure Irish was that they were predominantly Irish and of Irish tradition. The children of mixed parentage where the father or mother was English were very different from the like combination in England; a country's tradition, not the racial admixture of its people, seems to be the character-forming, temperament-forming factor. How many of England's most ruthless and imperialistic generals had Irish names like the General Dyer who shot the natives of India out of cannon, and how many Irish patriots who died for the country had English fathers and English names, like Pearse in 1916.

II

Some Irish people completely identified themselves with England, and when traveling abroad would refer to themselves as English. They would enter the English service in the colonies or in the Army and Navy and the home civil service. A small country, such as Ireland is, had but little outlet for the very talented, the adventurous, or the ambitious; consequently there were often tremendous competition and jealousy in connection with what desirable employment was available. The most sensible and adaptable took whatever work they could obtain if they wanted to live in the country at all. Government jobs with a pension were the great prizes; in pursuing them people pocketed whatever feelings they had against the British Government or rationalized them. "Sure, it's our own money anyway. The English have overtaxed us for hundreds of years." Consequently one found a rebel Irishman like Roger Casement in the British consular service, and some of the most ardent devotees of Irish freedom and separatism in the government services, mostly in minor jobs, though a few were in the higher branches, like a governor general of the Irish Free State who had been a high British official in India. There was, as I remember, unlimited free speech, and nobody restrained the expression of his sentiments even though officially he might be O.H.M.S.—on His Majesty's Service. At that, there was some justification for my uncle's insistence that overeducation of the middle class was one of the curses of the country—at least, education in the classical and literary sense. The country could not use all its most highly trained minds; it had too few resources, and centuries of bad government had left it with too little discipline. A great number of them went to the British colonies in various occupations; many young men I knew went to Africa to engineering and administrative jobs in devastating climates; others stayed at home, making the best adaptation they could, often getting slack and embittered.

A brilliant mind, such as at least one, if not all, of my uncles had, frittered itself away in frustration and resentments, with a mixture of love and hate for the country, such as Swift had, and a mixture of scorn and acceptance of English ascendancy. He and his friends sometimes drank heavily to forget the disappointments of their lives. What talents he had could have best found their function in journalistic and editorial work, but he scorned emigration to the United States, where he might easily enough have attained distinction in such a career. He and his friends, while liking English people personally, firmly believed that English officialdom all over the world conducted a propaganda against the Irish. My uncle knew the history of Ireland minutely and all the details of its exploitation. He could reel off the amount of taxation that had been put on the wool trade and the brewing industry to take them out of competition with English industries. But the House of Guinness used to claim that the attempt to tax Irish beer out of existence and to make the people drink English beer only proved how good theirs was, seeing it had survived all competition. Then, if anyone in his presence mentioned any of the names of the Anglo-Irish landowners, he would say, "That fellow got the lands of the McCarthys or of the O'Sullivans," and he was extremely vicious about some adventurer who not only got the lands of the O'Neills but stole their name and history and appeared before the world with the crest of the Red Hand. But as I grew into young womanhood I regarded my uncle as a patriot of an old-fashioned mode, chiefly because of his prejudice against the new movements, the literary movement and the language movement, for it was these in the end which rescued the country from the defeatism and provincialism it was sinking into. The younger generation christened the Anglicized Irish "West Britons" to mock their British provincialism. The new writers annoyed my uncle, and he would read a poem of Yeats's aloud and say menacingly to me, "I will buy you a new hat if you can tell me what that means." The last time I saw him he was still asking what that poem meant. The newest Ireland made him as crotchety as the British Government had made him in my childhood.

He was, I think, a fair sample of the psychology of a country which another country has subjugated or half subjugated, miserable under it, yet neither accepting outside rule nor fighting against it, skeptical of every attempt of the younger generation to assert themselves either politically or culturally. He was also a fair sample of the baffled intellectual with nothing to exercise his brains on. He was perpetually writing something—biographies, articles, odd scraps of verse which he published in the Dublin weeklies, never, in spite of his literary knowledge, learning to write with distinction, never really achieving anything in life that he wanted, remote from what interests and amusements the country afforded.

And the amusements could be thrilling, especially for anyone interested in outdoor life and horses. Though life was monotonous, it could at times be full of high delight. I have never had such pure intellectual pleasure on the one hand, or such hilarious fun on the other, anywhere as in Ireland. On a frosty October morning to go tearing after a hunt on a sidecar or a "trap," or as far as one could go in such vehicles, going the rest of the way on foot if one was not mounted, leaping ditches or climbing gates with everybody in wild excitement, with people on foot, on bicycles, on sidecars, on "traps," on ass carts, the young men on foot sometimes beating the horse in a race—all this was a sort of spirited life that could give an intense exhilaration. The hunt would meet generally on a frosty morning either in a graveled space beside the lawn of one of the large country houses, or else in an open square in the village, the horses prancing around impatiently, the nervous fox hounds with difficulty kept in control by the huntsmen. The women rode side-saddle, and, as I remember them, they were weatherbeaten and hard-featured, wearing dilapidated riding habits. The men were weather-beaten, too, and clad in the most variegated array of riding togs—the farmers with leggings over their trousers, the others in riding breeches, nearly all shabby except for the wealthy landowners and their guests, who would have smart London hunting clothes and red jackets.

The horses for the hunt were always trim and chic as horses always are in Ireland, though they were seldom thoroughbreds. I have known men in every rank of life in Ireland who loved horses more than they loved anything else, who could live without food or houses or love, but who never in the world could have lived without a horse, or without the drink that so often goes with the companionship of horses. In fact the love of horses was often regarded as a vice that distracted people from all habits of work and made them, as regards the ordinary business of life, good-for-nothings. It was not the habit to hunt with thoroughbreds. The horses I knew were half thoroughbreds, half farmers' horses, and grand-looking animals they were. They were horses of all work; they could be used for riding or driving or farm work. Sometimes a horse who had spent his youth as a hunter would in his stale days be forced into harness, and I remember a man who somehow managed to drive loads on such a horse, and they—man, horse, and cart—were one of the sights of the countryside as they came rearing along the road, the horse at one moment trying to shake himself out of the shafts, the next settling down to an imitation of the jog trot of an animal who has spent his life on roads and fields, and who never had jumped ditches or had torn after fox and hounds. The sight of a barred gate would prove an irresistible temptation to this horse, and he would rear and neigh and try to shake off the cart, but the hardy, expert horse handler who was his owner would manage to pull him in and make him jog along under the load. I am aware that the national Irish animal is supposed to be the pig, but my uncle would maintain that this was English propaganda. Anyhow, to anybody who really knows the country, the national Irish animal is the horse. I have met some Irishmen and women who did not care about horses, but with few exceptions they were dreary creatures.

III

Even in the case of people with considerable possessions, ready cash was not extensive except, perhaps, among the shopkeepers. But the country people, as I have already explained, had practically none at all, and living by barter or exchange was a common practice. Once, when home from boarding school, I lost a half sovereign on the footpath that led to a neighboring town, and the woman who found it figured out by a process of elimination who might be likely to have a gold piece in such careless keeping, and finally brought it to our house, saying to me with gentle severity, "Now, little colleen, you must learn the value of money; when you've a gold piece like that, you should tie it around your neck in a drawstring bag or put it in your stocking. Even in America you don't find gold on the streets, I'm told."

There were many "traveling men" on the roads, and while some of these were refugees from evictions and clearances, or were forced on the road by hunger, others, I am sure, were the remnants of guilds or unions of craftsmen and tradesmen who were in the habit of wandering from place to place in many European countries. I have seen the same type of "traveling men" on the roads in France, and they were nearly all the relics of itinerant trades, though some, as in Ireland, were simply natural-born tramps who were allergic to life in houses and labor.

Traveling tinsmiths, a gypsylike confraternity known in the countryside as "tinkers," would wander around in carts and on foot, selling new cooking utensils and mending old ones. These were the most outstanding and picturesque of all the itinerant trades, somewhat like gypsies in their habits and demeanor; in fact they might have had some gypsy blood. They would usually appear on the road in a procession of carts, horse carts, ass carts, mule carts, the women and children seated in the vehicles, the men walking beside the animals' heads. They took in payment for the utensils they sold or mended, empty bottles, farm produce, old clothes, or money when they could get it. Often they would steal chickens and ducks if they did not get them in barter, and sometimes people who missed poultry never knew whether they should blame the tinkers or the foxes for their loss. These tinkers would make a fire on the roadside and cook their meals, and the country people would go and watch them to see what they were eating, and if a fine fat chicken, as was usual, would be taken from the pot, some bystander would be sure to remark, "That's from John Shanley's spring flock," or "That's John Durkin's fighting cock." At their approach the housewife, who had washed her clothes and put them out to dry, would hastily collect them, for the tinkers stole shirts and socks when households were not on their guard. In the tinkers' train of carts were pretty young women and lots of vigorous-looking children. The ceremony of marriage among them was what they called "Leppin' the budget"; the budget was a bag containing the outfit for mending tins and saucepans. The young man and woman would join hands and together take a flying leap over the bag, whereon they were husband and wife according to tinker custom. They were undoubtedly a native product in spite of a probable admixture of gypsy blood, and they all had Irish names. One great tribe was called MacDonagh, and these were the terror of the roads, on account of their depredations, their command of language, and their possession of a traditional curse. A rich man's daughter eloped with one of them and traveled the roads with him until her child was born, and then she died on a bed of straw by a ditch, her newborn baby beside her. A charitable countryman, seeing her there, women about her, rode off for the priest, and he arrived before her death. Kneeling beside her, his stole around his neck, he heard her telling the handsome, weeping young tinker who was her mate that she had known the height of happiness with him and had been far too happy to live long.

Among the other traveling trades were ropemakers, saddle and harness makers, shoemakers, carpenters, tailors. When my uncles were small boys an itinerant tailor would stay at the house for a couple of weeks and, mounted cross-legged on a kitchen table, would cut out and make clothes for them, all sewn by hand, of course, for a sewing machine was then unknown. In an earlier day, among the road trades had been wool and flax weavers and glass cutters, and a scattering of these remained. Hand-woven linen was in common household use, and hand-woven tweed was used for overcoats and suits as it is to this day, though I think the earlier woolen weaver's craft has decayed in the last decade or two, and the cottage tweed is not so closely woven as it used to be. In fact I was told of a trick used to make a piece of goods a yard longer. Two asses were brought along, and one end of the piece was fastened to one of them and the other end to the other ass; then they were driven in opposite directions, finally stretching the tweed beyond its woven length. I have heard that this sort of trickery is also practiced by another method, by the Chinese, in making Irish crochet lace.

If the most popular of the road men were the musicians, the grandest of them appeared to be the glass cutters, who were indeed almost men of art and who produced highly prized work. They had a guild or union quite like a modern labor union which had this motto or device, "A pleasant road and a kind welcome for every traveling man." But of all the beautiful things that the glassmakers made, that the silversmiths made, that the other trades made, very little remained in people's houses, except, perhaps, in the houses of the big landowners, and they, too, often sold what they had when they needed money. There were very few old inherited things in the houses of the middle classes, and there were many reasons why this was the case. Life was uncertain and insecure; through the centuries there had been many wars and rebellions, burnings of houses, and consequent punishments, depriving people of their possessions. What remained to those who rebelled was not of much account, just as one might say that what will remain of inherited possessions to the Jews of Central Europe, or to the Poles, will not be great after this generation. What people in Ireland inherited was something inside themselves, often an arrogant pride of race, long memory of events historical and legendary, a curious sense of the past.

The past, even the remote past, seemed to be only a little way back, and even to walk side by side with the present. In my childhood the possessions people had held onto somehow for a couple of generations—silver, glass, mahogany—were often bought up by itinerant dealers driving around in horse carts and offering to an impoverished family a few badly needed shillings or pounds for native silver or glass, or for heavy mahogany that the owner cared little about. Sometimes the owner parted regretfully with possessions; often, not; I have heard a woman say, "What do I want with eighteenth-century chairs? The money will help to pay for my son in school." There was a case where a Jewish dealer had asked to see the contents of an old lady's attic and had bought several chairs he found there for ten shillings each. He had first offered less, but she held out for the ten shillings. When, afterwards, the chairs were auctioned in London and it was discovered that they were the remains of some owned by Marie Antoinette, and consequently brought a large sum, the dealer felt he ought to give the erstwhile owner more money. He took a special trip from Dublin to give her some extra pounds, but the old lady was adamant. "You gave me what I asked; a bargain is a bargain; I am an honest woman, and the family I came from never broke their word. I will take no more."

Often pictures and other items of value would be found in the houses of folk whose forebears had fought in Continental wars and had either brought back loot or honestly acquired things. In our house there were some dingy black paintings which always filled me with gloom as a child. But once when I described them to John Butler Yeats, the father of W. B. and Jack B., he got excited about them. "Black paintings are always interesting," he said. "They may be very good." But nobody cared about them, and the wife of one of my uncles later bartered them to a traveling dealer for some bric-a-brac, a reproduction of "The Angelus," and a bamboo tea table, and thought she had made a good exchange. It was like that all over the country, among all classes. When the old silver of the almost deserted house of the great Irish family of the Fitzgeralds, dukes of Leinster, was sold to America, the last regular occupant of their huge house, Cartan, County Kildare, Lady Nesta Fitzgerald, said to my husband, "Thirty-six furniture vans were filled with things out of this house. And don't you think people will feel odd eating off our plate with our monkey crest on it? Our monkey! Isn't it strange?" Perhaps I should say that the peculiar crest went back to an old legend about a monkey saving a Fitzgerald heir when their castle of Maynooth was on fire.

I think the disturbed history of the country made people of all classes careless about possessions while having a strong attachment to the past. It is hard to explain what it was that made people so careless about material things. In our house there were plenty of old books, and in the loft over the kitchen, perilously reached by a ladder, along with a few blunderbusses and pikes kept for the next "rising," there were pieces of broken furniture, some slender-legged chairs without seats, a couple of little damaged tables with groups of figures decorating the gold-painted tops. Now I know these must have been French. There were even manuscripts in Gaelic lettering, and undoubtedly all these were destroyed in one way or another. An old edition of Pope's *Homer* was exchanged for yellow-backed novels by Wilkie Collins and Anthony Trollope. I myself surreptitiously made the exchange. But I have noticed that I, too, care but little for furniture or household possessions, or even for possessions of any kind.

ဆ CHAPTER 8

Pursuing the Higher Studies

THE SUMMER that I was eighteen, after I had left boarding school, I got ready to go to Dublin to study for that university degree that was supposed to represent some security in life for me. "If you have a university degree," it was argued, "you can always earn a living." As in an earlier day young women were trained in piano playing, drawing, needlework, and a little French as an insurance against indigence, so in the first decade of the twentieth century the new-fangled higher education for women was considered the appropriate thing for me. What female relatives I had were against the scheme and considered that a suitably arranged marriage would be better security for my future, but the men of the family, even my grandfather, were strongly for the four years' training in Dublin. My writing uncle was now living in another part of Ireland, having married and lost most of whatever interest he had in me; however, he expressed his opinion by letter in a very decisive manner, and on a visit of a few days, later, added the weight of his presence to the argument. So I proceeded to get ready; my dark convent boarding-school uniforms were discarded together with my boarding-school trunk, and a new outfit was prepared. The long, heavy plait of hair which hung down my back was transformed into a sort of coiffure on the top of my head, and on my last Sunday before departing I wore my new ankle-length clothes to church with a large hat pinned perilously with two long hatpins on the bundle of hair on top of my head. The old people who had known me for so long as a tom-boy turned their heads to take in the vision stepping gingerly up the aisle. The church was a small chapel of the penal days, without bell or bell tower or sacristy or confessional—a remnant of the time when the people had to worship furtively—and the priest put on his vestments inside the altar railings in sight of the congregation. He was a handsome young curate. I met his eye embarrassedly, and in addition, becoming self-conscious under the gaze of Bartley and Brian and John and Mary, the long skirt somehow became entangled in my legs and I fell awkwardly to my knees, the hat slipped its moorings a little, and so, overcome by shyness and awkwardness, I made my entrance into young womanhood.

The convent school had set itself to eradicate whatever girlish vanity about their appearance their pupils might naturally have, with the result that I had very little concern with my looks and only an intermittent interest in clothes. The nuns had also instilled in us the resolution to correct our sins and faults a little every day and so advance in virtue. My dominant failings as expounded to me were pride and anger and a tendency to criticize religious practices which I was assured was related to the sin of pride, the first in order of the seven deadly sins, the one which had caused the fall of Lucifer. The deadly sins, in their order in the catechism, were pride, covetousness, lust, gluttony, envy, anger, and sloth, and while I was supposed to be free of four of them, or even five, still it was considered that my habits of daydreaming were part of the sin of sloth. I did not think that the nuns really knew the extent of the latter, or they might have been alarmed. My writing uncle, as I accompanied him to the train after his few days' visit, in a mood of unusual solicitude gave me a little talk on the studies I was to devote myself to, and I told him what the nuns considered to be my drawbacks; that I had a propensity towards three of the seven deadly sins—pride, anger, and sloth. "But, my God," he said, "all literature is about the seven deadly sins; you'll never be a writer unless you know about a few of them."

For a long time afterwards I never read a book without considering which of the deadly sins it was written around, though I thought at the time there was something wrong morally about his making such a statement.

The night before my departure the uncle who had been in America—all my uncles were now married—thought it fitting to give myself and his wife an account of his life in that country. And as an illustration he brought out a little book of the words of a work with the title, *Patience, or Bunthorne's Bride*, in which he had sung either a small part or as one of the chorus. Holding the book in front of him, without music, he proceeded to sing a lot of it, beginning "Silvered is her raven hair," and, in spite of what must have been the drawbacks of the performance, we were delighted. Early in the evening he concentrated on the wonders of the places where he had sung, but as he continued to lower the whisky decanter he got somewhat melancholy and tearful and told us how, in his later days before he finally came home, his artistic performances were in the nature of putting on a show in mining camps and salmon-packing stations. In this show he made a personal appearance in a song called "A Handful of Earth from Mother's Grave." The grave was on the stage with a cross at its head, and he, attired in a dress suit, would lift a handful of earth from the grave while a spotlight played on him. The song, he declared, used to make his audience sob, for devotion to mothers was very popular in the States, particularly in these wild places. Then he recited for us a few romantic pieces about the West, one called "Lasca," about Texas and the Rio Grande, and he made America seem so romantic that I was a little sorry that I was not going there with the emigrant boys and girls over the Hill of Weeping, instead of sedately to Dublin to pursue the higher studies. I felt that we had had a lovely evening; and before going to bed I was given a cup of mulled claret, and we all drank to my future.

Early in the morning, having breakfasted, as was his custom, on whisky, after which he fiddled with a cup of tea, he escorted me to the train. Though he had a poorer opinion of the family genealogy and family talents than my writing uncle, yet inspired by his singing of the night before, and also, doubtless, by his rousing breakfast, he gave the lecture usual in Ireland from an elder to a younger going out into the world. He discoursed on the fine stock we came from, on the intelligence and good looks of the family. "We've all wonderful minds," he said, "and we look very refined." He repeated this several times, and as for myself, I thought there might be something in all he was saying, for my uncles were handsomer and better-dressed than any other men I knew. In addition there was in them a sort of artistry and discontentment that made them romantic. However, the more I saw of the world, the more my notions of almost everything under the sun became different from theirs; yet to this day there have remained in my mind the ideas of artistic intelligence that I imbibed from my writing uncle, and I early acquired a feeling for literature as an art and a sense of the difference between the various kinds of literature that I did not find among many of my fellow students. One of them, to be sure, seemed to me to know far more than I did, to have read with a more avid eagerness, and to be more highly sensitive to every kind of art. I used to feel limited and stupid in comparison with her, though we were very great friends. But she dropped out before she finished her university course, her romantic interest in literature drawing her to London, where she got to know Fleet Street journalists, whereas I, by staying in Dublin, was to know all the men and women who made the Irish Literary Renaissance world-famous.

II

I got on the Dublin train attired in my new blue ankle-length dress, my dead mother's watch fastened to a long chain and stuck in my belt. Attached to the chain was a silver Child of Mary medal and a little silver cross, and nobody, not even a native of central Africa, could have failed to recognize in me the typical product of a convent school, for my tendency to three of the seven deadly sins was not visible in my outward appearance, certainly not the one that included criticizing the Church. A lot of young people must have got off trains in Dublin that autumn day to pass four years as students. One of them, a boy of about my own age, traveling in the same railway carriage, was armed with a large book about Dublin which had pictures of the eighteenth-century squares and the Georgian houses and Dublin Castle and St. Patrick's Cathedral. He was to study what, for me then, was a mysterious branch of learning—architecture—and he pointed out to me in a knowledgeable and superior way the points of interest in the picture of St. Patrick's and the part of Christ's Church that had been built at the time Sitric the Dane was king of Dublin. My interest in St. Patrick's was that it was Swift's church, where he was buried with the "*saeva indignatio*" epitaph written on his stone, where fierce indignation could tear his heart no more. The boy had his own dream; I had mine, and as for him, a few minutes after he stepped off the train, the Georgian houses he longed to see presented themselves to his gaze, so for me also something of a dream became alive. The drive on an outside car to the university residence house where I was going to live led all over the city from the north to the south side, so I passed through all the well-known streets. But it was not the stately eighteenth-century houses or the statues or Parnell's monument that held my attention. I just noticed them as I went by, but what awoke me to excitement was the figure of a down-at-heel, trampish-looking man walking slowly across O'Connell Bridge with a billboard attached to him back and front—a sandwich man.

On the billboard was printed in large letters on a sort of orange ground a notice that thrilled me so that I nearly fell off the swaying jaunting car: Irish Plays for One Week. *Riders to the Sea*, by J. M. Synge, *Kathleen ni Houlihan*, by W. B. Yeats, *Spreading the News*, by Lady Gregory. My companion on the train was stepping into his beloved squares and streets, but I was stepping right into the Irish Revival. I asked the jarvey to walk his horse slowly so that I could read again the magic names, the magic titles, from the back of the sandwich man. Yeats. Synge. . . . They might be walking the street that very minute. I had never been to a real theater in my life; what plays I had seen were amateur performances of the classics. I had never previously spent more than a night or two in a large city; the schools where I had been educated had been either in the country or on the outskirts of small towns, and my familiarity with even these was slight. The thought of seeing a real play by living writers who were Irish and one of whom used to be referred to by my elders as "old Parson Yeats' grandson," and whose poems had been in local guidebooks and on post cards— those poems that had lines containing the names of local places:

> I will arise and go now,
> And go to Innisfree.

or

> My brother was priest in Kilvarnet,
> My cousin in Moherabuie.

or

> I stood among a crowd at Dromahair—

brought a thrill of rapturous expectation as to the wonders of the life that was about to open before me. The interest in the textbooks that were at that moment in my trunk strapped to the well of the car—the interest in Anglo-Saxon grammar or middle high German or the *langue d'oc* and the *langue d'oïl* faded practically to zero. I wanted to hear Yeats's verse plays spoken on the stage; I wanted to hear Synge's personal prose and Lady Gregory's Kiltartan. The *Anglo-Saxon Chronicle*, the *Romaunt of the Rose*, and the *Nibelungen* belonged to a long-dead world and to other countries,

but this was all new and from our own country; they were voices
speaking directly to us, to me—especially to me I believed Yeats
was speaking—and they were all about Ireland, speaking to their
own countrymen. The voices who had spoken to my elders were
English voices, only English voices—Tennyson, Swinburne, Meredith. These had spoken to my uncle's youth as he walked the streets
of Dublin, and never an Irish voice. The new writers were especially
ours; they wrote about our life, our history, our legends. But I
pondered, as I have often done since, on why a country so proud
of its nationalism was really intellectually and socially so Anglicized
that when plays were produced by Irish writers they had to be
labeled in Ireland's capital city "Irish plays," and the writers described in the local papers as "Irish poets." As late as 1938, when
the country had had its own government for sixteen years, the
Irish Independent was still describing a speech by a poet in the
following terms. "The Irish poet, Mr. [So-and-so], next addressed
the audience." It almost seemed as if there were something rather
peculiar about being an Irish writer in Dublin. The truth, as I now
see it, is that the country's writers were not economically independent of England, and consequently not intellectually independent.

III

Arrived at the residence house, I found a couple of my boarding-
school companions. The girls, varying in age between seventeen
and the early twenties, were from various well-known Irish schools;
the older ones were studying for masters' degrees. The residence
house was in charge of nuns, though no nuns actually lived there;
there were other residence houses in the city, some Catholic, some
Protestant, some grander and more expensive than this one, but
I had been told before I came that this one had a freer and more
liberal atmosphere than the others. At the same time university
education for women was not as usual as it is now, and we were
far from being as unhampered in our movements as American
college girls. On my arrival I was told the rules by a sort of
chaperone who was domiciled in the residence house. No going
out after supper—supper was tea and bread and butter—without

express permission from various nuns. . . . For the first-year students, no going downtown at all without permission. But the heaviest blow to me, at first going off until I learned how the rules could be circumvented, was the information that the first-years could only go to such plays in English as were on the university course, and to such plays in other tongues as helped them with their language studies. This meant, in actual practice, Shakespearean stock companies, an occasional Sheridan or Goldsmith comedy; but the foreign plays were almost invariably French, for the Comédie Française in those days took in Dublin in their foreign tour. Myself and nearly all my fellow students among the girls were going in for the same sort of degree in modern languages and literatures—the girls at the time in Dublin rarely went in for a classical or mathematical degree, though we had to study Latin for all examinations except the last, and between the stiff intermediate course of the secondary schools and the stiff university course I really think we read the bulk of the Latin authors. We also studied a subject designated as natural philosophy which has left a slight residue in my mind of inclined planes, amperes, and capillary attraction. Even a lesser residue has been left from trigonometry and other flights into higher mathematics which the exams required. There were some rivalries between the products of the different secondary schools, but actually we had all been educated in the same way, brought up in much the same manner and with pretty much the same attitude towards life. Mentally, morally, and intellectually we were well trained; I think practically any of us on leaving boarding school could have passed the B.A. exams of almost any American university I know, but we were very ignorant of life and were more developed intellectually than we were in other directions.

The instruction we had received had been very idealistic: a lack of worldliness, an ignorance of money values, a conviction that the values one needed to take into account were spiritual values, a general innocence of how life was conducted, was the result of it. The elders who trained and educated us were broad-minded intellectually and politically and in theory generally, but they had a tight-bound code of behavior, not exactly a narrow one, but one that had been developed in a small world, and anyone who did not behave according to that code mentally, morally, and socially was looked down upon. There were tight little gentilities and considerable objection to anything that was untried or that was new in art or literature. Naturally a democratic people, and perhaps naturally aristocratic as democratic peoples are likely to be, the middle classes from whom so many of the students came had imbibed some of the worst as well as the best elements of British civilization; among the worst was the fantastic English snobbery widespread in Irish towns and that fantastic English formality which dressed men going to business in silk hats and frock coats and their maids of all work in starched frilled caps and uniforms. But in other respects we were more like young Continental girls than English girls. We had little of any of that affectation which so many young English people seem to have imbibed with their mothers' milk. The foreigners who occasionally came to study were very much like ourselves, and the young English girls of our age not very like us. The convent training developed unconsciously femininity and a graceful concealment or an unawareness of learning. Even the most erudite of our young women did not seem to show their learning as much as some of the Oxford and Cambridge girls who came occasionally to Dublin, especially the mathematical triposes and the classical triposes who sometimes seemed intellectual dragons; they knew all sorts of things like biology and modern science such as our more literary training discounted. Ours was a hang-over from the medieval world and was indeed so much like that of the French universities of a generation or two before that the Abbé Dimnet once wrote me that he and I had the same sort of background and the same sort of education until, as he said humorously, he had Anglicized himself. Modern, however, as was the education of the Girton and Newnham girls, what brought many of them over to Dublin was a comic relic of medievalism. The great English universities graciously allowed them to pass all the examinations but not to add B.A. or M.A. after their names no matter how brilliantly the examinations were passed. An astute provost of Trinity College—that is, the University of Dublin—decided that the college could add to its income by conferring degrees on the women who had passed the Oxford and Cambridge examinations. Accordingly, from time to time there would be an influx of mathematical triposes and classical triposes, and, in return for some guineas, girls who had already passed with high honors in Oxford or Cambridge could write after their names B.A. or M.A. (Dublin).

The university studies, on the whole, were simply an extension of our secondary-school studies, but that, instead of going forward in chronology, we went backward; that is, our secondary education had brought us to the nineteenth century in the languages we studied, but now we started at the beginnings of languages and literatures and went step by step through their development down the centuries. We were dosed with linguistics and early texts; at times it was all very far from being interesting, and I absorbed only the modicum that would enable me to pass the examinations. For some, these studies, dreary to me, were fascinating; to James Joyce, for one, who was still in Dublin when I first went there, and who had studied exactly the same courses and got a degree in modern languages and literatures as I did: all this stuff about the development of languages must have stirred some profound and significant part of his mind, for all his work can be traced back to his college life and his college studies. He is the most outstanding advertisement in literature for that sort of education. Then we learned vast quantities of literary history, ancient and modern, the modern in the languages in which they were written. Some of our teachers, in fact, thought the history of literature more important than the literature itself. But this hardly mattered in the Dublin of that period, for a live movement in literature was around us, and living men, some of whom were world-famous, were discussing poetry and drama in the clubs and societies all over town.

The vigorous intellectual life of the city was open to the students who wanted it, and even those who didn't could not have missed taking some of it in through the pores. If we learned about the past of literature in the classrooms, we learned about the present of literature, what literature was, outside from the men who were making it. Dublin was a small city, the suburbs stretched out to a distance, but the center, the old part of the city, was circumscribed and bristled with movements of various kinds—dramatic, artistic, educational; there were movements for the restoration of the Irish language, for reviving native arts and crafts; for preserving ancient ruins, for resurrecting native costume, an array of political movements; here, too, were the theaters and the tearooms and pubs which corresponded to the café life of the Continental city. In the center, too, were the headquarters of the clubs and societies, some at war with each other, but all exciting and, somehow, focused towards one end—a renaissance. Between Abbey Street and College Green, a five minutes' walk, one could meet every person of importance in the life of the city at a certain time in the afternoon.

The city was then drama-mad, and every actor with an ambition to play any drama, ancient or modern, tried it out in Dublin; if it passed the test of a Dublin audience, it could pass anywhere, it was the fashion to say, and Dublin believed the dictum. Certainly we saw the most diverse kinds of dramatic entertainment, all the way from *Oedipus Rex*, played by Martin Harvey and staged by Reinhardt, to Mrs. Patrick Campbell in *Hedda Gabler* and Sarah Bernhardt and Mrs. Patrick Campbell in Maeterlinck's *Pelléas and Mélisande*. There were Hamlets in infinite variety, the outstanding ones being H. B. Irving's, Martin Harvey's, Forbes-Robertson's, and Benson's. I still think Martin Harvey's Hamlet the most enthralling I ever saw, and Sir Henry Irving's Shylock the best, infinitely the best, the most curious and the most arresting. When Ellen Terry played Portia, no doubt her acting was superb, but the personality that came across the footlights to us young persons in the cheap seats was that of a middle-aged woman with that curious deep voice, all youth gone out of it, that English middle-aged women so often have. The other Shakespearean plays, the less well known, were played by repertoire companies of whom I remember best the Ben Greet Company and the Bensons.

The Bensons had been engaged to play one of the early dramas of the literary movement, *Dermott and Grania*, by W. B. Yeats and George Moore, the manufacture of which Moore has given a sidesplitting account in *Hail and Farewell*. To give this composition the right Irish, or rather un-English, flavor, the play was first written in French by Moore, then translated into English, then translated by Dr. Hyde into Irish, then turned back into English by Yeats and Moore. But this was before my time and before the founding of the Abbey Theater. The Comédie Française, as it always did in its provincial tours, took in the needs of the students, and the French seventeenth-century classical drama was played, including the pieces on our course. The acting of the Comédie Française was strikingly different from that of the English companies and was supposed to be the type that native Irish players could take for a model; indeed it was passed around that the real name of the great French actor Coquelin was Coghlan, and that his family had originated in Limerick. But at this period the Irish were claiming almost everybody of distinction as Celtic or Gaelic if not Irish. Coquelin certainly looked a Celt, but many Frenchmen do; he played with sweeping verve and force; when he came on the stage, not only the audience, but the actors and actresses, took on a new life; they seemed vitalized by every blink of his eyelid, every stir of his hand, as well as by every syllable that came out of his mouth. A vibration was set up between audience, actors, and play that made them all a part of each other. I remember Coquelin's playing in *Le Bourgeois Gentilhomme* and *L'Avare* as I remember the acting of no player in English: it was art so perfect, so vigorous, so individual, so alive that it was life itself, but life framed and intensified. He was the only great actor I ever saw.

The English actors and actresses on the stage were always anxious to appear ladies and gentlemen, and it used to be said that breeding showed itself in an actor the moment he came on the scene. However, the French had no such notions; to be artists on the stage, to put themselves into the part, was obviously all they cared for. Besides, the traditions of the house of Molière and of the strolling players whose heirs they were clung to them. The women of the cast played with a vigor that would have been considered unladylike on the English stage. When they scolded they scolded, when they cried they cried with abandon. When Coquelin laughed he threw back his head and let forth a sound that made the theater rock with mirth and sympathy. His Protean personality, his immense humanity, animated everything he said and did; he not only was a totally different person in each new role, but he could be different night after night in the same role. The next greatest acting to his, I think, was that of some of the actors of the Moscow Art Theater whom I saw years afterwards.

Even in contemporary-society dramas like *Frou-frou* and *Maître des Forges*, brought to Dublin by the then popular French actress, Jane Hading, the actors and actresses showed little of that sort of restraint that in the Anglo-Saxon world denoted good breeding. They came from a different civilization, and both their plays and their acting showed it. Their acting, at once robust and disciplined, suited their plays exactly. On the other hand, the plenitude of life and passion in Shakespeare could have stood a little less good breeding and good form than the English actors were committed to. The Dublin sophisticates were in the habit of saying that Shakespeare was better played by the beer drinkers of Munich and Berlin.

ह्ळ CHAPTER 9

Early Days of the Abbey Theater

I WAS a moderately seasoned theatergoer before I saw any of the Abbey plays. In fact the theater had only recently emerged from the halls and back streets where it had its beginnings, and entered into possession of Mechanics' Institute in Abbey Street, which Miss Horniman had had reconstructed, partly, through her intense interest in drama, but also because of her admiration for Yeats, both for the poet and the man. Yeats had to fight hard for artistic ideas in Ireland: once, after he had made a fighting speech from the stage of one of the halls which served for productions, Miss Horniman was so moved that she came forward and said to him, "I will give you a theater." The Abbey Theater was the result of this promise. One hopes that Miss Horniman, who was a patriotic Englishwoman, ignorant of Irish history, did not regret her prompt generosity, for she had many difficulties afterwards with actors and dramatists.

For a conglomeration of reasons, some of the heads of our residence house—dormitory it would be called in America—as well as many of our teachers, had a very unfriendly attitude towards the new literary movement. First of all there was the antagonism which nearly always exists between the academic world and the writing world, between people who regard literature as a branch of learning in which they have a sort of vested or even hereditary ownership, and people for whom it is an art like any other art to which each new generation adds its own contribution. Then there were those people, common enough in every country, who did not regard it either as art or learning but as an instrument to advance a cause or improve morals or safeguard religion; in short, a group who believed that literature should be propaganda for something or another. Yeats, in his play *The Countess Cathleen*, had shown an insufficient acquaintance with the doctrines of the Church concerning salvation, and when, some years previous to our time, the play had been produced, the clergy and some young men students at University College protested against it because it showed the heroine redeemed although she had sold her soul to the devil. One James Joyce refused to sign the protest. Indeed from both the Protestant and the Catholic standpoint the whole Abbey and literary group were supposed to be irreligious. What was called the Castle set and the anti-nationalist set, known in Dublin as West Britons, pronounced the literary movement distinctly Fenian in tendency, and the rebel things Yeats had done along with Maud Gonne were brought up against him. At the other side of the line the extreme nationalists and the Gaelic League thought the whole group was not nationalist enough and were indignant that never a play in Gaelic was seen on the Abbey boards. Then it was said of A.E. that he worshiped pagan gods, and of George Moore that his immorality made him an outcast: he made no secret of having a mistress who had followed him from England. Yeats's imaginary lack of scholarship was the subject of solemn consideration among some academic groups. He had shown uncertainty about a Shakespeare folio and was hazy about the pronunciation of French words. The rural accents of some of the others were unfavorably noticed, and as their plays were about peasant life they were said to be vulgar. "Why can't the educated middle classes be put on the stage?" it was asked. "The middle classes are the most interesting people in the country. Why aren't they written about?"

The morals of one of the younger dramatists were questioned because a character in a play of his referred to her confinement, and he was cautiously advised to let his characters have their babies before putting them into his plays. Edward Martyn was the only one of the band I ever heard spoken of in these circles without criticism;

indeed I heard a mountain of talk against the others before I beheld even one of them.

Then one day, as I walked up the steps of the National Library, that library celebrated by Joyce in *Portrait of the Artist as a Young Man* and in *Ulysses*, I noticed ahead of me, dressed in black, a tall figure. My companion nudged me. "Yeats." At the sound of his name he turned sharply, and I encountered for a second a pair of necromantic eyes sunk in dream and seeming barely conscious of his surroundings. Again, as we climbed the stair inside the building, he turned slowly and stared steadily at us. I gasped, "Mr. Yeats," not knowing whether he noticed me or not. That he actually did he told me long afterwards, and that he remarked me whenever I came into his orbit, for, with the hostility he had to encounter, he was on the lookout for a likely following for the movement in which his life and genius were enlisted. I followed his progress up the broad stairway, and I arrived at the library counter beside him, my companion dropping behind to talk to a young man student. "Can I see Mr. Magee?" Yeats asked the clerk. Another excitement, for Magee was the real name of the critic who wrote under the name of John Eglinton. I hung around the counter, surveying the poet whose work had been responsible for so much ecstatic excitement in the lives of the young people I knew, including myself. He must have been around forty, but he seemed to be in the late twenties. With his very black hair, his olive complexion, his strange eyes, his height, he did not seem to belong to this common world. His great intellect, his imagination, his emotional power showed not only in his face but in his gait, in his voice, and in the beautiful hands which played with the desk pencil—in his whole being. Even then, before I knew much about human behavior, I realized that the distant, somewhat haughty tone in which he addressed the clerk came partly from a complication of shynesses: he was not really at home with people or in the everyday world, though he became a little more so later in life.

Mr. Magee was not in the library, and, with a slight inclination of his head to the clerk, Yeats turned and walked out through the library turnstile. Leaving my books on the counter, I raced after him, following a few yards behind as he turned down Kildare Street and then down Nassau Street to the Nassau Hotel, which was a sort of headquarters for the leaders of the literary movement. It was a small, old, unimposing hotel, of the kind often to be seen in provincial French towns, and like them, eighteenth-century. As I walked behind I noticed that he was speaking to himself as if he were repeating verses or making them. This was a habit with him, as I noted many times afterwards; he composed aloud, and in the street he seemed quite indifferent to the passers-by. Turning into the hotel, which opened, not onto the street, but onto a little inside court, he tossed away a half-smoked cigarette. I picked it up and kept it for years in an old horn snuffbox, so great was my youthful hero worship. But a fellow student outdid me: she, somehow, secured a castoff tie of Yeats's which she sported on a blouse. Even as I now write, after meeting through the years many who had stirred the world in various ways, I still think Yeats was the most remarkable person I have ever known—by many, many degrees the most remarkable.

The students in our residence house became persistent Abbey Theater goers; what our elders and professors gave out about it made no difference to us. The intellectual excitement brought into our lives by the theater, its dramatists, and the literary movement generally roused our minds to more of a pitch than all the learning we were imbibing. But to do them justice, the heads of the residence house did not ask us to conform to their ideas of literary excellence, but permitted us to go to all the performances. We started a club called the Twilight Literary Society from Yeats's *Celtic Twilight*, of which I was president; it was small, composed of about twelve literary enthusiasts, but small as our body was, it managed to cut some ice in the literary and artistic circles of our capital city. The city was not too large, and it was not difficult to take part in every intellectual proceeding in the whole town: we were visible at every artistic and intellectual function—exhibitions of pictures, private views, meetings of the National Literary Society, the Antiquarian Society, the Theosophical Society over which A.E. used to preside, the Gaelic League, the Feis Ceoil (Musical Festival). We were young and eager, and this was our way of having a grand time. We were not satisfied to go to one performance of each of the plays, but went to every performance until we almost knew the plays by heart. Our excitement after an opening night was so great that we would stay awake most of the night discussing the play. New literature and new ideas are perhaps always for the young who accept them readily and enthusiastically.

II

The Abbey Theater, then in its early days, opened only one week a month, and despite the fact that it was a week of great excitement in Dublin, the performances were but sparsely attended. It was only when its outside fame began to decline a bit that the theater became popular with the natives, and at present, the period in which I write, it is certainly three or four times as full as it was in the days of its great plays. We students in the cheap seats were delighted with all the plays, good and bad, and with all the actors and actresses as well as with the audiences. The actors at this period were amateurs in the sense that they worked at other occupations during the day, and, in the beginning, anyway, gave all their services voluntarily. A little later they got small salaries. I think only two of the company had any experience in acting previously: these were the brothers Fay who had played in some sort of vaudeville. Willie played in comedy and Frank played mostly in poetic dramas, but all the actors and actresses had beautiful voices, Frank Fay and Sara Allgood especially. When they played in a Yeats play they would speak the verse nobly, in a way that would often make the thrilled audience rise to its feet at the end and applaud. I have seen young Dublin mechanics sit entranced at verse plays; their taste had not been spoiled by much theater going, and in those days there were no movies. Besides, they loved to see the legends of the country and the people of the country put into plays. When Yeats's *Kathleen ni Houlihan* was performed they would rise to their feet in a display of emotion that was not perhaps more moving than Yeats's emotion when he came on the stage to acknowledge their calls. In fact the audience, though few, were such as to arouse any author to summon up his best powers. I have never anywhere seen such a responsive audience; they had an instinct for literature, whether they were students or workingmen in the pit, or the bourgeoisie or aristocracy in the stalls.

There were not many excitements except artistic, political, or religious excitements, and the artistic excitements were literature and painting; there was not much music or sculpture, and perhaps the reason literary and art movements were so rousing was that they really expressed the country; they were native. The important concerts were naturally of foreign music, as they are in every English-speaking country, and a people isolated from the rest of the world for too long had no great interest in it. However, the national festival, the Feis Ceoil, which set itself to discover native musicians, composers, and singers, aroused an interest in the whole country; in fact all the movements were bound up with nationalism and patriotism. Among the singers discovered at a Feis Ceoil was John McCormack; James Joyce also appeared as a singer at this festival, and but for some misadventure which I now forget—I think it was that his shortsighted eyes were not equal to the test of sight reading—might have been first presented to the world as a singer.

Except for a couple of singers, I do not remember that the Feis Ceoil discovered much distinguished musical talent. The efforts at musical composition were, I think, very much what the French call *voulu*, part of a determined desire to revive everything that Ireland had once stood for, or that it was imagined she once stood for. There were attempts at writing opera as well as every other sort of musical composition, and people patriotically attended performances of musical works that came out of native brains, no matter how bored they were. These works had poetic-sounding Gaelic names, inspired by Irish legends or mythology. One, an opera by a composer fairly well known at the time, O'Brien Butler (afterwards lost on the *Lusitania*), was called *Muirgheis*, meaning The Sea Swan; a composition by another with a less Gaelic-sounding name, Pellisier, had an even more romantic title. It was called *Connla of the Flowing Golden Hair*; the composer himself had a flowing walrus mustache which seemed to wag when he smilingly took a bow after a performance. At one of these musical affairs George Moore and the then youthful Padraic Colum sat in front of a row of us girl students. At an intermission George Moore, raising his two hands in the air, said in what seemed to us tones of awe, or anyhow staggered astonishment, "I declare to heaven, I don't know whether this performance is the pit or the peak—it must be one or the other." The musical composition assuredly got production only because of persistent accusations that the native composers, whoever they were, got no showing. The local satirical poetic talent was exercised on the composers, and Pellisier's mustache was good for clever lines. Vaguely I recall a rhyme about:

> Little jokes that once were dear
> To long-mustached Pellisier.

Actually, there was one fine composer living about this time in Dublin, Arnold Bax. But he was young and English, and nobody knew much about his composing, though he was well known in musical circles in London. Dublin was certainly not lacking in musical appreciation. It had a couple of good amateur orchestras, several good instrumentalists, one or two well-known native conductors, besides a couple of imported ones. But, musically speaking, the real interest was in opera and in singing generally, as is shown in Joyce's books. In the big theaters where the London and foreign companies played, the denizens of the top gallery—the "gods" where the seats were sixpence—always had amongst them plenty of singers, some with a fair local reputation, who sang for the audience during the somewhat long intermissions. When the curtain fell on an act and the rather dreary commercial orchestra ceased its sounds, someone would call up to the "gods," "Raise us a harmony," and the harmony would start, sometimes several voices together singing a patriotic ballad or an old come-all-ye, sometimes a solo singer would give an aria from an opera—"Hi, mister, give us a stave from *Figaro*." Or it might be *Pagliacci*, or some other favorite. In response a young man would stand up and troll forth in a sort of Italian "*la ci darem*." But the audience was happiest when they could join in some patriotic ballad like "The West's Awake" or "The Croppy Boy" or in the chorus of one of Dublin's familiar street songs like "Molly Malone":

> She was a fishmonger
> And that was no wonder
> Her father and mother were fishmongers, too,
> And wheeled a wheel barrow
> Through streets wide and narrow
> Crying, "Cockles and mussels, Alive, Alive O!"

The song concluded:

> She died of a fayver,
> And nothing could save her,
> And that was the last of sweet Molly Malone.
> But her ghost wheels a barrow
> Through streets wide and narrow,
> Crying, "Cockles and mussels, Alive, Alive O!"

At the end of each stanza, the less genteel part of the audience, on whom the Anglo-Saxon virtue of decorum sat lightly, would break out resoundingly in one grand chorus:

> "Cockles and mussels, Alive, Alive O!"

And the "Alive O!" of the chorus would be repeated several times with an augmenting volume of voices and an increasing lugubriousness. A London actor like Martin Harvey, who liked life and vitality in an audience, would be delighted with these sing fests, but others were of the opinion that the energy put into the self-expression made the singers less capable of attention for the next act.

Anyhow, these goings on were not allowed in the Abbey Theater, where, during the intermissions, one part of the audience sat in its seats listening to an exquisite little orchestra of a few instruments, or to a violin solo by a very distinguished artist, Arthur Darley, and another part betook itself to the tearoom and engaged in violent discussions about the play or the acting.

But the great diversion during the intermission was the audience. The leaders of the various national and patriotic movements, though all the movements were national and patriotic, were to be seen in the theater, especially on first nights. As the theater was small, practically everybody among the habitués got to know everybody else. The general meeting place was the tearoom or the theater vestibule where the portraits of the literary celebrities hung. In addition to the well-known Dubliners, there would be famous Englishmen and Continental Europeans; it would be no unusual sight to behold a spectacled, bearded foreigner trying to talk to A.E. or Lady Gregory with an open dictionary in his hand to which he would refer frequently. It may be that only in a comparatively small city like Dublin, where the population was not much more than half a million and where all the movements had their headquarters in the center of the city, such easy familiarity between writers and audience was possible. However, I think such familiarity quite possible in Paris.

The three directors of the theater, Yeats, Synge, and Lady Gregory, were in the audience at every performance; the week of the Abbey plays and the week after were full of all sorts of intellectual excitements—meetings of the National Literary Society at which Yeats would so frequently speak, meetings of the students' societies at which Yeats, Lady Gregory, and Lord Dunsany, as well as the younger writers, sometimes appeared. Then there were discussion groups, like the Contemporary Club, a men's club which once a month admitted women; meetings of the Arts Club, meetings of odds and ends of societies such as the Theosophical Society, the Archaeological Society, innumerable Gaelic League meetings, not to speak of the Agricultural Organization Society, which Horace Plunkett, Lord Dunsany's uncle, had founded and of which A.E. was the leading light.

Yeats and Lady Gregory would make an entrance into the theater together, as this was the period of their fruitful literary partnership, and as it was a small theater they were visible to all. The sartorial getup of the celebrities greatly interested the audience. Yeats would be attired in a black velvet jacket and flowing tie, though, on important occasions, he would appear in full evening dress. I think he was always attached to clothes and personal adornments; anyhow, his appearance certainly was picturesque, though by no means the only picturesque male in the Abbey Theater.

In those days there were many men in Dublin who returned to the wearing of Gaelic kilts, which differed from the familiar Scots kilts by being plain saffron or green in color; sometimes the kilt would be saffron and the brath green, fastened to the shoulder of the jacket with a Tara broach of silver or copper. For a tall, well-built figure the kilts are the most becoming of all forms of dress for a man, making him look both romantic and virile. Several of the writers affected them: Darrell Figgis, who wrote poetry and novels and had a career later as a politician in the new Irish state, Thomas

MacDonagh, who wrote poetry and later taught in the National University, and who signed the proclamation of the Irish Republic in 1916; kilts were occasionally worn by the brothers Pearse—Padraic, who founded a bilingual school, and Willie who was a sculptor. The last three were executed in 1916 as leaders of the insurrection and signers of the proclamation of the Irish Republic. Figgis also had a violent end. He committed suicide as part of the outcome of a tragic love affair. But the most picturesque of those who arrayed themselves in kilts was Lord Ashbourne's son, William Gibson, afterwards himself Lord Ashbourne, who, when he succeeded to the title, insisted on addressing the House of Lords in Irish. He was one of the Celtophiles who refused to speak the English language and confined himself in conversation to French and Irish. To meet him striding around the foyer of the Abbey Theater or up O'Connell Street in his kilts and to be greeted by him in Irish, "*Dia 'gus Mhuire duit,*" or "*Bon jour, mes petites dames,*" was to have experienced an added excitement to the day. More romantic in ancestry and in title, if not in appearance, was Lord Castletown of Upper Ossory, in Irish the MacGilla Padraic, a Gaelic Leaguer, a descendant of the kings of Ossory who in their prime had looked down on the kings of Tara. Castletown, like Yeats, was ubiquitous. In an odd way he was both in everything and out of everything. He also headed or invented one or several of the various movements for saving the country. His name was on the stationery of nearly all the organizations, and he was forever presiding at meetings; there were several like him, honest-to-God descendants of historic Irish families, some flaunting the title "The," denoting that they were head of the clan. A good many of these old Irish families were less nationalist and democratic than one might expect, and for that reason were not entirely accepted in the inner circles of any of the movements. Occasionally picturesque fellow Gaels from Scotland, attired in the tartan kilts of their clans, would appear, talking the same language as Irish, but with a different intonation; and they sang the most rousing songs, for like all Celts they were given to singing. The boat songs of the Hebrides seemed somehow to have more life to them than the native Irish songs, which so often were love songs or religious songs and a little on the mournful side.

III

In decorating themselves in a traditional Irish manner, the female sex were not behindhand, especially the youthful members thereof. It may be doubted, however, if the women's garment which really had been concocted from pictures was especially Irish: it was probably simply the costume of the medieval European lady with a few fancy Celtic fixtures attached. A girl poet, friend of mine, Moirin Fox, never wore any other garb. She would appear in the Abbey in gorgeous purple and gold, a torc on her forehead, a Tara broach fastening her brath, and various other accouterments of the ancient Irish, including the inevitable amber. The rest of us only occasionally appeared in Gaelic costume, which, of course, had to be of Irish manufactured material. For dressy wear I had a white garment with blue and green embroidery, a blue brath, copper broaches, and other archaeological adornments. For more ordinary wear, I had the Irish costume in blue green, a brath of the same color with embroideries out of the *Book of Kells*. These, as I remember, were chiefly of snakes eating one another's tails. With this went a blue stone necklace, a little silver harp fastening the brath, a silver Claddagh ring, and a silver snake bracelet which I'm afraid was early Victorian rather than early Celtic. This getup was all right for the Abbey Theater or Gaelic League dances, but once when myself and a friend, Siav Trench, in a similar getup and a more striking color scheme, walked together down a street where the fishwomen were selling their fish, we were openly derided. The fishmongers called out, "Will yez look at the Irishers trying to look like stained-glass windows? What is the country coming to at all, at all? Them Irishers are going daft!" We were not too sensitive to ridicule, but we did not again wear such garments in parts of the city where anything out of the ordinary was mocked at so vociferously.

Though we had a grand time decorating ourselves in this manner, truth compels me to state that, in strikingness of appearance, the male sex put it all over the female at all national functions. Douglas Hyde, with his strange dark face, seemed a prehistoric Celt or one of those the history books called Firbolgs, rolling off rapid Irish through his long black mustache. A.E., with his full brown beard, looked like the Celtic sea god Mananaun Mac Lir, whose role he once played in a drama of his own. Synge had the most sensitive face of all the writers. He seemed to me very different from the description that George Moore was to make of him "as a man of such rough and uncultivated aspect that he looked as if he had come out of Derrinrush." To me he seemed far from this with his nervous pale face, high forehead, and retiring manner. He looked very much like the Fritz Kreisler of thirty years ago, who then dressed very much like the Synge we knew. He was different from the others in the Abbey in that he did not talk much to anybody.

The younger writers—and I have never seen anywhere so many young people cutting figures of importance—attired in various degrees of shabbiness, talked a great deal both in public and private. Lord Dunsany did not seem to care much for Yeats or Lady Gregory, but was very affable to the students. He belonged to an old Irish family, the Plunketts, who had started out as bold Norman adventurers. Themselves and their castles were described in warning terms in the Irish Annals of the Four Masters: "On the road between Kells and Drogheda, there be the strongholds of two great robber barons, Plunkett of Fingall and Plunkett of Dunsany, and if the traveller fails to fall into the hands of Fingall, he will assuredly fall into the hands of Dunsany." But our Dunsany had nothing of the demeanor of a bold robber baron. He was romantic and poetic-looking, and when he spoke at clubs and literary societies he was very persuasive, and he chanted poetry almost as beautifully as Yeats, and with immense excitement and enthusiasm, and he read his own plays to delighted audiences. Part of his castle of Dunsany was built before America was discovered, but it fell foul of some of the later English invaders, and so some of it was of fairly recent build. Indeed I have heard one of those sophisticated Americans who know everything about periods and architecture call the later part "Sears, Roebuck." The Dunsany of the Cromwell period, with all the native Irish and the heads of the great Irish families, were ordered to "Hell or to Connacht." The Lady Dunsany of that period died on the trek westward like many others, and Cromwell turned his cannon on Dunsany Castle and damaged a lot of it. The Lady Dunsany of our period was a brilliant and charming Englishwoman of great naturalness and humor, who, like the ladies of the French salon, had read many books, known many intellectuals, and seen many lands. She made herself a gracious hostess to her husband's friends in the literary movement, though her patience must have often been severely tried by the rebel Irishmen she entertained. Many people thought that Lord Dunsany did not get the showing in the new movement commensurate with the importance of his work, for his plays always drew a considerable audience, and he himself was quite an inspiriting figure.

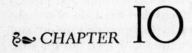

ခဲ CHAPTER 10

A Country's Awakening

AT THIS TIME, not only the literary and dramatic movement and the Gaelic League, but all the other diverse national movements—political, Sinn Fein, economic, industrial—were beginning to make the pulses of the young and eager beat faster and faster. The older and staider people guessed that it would all end in one more fight for freedom from the British, and they shook their heads—such fights had always failed and had actually done more harm than good to the country, they maintained. For centuries, in almost every generation, there had been uprisings; the country was littered with ruins from wars and rebellions and at one time or another armies and leaders from the Continent, French or Spanish, had come over to help, but the issue was always defeat. "They went forth to battle, but they always fell," the old poem said about the Celts, and it was repeated so often that even they themselves began to acquiesce in the belief abroad that they were a romantic, poetic, charming, and ineffective people, destined to failure and incapable of governing themselves. Indeed every activity in the country seemed to go down in failure. There was no money to back any enterprise, and the stench of frustration and oppression was widespread in the land—that is, until all these movements, started at the end of the last century or the beginning of this, converged and began to stir the country to life once more.

Before our generation the names of those who had died for Ireland were the dearest names of all—Sarsfield, Wolfe Tone, Lord Edward Fitzgerald, Robert Emmet. Many a young man and woman grew up dreaming of dying for Ireland and leaving behind a name immortal in the country's memory. Dying for freedom, suffering for freedom, was the great road to fame and renown, the sure way of having one's name remembered forever. But in our day, under the new leadership, young people began to think that living for the country and doing something for it might be as good as dying for it. The hero of one of the old sagas, Cuchulainn, had uttered that sentence, "I care not if my life have but the span of a night and a day if my deeds be spoken of by the men of Eirinn," and many of my fellow students, not only the young men but the girls, wrote the sentence in their notebooks or beneath their names in the old Irish texts that everybody was beginning to read, most of us, to be sure, in Lady Gregory's or Standish O'Grady's English versions. Some of my fellow students, however, were good Gaelic scholars and could read the original texts or a modernized version of the original texts.

It was now twenty years since Dr. Douglas Hyde founded the Gaelic League to revive the Irish language, to return to the native culture, to de-Anglicize the country. Many parts of the country were still Irish-speaking, especially in the West, and of course in the islands on the western coast it was the only language. In English-speaking Dublin the passion for learning Irish showed itself among all ages, all classes, and all professions. In the evenings, after the day's work, shopkeepers, artisans, housewives, students would go to the Gaelic League branches to learn to speak and read the language and to write in its strange characters. Some mysterious romance lay behind every sentence they learned. On holidays and during vacations young men and women would make pilgrimages to the Irish-speaking districts and there practice talking what of the language they knew with people whose forebears had clung to the ancestral language. Summer schools under distinguished scholars were started where adults went to learn, not only the language, but the athletic games and the native dances. These dances had romantic names—the Waves of Tory, the Bridge of Athlone, the Walls of Limerick—and there were jigs and reels danced to old tunes that were athletic exercises in themselves. Even the most vigorous of us in our teens would be breathless after romping through a rousing jig or reel.

Like every activity in life that is a success, it was part play, a good time was had by all. The English Government, on the alert for political and rebel movements, paid no attention to the cultural movements. The attempts to destroy the native language and substitute English had succeeded pretty well, and there still remained the remnants of the penal laws against using Irish. Anybody who had his name printed in Irish on a vehicle was summoned to court and had to pay a fine. Thus, if one Irish-speaking James MacCarvill of Newton called himself by his right Irish name of Seumas Mac-Cearbhaill of Baile nua, he was summoned to court and fined. But there was no law in the way of the Gaelic League, the literary or dramatic movements, so they all flourished. In fact, if anything, England encouraged them, probably thinking they would take the people's minds off the struggle for freedom.

About the new Irish literature, intellectual England was enthusiastic. Massingham, the great editor of the *Nation*, welcomed the work of the Irish writers, as did the Manchester *Guardian*. The players and dramatists were made much of in Oxford and in London. The irruption of these inhabitants of John Bull's other island into London had some of the features of Columbus's bringing home specimens of the natives of the land he had discovered or of the first official Japanese visit to America—they were strange, unfamiliar beings; their appearance, their coloring, their peculiar names were carefully described. Arthur Symons, whose *Symbolist Movement in Literature* was read avidly in Dublin, spoke warmly of the plays and the players. He wrote of one of the actresses, Maire Nic Shiublaigh, whose name was a tongue twister for a Saxon, "One of the maidens is beautiful, with a strange, wan, disquieting beauty." She was a friend of mine, and like me she had anemia, which accounted for her wanness and maybe for her disquietingness. But there was no doubt about her beauty, and her voice, like her face, was lovely, though not so rich as Sara Allgood's voice, of which Mrs. Patrick Campbell said, "It is the most beautiful on the English-speaking stage." Sara's wonderful voice and rich personality and Maire's beauty and strange golden eyes are mixed up with all my memories of Dublin of those days and with Yeats's poetry and plays, which they both interpreted at the Abbey.

All my generation interested in drama,. not only in Ireland but in England, remembers Sara's playing of Kathleen ni Houlihan. But to our elders in Dublin it was Maud Gonne's creation of the role that was significant. Those who saw her on the first night said that when she came on the stage, with her marvelous beauty, her height, and the memories of her militant patriotism, people's hearts stopped beating, and many, including Yeats himself, wept. He has written of his emotions on seeing, coming on the stage of the little hall, "Such a beautiful woman to play my poor old Kathleen." But then we must remember that it was to Maud Gonne he wrote his wonderful love poetry:

> A woman Homer sung
> Till life and letters seem
> But an heroic dream.

But for us, the younger ones who had not seen Maud Gonne's performance, there was Sara Allgood's, with her rich glamorous voice—I really believe a more golden voice than Sarah Bernhardt's, which I also heard in Dublin about this time. Now, after more than three decades, it sounds in my ears, with Sara playing Aoibhell of the Shee in Lady Gregory's *Kincora*, her chanting in Yeats's *Deirdre*, "Why is it, Queen Edaine said?" or as a keening woman in Synge's *Riders to the Sea*, and the rich humor of that voice in comedy parts such as the Widow Quinn in *The Playboy of the Western World.*

Hugh Lane was always having picture exhibitions, shows of all kinds, from the pictures of Watts to those of the French post-Impressionists. If the artistic intelligentsia preferred the Corots and the Monets and the Manets, the rest of Dublin, I think, preferred the Watts pictures, for people in the mass prefer a little moralizing in their art and something that may be a help to coping with life. Dublin was reduced to a sort of mystic meditation by Watts, by that picture which had inscribed under it, "What I Gave I Have, What I Kept I Lost," prints of which were to be seen

in almost everybody's house, as well as that other of "Hope" blind-
fold, seated on a globe.

II

What one heard most about was, of course, literature, especially
poetry. Though thrilling poetry had been written in Gaelic and
lyric poetry at a time when it was not being written in English,
actually not a great deal of real poetry had been written by the
Irish in English. This was no doubt partly due to the operation of
the penal laws, when all education for the natives had been pro-
hibited except such as they could get secretly or in schools and
colleges on the Continent: this often meant, in practice, that those
so educated might know French very well, but not much English.
Of course, among the poets before our time there had been Thomas
Moore, beloved by the older generation, but for ours he had almost
no appeal. What we cared for was the poetry that sprung out of
Gaelic inspiration, that of Mangan and Ferguson, Callanan, or such
as showed certain native satiric qualities as were in the anonymous
ballads like "The Night Before Larry Was Stretched," and "Johnny,
I Hardly Knew Ye," the same qualities which Swift showed in prose
and verse; Swift was really a Dublin poet—the town was haunted
by him, I often thought; his street songs were still sung; the Sinn
Fein movement championed his political ideas, and we students all
read his verse and prose. Then, Dr. Douglas Hyde's translations of
The Love Songs of Connacht threw us all into the same sort of
excitement that Herder's translations of folk poetry or Percy's *Rel-
iques of Ancient English Poetry* had thrown people into in the
eighteenth century. These anonymous West-of-Ireland songs were
mostly women's love songs, and they were unlike any love poetry
we read in other languages. They had a directness of communication, an intensity of emotion which, I think, is the special Celtic
gift to literature. It was odd that in a country where romantic love
was not part of the social organization, where it was even mocked
at, where marriages were arranged and were even a sort of deliberate alliance between families, there should have been love poetry
of such a high kind. We read these songs in the original and in the
striking translations so often that we knew them by heart. The

occasional carelessness of Douglas Hyde's language seemed to be all right in these versions of folk poetry. A stylist could easily find fault with some of the words in the following:

> Ringleted youth of my love,
> With thy locks bound loosely behind thee,
> You passed by the way above,
> But you never came in to find me.
> Where were the harm for you
> If you came for a little to see me?
> Your kiss was awakening dew
> Were I ever so ill or so dreamy.
>
> .　　　.　　　.　　　.　　　.
>
> I thought, O my love, you were so—
> As the sun or the moon on a fountain,
> And I thought after that you were snow,
> The cold snow on top of the mountain,
> And I thought after that you were more
> Like God's lamp shining to find me,
> Or the bright star of knowledge before,
> Or the star of knowledge behind me.

but we knew it was grand love poetry. It was the poetry of youth, yearning, and unsophistication. And not only this, but it was the special expression of the women of the race we belonged to, women who were married to men whom they barely knew, who took it for granted that marriage was a destiny they had to accept, but love was an aspiration of the heart and spirit to be expressed in beautiful words by people who had never handled a book except a prayer book.

The Love Songs of Connacht and the new translations of the old sagas set everybody on fire with a desire to have a national literature and to revive a national life. A spirit that had been long asleep awoke. It was surprising that the English Government, which proclaimed Land League meetings and threw the Irish members of Parliament into gaol for some little political offense, took no notice, or only favorable notice, of this new ardor for native culture. One would think that even a child of ten would have realized that all this was bound to develop towards another and more determined fight to throw off the English yoke. But the truth was that English officialdom never knew Ireland very well. The English nation did not understand the Irish nation in spite of all the intermarriages over hundreds of years, in spite of the fact that the amount of Irish blood in England is surprisingly large. A difference in religion has, of course, to be taken into account, but besides this there was a difference in education. Irish education, to an astonishing degree, was on the Continental model, and not only that, but most educated Irish people had received some part of their education on the Continent, whereas this was not at all to the same extent in England. Of course, a minority of Irish people had received some part of their education in England, but these did not have much influence on the trend of thought, especially on the new kind of thought, in the country.

It would be fallacious to suggest that the country as a whole read the best work of the literary movement either in Irish or English. In the Irish-speaking districts the people had their own traditional poetry which they sang or lilted without a musical accompaniment and sometimes recited. In the rest of the country there was a popular poetry which had some direct bearing on the lives of the people; there was also a certain amount of literate verse such as is written everywhere by people with rhythmical talent. There was William Rooney, who wrote the poetry that everybody in the political organizations recited; there was William Dara, whose verses the students read, and probably other people, though I never met them. Long afterwards, in the 1930s, James Joyce, who had been a student some years before me, recalled so much of William Dara, as did I, that, sitting in a Paris café, we were able to repeat his verses line by alternative line. There was much Kathleen ni Houlihan, Dark Rosaleen poetry written, and there were several well-known women poets, some with considerable influence. There was Ethna Carberry, whose work closely touched the experiences of the people. Every one of the numerous mothers who had a son or daughter in America was pierced to the heart by her

> O Paisteen Finn, but it vexed her sore,
> The day you turned from your mother's door
> For the wide grey sea and the strife and the din
> That lie beyond where the ships go in.

Has the world been good to you, Paisteen Finn?
Has the yellow gold that you sought to win
Been worth the toil and the danger dared?
Has plenty blessed you and sorrow spared?

The young girls, sighing for romantic love, delighted in her "Cold Sleep of Brighidin":

My heart's desire, my treasure, our wooing time was brief,
From the misty dawn of April till the falling of the leaf;
From the first clear cuckoo calling
Till the harvest gold was falling,
And my store of joy was garnered with the binding of the sheaf.

The author of these poems romantically died young after she had been the bride for less than a year of Seumas MacManus. In her day she was probably the most widely read poet in Ireland, and I should not be at all surprised if her death was not more mourned throughout the country than the death of Yeats, whose poetry required more experience and more training in literature to understand.

The variations in intelligence in Ireland are very great, greater than I have observed in any other country. At the very top about ten per cent of the population are mentally and emotionally so highly gifted that they are hard to beat or even equal in any country; at the other end there is a denseness and stupidity that is also hard to equal or to beat. Nobody is more critical of this low level than the Irish themselves; it is doubtless the result of centuries of oppression, of the penal laws which not only reduced people economically but outlawed schools and churches, and the terrible system of land tenure which not only kept the people in perpetual poverty but in perpetual fear of eviction if they could not muster the rent or if the children in America could not manage to send home what was necessary. Not only had the peasant to pay a purchase sum for the land, for the privilege of working it, but he had also to pay rent to the head landlord, an absentee very often who never saw the people who supported him or the land he drew his rents from. That poverty, ignorance, resentments, frustrations were the result, that minds became dulled, sometimes even more than a little crazy, that a part of the people in the countryside took little interest in what was called the Irish Revival, was not surprising; they had enough to do to keep alive at all without any margin of energy for artistic interests or to bother much about the poetry writing, playwriting, and painting that was going on in the capital. The real passion of the people was for freedom, to own their land and their country, and this was stimulated by all the new movements. The energy generated spread all over the country, even among people who did not know or care for the movements that carried it. There were great personalities, real leaders behind these movements, people not only of high talents and patriotism, but of strong character, great disinterestedness, and unshakable courage.

ᗖ CHAPTER II

Lady Gregory of the Abbey Theater

A CERTAIN AMOUNT of the outstanding leadership was feminine: on the political side there were Maud Gonne and Countess Markievicz (Constance Gore-Booth, the daughter of Sir Henry Gore-Booth, a neighboring landowner from Yeats's native Sligo). But it may be that history will decide that the most remarkable was Lady Gregory—in fact, she very likely was one of the most remarkable women of her time. There must have been many people in Dublin who really liked her, but actually I remember very few. There were, of course, some people connected with the Abbey Theater, and there was always Yeats, who remained devoted to her to the day of her death. Indeed their friendship was that best of all literary friendships, one between a man and a woman who admire each other's work and personality. In art women are great allies of men, and Yeats, a man of genius, had many women allies, but perhaps outstanding men in any avocation have. It seemed, however, very odd that in a movement making a bid for the support of Dublin and the Irish people generally, both gentle and simple, one of the leaders should be so aloof and condescending as Lady Gregory was. The Irish are not as likely to be snobbish as are the English, but when Irish snobbery exists at all it is fierce, fantastic, and absurd, and without the basis in inherited class pattern that gives it its driving force in England. Snobbery in Ireland comes partly from originally being an attitude of the invaders toward the invaded. Lady Gregory was a snob and kept herself apart from Dublin life. She not only did not appear at the numerous Dublin literary evenings, of which A.E.'s Sunday evenings were the most frequented, and where distinguished foreigners met each other and the natives. One never saw her at Commissioner Bailey's, where even the English governors of the country showed up and rubbed shoulders with the aborigines; one never saw her at national festivals or at picture exhibitions, except such as her nephew, Hugh Lane, organized.

Some of her family had been known for their efforts at proselytizing the country people and for distributing tracts and Bibles, but she herself did not take part in these godly works, at least not after she reached maturity. A young relative of hers was a fellow student, and this girl used to call Lady Gregory "Aunt Augusta," with the result that we students always referred to her behind her back as Aunt Augusta. Once in a while she showed up at a literary meeting if Yeats was scheduled to speak, and on one of these occasions, I remember, the student chairman asked her to contribute to the discussion. In a manner that chilled us all she rose to her feet and said with her elegant lisp, "I never speak except through the beautiful voices of our players in our little theater."

However, after one of those visits to America that were so decisive in the lives of Irish intellectuals, she came back a fluent public speaker, and she practiced her newly found accomplishment from time to time. I remember once, just after her return, as the audience sat in the Abbey Theater waiting for the play to begin, the curtain slowly rose, and behold! instead of the play and players, there was Lady Gregory alone, in the middle of the stage, very smartly attired and looking more like Queen Victoria than ever, especially as she had now on her head a lace cap of a sort of Spanish allure. With a platform assurance acquired in America, where she had spoken at clubs and colleges, she addressed the audience in a fairly long speech. We had heard that she had been popular in America, especially in the women's colleges and with the girl students, and had even announced with her famous tact that when her granddaughters grew up she would have to decide whether she would send them to Smith or Vassar. She did not mean a word of it, because she knew perfectly well that if they bothered about a college education at all they could be better educated in Ireland.

Lady Gregory's title probably stood her in good stead in her lecture trips, for in those days any old title seemed glamorous. Her husband, Sir William, had been knighted by Queen Victoria for services in the colonies, but as George Moore was fond of pointing out, the Gregory title belonged to the lowest order in the British Empire. Lady Gregory herself was obviously pleased with it, and I think the longer she lived the more of a feeling of importance it gave her, and not only her but her friends, and especially Yeats. Though she did not go round to Dublin houses or literary evenings, Synge seldom did, either, but we knew he preferred the company of the country people and liked living in cottages in Aran and Wicklow, and anyhow, though shy, he was always affable and courteous, but Lady Gregory behaved as if she were a grand duchess, and as if the people of Dublin were somehow her subjects. She did not care enough about people to have a native friendliness to them and so was by nature tactless. But with discipline and cultivation she had acquired a perfectly fearsome artificial tact, as young women at a finishing school acquire artificial charm. It was the kind of tact that might pass muster if exercised by a highly intelligent person on a stupid or uneducated one who could not see through it. But Dublin at that period reeked with intelligence and nimble wits of all kinds, and so Lady Gregory's tact was resented and ridiculed, though it enabled her often to get the better of those in disagreement with her. I remember once partly overhearing an argument between her and one of the Irish members of Parliament at the Abbey Theater, in which she must have gained the upper hand. On her leaving the seat beside him with her studied graciousness he pressed his fingers to his forehead and said in a very loud and harassed voice, "Oh, God, oh, God, this Protestant tact! I can't bear it!" However, I think the tact maintained a degree of surface friendliness with people who were privately exasperated, and it was said to have gained financial support for the theater from well-to-do Unionists. I here quote the opinion of her by a member of the early Abbey group: "Her diplomacy was successful, but because it combined resolution with an artlessness of manner and a flattery of address, it was very annoying. She had kindly, friendly eyes, but a mouth that was inflexible."

Augusta Gregory belonged to an old Galway family, the Persses, of which the first member must have come in with the foreign invasions, and he claimed descent from the Percys of Northumberland whom we had heard of in Shakespeare. But her family had been a long time in Ireland, and she was as Irish as anybody in a land where, with so many wars and invasions and even émigrés of many kinds, almost everybody had some drops or streams of foreign blood, as indeed must have been the same in almost every European country. In addition, Lady Gregory deliberately and conscientiously acquired as much Irishry as was available. She studied the Irish language, Irish history, Irish mythology, and Irish folk tales. She consciously or unconsciously prepared herself for her career as an Irish writer and a leader of the renaissance. She became an illustrious figure, and yet, but for a peculiar dispensation of fate, she might have lived all her life in a little Galway village, an old maid of bookish taste and an interest in Irish tradition and old Irish literature. She seemed indeed headed for such a life when, at the age of thirty, she married old Sir William Gregory, also of a Galway family. He had come home from Ceylon, where he had been the British governor of the island. With her marriage she acquired a title, became the mistress of a beautiful old house and of wealth gained by a previous Gregory in that East India Company which was the wedge by which India became part of the British Empire. The Gregory fortune, like a lot of British fortunes, had come mostly out of Asia.

Augusta was one of a large family; she had several brothers, and some of them, especially one whom I knew pretty well, intensely admired her feat in espousing Sir William. The intelligence of the Persse family seemed to have gone into the distaff side. Lady Gregory's sisters had distinguished progeny, but the male members of her family, or what I knew of them, were not very bright. The one I knew best was one who used to come to tea with us in our early married life, and who liked to read chunks of the Bible to his Catholic maidservant, who had previously worked with us, and who was inclined to think that listening to Bible reading was a matter for confession.

Sir William Gregory took his young wife to London, where he himself was quite a figure, and launched her on a social career which was later to become a literary career. The old gentleman died not long after their marriage and left her a well-to-do widow with an only son. But for the few years of her married life she seems to have spent part of the time in London, where she met many distinguished men. However, her manner must have been a little on the awkward side, for George Moore records lunching with her at Coole, shortly after her marriage, where he noted her ill-at-ease and timid air, and of afterwards seeing her in her house in London, which was visited by many famous people. Once again he notices her tactlessness and Sir William's embarrassment at it. Sir William he describes as a man who had the Lord Palmerston air, as had his father, George Henry Moore, but who was less interesting and more of an opportunist. However, an Irishman is likely to describe another Irishman who has taken lucrative service with the British as an opportunist, or even any Irishman who has made money in any way.

II

If the first important event in Lady Gregory's life was her marriage to the elderly Sir William, the second was surely her meeting with Yeats. History and biography have it that this took place in Edward Martyn's house, Tullyra Castle, where Yeats and Arthur Symons were staying in the summer of 1896. It was Symons's first visit to Ireland, where, I very much doubt, he was very much known at the time; later, however, he became a sort of god of the younger college set because of his book, *The Symbolist Movement in Literature*, which we devoured. His own poetry was too often heavily influenced by Yeats, who, in turn, was influenced by Symons's translations from the French, for a brief period. On this occasion he claimed to be a Celt of Cornwall visiting fellow Celts. The craze for Celtic things and Celtic mysteries was just beginning to sprout, and visitors from America, England, and the Continent had started coming to Ireland in search of Celtic magic and Celtic twilight. The craze lasted for about twenty years, or up to a little while after the last great war—that is, the one which began in 1914

—but the magic was certainly there during that time, and the glamor and the faerie enchantment, and it as assuredly nearly all departed before the fourth decade of this century. Gods and fairies did fold their wings and rest for a brief period on historic hills, enchanted mounds, and ancient ruins, and then, after another space, they fluttered their wings and fled.

To make a long story short, Lady Gregory, a wealthy widow, aged forty-five, full of intelligence, energy, ambition, and patriotism, and under the influence of the Celtic enchantment, drove over to Edward Martyn's and invited his guests, Yeats and Symons, to luncheon at her house, at Coole near by. Edward Martyn was critical of Lady Gregory; at least he was ten years later, when this chronicler was a student, but he was never unfriendly to her. He had a fine local country humor and was in the habit of remarking, "Those Persses can put a face on anything; they make everything they do seem important. Look at the Galway Blazers! You'd think, the way they talked about them, they were the best pack in Ireland. They're nothing—nothing at all," he would chuckle. Lady Gregory, it is hardly necessary to say again, was a Persse, and whereas she had undoubtedly the Persse talent for making things she or her family did seem important, yet the fact remains that what she herself did had great importance indeed for her country and her country's literature. Symons, however, was allergic to her, and it is recorded that he used to refer to her with fury as "La Strega," the Witch. His dislike of her could not have been of that kind that men sometimes get up for women of great intellectual gifts, for at that time, and for long after, nobody knew much about Lady Gregory's gifts. Her literary work had been limited to collecting folklore and editing her husband's journals.

Hardly had Yeats and Symons entered the library of Coole House than, as is reliably recorded, Lady Gregory asked Yeats if she could not help in the Irish literary movement. Yeats, who was very psychic about other people's gifts and potentialities, answered her, "If you watch what we are doing, you will soon find your work." They talked much of Yeats's project for an Irish Theater, and this put Lady Gregory on the way of finding her work. She started by giving and collecting money for the theater, but soon she became an active and popular dramatist, insofar as an Irish dramatist in those days was popular. It is hard to estimate how great were her services in the foundation of the national theater: certainly Yeats could not have built it up or run it without her.

It was the fashion in certain circles to say that Lady Gregory was bad for Yeats and bad for the literary movement, bad for the nationalist movement. Everybody had different reasons for these animadversions: some said she was an ambitious woman who was using Yeats and the movement to get a public for her work. Maud Gonne, whose emotions were more for the national than for the artistic cause, said that when writers came back to Dublin after a sojourn in Coole Park, they were less interested in the national aspirations and more in their own lack of money. A group of Yeats's friends held that Lady Gregory was infecting Yeats with snobbery, with highfalutin notions about aristocracy, and with the despised ascendancy affectations. I think all the groups were almost completely wrong, though there was a modicum of truth in what they said. But exaggerating the truth is almost the subtlest form of lying. Of course Lady Gregory was a snob, but snobbery did not always rule her life; of course she was ambitious, but ambition was not always her dominant quality. But her talents were her own, they were remarkable, and of the greatest value to Ireland and to Irish literature; it was a very good thing that they got public recognition. If she had had the talents without the ambition she would not have achieved much, for in every country there are women of high talents, but for some strange reason, ambition among greatly talented women is not common, perhaps because strong emotions go with great talent and the satisfying of emotion appears to be a major instinct with women; ambition is more likely to be found among mediocre, energetic talents; it is likely to be uncommon among gifted women who happen, like Lady Gregory, to be persons of wealth and position. These, for the most part, are contented to gather around them men of talent and run a sort of salon; this has been the hereditary role of such women. If Lady Gregory had simply been one of this kind, and there was that side to her, Ireland and literature would have been deprived of a great deal.

As for the accusation that her influence was against nationalist sentiment, there was very little to that. The kind of nationalist sentiment then popular in Dublin was not Lady Gregory's sort, but nobody could doubt the nationalism of her plays. What she wanted to do was to help re-create the spirit of the race, to waken into consciousness, with the help of literature and a revived racial tradition, what had once been potent in Europe and had produced so many trained and scholarly minds. She devoted herself to all the remains of Irish literature she could find, and not only to the old hero tales of Cuchulainn, and the Red Branch, but to all the relics of folk literature that could be found in the County Galway. She worked at the English language as it was spoken in the villages around her, English spoken beautifully with an Irish idiom; in fact it may be wondered if there would be any distinctive Irish literature at all if this idiom should go out of the English spoken in Ireland. Lady Gregory could write this sort of English very interestingly; she wrote her plays in it, her translations from Molière and Goldoni, and her versions of the old hero tales—*Cuchullain of Muirthemne* and *Gods and Fighting Men*. The literary lights in general might praise Standish O'Grady's versions as being finer and more heroic, but we young people were enraptured with Lady Gregory's writing and read these books over and over again. It was the same with her plays: they made an immense appeal to us; some rich emotions not obvious on the surface of her relations with people went into her work, as well as a great knowledge of local Irish life. *The Workhouse Ward, The Rising of the Moon*, and *Spreading the News* are little masterpieces, and indeed one might reconstruct quite a bit of Irish civilization, past and present, from her writings if every other way of doing it disappeared. There was something in her plays that went right into the hearts of her audience in the theater, even in her not very good historical plays like *Kincora*. After so many years I can still say long pieces of that play by heart, and I remember the characters—Queen Gormlai, as played by the beautiful Maire Walker, and her farewell words as she left Brian Boru to go off with the Earl of Orkney, "My thousand farewells to you, Brian of the Victories," and I remember Sara Allgood's beautiful voice as Aoibhell of the Shee, the Fairy Woman who protected King Brian, and many of the lines of Brian himself. Even though heard in impressionable teens, people do not remember plays for most of their lifetime without there being something very striking in them. I believe Lady Gregory to have been a fine dramatist and a fine writer, though perhaps often too local to make much of an appeal to a metropolitan audience.

She belonged to an Irish national theater, as did all the players and all the writers whose work was produced, with the exception, of course, of the foreign writers and of Bernard Shaw, whose *Shewing up of Blanco Posnet* had its premiere in the Abbey. In all she wrote there was something noble, for despite her deliberateness, her calculated behavior, she was high-minded and loved all fine and noble things, as people brought up on great literature are likely to do. Her love of Irish literature, old and new, was intense; she did all she could to keep alive the memory of those who wrote in the native language. It was she who put up a monument to the eighteenth-century Gaelic poet Raftery; she helped spread his fame so that practically every literate person in Ireland knew some of Raftery's poems in the original or in an English translation—if not his love poetry to Mary Hynes, at least his poem about himself, one of the most exquisite characterizations of a poet ever made. Here is Douglas Hyde's literal translation:

> I am Raftery the Poet
> Full of hope and love,
> With eyes that have no light,
> With gentleness that has no misery.
>
> Going westward on my pilgrimage
> By the light of my heart,
> Feeble and tired
> To the end of my road.
>
> Behold me now,
> And my face to the wall,
> Playing music
> To empty pockets.

For the folk poets who wrote in Irish generally played a musical instrument of some sort at wakes and weddings, mostly to empty pockets, and were part of the numerous wanderers on the roads. Raftery was blind and used to be led from house to house by a member of each family he visited, as I used to lead the blind "priest" who gave me the curse with his blessing. Raftery, his life and his poetry, had a great deal of influence, not only on Yeats,

Lady Gregory, and Douglas Hyde, but on almost all the younger Irish writers of the period.

For all that was said and felt against Lady Gregory, and nobody can escape being attacked in Ireland, she was not only a patriotic but a fighting Irishwoman. She fought the opponents of Irish tradition, the mockers of the Gaelic inheritance—and these persons were well planted in Ireland; there were even native Irishmen like Professor Mahaffy, of Trinity College, with a typical Irish face and a typical Irish wit, who declared, without knowing a thing about it, that old Irish literature was of no value. There was Professor Atkinson, who was so overcome by racial antagonism that he announced, as a counterpropaganda to the Irish renaissance, that there was nothing in old Irish literature that was not either silly or indecent, who repeated what Yeats called "the traditional slanders against Ireland." Lady Gregory fought all the slanderers, gave them back better than they gave, and got under their skins. She did it with passionate patriotism and learning, and with the help of Douglas Hyde and that other great Celtic artist-scholar, Kuno Meyer. She fought for the new Irish literature as well as the old, and for the Irish national theater and Irish culture, with a prestige that was perhaps all the more potent because she was a wealthy woman and the mistress of an old house and estates. In dealing with Unionist loyalists and persons of recent English descent, the famous tact might have been of some help. But I think it was not so much the tact as her honesty of purpose, her single-mindedness, her hard disinterested labor for what she believed in, that kept for her the friendship of so many people in England and Ireland who were inimical to Irish nationalism. For devotion to a cause generally arouses respect even among the enemies of the cause, and anyhow, not all Unionist loyalists wished Ireland to remain merely a western province of Britain; they favored cultural, if not political, independence and were willing to do what in them lay for the Irish Renaissance without compromising themselves. Then it has to be said that a certain amount of the antagonism to Lady Gregory was of the kind that people of wealth and position are likely to encounter among the economically unprivileged. With all her faults and snobbery, she was a great woman, a real leader, one of those who woke up Ireland from the somnolence and lassitude it was too prone to fall into. It is very doubtful indeed if Yeats could have produced as much work as he did without her help. It is almost certain that, but for Lady Gregory, the Irish national theater would have remained a dream, or ended in being that failure that so many hopeful undertakings in Ireland became.

„ CHAPTER 12

The Yeats I Knew

IF ANYBODY told Yeats that he had just seen a ghost, or had had a strange dream, or had been a pupil of William James, or had heard D'Annunzio repeat his sonnets, or had seen Duse so unstrung after receiving a letter that she could not go on the stage, he would become all excited and curious and oblivious to everything around him. I mention these special incidents because I have been present when they happened. Anything connected with the life of the spirit or the emotions or the beliefs of mankind—anything, no matter how farfetched, that human intellect or even superstition had ever owed allegiance to—stirred up an eager movement in his mind. "I am a man; nothing human is alien to me," one of the great ancients said. "I am a poet," Yeats might have said, "a man of imagination; nothing of human imagination is alien to me." Because most of us have limited capacities, this attitude of his often gave people the notion that he could not cope with external life or practicalities. Yeats, I should say, had few incapacities of any kind; anything he might have wanted to do, provided it interested him steadily, he could, by turning his faculties onto it, have done. Naturally, having the creative and not the acquisitive mind, he could not have been interested in acquiring anything for acquisition's sake; he had no interest in getting money except as it could be used for a creative purpose like founding a national theater; he acquired a lot of knowledge, but it was of a kind that his mind could create something out of; stocking up on dead knowledge as people in universities often do would not have seemed worth while to him. Knowledge of any kind was, as it were, bricks out of which he could build something.

If I say he was well equipped for coping with practicalities, I mean such practicalities as seemed worth a man's devoting his life and powers to and as could form a reserve of intellectual and spiritual interests for humanity. He was very far indeed from being the type of person he was often satirized as—one of those aesthetic, vain, ineffectual people who are sometimes in the arts because they have so little interest outside themselves. Max Beerbohm had caricatured him as a long, lean, unvitalized hobbledehoy, with a fishlike mouth, in a fantastic posture, introducing George Moore to a Christmas-card little figure with a crown on her head, supposed to be the queen of the Irish fairies, and this became the current conception of him in England, where, though he had many warm admirers, he was never understood at all; indeed, it was hard for the Anglo-Saxon mind to understand a man who regarded every invention of the human imagination, no matter what shape it took, as worthy of a certain amount of belief and even of allegiance. Didn't he write that man had invented all things? "Yea, moon and stars and all out of his bitter soul."

Far from being in any way unvitalized, his personality exuded vitality, and his appearance was striking in exactly the opposite way from Max Beerbohm's caricature. His whole being was so charged with psychic energy that one became aware of his presence in a street, a hall, or a room before one actually saw him. In a country where the mixtures of strains brought in by Norman, Danish, and English invasions were very obvious in reddish hair and fair complexions, he belonged to what was called the black Celts, actually supposed to be the earliest race in Ireland and known by various names—Firbolg and DeDanaan—and believed to possess magical powers. One could believe very easily that Yeats had magical powers; he was very strange-looking, with dark, sorcerer's eyes, very black hair, and an olive-skinned face molded by intellect and imagination into a strange and sometimes startling beauty.

He was so sunk in dream that when we met him in the street it seemed as if only his bodily presence passed by those dim eighteenth-century houses that he loved to talk and write about, and as if the rest of him were off in some realm beyond the human and everyday. As I say, one could easily believe from his appearance that he had some sort of magical powers; he had belonged to esoteric societies like the Order of the Golden Dawn and others devoted to the work of old magicians and occupied with the ancient wisdoms and beliefs outside the domain of ordinary human life. We knew he was learned in magic, and as he walked alone in the streets he would seem to be talking to himself, his lips moving rhythmically as if he were making verses, for he composed aloud as many poets do. But we students would delight in thinking that maybe he was composing magic spells, for he would seem to be in a sort of walking trance. If he met somebody he knew he would give an absent-minded salute with his right hand raised high. It was the old European salute of the man on horseback, not unlike the modern fascist salute, and it was common enough in Ireland even from men to women. Yeats gave it absent-mindedly with his hand gravely raised in a sacerdotal manner and as if he were but vaguely aware that someone or something he knew had passed by.

It was wonderful in those student years, after listening to some minor professor treating literature as if it were a branch of pedagogy, to go to one of the clubs where Yeats frequently held forth. After long hours of work in the theater, after what he himself called in a poem "the day's war with every knave and dolt, theater business, management of men," he would often come to the students' societies and talk to us of poetry and criticism and of the poets he had known—Dowson, Oscar Wilde, Lionel Johnson, Henley, Beardsley, John Davidson. Contrary to what I have seen in print several times in America, Yeats never knew any of the French symbolists; he had met Verlaine once, but he had never known Mallarmé, never gone to Mallarmé's Tuesday evenings, and all the criticism of his poetry built on the notion that he had part in the celebrated Mallarmé group is unrelated to reality. His French was hazy, and he had no first-hand acquaintance with French literature, symbolist or any other species. From Arthur Symons he had picked up some knowledge of the French symbolists, particularly of Mallarmé, some of whose early work Symons had translated and whose celebrated text he was fond of quoting: a poem is a mystery for which the reader must seek the key.

However, his knowledge of French symbolism was slight and

used to be mocked at by the bright, knowledgeable young persons, particularly of the male sex, who took their degrees in modern languages and literature and who had sojourned in Continental schools and universities. But he had known all the poets who had met a miserable end. "I am the last of a doomed generation," he was fond of saying. There was Lionel Johnson, who had fallen off a high stool in the bar of Mooney's public house in the Strand and had cracked his skull, died of it, and had been made the object of a coroner's inquest. "He had never grown except mentally from the age of fifteen," Yeats used to inform us. There was Dowson, who had died before he was thirty as the result of his reckless life and his heavy drinking. There was John Davidson, who had committed suicide. There was Oscar Wilde, who had been gaoled for sexual inversion.

There were still alive in those days old Dublin ladies who had known Oscar as a young man. "My poor Oscar," one of them would say. "The English put him in gaol for something—I never did know what." I think she thought that it must have been for some patriotic activities, as his mother, under the name "Speranza," had written widely known patriotic poems and was considered a great rebel. And there was another who used to say, "What are Georgie Shaw's plays in comparison with Oscar's?" Bernard Shaw was still Georgie in some Dublin circles.

Yeats would read the poems of "the doomed generation" writers in that chanting voice in which he believed all real poets read their poetry, and he would tell us of their lives. It had been the fashion among them to have unhappy love affairs and at the same time to indulge in debauchery like that of Baudelaire and Verlaine and Dowson; it was the fashion also for them to believe that they could keep their minds and spirits pure no matter how they soiled the body and no matter how gross the physical pleasures they indulged in. Yeats himself had the most romantic unhappy love affair of them all, the one with the beautiful Maud Gonne, to whom he had written his love poetry. But Yeats had the character they seemed to have lacked; both in art and in life he was a highly disciplined man, and he gave his allegiance to causes, friendship, and literature. He was a man who had to work for a cause or probably he could not have realized himself at all.

As he walked along the street or appeared in the Abbey Theater or at any one of the innumerable literary and dramatic societies, he stood out from the indifferently dressed men around him as carefully garbed, with a studied bohemian elegance, an elegance influenced, no doubt, by the aesthetics of the nineties and by Oscar Wilde. Sometimes he would be in dead black, with a flowing tie, sometimes in a strange shade of brown; in the evenings he wore a black or brown velvet jacket. This dressing set off his personality, as did his rhythmic speech and his gestures. I suppose there was a great deal that was studied about his appearance in those days, and the charge of posing that was often leveled at him had a certain foundation—that is, if one had not enough insight to take the whole personality into consideration. A good deal of his posing was due to the fact that he really was not very much at home with ordinary people, did not know much about life as lived by the rest of us and had not a great variety of friends. Then, human energy and human interest even in the most powerful personalities are limited, and unless people can put on some mask, the outstanding ones can be drained of energy by the demands upon them of people and of the world. Yeats, then, played the role of the artist, the man who devoted his life to the practice of art and the furthering of art. It was often said of him in Dublin that Lady Gregory's influence had made him snobbish; I really do not think he needed any external influence to make him snobbish; at this period he was afflicted with a variety of snobbishnesses that were a sight to behold and an experience to encounter. First of all, his genius, the nature of his intellectual interests, placed him to some extent apart from the bulk of humanity; then, in addition to the common Irish notion of high descent, he had, like Villiers de l'Isle-Adam, the ideas of the romantic poets of a noble and chivalrous ancestry, an ancestry devoted to high causes. If he had had his choice he would have liked to be at the court of a Renaissance prince or duchess, or even with Goethe's Duke in Weimar. Added to this romantic snobbery, he had a curious bourgeois snobbery mocked at by George Moore, and it was very hard for Yeats to mock back at Moore. Yeats might be able, as he certainly was at times, to adopt the grand air of a Renaissance prince, but he often failed in ordinary good manners, and he certainly was no match for the easy courtesy of an estated gentleman like George Moore or the considerate Lord Chesterfield manners of James Joyce. Yeats often gave an odd impression of being not only ill-mannered but insensitive; James Stephens once told me that he had cultivated this mask of insensitivity as a protection against the world and against the slings and arrows that were so often launched against him.

II

Nevertheless, there was an unaccountably coarse streak in him such as I have never encountered in any other outstanding artist. But he seemed to have none of the vanity that so many writers have, and, absorbed and absent-minded as he was, he gave no impression of self-centeredness. His enthusiasms were for causes—the cause of art, the cause of Irish nationality, the cause of love and friendship. His very snobbery was in the cause of the superior human being devoted to the higher disciplines and to beauty. He made a cult of discipline which in later life made him take a romantic view of the fascist movements in Europe. Yet in a strange way he did not equate discipline and self-control. "Art gives everything," I have heard him say, "to self-surrender, never anything to self-control." It was his devotion to art, to his country, that made him work so hard in Dublin to make people understand poetry and literature. He worked so hard that I think much of his mysterious illness in later years which the doctors diagnosed by such queer names was due to the fact that these labors of his in his prime had so exhausted him. I have seen him put such immense emotional and intellectual energy into a talk to an audience of about twenty or thirty, some of them inimical, as would have projected a major scene in one of his verse dramas, and neither for this nor for his work in the theater did he get any financial return; he did not even at the time get much of any other sort of return, either—little gratitude, and that only from a few. In one of his poems to the beautiful, stormy woman who inspired so much of his love poetry, he wrote:

> My darling cannot understand
> What I have done or what would do
> In this blind, bitter land.

And yet a great poet of his type, an intellectual and artistic re-
former, would certainly have found more opposition in a larger
country where the practical man of affairs dominated; for him an
industrial country might also have been a "blind, bitter land." But
he never wavered; no matter how strong the opposition he encountered he went steadily toward the goal he had visualized, the creation of a national theater and a national literature. "The dogs bark,"
says an Arab proverb, "but the caravan goes on." There was plenty
of barking and snarling in Dublin, but day by day the caravan went
on.

In his own esoteric way he took note of our student exchequer.
I was deputed by the little college society of which I was president
to approach the Abbey box office and explain that the cheapest
ticket, one shilling, was a little above our student budget, as we
went not only to each play but to every performance of it, which
meant every night for a week. The Abbey secretary, Fred Ryan, a
young man whose life was also devoted to causes, interviewed me
with some perplexity.

"I don't think our license permits us to change the price," he
said. "You will have to see the head director, Mr. Yeats. He is now
at rehearsal. I will find out if you can see him."

He came back in a minute from his investigation. "Mr. Yeats will
see you in about ten minutes."

I waited in the foyer of the Abbey Theater in an ecstasy of nervous fright and delight. In a little while W.B. came out from
rehearsal, exhausted and remote from the world, his lips still mur-
muring lines. Fred Ryan held a low colloquy with him and then
presented me.

"This is the president of the Twilight Literary Society. The society is asking for reduction in the price of tickets."

W.B.'s eyes were dimmed. His gaze went beyond me. But he
woke up.

"I remember," he said. "You wrote the box office a letter about
this, didn't you?"

This was matter for surprise: it had never struck me he would
read the letter himself.

"Would eightpence be all right?" I interjected nervously.

"Eightpence!" he repeated dreamily, raising his arm in the familiar gesture. "Eightpence!" he repeated. He nodded to Fred Ryan

and walked out the door. Ryan and myself were left a little uncertain of the result. "I think it's all right," he said in a soothing voice. "Mr. Yeats wants you in the audience. We will give you twelve tickets for eight shillings." The society, I should mention, numbered twelve.

From that time on the club at each performance seated itself in the front row of the pit, the row next to the back row in the stalls where the three theater directors, Yeats, Lady Gregory, and Synge, often placed themselves. The audience was so slender in those days that we visibly augmented it, and Yeats would cast a pleased eye on us as we entered in a body. We could be depended upon to listen ecstatically to a verse play and to applaud with hands and feet. Nobody else in the theater was so delighted as we were or so young. We were pretty good scholars in literature and had a real sense of poetry. "The pit in the Abbey Theater," said Yeats in a London lecture reported in Dublin, "has an ear for verse; they know at once between one performance and the next if I change a line or a word in a line." "He means us," the Twilight Literary Society said. As I came to know him, he would tell me that I was his ideal of a youthful nihilist. Nihilism was the romantic form of revolt in Yeats's early days; his friend Oscar Wilde had made a play about Vera, the girl nihilist. I was so pleased to be Yeats's ideal of anything that I did not care what the word signified. I think in his mind it stood for a youthful fighting spirit that went with a reading of Russian novels, French symbolist poetry, and Nietzsche.

Now and again after listening to a verse play, at the intermission or in the tearoom, he would come and repeat lines with the changes he had made after a performance or two. On one of these occasions he repeated the marvelous ending of *The Green Helmet*:

> I choose the laughing lip
> That will not turn from laughing whatever rise or fall,
> The heart that grows no bitterer although betrayed by all,
> The hand that loves to scatter, the life like a gambler's
>   throw,
> And these things I make prosper till a day comes that I
>   know
> When heart and mind shall darken that the weak pull
>   down the strong,
> That the long remembering harpers have matter for a song.

He said them two or three times, explaining why he had made changes, and the lines always remained with me after he said them, for I had a quick ear for verse and my youthful mind was not too burthened with memories and experiences at the time.

Following the Abbey example, Sir Hugh Lane, Lady Gregory's nephew, reduced the rate for us at his picture exhibitions and art lectures. He ran the painting side of the renaissance, but I do not think an especially Irish school of painting was developed through these. The most Irish of the painters always seemed to me to be the Yeatses, father and son, J. B. Yeats and Jack B. Yeats. At the lectures in the Royal Hibernian Academy, the front row of arm-chairs would be reserved for us, and Hugh Lane, handsome and languid, with an air of wearied cultivation about him, like a French-man of ancient descent, would himself act as a sort of usher when he saw us enter. "These chairs are for my college girls," he would say, shooing away from the front row Dublin dowagers and the patrons of his art projects. Once he delayed no less a personage than George Moore, who was to give his famous lecture on the French impressionists, because we were kept some minutes in our residence house by another lecture. The audience got a little restive, and I can never forget the look of astonished rage an important Dublin lady threw at Sir Hugh when she beheld the awaited guests being ushered in by him and saw him nodding to the chairman so that the proceedings could now begin. "Hugh," she asked, making use of the good acoustics of the hall, "who are these young whipper-snappers?" As I have said before, young people were cutting a great swath in the Dublin of those days. The poets and playwrights were nearly all young; even the Sinn Fein party, headed by Arthur Grif-fith, who seemed to us rather oldish, must have been, the bulk of them, in the twenties or very early thirties. Yeats himself was only in his early forties, but he had even then a very grand air of author-ity. I think all the fighting he had to do must have both developed and altered his personality from that of his dreamy youth. The friends of his twenties would talk of the gentle, affectionate, ingenu-ous boy they had known, while the man we knew was hard, strong, reserved, deliberately living behind a mask—that mask, as he ex-plained to us, that all artists must find for themselves.

He knocked on the head so many hoary ideas of patriotism and literature, ideas that tradition enshrines in small countries or countries dominated by another, that of course he aroused resentment and suspicion. Before he had made himself into a sort of literary dictator, the subject for discussion at literary gatherings was not literature but patriotic ideologies, and at every assembly there was a number of older literary men who would get up and contradict him and announce that until freedom was won it was the duty of literature to advance the national aspiration. When Yeats informed us that favorite lines like

> For thy hapless fate, dear Ireland,
> And sorrows of my own

were but conventional sentiment and could not move us deeply; when he became mocking about "Believe me if all those endearing young charms," and similar effusions of the national poet, Tom Moore, he reduced over half his audience to almost speechless rage. Somebody would recover sufficiently to say that Yeats was living in an ivory tower and all the other things men say when they are faced by somebody who takes seriously the discipline and training of art. Irish audiences were not unique in that they liked speakers to deliver themselves of the humanitarian and political platitudes in fashion, on which their brains had not to work hard to understand.

III

The toughest fight I saw him in was what came to be known as the "Playboy row"; in this many of his usual supporters were against him, for the national sentiment in this case was mysteriously wounded. Synge was not popular, chiefly because his plays were so different from anything the audience had ever seen, and mysterious rumors were circulated about him. The subjects and personages of his plays, though native, were in a way incomprehensible to a part of the audience who were always on the lookout for anti-Irish propaganda. He was seldom treated fairly by the Dublin press; neither, of course, was Yeats, who was also at times treated scandalously in the English press. A well-known writer once reviewed a book of his by confining his remarks solely to the illustrations and winding up with the statement: "The letterpress is by W. B. Yeats." No doubt he thought this was very smart, but in time's revenges who cares what he thought, who even, beyond the present narrator, remembers his name? When, in Synge's *Riders to the Sea*, the body of the drowned man was brought upon the stage, certain of our professors who, a hundred and fifty years after Lessing, were still discoursing on the rules of composition, informed us that this was against all the laws of art, especially the Aristotelian laws of tragedy. One of the most enlightened of the national weeklies invariably referred to this little masterpiece as a "corpse curtain raiser." If the Abbey Theater writers were hurt by this sort of treatment they did not show it: "the caravan went on." Yeats seldom or never bothered to fight for his own work, but he put up a continuous fight for that of his friends. He was a wonderful fighter, eager, sardonic, tireless, and undoubtedly he had the racial quality of liking to trail his coat. His biographer, Joseph Hone, notes the fighting lineaments of his face, his pugilist chin.

The battle he waged for *The Playboy of the Western World* was a display of fighting strategy, of immovable courage, of indifference to public hostility such as I have never seen anywhere in anybody else. For a couple of weeks, during the rehearsal period, reports spread through Dublin that there were improprieties in the play and that the womanhood of Ireland was being slandered, and these rumors were received with hilarity by some, with solemnity by others. At the opening night the attendance was far larger than usual—in fact the largest I had ever seen in the Abbey—and there were tenseness and expectation in the air. The first act went well: it is a wonderful act, and people rocked with laughter. But as the performance went on, a restlessness became evident: a young man was being made a sort of hero on the stage because he had killed a tyrannical father—the father, of course, turned up later, hale and hearty, with nothing worse than a bandaged head. Finally the restlessness turned into a complete uproar when the young man used the phrase, "If I saw before me a drift of chosen females in their shifts." The man near me who began the hissing in the pit was Francis Sheehy-Skeffington, and he was certainly neither narrowminded nor anti-Abbey Theater. Why did he hiss? Why did the theater in the end become a mass of angry, swaying humanity? I could not understand.

Yeats was lecturing in Scotland on the night of the first performance; he was telegraphed for, for he alone could handle the trouble and cope with a demand by sections of the public for the withdrawal of the play. "Audience broke up in disorder at the word 'shift,' " the telegram to Yeats said. But, looking back on the whole business, I have come to the conclusion that the audience had been previously worked up to expect something immoral in the play, and the moment the word "shift" was pronounced, it was suspected that the worst was coming.

On receipt of the telegram Yeats hurried back to Dublin, all roused by the prospect of a fight in a good cause. He announced that the play would continue for the advertised number of performances. Lady Gregory had called in the police, who, as they lined the theater, were themselves frequently overcome with hilarity at speeches in the play, and though they tried to keep solemn faces, the whole force collapsed with laughter at the lines, "The peelers here are droughty poor fellows." It was altogether a comic scene both on and off the stage. The demand for withdrawal continued; Yeats announced—these were his exact words—that neither the house nor the race that bred him had given him a pliant knee, and he was not going to bend before the public. He promised he would throw open the theater for a discussion after the play's run had been completed.

On the night of this public discussion the streets approaching the Abbey were crowded with police, and there was an excitement as if revolution had started. The resentment at the management's appealing to the law—British law at that time—for protection for the play further angered the already wrought-up crowd. They had the inherited memories of generations of harsh treatment by British law, of abortive rebellions, and the horrors of the evictions from land and home were still alive in the minds of the older men and women.

A motley mixture of workmen, students, and bourgeoisie in evening dress filled the theater, most of them with denunciatory speeches ready to deliver. Yeats took the platform in full evening dress and faced the crowd. Step by step he interpreted the play, delivering in the process some of his most complex theories of art, one moment cowing the audience, the next, shouted down by them. Synge, the author of the play, who was no fighter of this kind, stayed at home. When the standard speech about freedom, patriotism, anti-Irish propaganda came from somebody in the stalls, the audience cheered. But even on the patriotics, Yeats was equal to them. "The author of *Kathleen ni Houlihan* addresses you," he said. The audience, remembering that passionately patriotic play, forgot its antagonism for a few minutes, and Yeats got his cheers. At one moment a student supporter of his took the platform beside Yeats and made a remark which caused nearly all the few women in the audience to walk out. Myself and another girl student were the only members of the female sex in sight; we were surrounded by a group of angry males, ordering us, if we were virtuous girls, to leave the theater. We stood our ground, and Yeats, who in spite of his well-publicized dimness of vision could see when it suited him, saw our difficulties from the platform and sent a couple of theater attendants to escort us to the stalls among the men in evening dress, who, however, did not regard us with a friendly eye, either. I never witnessed a human being fight as Yeats fought that night, nor ever knew another with so many weapons in his armory. He was then in his forties, but he looked under thirty, a fearless, dominating man in spite of, or perhaps because of, all his dreams and visions and esoteric philosophies.

In the end he won the battle for John Synge, and *The Playboy* became one of the favorite plays in the repertoire of the Abbey. Later audiences hardly understood what the fight could have been about. But the rumor of the play's wickedness spread to America, and when the Abbey company went there on tour, Irish audiences made an uproar similar to that in Dublin, and in one city, Philadelphia, the Irish societies got the company arrested. Although, years later, I met in America some of those who demonstrated against the play, I do not think I ever met anyone who was perfectly certain why he or she protested. No two had the same reasons. One intelligent woman told me that there was something pathological about the play that repelled her. Others seemed to be obsessed by odd ideas—that a drunken man was on the stage and drunken men did not appear in American plays; that the scenery, an Irish cottage, represented a state of squalor such as was uncommon in Ireland; that the father left his daughter alone with a strange young man, and that no Irish father would do such a thing (it may be remarked that the impropriety of such a proceeding would hardly occur to an Irish parent). Then, further, I was told that some New Englanders who looked down on Irish people had their reasons bolstered by the type of character represented on the stage. *The Playboy* was supposed to have degraded the Irish race. Irish immigrants often develop an inferiority complex, as indeed do other immigrant stocks, and this is particularly true, I believe, in the New England states, where racial prejudice has an odd hold on some of the older stock, though it is non-existent in others. Yet, as a matter of fact, the bulk of the New England people I have known have been of Irish descent—Ulster Irish descent, the same as my own.

Actually, I think, a strong though unconscious cause of the hostility to *The Playboy* was its novelty and strangeness; it was a new species of drama, and as Elizabeth Barrett Browning said long ago, the new, to please the audience, must be orthodox. "You must not pump spring water unawares upon a gracious public full of nerves." The hostility to Flaubert's *Madame Bovary* and to Baudelaire's *Fleurs du mal* was partly for the same reason—the public was caught unawares.

It was not only for John Synge that Yeats fought; he would put up a battle or a barrage of propaganda for anybody whose work he admired, whether this work was in literature or was, as in the case of Hugh Lane, for a modern art. He was a really fine critic in the sense that he was a subtle expert in literature—as I believe all great poets are, on account of their excess of intellect and excess of emotion. However, in what I have called elsewhere the criticism of judgment, he was sometimes governed, not by a cool estimation of values, but by another sentiment—partisanship for his friends, gratitude, or response to something that appealed to an esoteric interest of his own.

I remember his extreme enthusiasm for the work of Rabindranath Tagore. Will Rothenstein, the artist, had discovered Tagore while on a visit to India and had brought back some of his work in Tagore's own English version. This he showed to Yeats, who became fascinated and conducted a propaganda campaign for it which spread extensively and found strong roots in parts of America, especially in Chicago. In the summer of 1912, as I was walking in London in the neighborhood of the street where Yeats had his flat—one of the dreariest parts of the city, I always thought, near Euston Station, where one got the train to Holyhead for the Irish boat—I encountered the poet carrying a bundle. It was manuscript or galleys, I forget which. As always, I was glad to see him, but I was hastening to some appointment and did not want to delay. But he fixed me with an eye like the Ancient Mariner and started to read from the manuscript or proofs. As we were blocking the pedestrians, and as Yeats's gestures as he read were beginning to attract attention, I steered him to the nearest tearoom, an incredibly dingy place that smelled of a kerosene cooking stove. He ordered tea, sat down and read steadily. His excitement was so intense that he did not notice that the toast tasted of kerosene smoke and the tea of something similar. As he paused now and again in his reading to take a draught of the awful tea, he gave me a discourse on the meaning of the poem, on Indian philosophy and the probability that Tagore, who looked like the pictures of Christ, would start a new civilization. The old one was coming to an end—a persistent intuition of his. My response seemed lacking in enthusiasm; I began to feel feeble-minded, and I put this down to the fact that I had just been married. "This is the greatest poet in the world at the present time," he announced. Like A.E., he stood in awe of certain aspects of the Indian mind, aspects which to a female intelligence seemed a little woolly. I think he was eventually responsible for Tagore's getting the Nobel Prize.

The generosity of his intellectual admirations was indeed memorable; it was his tribute to all things of the mind and the spirit. It used to be said in Dublin, "If you are a friend of Yeats', you do not have to fight your enemies; he will fight them for you." As to his friends or enemies, I doubt if he ever forgot a friendly deed or forgave an unfriendly one; indeed, he had the hard Irish memory for wrongs once done him or his friends. "The Greeks," Yeats would say to us, "thought it as great a virtue to hate your enemies as to love your friends." He did both.

ह~ CHAPTER 13

"A Woman Homer Sung"

ONE EVENING in my university days in Dublin I went with some
fellow students to the Abbey Theater, which was doing its monthly
week of plays, at that time mostly the plays of Yeats, Lady Gregory, and Synge. Then, though it was producing only one week a
month and though it was at the height of its fame, the theater was
so badly attended that the habitués, or nearly all of them, knew
one another, and the audience was a sort of social gathering. Between acts one drank tea, chatted to one's friends, discussed their
work with the authors. As usual, we watched for the entrance of
Yeats and Lady Gregory. One of the plays was to be *Kathleen ni
Houlihan,* and some of the most fiery patriots in town were in the
pit audience waiting impatiently for the raising of the curtain. But
ten minutes, fifteen minutes passed and the curtain did not go up.
Somebody or something was being waited for. At last we saw Yeats
hastily enter, accompanied, not by the short Queen Victoria-like
figure of Lady Gregory, but by a tall woman dressed in black, one
of the tallest women I had ever seen. Instantly a small group in the
pit began to hiss loudly and to shout, "Up, John MacBride!"

The woman stood and faced the hissers, her whole figure showing
a lively emotion, and I saw the most beautiful, the most heroic-
looking human being I have ever seen before or since. She was
about six feet tall and of both romantic and commanding presence.
Her height would have drawn attention anywhere, but it was her
beauty that produced the most startling effect. It was startling in
its greatness, its dignity, its strangeness. Supreme beauty is so rare
that its first effect is a kind of shock. Yeats, standing beside her,
looked bewildered as the hissing went on; his face was set in lines
of gloom, but she was smiling and unperturbed. Soon a counter-
hissing set up, the first hissers being downed by another group, and

then I realized who she was. Maud Gonne, heroine of the Irish revolutionary movement, the woman the French called the Irish Joan of Arc, whose beauty and personality had given a dream to all sorts and conditions of men, from royalty to peasants. She was a legend to us young persons in our teens. She was the woman of whom Yeats had written:

> A woman Homer sung,
> That life and letters seem
> But an heroic dream;

the woman who had figured in *The Countess Cathleen* as the lady who had sold her soul to the devil in return for the lives of a famine-stricken people. She was the Dectora of *The Shadowy Waters*, the fairy-woman Niav of *The Wanderings of Oisin*; she was Aoife; she was all the strange and lovely women Yeats had written of. The young men were hissing because she had recently divorced, under circumstances that in Ireland seemed a scandal, one of their heroes, John MacBride, who had fought against the British in the Boer War; later, he was to be shot as one of the leaders in the insurrection of 1916. In a while the disorder died down and the plays proceeded, including *Kathleen ni Houlihan* in which Maud Gonne had played the name part years before in its first production.

A few days later I saw her on the street, the passers-by stopping to look at her, and I noticed that in spite of her tallness there was nothing oversized or Amazonian about her. She looked very feminine in her Paris clothes, and with what Yeats called her "delicate high head"—that was it—for all her height there was something exquisitely delicate in all the lines of her, she was perfectly proportioned, and not only that, there was a physical delicacy about her— she did not look very robust. And yet she was full of an electric, psychic life; she was alive to the last hair of her head. As she stopped to speak to an acquaintance some wandering strands of hair showed from under her small turbanlike hat, that bright bronze hair that Yeats had written of:

> Fasten your hair with a golden pin
> And bind up every wandering tress.

That bronze red hair was not so uncommon amongst Irish people, but in her case it went with bronze-brown eyes, an inheritance from her French blood, and that made a rare combination. She must have been at least forty years old, but she seemed ageless. Seeing her there was almost like meeting Helen of Troy on the walls, though later, as I knew her, I came to consider Yeats's comparison of her with Helen as a somewhat unreal one. Except for her beauty there was nothing of Helen about her. She was made of sterner stuff—"high and solitary and most stern"—and would never have eloped with a milksop like Paris, a haunter of ladies' chambers. The men she liked were fighting men, combative in body or in spirit, who were not too easily ensnared by women. In those first days I saw her rarely, as she did not then live in Ireland but made her headquarters in France, visiting Dublin occasionally. She was not easy at first to understand, not because of her complexity, but because of her strange simplicity. She was the most single-minded person I have ever known. Her single-mindedness was as strange as her beauty; all her life she was dominated by one idea, one passion, and this settled the external circumstances of her existence— her loves, her friendships, and her hatreds. It was the idea of freeing Ireland from English domination. I can imagine no event in her life that did not come out of this passion, and she made everything she had—her beauty, her power over others, her money, her social position—a handmaiden to it.

Her history was an interesting one. Her family was wealthy and socially important; her father, an Irish officer in the British Army, for a while shared the command of the forces quartered in Dublin. Like many Irishmen in the British service, he was a Nationalist, but others of the family were Unionist—that is, they believed in maintaining the union between England and Ireland. As is not uncommon in Ireland, there was a mixture of English and of French blood in her family; the name Gonne was a French one. Her mother died when she was a small child, and her father brought her up in a soldierly code of fearlessness and indifference to danger. At seventeen she was presented at the Viceregal Court in Dublin Castle. The Court, dramatically enough, being presided over by that connoisseur in women, Albert Edward, Prince of Wales, later Edward

VII, and his Princess Alexandra. The lovely debutante caught the practiced eye of the Prince, who had made beautiful women such a mode that beauty was a passport to any society. It was at the period when people used to stand on chairs to get a good look at beautiful women entering a hall or a reception. Maud Gonne's debut was a triumph. At the Court Ball the Prince of Wales cut in on his son, who was dancing with her, and escorted her himself to the royal platform. Tradition has it that she sang that rebel song, "The Wearin' o' the Green," to the royal ear on this occasion.

Immediately a lively and mundane old aunt took up the triumphant debutante with the idea of launching her on a dazzling career. French *couturières* and beauty experts were brought in to heighten all her effects. As Eugénie de Montijo was displayed by her mother in the smart watering places of Europe, finally landing an emperor, so the old lady displayed her dazzling niece, foreseeing a resplendent career for her. It was while being chaperoned by this aunt that Maud Gonne came once more into the orbit of Queen Victoria's heir. But now her father, Colonel Gonne, intervened in time to cut short the royal attentions and to carry her off to another city. From that time on her admirers numbered amongst them the most famous men of her time. But the one who was to make her most famous—nay, immortal—was the son of an Irish portrait painter, John Butler Yeats, to whom she was introduced by an old Irish political exile, John O'Leary.

In her aunt's house she met the man, the French statesman Millevoye, who was to divine her political gifts, her sense of tactics, the resourcefulness with which she could plan a campaign and carry it through. For women to be used as pawns in the games of European statesmen was usual enough: they allowed themselves to be made use of and got little in return except the brief glory and homage that their beauty brought them. Maud Gonne was made of different stuff from these enchantresses. She knew well enough the power of her beauty, for she had heard and read often that she was one of the most beautiful women in Europe—old W. T. Stead went so far as to say in the world—but she was not going to let her beauty be unscrupulously used by others. When Millevoye, the statesman who was planning the comeback of France after the debacle of 1870, proposed that he and she form an alliance, he to help her in her work for Irish freedom and she to help him in his projects for France, especially in the countering of British influence and the regaining of Alsace-Lorraine, she hesitated at first: the French enemy was Germany; the Irish, England; and she thought that a move on two fronts was not practical. Millevoye's policies were, of course, more complicated than hers, more professional and more responsible. France was a leading Continental power, an object of intrigue in all the chancelleries; Ireland was a little vassal state, an island beyond another island on the western outposts of Europe, and the chancelleries had no reason to bother about it one way or the other. Millevoye was the leading spirit in the anti-British group in France, combating Clemenceau and the pro-British group. He was connected with numerous influential groups and organizations, with General Boulanger and the Boulangistes, with the League of Patriots, and with the party who wanted an alliance with Russia.

The first job he entrusted her with was the smuggling into Russia and into the hands of the Czar's chief adviser of an outline of the French proposals for an alliance. The Millevoye group knew the Germans were sending similar proposals, and it was a race as to who should be first to get to the Czar's adviser. Maud Gonne sewed the documents in her dress; Russia was the only country then that demanded passports; an irregularity in her passport caused her to be held up at the frontier. She used her charm, vamped an important Russian official, and managed to get on the train for St. Petersburg that would permit her to be ahead of the Germans. There was a dizzy moment when she found herself alone in the railway carriage with the vamped gentleman and noticed that everybody else was being kept out. But she had been in similar tight places before, and Millevoye saw to it that she always carried a little pistol in case the gentlemen were not amenable to soft talk. This one was: she told him she was an Irish girl, and that the relations between men and women in her country were not based on elementary sex notions but were more on the line of old romance—in short,

> Though they love women and golden store,
> Sir Knight, they love honor and virtue more.

He was vanquished; for the rest of the journey he listened to her conversation, undoubtedly with the same delight that I have seen men listen to her: she would look at them gently with her bronze-brown eyes, talking in her beautiful and dramatic voice about what interested them most. She had a mind as well as an intelligence and could bring light and heat to many subjects.

But if she served Millevoye's group well, their services to her cause were even more effective. European countries had only the most secondhand ideas as to what Ireland's claims were or what was happening in that country. The all-powerful British information services saw to that. Now with the aid given her by the Millevoye group, Maud Gonne, who could make an impassioned speech and write an effective article, succeeded in getting a wide publicity for Irish affairs. Lectures were arranged for her all over France as well as in Belgium and Holland, the students forming a bodyguard for her. Millevoye got important newspaper publicity for the Irish cause, and the powerful *Figaro*, a newspaper read in every capital in Europe, carried articles on the Coercion Acts, the famine, evictions, burning of the peasants' houses, the treating of Irish political prisoners in Dartmoor. The British Government found themselves up against, not one of the sleek enchantresses who work behind the scenes; they were up against a woman of consummate fighting powers, an able tactician, an ardent patriot, one who turned men's heads, not to keep them in silken dalliance, but to make them help her in her work. Men ruined what men often think more of than anything else—their careers— to aid her in her efforts for Irish freedom. In herself she was for them the impersonation of the Irish cause, and she made it seem incredibly romantic. Two years ago an old gentleman in the French Education Office told me, with a nostalgia that only a Frenchman can express, of that golden day nearly a half century before when Maud Gonne came to lecture at the university where he was a young professor, fascinating the young men, professors, and students.

She had Englishmen with her, as well as French and other nationalities. It is not possible to forget that Irish aspirations had many strong English supporters. Some of them devoted their lives to the struggle and even endured, as did Wilfrid Scawen Blunt, sentences in gaol. When Maud Gonne went to the scene of an eviction or to a political meeting she would be followed, not only by her friends and allies, by journalists from European papers, but by the harassed men who loved her and who feared for the dangers she was running. She would travel round on horseback guarded by her dog, Dagda, and her little pistol. On one of her campaigns she found Millevoye in a ramshackle inn in the wilds of Donegal, having succumbed to the rigors of the climate before he could overtake her, and the gallant Sir John X, then an English member of Parliament, jogging round after her on the stony roads in a jaunting car, with a diamond pendant to entice her away from the field of battle. Secret service men followed her around, too. She was perpetually trailed by those shady individuals employed by governments to shadow the leaders of revolutions in vassal states. They could do little against her except spread scandals of one kind or another. At one time government hirelings spread a story that she was an agent in British pay; in a spy-obsessed country this might have been believed, for it was published in a British-subsidized weekly. But she who never hesitated in a fight took an action for libel against the editor of the paper, and though he had the backing of the Solicitor General, she won the verdict. Arthur Griffith, the founder of the Sinn Fein party, the party that eventually won what freedom Ireland has now, dropped round with a horsewhip and gave the libeler a thorough hiding. It was not the first time a man had been horsewhipped by a devoted admirer for saying something against Maud Gonne. The victim generally kept quiet about it; however, this horsewhipped gentleman took the case to court, and Arthur Griffith got a term in gaol.

Indeed, as Yeats's poems say, "She lived in storm and strife," for

> What could have made her peaceful with a mind
> That nobleness made simple as a fire?

Men and women with a passion for freeing their country have a psychology all their own; it can be a passion of such intensity that makes all other passions tame beside it. Yet very few people with this passion are real social revolutionaries: outside the determination to free their country they are often conservative and even reactionary. Maud Gonne had the social-revolutionary as well as the national-revolutionary fervor; like many revolutionaries she had often an unscrupulousness in furthering the end she had in view: she might have preferred other means, but the end had to be reached. Once, during a famine, when she ordered the starving people to help themselves to the landlords' flocks or any other eatables they could lay hands on, she found that their religious training inhibited them from doing this heartily; then she ransacked the doctrines of the Church and the encyclicals of the popes until she found justification enough to encourage them to do as she demanded. She brought out a pamphlet with extracts from Saint Thomas Aquinas that filled some of the clergy with horror. Then there was a prominent uncle of hers who found that his crested and engraved stationery had been used to get her into Dartmoor prison to interview the Irish prisoners.

It was not always the political fight that engaged her. She strove hard in the less exciting battle against poverty and illness in the Dublin slums. She was absorbed in this work and in providing meals for school children when, in 1914, a yacht full of guns for the Irish revolutionaries was steered by a mysterious woman into Howth Harbour. The woman, to her regret, was not she, but a quiet mouse of a girl, Mary Spring-Rice, cousin of the then British ambassador to Washington. Maud Gonne did not appear prominently again until after the 1916 insurrection, when she was imprisoned in Holloway gaol. While she was serving a sentence there, the news reached her that Millevoye died: their alliance had long since lapsed, their ways had parted; their policy had failed, that of her and Millevoye's enemy, Clemenceau, had won; Edward VII, to whom she had made her bow as a debutante and whose admiration for her had been marked, had made France all for Britain.

Out of gaol, she took up the fight again. After the war, for the first time, I think, under British rule, a member of an Irish family, Lord French, was viceroy. This bewildered gentleman, divided in his allegiance, when driving through Dublin in state with all the trappings of the King's deputy, would behold two beautiful middle-aged women making speeches to an insurrectionary populace. He could not without scandal order their arrest, for one was his sister, Mrs. Despard, and the other the woman he once admired, Maud Gonne.

To try to discover what composed the charm of a woman like Maud Gonne is difficult: there was only a minimum of the conventional enchantress about her. She wore chic clothes carelessly; choosing hats was a bother, so she wound veils round her head, turban fashion. She used, as far as one could see, no cosmetics. Beauty alone could never have won her the lasting devotion of men and women, or the tribute of immortal verse that Yeats has given her. Men fell in love with her and stayed in love with her, and though they married afterwards, as most of them did, it was noticeable that they married rather plain and charmless women. It was as if, having once known all beauty and all charm, they did not care ever after for any of its lesser manifestations. She had three qualities that I have seen in all the real charmers I have known: she had a romantic personality; she had rich emotions and a warm heart—indeed, one of the winning things about her was her affection for other people; she had a considerable touch of artistry, and artistry even without beauty can have a fatal charm of its own. She could paint interestingly: she gave me as a wedding present, among other things, a memorable picture she had painted, a picture of a red-haired woman going forth to battle, her shield in her hand, a flock of ravens around her head—some old warrior-queen, or perhaps the Irish war goddess, the Morrigu. Besides these, she had a mind that could brood and think, making her always interesting, though her mind was not the literary mind cultivated in Dublin in the first quarter of this century. It was a soldierly mind like that of a chief of staff, and at the same time, mystical and mysterious. With Yeats she had dabbled in the occult, and believed in second sight, telepathy, and fairy lore. She had a sort of Protean personality moving on various planes, all unified by her single-minded passion for her country. She could be a violent fighter; she could be gentle and appealing; she could be fearless; she could be pathetic; she could be coldly realistic and romantically glamorous. But you will find all of her, every shape of her, in Yeats's poetry and plays. "Who can tell which of her forms has shown her substance right?" the poet, dying, wrote of her in a poem published posthumously. She had obsessed his mind and imagination for half a century. The last time I was in Ireland, as I was driving hastily across Dublin with an American friend and an Irish writer to catch a train, we were held up at College Green. A political meeting was taking place, demanding an Ireland completely independent of England. A tall old woman dressed in black, floating veils about her head, was addressing the assembly. "Did I not tell you," said the writer, "that we have the most beautiful ruins in Europe—there is the most beautiful ruin of them all."

ॐ CHAPTER **14**

Working with Padraic Pearse

WHEN I HAD GRADUATED I did not want to leave Dublin; all my interests, all my friends, were there. To me the city was full of excitements; the whole driving force of the country was centered in it. I did not care about money, but to live, I had to have a job; so I settled down to teaching, which was one of the very few occupations my education fitted me for. First I taught university students a branch of that subject called in colleges, English, which seems to embrace everything connected with literature. But with these students my relationship was casual and limited to class teaching, and nothing casual ever interested me, so eventually I went to teach in one of Padraic Pearse's two schools. I knew nearly everybody connected with them: the teaching staff was young, and we seemed, all of us, to be traveling on the same road.

Padraic Pearse was one of the striking figures that this period in Ireland threw up. He was the son of an Englishman who had been trained as a sculptor but who had settled in Dublin with a business in ornamental ironwork and marble, married an Irishwoman, and brought up his family in Ireland. Racially, therefore, Padraic Pearse was only half Irish, if so much; but psychologically he was more completely so than anyone I have ever known. For people to belong psychologically to one country and racially, whole or in part, to another, is not an uncommon phenomenon. I have known Irish people who with a little English blood were psychologically entirely and angrily English. But I never knew anyone who had quite the traits of Padraic Pearse. He had a powerful mystical personality which seemed to have its roots in some region beyond ours to which his mind escaped from time to time. Psychically there was something of Yeats in him, but this was only evident at moments. They were not very intimate, being both absorbed in the work they had to do, but I never saw them together without being strongly aware of some inner resemblance. They had an intense expression, both; mysterious eyes that looked concentratedly and fascinatedly at something the rest of us did not see. One of Pearse's eyes had a slight squint which added to the strangeness of his gaze; his expression was kinder than that of Yeats. He was, of course, many years younger and did not live long enough to be disillusioned with mankind.

In general appearance Pearse was a tall, prophetic-looking young man, somewhat heavily built, reserved in private conversation, but very fiery on a platform and always full of humor and even whimsicality. Both he and Yeats were born leaders; they could get followers and they could get unquestioned loyalty; both gave the impression that they were engaged on a work to which they were driven by some inner compulsion—maybe destiny is too highfalutin a word; but they gave the impression that they were obeying some call and that personal choice had little to do with it. Yeats had a natural dictatorialness, especially about such things as literature and poetry, and rightly so; he could be, when he felt like it, fascinatingly arrogant and a devastating fighter, but Pearse was a fighter of a different kind; he was never arrogant; he was always gentle though he, too, was a very strong man; in fact there was nothing feeble at all about the men I knew then. Pearse was by profession a barrister, by temperament and performance a poet, by choice an educationalist. When he first worked out his ideas of education, of an education that would enable young people to fit into the life that Ireland offered them and be useful to their country, he was a very young man; he was in his twenties when he founded the first of the two schools; he was still a young man when, after the rebellion of 1916, he was shot by a British firing squad in a barrack yard.

The first school he started, St. Enda's, was for boys; the second was a girls' school called St. Ita's, both named for old Irish saints who had monastic schools. In these schools he tried to combine some very modern ideas of education with the older Irish notions of fosterage where parents sent children to live with some person or family distinguished for their attainments and whose ideals and ideas were considered worthy of adoption. He wanted education to be, to some extent, the vital influence of personalities. For this he tried to get into association with the school all the outstanding people in the country who were sympathetic to the national idea. He also acquired an interesting group as teachers or lecturers. Not all of us, I am very sure, were equal to what he wanted, but at least we responded to his ideas. He himself was the most high-minded person I have ever known; it was unthinkable that he should ever have thought a mean thought or done a mean action; it was even hard for him to imagine others doing them.

Of his teaching staff, those I remember best were his own brother, Willie, who taught art; Thomas MacDonagh, poet and critic, both executed after the insurrection in 1916; Louise Gavan-Duffy, one of the finest teachers, was the youngest daughter of Sir Charles Gavan-Duffy, who had himself barely escaped execution in a previous insurrection, but was, instead, "transported" to Australia, where he became an outstanding statesman. This remarkable man had had three existences: he was married three times, had had three families, a career in two hemispheres, had lived in three countries, and had been a friend of many of the well-known people of his time. Louise, his youngest daughter, had been brought up in France, but, like others, had come back to help in the new awakening Ireland, and had, like myself, taken a degree in the National University. Almost everything significant in the Dublin of that period was run by the young; youth, eagerness, brains, imagination, are what I remember of everybody. There was something else that was in all of them: a desire for self-sacrifice, a devotion to causes; everyone was working for a cause, for practically everything was a cause. There was the literary movement—an unexpressed people had to be encouraged to express themselves according to something in the national tradition, and whenever possible, in the native language; there was the Gaelic League—an old culture, an old language partly destroyed, had to be brought back and cherished; there was the Sinn Fein movement—the government of Ireland had to be got away from England, from Westminster, and into the hands of people who understood the country and its needs; the industrial movement—an impoverished and unprosperous country had to be helped to prosperity by starting industries and inducing people to buy what was made in the country. Later came the militant or physical-force movement—England was not going to give self-government, then force was to be organized to wrest it from her. Everybody I knew was working in one or several causes, some people were working in all of them. Any public meeting by any organization for any movement would very likely be addressed by a selection of people prominent in all the other movements. The witty Sarah Purser who, as I write this, has just died at the age of ninety-six, used to say they were like a stage army—they marched round and round. Whatever sort of gains could be got out of work in Dublin, material gain was not one of them.

The staff of Pearse's two schools were knit into all the causes; some of them were in two or three, some in the rest of them. Looking back, it seems incredible that so many young people were eager to devote their lives to the service of causes and ideals rather than to the normal things of youth. That they should take on themselves the arduous task of running a school, of bringing up and educating boys and girls, a task so full of drudgery and routine, seems unbelievable. But then it seemed equally incredible to some that parents would want to entrust their children to a group of young people whose chief recommendation was their ideals, their scholarship, their sense of art, and in other ways their lack of experience. But entrust them they did, and the progeny or youthful relatives of some of the best-known people in the country came to St. Enda's or St. Ita's school. As in almost every other enterprise in the Dublin of the period, an atmosphere of literature and art pervaded everything; many of the pupils came from writing and academic families, and the visiting relatives were an excitement of the school, especially the visits of George Moore, who used to come to see his nephew, Ulick, the son of "my brother the colonel who ought to have been the cardinal." George would arrive in the usual atmosphere of studied comicality that surrounded him; he would descend from the jaunting car, argue over the fare with the jarvey who had driven him, bow solemnly, and say, "If it comes to abuse, let us part." This was his ordinary reply to the

argument put up on all occasions by every Dublin jaunting-car
driver. Jaunting cars or horse cabs were the only mode of locomo-
tion in Dublin outside trams in those days, and the fare rate was
very loosely fixed, and the jarvies expected more than the regulation sum from every well-dressed person. George would ascend the
school steps in a stately way, leaving the jarvey looking villainous
and calling names after him—"It's easy to see the difference between you and a gentleman." On one of these visitations the servant
who opened the door informed him that his nephew was down
with the measles. George, without another word, dashed back down
the steps, climbed onto the car, the same car which had brought
him, the jarvey still engaged in inventing insults, and drove away
for fear of catching the measles. For days he kept telephoning
Pearse, inquiring as to the beginning symptoms, as he was full of
fears he was developing the ailment, a spot having appeared on his
chin, and his temperature, as he believed, having gone up. This sort
of fear, or any sort of fear, was the last thing Pearse wanted his
pupils to acquire, for courage, all the courages, were fostered in the
school, and I do not think George's visits were encouraged in spite
of the fact that he was then at the height of his fame. No living
writer has that sort of importance now; then everybody bowed to
George Moore as the great innovator in the novel, the introducer
of the realistic method in English. Arnold Bennett had written, "I
think Mr. George Moore is a greater novelist than our dear old
Thackeray." So great is the overestimation of the innovator in
his own time! I do not think Ulick knew much about Uncle
George's literary fame, though he liked to touch him for pocket
money. But the really striking visitors were the renowned European
Celtic scholars. They were cosmopolitan only in the sense that
they were from so many different capitals; otherwise they were
men of the study, of the library, absent-minded and shy.

II

Celticism was, at this period, it seemed, all the rage; the romance
of the Celts "who went forth to battle but who always fell," who
were among the few European peoples with their own mythology,

their own gods and heroes, engaged attention in many lands, and the last militant standard-bearers of the Celtic idea seemed to be the inhabitants of that island lying beyond another island in the western outposts of Europe. Consequently, during the years I write of, every happening in Dublin aroused an interest perhaps out of proportion to the significance of the happenings. The Gaelic idea in action in Pearse's schools and the hopes it aroused among dev-otees of the old Celtic culture, the hopes that once again this would become important in western Europe, brought to the school those visitors and students who made the pilgrimage to Dublin. These devotees were always showing up, and some of them knew the Irish language but not the English language, queer old scholars, all the romance of whose lives had somehow been con-nected with this conquered island in the North Atlantic, in its language and its history. The only man of the world among them, or one who was not entirely a dreamer lost in texts and traditions, was the famous German Celtic scholar, Kuno Meyer, who gave courses in Dublin in the School of Irish Learning, but who, most of the time, was attached to an English university. He was very fond of England as well as of Ireland, and I think the first World War killed him. Meyer was the poet scholar, the artist scholar, and he wore his rare learning with a grace not usually associated with German philologues. On account of the beauty of his translations he was one of the first to attract an interest in the old Irish litera-ture which he passionately loved as some men love the Greek, and consequently he was a good deal of a hero in Dublin. Some of the charm of this man, his intellectual distinction, has been got down by George Moore in his *Hail and Farewell*. How well I remember his figure at a reading stand, his shoulders stooped both with arthritis and his bending over books as he read in his beautiful voice and his perfect English his translations of old Irish poetry, all done as naturally as if he had written the poems himself.

There would come a romantic Viennese scholar named Pokorny, who lived to fall under the wrath of Hitler. There was an array of Celtic Frenchmen, mostly Bretons, who would even talk of the separation of Brittany from France. There were Scotsmen whose names I do not remember, looking so tall and aristocratic in their kilts which they called filibegs. Then there was a bucolic Welsh-

man, Sir John Rhys, the dean of Celtic scholars, who looked what
he probably was, a Welsh farmer, but who for his Irish visits got
himself up to look like an Irish farmer with frieze coats and black-
thorn sticks. He commended everything in a booming voice four-
fold. Both he and our own old Dr. Sigerson, of whom I am writing in the next chapter, were enchanted with Pearse's plays written
in Irish. One of these was a passion play acted by the teachers and
students of the schools in the Abbey Theater and which caused a
minor dramatic sensation so that accounts of it were not only in the
London but in the Continental papers. The beautiful girl who
played the Virgin mother was the daughter of an Irish Argentinian,
Señor Bulfin, and oddly enough, though she had no Spanish
blood, looked like a Murillo virgin. I played Mary Magdalen, a
small part for which I was cast chiefly on account of my long reddish hair that, like that of Browning's heroines, wound three times
round my neck. In the rehearsals the feet-washing incident was
cut out so that my hair served no useful stage purpose except to
hang down over a purple-and-gold dress. The twelve apostles, all
of them, were played by schoolboys, for, as in all schools, as many
as possible of the pupils had to be got on the stage for their parents
to admire. When, on these occasions or at the dinner that followed,
Pearse would announce that if Ireland did not get self-government
soon, he and his generation would have to fight for it, he would
be loudly applauded by all the visitors, Henry Nevinson, the
famous journalist and war correspondent, and other visiting Englishmen being especially enthusiastic over such sentiments.

It was characteristic of the period that when the schools designed
any outside activity it was likely to be either literary or dramatic.
When a literary monthly, the *Irish Review*, was started, extempo-
raneously as most things at the time were, the editorial and advi-
sory board was partly composed of members of Pearse's teaching
staff. The managing editor was Professor Houston, of the College
of Science, whose money paid for the first issues of the *Review*,
all other services, including those of contributors, being voluntary.
At the start and perhaps all the time I was the only girl in this
group, and being some few years younger than the men, I was well
bossed and patronized by them. They were determined to write
the body of the magazine themselves—poetry, the stories, the plays,

the articles, and the editorial notes. But they decided to let me do some book reviewing in the back pages in small type. Troubles soon began, for the older and established men of letters did not want to be brushed aside by obstreperous youth in a new Irish periodical; they were bent on sending in their contributions. George Moore sent in a short story called "The Flood," asking that it be printed in the opening number of the magazine and on the front pages. The bright boys of the editorial board, however, decided that the story was an imitation of Zola and that it would be a mistake to print it in such an up-to-date magazine as they projected. Besides, Padraic Colum, of the editorial board, fancied himself as a political commentator, and he wanted some items of his in this line to open the magazine. But the young men were no match for George Moore. He sent for Professor Houston, who was considerably the elder of the group and exhibited such an interest in the project that he completely won the managing editor, and eventually the review was scheduled to appear with Moore's story as the principal feature, and on the opening pages.

The *Collected Works* of John Synge had just been published in Dublin, and Houston, having heard of Yeats's opinion of my supposed critical prowess, gave the books to me for an essay review. In the interview about his story, Moore had asked Houston who was writing the article on Synge. The managing editor somewhat deprecatingly answered, "A girl is doing it." George Moore, with a characteristic outward gesture of his hands, said, "My dear man! A girl! What girl? Whose girl?" Now, at the stage of my life when I am writing this, if anyone told me a young girl or a young man was writing an article on a famous and provocative author, my reaction would be exactly the same as Moore's, for criticism is a mature art, and the young never really do it well. However, I had been soaked in Synge, and I did my best with the article, and when the magazine made its appearance the opening pages were by George Moore in large type and the last pages by me in smaller type. As ill luck would have it for the young men who were bent on writing the whole magazine themselves, most of the notices in the English periodicals concerned themselves with the first and last pages of the *Review*; that is, with George Moore and myself. As it continued to appear, the *Review* published work by nearly all the writers in the country: Pearse gave them his Irish Anthology, collection of Gaelic poems with translations, and James Stephens his delightful *The Charwoman's Daughter*, which ran for eleven issues of the magazine as a serial. Its chapters were first read aloud before the fire in the drawing room of Professor Houston's eighteenth-century house in Rathfarnham before publication.

The interest in the review was surprising. Offers from American publishers came in, the first to James Stephens from Little, Brown, of Boston, through the late Edward O'Brien. The proposal of an advance of five hundred dollars—a large sum in Dublin of those days—for *The Charwoman's Daughter* amounted to about twice the yearly income Stephens was earning at the time as a clerk in a lawyer's office. He was the most envied man in literary Dublin, but this envy was manfully overcome in a real admiration for Stephens, his originality and enchanting fantasy. This book of his was published by Little, Brown under the title of *Mary Make-believe*. He was the first of the young writers to have a book published in America, though most of the others had appeared in American periodicals.

The magazine remained great fun; we all took turns at the editorial desk for short spaces and quarreled happily among ourselves and with the contributors.

From this distance of space and time it all seems very exciting and romantic, but actually there was much hard work and drudgery, and we who worked in Pearse's schools and in associated causes had little of the pleasures of youth with its few years, except what Madame de Staël called "the pleasures of intellect and imagination." Pearse himself could have had no youth at all in the ordinary sense. A feeling of responsibility to the country and its future was always with him. He knew Ireland from end to end, in all its history and legends, its harassing, unnecessary poverty, destructive to all life and spirit. "I have seen such sad childings, such bare marriage feasts, such candleless wakes," he wrote in his play *The Singer*, the chief character of which, MacDara, expresses so much of Pearse's meditation and character. "I felt it proud and wondrous to be a teacher. . . . I gave to the little lad I taught the very flesh and blood and breath that were my life." This was all true of Pearse himself; he loved his pupils and his schools, but there came a time when he was drawn into another cause and another duty beckoned. The country was being run as the minor dependency of an empire and governed from Westminster, England. The very things that seemed right and necessary for Ireland seemed wrong to its rulers. Everything was at cross-purposes; loyalty and patriotism for one country meant treason for the other. The young men I knew, proud, high-spirited, eager to serve their people, had reached the limit of their patience; they saw Ireland as the one European country that was getting nowhere.

The high British officials were often decent fellows, but their knowledge of the land they ruled was farcical. Their manners had that easy condescension combined with that affectation, an almost instinctive affectation as an American has called it, considered so chic by the English governing classes before the first World War. I remember once at a party at the home of Commissioner Bailey, the government Land Commissioner who happened to be an Irishman and who did his job by ignoring the Castle government as much as possible, there was an English official who was making himself pleasant to a group of mixed Dublin intellectuals and society people.

"Come now," he said engagingly, "what are you making of the new university we have given you? What else do you want us to do for you? I assure you we'll see if it can be done. What really do you want from England?" He was not nonplussed by the laughter that greeted his remarks.

"We want nothing from England; we want you all to get out of our country."

"Then who do you want to rule you?"

"We want to rule ourselves."

"To rule yourselves! But you can't rule yourselves." Then I heard him say in an undertone, "I must tell Mr. Birrell about this."

Pearse and his group were willing to take any reasonable settlement of the Irish claim, such as would give control of Irish affairs to Irish people. But, seeing no settlement coming, they became more and more convinced that the old revolutionary party was right. Irishmen, somehow or another, must get control of the government or the country would sink into a more and more hopeless condition. This feeling became a mystical passion with young

men and women, so great that it dominated every other. I have
heard, and read still oftener, that the elemental human needs are
food and love, but I have known men and women in whom these
needs were slight in comparison with the obsessional need of freeing their country. Men may risk death for love or hunger, but I
have known those who set out knowingly for certain death in the
flower of their youth in a fight for freedom. Many of the young
men I knew believed that the very sacrifice of their lives, the shedding of their blood, would eventuate in freedom for their country.
I do not know what they thought freedom would bring or if, by
long pondering on it, their minds had not made a sort of ideal
image of it. But anyhow they all joined together, drew up a declaration of withdrawal from the British Empire, appointed Padraic
Pearse Provisional President of an Irish Republic, and on Easter
Sunday, 1916, went out in what battle array they could muster and
seized what they could of the government offices. They were
downed that time by the might of an empire, and the signers of the
declaration were all condemned to death. The end of Padraic
Pearse, his courage and his dreams, took place in May 1916 in a
barrack yard where a firing squad of soldiers shot him for rebellion against the British Government and buried his body in
quicklime. I read the news in an afternoon paper in New York,
stepping off a train at Grand Central, and the shock of the loss of
all he stood for still remains with me. He, too, had his dreams of life
and love like others, and sometimes he feared these might pluck
him back from his purpose and his duty. He has expressed it all in
a poem written originally in Irish, translated into English by one
of his colleagues in the school, Thomas MacDonagh, shot also
on the same day by the same firing squad:

> Naked I saw thee,
> O beauty of beauties,
> And I blinded my eyes
> For fear I should flinch.
>
> I heard thy music,
> O melody of melodies,
> And I closed my ears
> For fear I should fail.

I tasted thy mouth,
O sweetness of sweetnesses,
And I hardened my heart
For fear of my ruin.

I blinded my eyes,
And I closed my ears,
I hardened my heart,
And I smothered my desire.

I turned my back
On the dream I had shaped,
And to this road before me
I turned my face.

I have turned my face,
To the road before me,
To the deed that I see,
To the death that I shall meet.

He met the death he had visioned in this poem.

౭ CHAPTER 15

A.E., Dr. Sigerson, Sarah Purser

OF COURSE not everybody in Dublin was young, and not everybody was fighting. There were a number of moderately placid and settled people whose families had been identified with the city for a very long time; the ancestry of some of them went back to the period when Sitric the Dane was king of Dublin, for Dublin, like all European cities, had a population of mixed descent. Some of these lived in the old houses, and the houses and themselves seemed to have exchanged characteristics—solidity, hospitality, stodginess mingled with gaiety, courtesy fixed by tradition; a historical past and its lineaments showed in both. They were the products of history, and they took unkindly to changes; some of the young people tried to make their elders put in a telephone or electricity, but these contraptions did not work so well. One or two Vandals acquiring Georgian houses tried to improve them by putting bay windows in the second floor, the drawing-room floor, but the old houses threw the windows out—they were always cracking, the bricks around them falling to pieces, the very brick and mortar hated them.

Two of the picturesque personages of old Dublin to whom I was deeply attached and to whom I felt very comradely, though I was about half a century their junior, were Sarah Purser and George Sigerson—Sigurd's son—Sigerson being a descendant of the Norse invaders of Ireland, indeed, as he used to say, from one of the captains defeated by Brian Boru at the Battle of Clontarf in 1014. He had a curiously Scandinavian appearance and bore a strong resemblance to the portraits of Ibsen, though he was not quite so modern-looking. Known in Dublin as simply "the doctor," by profession he was a neurologist and a professor of neurology at a time when people knew very little about such things; he had been a pupil and friend of the great Charcot of Salpetrière in Paris, who had had also among his pupils Sigmund Freud and Pierre Janet. The doctor, in addition to his neurology, was a well-known Celtic scholar— maybe not so thorough a one as some of the great Continental ones because, naturally, he could not devote his whole time to scholarship. But he was a native product, and we had the affection for him one gives to kindred; we all knew his book of translations, *Bards of the Gael and Gall*, some of them even by heart. He lived in an old house in Clare Street, a street that was a continuation of stately Georgian Merrion Square, though the houses were not so large or so grand. The doctor's Sunday-evening dinner parties were a great feature in the limited social life of the town; there was the atmosphere of a French salon about them, for Dr. Sigerson was very Frenchified, and his house was full of French furniture and bibelots, literally full, for to navigate his drawing room without knocking over a little gold table or a vase or a clock or a little statue was a gymnastic feat. He would sometimes have his guests meet in his consulting room, which, as is usual in doctors' houses in England

and Ireland, was off the dining room. After a glass of sherry the connecting doors would be thrown open, the doctor would gravely offer his arm to the youngest lady present, who was sometimes myself, and march with her into the dining room, placing her on his right, with the most important lady on his left. He himself would lead the conversation—it was always conversation in which the whole table took part—all the time tackling the roast with a huge carving knife which he first sharpened loudly. Among his guests there were nearly always some famous and distinguished people; occasionally these would be visiting Continentals, or Americans, for the American consul in Dublin, Donn Piatt, was his son-in-law. Donn Piatt himself was the son of the American writers, the Piatts, and so had various American connections. His son was at one of Pearse's schools. The doctor's other son-in-law was Clement Shorter, the well-known editor of the London *Sphere*, who had married the poet daughter, Dora Sigerson, who is represented in the *Oxford Book*. She was one of a group of women poets, very famous in their day and much photographed, whose work would be in all the anthologies but who is now rarely heard of. At these dinner parties the food and wine were really the best on any Dublin table: there was always a perfect roast with fine red wine or sparkling Vouvray, after which the guests would go up to the cluttered drawing room, the women about fifteen minutes before the men, and drink China tea. Then the latest Paris purchase would be examined—a little miniature, a fearsome-looking clock, or a table with pictures painted on it. If a poet was present he would be asked to repeat a poem or two. I remember Padraic Pearse repeating the doctor's own translation of Cuchulainn's lament over Ferdiad, just as he would often repeat it to the teachers and pupils of his schools, for he thought no poem represented such high chivalry. He would repeat it with intense emotion, his strange eyes aflame. On this occasion, our host, a cup of tea in his left hand, beat time with his right:

> Play was each, pleasure each,
> Until Ferdiad faced the beach:
> One had been our student life,
> One in strife of school our place,
> One our gentle teacher's grace
>   Loved o'er all and each.

Play was each, pleasure each,
Until Ferdiad faced the beach:
One had been our wonted ways,
One the praise for feat of fields,
Scatach gave two victor shields
    Equal prize to each.

Play was each, pleasure each,
Till Ferdiad faced the beach:
Dear that pillar of pure gold
Who fell cold beside the ford,
Hosts of heroes felt his sword
    First in battle's breach.

Play was each, pleasure each,
Till Ferdiad faced the beach:
Lion fiery, fierce and bright,
Wave whose might no thing withstands,
Sweeping with the shrieking sands
    Horror o'er the beach.

The doctor had a Johnsonian manner of address and a Johnsonian humor which often left us gasping. In the most unruffled way he would deliver himself of a demolishing dictum. Once, at the dinner table, a poet unasked proceeded to repeat his latest effort. At the line resoundingly given:

There grows the swart smock weed and the blue sea poppy,

the doctor held up the carving knife.

"Stop," he said. "What is—a—smock weed?"

The flustered poet, at a loss, said, "But, sir, you know what a smock weed is. A smock weed . . . well, everybody knows what a smock weed is."

"There is no such thing," said the doctor, "as a smock weed. Since the poetry of this country began to be written by Mr. Yeats, nobody knows what words mean any more."

There was a chronic quarrel between Yeats and Sigerson which was one of the diversions of literary Dublin. It was said to have begun long before at a crystal-gazing séance Yeats had held before or after one of the famous dinner parties. Yeats, looking raptly into the crystal, announced, "I see a majestic, shining figure waving over an abyss; I see also other shapes—scarlet, green, purple, fluttering around."

"Mr. Yeats," said the doctor in his best Johnsonese, "you see no such things. What you are looking at is a reflection from the apothecary's shop across the street. If you look out of the window you will see a row of jars filled with colored water—scarlet, green, purple, and the shining brass fixtures supply the shining figures."

The doctor seemed to be perpetual chairman of the National Literary Society which Yeats had founded along with the Irish Literary Society of London, and every Monday evening he would appear there to introduce the lecturer of the occasion. If Yeats happened to be present, which was frequently, he would interpose a remark into the flow of the doctor's periods, a remark which might be embarrassing to any other speaker; the doctor would magnificently ignore him, and later in the evening would not discourage the satirical remarks the audience would occasionally make the poet the butt of, such as, "Mr. Yeats seems to be unaware that the dress the actress wears in his play *Deirdre* is Elizabethan in design and Victorian in material." Yeats would smile blandly and say, "I know it very well, but if an actress insists on wearing a dress which suits her style, what can I do about it?"

At his dinners the doctor would sometimes delight in dividing his guests into Gaels and Galls; that is, those whose names were Celtic were put at one side and those whose names were Saxon or Norse on the other, "for the Norse," he would say, "had as much right to Ireland, especially to Dublin, as the arrogant Celts who were claiming everything." He would refer to the high-king, Brian Boru, a great hero in Ireland who had defeated the Norse in the eleventh century, as "that usurper, Brian."

On his own job, neurology, the doctor could be very exciting on the rare occasions when he spoke of it, and he would tell us of the experiments into hysteria and mental ailments conducted by his friend, the great Charcot at Salpetrière, and how he, really, was the precursor of all modern movements dealing with the subconscious. Sigerson had then in his possession numerous letters from Charcot, who had come to Ireland to lecture. In this matter he aroused my interest to such a degree that, years after, I attended the lectures of Charcot's pupil, Pierre Janet, at the Collège de

France, and some of Georges Dumas' at the asylum of St. Anne. Dr. Dumas followed Charcot's technique in bringing the patients on the stage. I must say that the criticism that was often made both of Charcot and Dumas, that these affairs were too much of a show, seemed to me to have some justification. Some of the patients were obviously delighted to find themselves on a stage and before an audience. They talked steadily about themselves and their visions, but not more fantastically than I have heard people talk about themselves in daily life. In answering Dr. Dumas's questions they gave such an interesting revelation of human quirks and emotions that I began to understand why, in the past, writers made such a point of visiting asylums to study character. It was like looking at people through the other end of the telescope and seeing human qualities isolated and immensely enlarged.

II

Not more than a half mile from the doctor's was one of the most singular of old Dublin houses, Mespil House, where Sarah Purser lived. It was a big Georgian house standing in its own grounds in the middle of the city. Doubtless it had been somebody's country house in days gone by when that part of Dublin was outside the city boundary. The house was so remarkable, so full of character, and, at the same time, so weird—there must have been a ghost in every room—that it would have reduced to lonely eccentricity anybody of a less vivid and warm personality than Sarah's. She lived here full of bubbling gaiety, alone, except for her servants, in a house that, complete with its tarn and gloomy trees, was like something out of Poe. She and the house both seemed survivals out of history. Before I was born she had been a famous portrait painter. When W. B. Yeats was a boy she had seemed old to him, yet she survived him by some years. She had figured in the diary of Marie Bashkirtsev as Sarah, the Irish girl art student in Julien's studio in Paris. She had painted almost every well-known person in the country, she had been mixed up in every Irish cultural movement, had backed the Abbey Theater, Hugh Lane's exhibitions; she had given scholarships in painting, founded a studio for the making of stained glass named An Tur Glionne, The Tower of Glass, which sent out its beautiful stained glass to all parts of the world. Her family had been famous Dublin scholars, and there was about all of them something so characteristically Dublin that it is impossible to imagine them as the products of any other city—their accents, their manners, their wit, their downrightness, their patriotism made them indubitable Dubliners. Sarah was well known to visiting Americans, whom she was fond of entertaining in her strange old house. Once a month she gave a party to all her friends in the perfectly huge drawing room, its walls covered with pictures, its furniture beautiful and gay in spite of an all-pervading air of dampness in the room, for I think Sarah kept it closed except for these occasions. In Mespil House she kept up the eighteenth-century fashion of having her servants on board wages, and was very proud of the economic way she ran the place. "I run it on seven hundred pounds a year, my dear," she would declare triumphantly. "No waste at all." As is likely to be the habit of people whose families always had money, she spent none in extravagances.

When we were living in Paris she would come over, stay in the same little hotel in Montparnasse as we did, in a room like a student's up four flights of stairs, and though she was then past eighty —she lived to be ninety-seven—she would roam around cafés at night drinking this and that and talking to her friends and their friends until long after midnight. In the daytime she would frequent studios and dealers' shops, looking at pictures and sculptures and driving hard bargains in her purchases for Dublin galleries. All her life she was an unmitigated artist, and nothing in art new or old, I think, was alien to her. So indifferent was everybody I knew in Dublin to wealth that I had not realized Sarah was a rich woman until once after seeing her off on the Calais train I got a telegram from her saying she had forgotten her jewel case in the taxi and asking me to get the police to recover it. In Paris things found in taxis are, as a rule, handed over to the police, and, right enough, our hotel proprietor received a visit from the taxi driver, who informed him that he had left a case found in his taxi at the police station and expected a reward. To get lost things back, it was the regulation to pay the police ten per cent of the official valuation, which then was sent to the Paris hospitals. I conceived Sarah's jewels to be one or two of those gold necklaces and bracelets, a turquoise broach, and maybe pearl earrings, which is all that most family jewelry in Ireland amounts to. I started off with about two hundred francs in my purse, interviewed a loquacious police official who handed me an *affiche*, the contents of which at first I could not grasp.

He proceeded to explain that on the production of the proper authorization and identification, plus a hundred thousand francs, ten per cent of the valuation, he would transmit the jewels to their owner. I was staggered to hear that the contents of Sarah's battered old jewel case were worth a million francs, and I had not the hundred thousand to redeem them. Furthermore, I could visualize Sarah's face and her tongue if I sent her a bill for a hundred thousand francs, and was in despair until the hotel proprietor came to my aid. He knew the right approach to the police, and had no hesitation whatever in telling all the fictions that came into his head. He put up a lacrimose yarn that the jewels represented Sarah's life savings, all that she had to transmit to her numerous descendants, that she was so old and senile that she really did not know what she was doing or where she put anything, and then he added a talismanic sentence: "Her distinguished family in Ireland were well-known friends of France." Finally, for a few hundred francs, Sarah got her jewels back. I trembled to think of what she would say if she ever heard the details about her senility that the hotel proprietor so eloquently related. Being vigorous in mind and body, she delighted in telling everybody her age. "I'm now the age Goethe reached," she would say when she was in her eighties. But as the years went on there was nobody she could compare herself to, for she had outlived them all. In my young days I had thought that Sarah, like the sun and the moon, would be there forever, but indeed I had thought the same about most old Dublin friends. Some, like Sarah and Dr. Sigerson, had been celebrated before I was born, others while I was still a child; I was accustomed to hear their names or see them in print, and this somehow made me inclined to imagine that they were fixtures like monuments.

III

The same sort of niche in my mind was occupied by A.E., who was, however, a generation younger than Sarah or Dr. Sigerson. A.E. did not go to any of the doctor's Sunday dinner parties for the reason that he had his own Sunday evenings. These were not dinner parties like the doctor's, but on the order of what the French call *réunions*. People came around to talk, read bits of their work, and bring up problems of technique in art or literature, and discuss philosophy. A.E.'s reunions had their start, I imagine, with meetings of adherents of hermetic and theosophical societies, for both A.E. and his wife had been theosophists. Not much of the hermetic tinge was there in my time, or if there was, I did not notice it, but there was the best talk on art and literature I have ever heard anywhere. One learned in a practical way how a poem was made, how a play was made, how a novel might be made, for the practitioners were there and delighted in expounding. If one listened to the talk at the other side of the room, one could learn about national politics. It was possible, too, to hear about ways of marketing butter and eggs, for A.E. earned his living as an organizer for the Irish Agricultural Organization Society which Sir Horace Plunkett, Lord Dunsany's uncle, had founded. Sometimes farmers for whom poetry and painting were strange worlds came to talk to A.E., the agricultural organizer who had roamed Ireland on a bicycle and had given lectures in local halls and schools on matters connected with farming and co-operative societies, and who was the editor of a farm paper called the *Irish Homestead*. The few farmers who came into that picture-littered room wore tweeds like everybody else, but their coats generally had tails, and there were pockets in these tails out of which a handkerchief would be half hanging. Occasionally a farmer would look at A.E.'s canvases hanging on the walls, pay a few pounds for one of them—A.E. never charged more than a few pounds—and walk off with it wrapped up in a newspaper.

Yeats had no residence in Dublin at this period, but when he settled in one after his marriage, one could not help noting the difference between A.E.'s house and Yeats's. A.E. liked to have every sort of person and had no awareness of class differences or the difference between the mind of a man and the mind of a woman. W.B.'s guests were selected; one could not bring any chance-met acquaintance into his as into A.E.'s house; one did not go oneself without an invitation. In A.E.'s one talked on draughts of tea or coffee, but in W.B.'s one's tongue was loosed on sherry. Yeats, no more than A.E., held any notions about female inferiority to the male, yet he would sometimes have evenings for men only, perhaps because the Dublin writers were mostly men. Though these two had been close friends and, to a certain extent, remained friends, their interests at some point had gravely diverged. In a way hard to explain, Yeats was more professional and more practical, though on the outside it looked as if A.E. was engaged on the more practical avocations. I am not using "practical" here in the common sense of a money-making ability. But when Yeats really set himself to do anything, it got done in spite of all antagonism and opposition. Perhaps it was that A.E. was too kind a man to have faced with equanimity the antagonism of other men. Yeats did not mind people's antagonism at all; in fact it spurred him on towards his goal.

Though really belonging to what is called, in the vocabulary of the moment, the petty bourgeoisie, A.E. was an aristocrat, with all those qualities that have been so impressively summarized by the Russian philosopher Berdyaev as marks of an aristocracy: he was magnanimous, he was unenvious, he was courageous, he had no prejudices, he was a free being. I never knew him to take personal offense, though he sometimes showed a fury like a god in a rage at things said against his country or his countrymen. His open letter to Rudyard Kipling, who had jibed at Irish nationalism, was such a reproof and on such a large-minded plane that Kipling's reputation as a writer was shaken, even unjustly shaken. On another occasion, when someone asked him what should be done with the correspondent of the Tory *Morning Post*, who had been cabling mendacities from Ireland to his paper, A.E. answered in my hearing, with a fearful flash in his eyes, "Lead him to the frontier and pitch him over." "But we've no frontier, A.E.; we have only the sea." "So much the better; pitch him into the sea." Though attached to his friends, he was never, I think, so swayed by personal devotion as was Yeats, and though a good fighter who fought to the end on many issues, A.E. always suffered in a fight where W.B. enjoyed every minute of it.

A.E. and Yeats had first met as art students at the Dublin Art School, but whereas Yeats was to drop painting, A.E. kept on painting diligently. His pictures were mostly landscapes with remote fairylike figures, though on rare occasions he would paint a portrait of one of his friends or of someone with whom he liked to talk. Once he painted my portrait; it was after I had been years in America and was back in Dublin for a little while. I think it was because he wanted to get in a few remarks on modern poetry, about which I had been writing, that he asked me to sit for him. He discoursed so much on the subject that I had some difficulty in getting a word in edgewise and found the best way of intervening was to whirl off some strange piece of poetry; he knew no language except English, and I thoroughly enjoyed rattling out verses in French or German. It was for this reason, perhaps, that he gave me a large mouth in the portrait as well as wild red hair—the redness was all right, but I had taken pains to have the wildness toned down with a finger wave. "Why have you given me such a large mouth, A.E.?" I asked. "Well, you see a mouth is very important in a portrait, and as nature gave you practically no mouth, I had to invent one for you." And then he would say, "How nice it is to be able to leave nature out."

His was never the biting Dublin wit—sometimes Dublin wit was nothing but plain downright malice—but A.E.'s had always something affectionate and whimsical in it, and one remembered it like a caress. It was this, I think, that helped to make him, along with his great magnanimity, the most popular, next to Douglas Hyde, of the men of the Irish Renaissance. His appearance is familiar to Americans, for he came here often to lecture and was widely photographed. The sudden entrance of this tall, broad-shouldered, bearded man into any assembly would give a thrill to the beholders, for he looked a prophet, a seer, a high priest of some divinity. He was a familiar figure in many milieus, for he mingled in all the activities of his country, whatever form they took—politics, art, literature, education, the theater, the labor movement—the last indeed with passion. During the bitter and revolutionary transport workers' strike of 1913 he took the platform for the workers and made a sensation by announcing, in that beautiful voice of his, "All the real manhood of this city is to be found amongst those who earn less than a pound a week." His sympathy with labor was not the literary and sentimental attitude and attitudinizing now common among writers, but of such a nature that the workers looked to him as one of their spokesmen and counselors.

I look back on these three people, A.E., Dr. Sigerson, Sarah Purser, each so different from the other, as contributing lavishly to the special charm that was in the life of the Dublin of the period: they were so many-sided, so vigorous, so large-minded, so friendly, so free of prejudices, barring a prejudice against the British Government. Can it be that the strong life, the impassioned intellects that were theirs, have gone forever from the earth? It may be that they represented something that has gone out of the modern world. They were an island type and could never have been produced in a big country. Each in his or her own way had that which gives such character to a people—a warm and rooted provincialism. They would never have had the chance to develop into what they were in a very large country or a very large city; they would never have had the chance to develop that curious sophistication, intellectual, artistic, that broad humanness which is what I remember most about them. The next generation did not measure up to them. To say that I am entirely glad or entirely pleased that one of the accidents of life, combined with some temperamental urges of my own, threw me among them when young, would not be true, for having known them well, I was forever afterwards disappointed with all the other life I knew. It may be memory playing tricks with my imagination, but they were the most brilliant, the most affectionate and warmhearted people I ever knew, though I am under no illusion that they were common in a country of which they were typical. The typical of any country represents not the common or the majority, but those with the aggregate qualities at their peak.

ဗာ CHAPTER 16

Marriage: Sir Roger Casement and W. S. Blunt

AT INTERVALS one or another of my young men friends or colleagues would propose to me, but we would laugh it off. I had, as far as I remember, no sentimental interest in them, only an interest in the causes we were all working for and in the poems and plays they wrote. All the young men of my circle wrote poetry; most of them wrote plays, and nothing I could say—and I was sometimes very snappy—could restrain them from reading them to me. Girls do marry, however, though this is not so usual in Ireland as elsewhere, and I supposed I would eventually marry somebody, though I certainly did not covet the role of some of the young married women I knew, with the monotonous domesticity, the dreary commonplaces, and often loneliness of their lives. In addition to other causes I was deep in the woman's suffrage movement and had read all the books about the position of women, which corresponded in a way to that of the oppressed races. The women I knew were not in the least intellectually inferior to the men; that is, perhaps leaving out men of genius like Yeats and a couple of the outstanding writers, though in physical endurance they certainly were, and this included myself. This, maybe, was the crux of the whole notion of women's inferiority in a civilization where force was and still is the decisive factor.

I did not have any taste for exchanging the independent and interesting life I was living for pottering around a kitchen, planning meals, hanging curtains, and so on, and I let my young men friends know my sentiments about this. One of them, however, declined to listen to me and kept assuring me that he was the person Heaven had destined me to marry and that I could not escape my fate. I always thought, as he was a very fine and courageous person, that he would be a nice man for somebody else to marry, which was what eventually happened—in fact he married before I did. But he made one final determined effort before dropping me. He called at my little flat, armed with an engagement ring, and told me in a very cave-man manner that he had arranged everything, that I was to marry him on a certain date in a certain church, and that I had better accept my destiny. The argument that ensued reduced me to a state of panic such as I had never known, for I was afraid I might be unable to hold out, especially as he said I had encouraged him and ought to have some sense of responsibility about it. But I managed to be strong-minded, and the harassing interview ended with tears on both sides, with his throwing the ring into the fire and leaving in a high state of emotion. I was stretched out in a condition of copious weeping when, some minutes later, another of my young men friends, a well-known Abbey author, Padraic Colum, called. Tearfully I told him of my ordeal; the ring was still lying unconsumed in a corner of the grate; he fished it out with a tongs, left it on the hearthstone to cool so that it could be mailed back to the young man who had brought it; then he settled himself gravely in an armchair and proceeded to lecture me. "I think," said he, "that to save yourself trouble, you should marry me. Then these fellows will all leave you alone and you won't have to go through any more of these scenes." He pursued this train of reasoning, and eventually I dried my eyes and said, "All right, Colum; maybe that would be best."

At the end of this scene I think he was a very sober young man at finding himself engaged to be married, for I imagine he had pondered on the marriage state about as little as I had. There were many dismal prognostications as to what would befall us, for two more unpractical young persons would be hard to meet. A mature friend of Colum's called on Violet Russell, A.E.'s wife, and said dolefully, "Have you heard the news? Colum is going to marry a university girl who does not know how to boil water or wash a pocket handkerchief." Violet was unperturbed. "Well," she said, "she can learn, as I had to. I married a penniless writer and artist, too."

We were married in midsummer in a church called the Star of the Sea, by an old scholarly bearded priest. After the ceremony we took the early boat to Holyhead, as Wilfrid and Alice Meynell had invited us to spend our honeymoon in their cottage at Pullborough in Sussex. We were to stay a few days first in London, as some of the Abbey Theater players had arranged to put on a one-act play of Padraic's in a vaudeville theater, which was expected to have a considerable run and for which he was to be paid a weekly sum. On the train between Holyhead and London as we sat at luncheon in the dining car we counted our united finances; they amounted to so little that I felt a cold shiver go down my spine, but my newly acquired husband was unmoved. He pointed out that he was getting money from a publisher in London, and besides, there was his play coming on. I cheered up, but we did not reckon on what was to happen. Lady Gregory, as a director of the Abbey Theater, had some control over the engagements of the actors through their contracts. The arrangement about Padraic's play, *The Betrayal*, was squashed and a play of her own substituted. We had to resign ourselves to the disappointment, which was, however, made less black by the warmth of the Meynells' kindness, and by their indignation at Lady Gregory's action.

We were entertained a great deal, for London is a kindly city and Londoners more hospitable than Dubliners. At a lively luncheon Wilfrid Meynell gave in a restaurant I found my attention often wandering to a bearded, tanned, Castilian-looking man who sat at a table near and, his luncheon finished, was interestedly watching us. I seemed to be the only member of the party who noticed him, and he smilingly returned my gaze. After a while someone leaving the restaurant approached him; the exact appearance of this man, clean-shaven, blue-suited, with monocle, cane, gray suède gloves, assured English upper-class manners, remains clear in my memory. He held out his hand to the bearded Castilian. "Back in England, Sir Roger," he said in a loud clear voice. "Won't you join me in a coffee and a liqueur at the club?" "Thank you," said the Castilian, "but I am waiting to speak to Padraic Colum, who is over there with his bride." At the sound of the voice Padraic jumped to his feet and brought the striking-looking stranger to our table. "Sir Roger Casement." The gaze of all at the tables was fastened on him.

He was really magnificent-looking, and then at the height of his fame because of the part he had played in showing up the

atrocities committed on the natives in the rubber plantations of
South America and Africa. There was about him that strong psychic
life that was characteristic of so many of the elder generation of
Irish people of the time. It seemed amazing that he had come out
alive from some of his experiences among the exploiting rubber
traders. It was his love of the human race which led him to risk
his life to rescue the enslaved blacks of Africa and the Indians of
the forests of South America, as well as the typhoid-ridden under-
fed people of the West of Ireland. He had seen terrible sides to
human nature, but here he was, bronzed, and apparently happy, on
his way back to Ireland to work for causes in his own country
which needed him as much as the wretched, exploited natives
of Africa or Putumayo. So striking-looking was he as he stood at
the table that the patrons of Pagani's stopped eating and stared
at him. As to the sort of impression he usually made, we have
a description of it by Stephen Gwynne, a well-known writer and
member of Parliament. "Figure and face, he seemed to me one
of the finest-looking creatures I had ever seen, and his countenance
had charm and distinction and high chivalry." It had indeed all
that, and his voice with its singular intensity added to the dramatic
effect of his presence. Like Faust, two souls must have struggled
in his breast, for he was a British consular official and at the same
time an Irish patriot, a Fenian, as his English colleagues used to
call him who made no secret of his desire to help to free Ireland.
As he said himself, he went to remote places in South America as
consul "to have money to spare for Ireland." His salary could not
have been very large, but he sent contributions to practically every
Irish cause and was a firm backer of Arthur Griffith and his newspaper, *Sinn Fein*. Now as we saw him he had just come back from
South America, one of the most noted men of the day, and he was
about to retire from the consular service to devote the rest of his
life to Irish affairs. Later we were to see him often in Dublin between the time of our marriage and our leaving for America.

II

A few days after this we went down to Pullborough in Sussex
to stay in the Meynells' cottage. A group of Meynells lived in

cottages scattered around—Monica (Mrs. Saleeby) and Sylvia (Mrs. Lucas), to both of whom Francis Thompson wrote such beautiful poetry. Here we were not far from Wilfrid Scawen Blunt's house, New Buildings, and he came over to see us, driving down the narrow country roads four-in-hand, the hoofs of his lovely Arab horses barely seeming to touch the ground. He was at this time over seventy, but what strong life he still had, and what a passionate and romantic existence he had led. He had taken up more lost causes and loved more lovely women than any other man I ever knew. He had supported rebels all over the world, principally Arab and Irish. Before I was born he had been jailed by the British Government for his intervention in Irish affairs. All my generation had read his love poetry; his Love Sonnets of Proteus, or a great many of them, were written to a beautiful and dashing courtesan who had had many lovers in high circles. It seemed to have been a great affair, and if it did not last, the poetry it inspired did, and some of it is enshrined in the *Oxford Book:*

> When cities decked their streets for barren wars
> Which have laid waste their youth . . .
>
> .   .   .   .   .
>
> Then I remember that I once was young,
> And lived with Esther, the world's gods among.

In his late twenties, after some time in the diplomatic service, he had married Byron's granddaughter, Lady Anne Noel, the daughter of that Ada, "sole daughter of my heart and home," who had married the Earl of Lovelace. In spite of the passion they had had for each other, their similarity of tastes, the delight they had in traveling together through the Arab world and breeding Arab horses, they were now separated, Lady Anne living at the family estate, Crabbet Park, and breeding Arab horses, and Wilfrid living in New Buildings and breeding Arab horses. Their friends accounted differently for their separation. "Too much Belle Millbank in her," Wilfrid's friends said; her friends had a different story—the difficulties of living with a man of such Protean personality and sometimes eccentric habits. When we went to see him or have lunch with him, we had to go up the avenue literally stumbling over rabbits, for he would not have them destroyed.

He had been in the diplomatic service when a young man, and it was while in the service in South America that he met that Arab scholar and traveler, Sir Richard Burton. Burton excited him about the Arabs and started him on his travels into the Arab world. And like so many Englishmen, he was fascinated by the Arabs forever afterwards and championed them when any of their territory came into conflict with British imperialism. He denounced the British policies in Egypt and the Sudan and took the side of that strange man, Arabi Pasha. He always championed the Irish; indeed, he had wanted to become a member of the Irish parliamentary party, but Parnell, then the leader, was averse to having an Englishman as an Irish member of Parliament. Blunt took no offense as a smaller man might and continued to back Parnell and the Irish cause with might and main. During that revolutionary struggle in Ireland known as the Land War, he was arrested and flung into gaol for taking the chair at a proscribed Tenants' Meeting: the landowner against whom the meeting was directed was Lord Clanrickard, who had years before been Blunt's colleague in the diplomatic service.

Lady Anne Blunt, who had accompanied her husband on these campaigns as well as on his travels amongst the Arabs, was, as behooved Byron's granddaughter, a great lover of liberty. Blunt, when young, was himself a very Byronic character and, by accident or design, followed Byron's example as a traveler, a love poet, and a fighter for forlorn causes; indeed he was the typical romantic aristocrat, but to be such one has, of course, to have not only wealth and high position but imagination and talents. Wilfrid Scawen Blunt had them all. He, Yeats, and Casement were the handsomest and most romantic-looking men I have ever seen, but whereas Casement and Yeats were poor and hard-working men who often had known pinched times, Blunt was of the wealthy and well-placed English upper classes, a great English "milord." Probably no people on this earth ever were freer or had more opportunities for both work and pleasure than the English upper classes, especially the men. They were on a pinnacle in their own country, waited on by a serving class who were really a sort of slave class. They had what were called rank and privilege and the entree to the great places of the world; at this period they were still kowtowed to all over Europe, and to see one of them descend at a grand European hotel, welcomed by bowing lackeys and followed by a valet or two bearing his effects, was a memorable spectacle. Some of them, a lot of them, were undoubtedly hidebound and reactionary, but there were always enough of them with no prejudices of any kind, either of class, race, religion, or anything else, to give this type of Englishman great prestige everywhere and a reputation as being free, enlightened, chivalrous, and adventurous. "They were the most fascinating people in the world," I have heard a rich German-American who had lived years among them exclaim enthusiastically.

Not many of them were as gallant fighters against oppression as Wilfrid Scawen Blunt, but there always have been enough of such men in England to make that country seem almost their habitat; so, without being a common type, Blunt was a characteristic type. He was a gentleman in a sense that anybody could understand, difficult as it is to follow what the English mean by that word. Being a gentleman, however, can and does sometimes include all the most excruciating genteeleries, so Blunt was something beyond a gentleman. He was a hereditary European aristocrat, at home anywhere, in camps and courts, in tents and castles. He could share with equal pleasure a meal in the desert in the black tent of an Arab chief, or in the house of a West-of-Ireland squireen where the host, in honor of his guest, changed from yellow boots and leggings to black ones, and the hostess put on a clean blouse over her tweed skirt, she presiding, as Wilfrid told us, at one side of the table carving a ham, while the host presided at the other end carving a goose, all washed down in the process of eating by whisky or poteen or smuggled claret. Wilfrid was a product of a long evolution, physical, mental, moral, of all the cultures and the ideals—Greek, Roman, Christian, Islamic, Hebrew—also the product of the English love of freedoms. Then he had been bred a Catholic, and this helped to make him the romantic aristocrat on the Latin pattern like Chateaubriand rather than on the English pattern or like the Cecils, the Churchills, and the Roseberrys, who though they fought on the day of danger, did not absent themselves on the day of awards.

Yet with all this, Wilfrid Blunt's conversation was mostly gossip —gossip, of course, of a high kind—imperial gossip, as it were, about the goings on in embassies and foreign offices and cabinets, about

politicians and the beau monde of all the European capitals, about
the hatred of certain French salons for Edward VII, who had
brought about the Franco-British alliance, which they believed
would lead to war with Germany. Then he talked out of his intense
hatred of unscrupulous imperialism, of any people ruling another
against their will. England, he considered, was far greater before
she attached an empire, when she was a little country devoting herself to the production of great literature and a happy breed of men.
Disraeli had made her a land grabber. But I wonder did Wilfrid
forget about the East India Company and Clive and Warren Has-
tings? Then, after this imperial history, he would gossip about some
country house where women were invited without their husbands
but with their lovers and told to leave their doors unlocked at
night. Then there was such and such an Indian prince who was
really playing in with England, but another, a certain maharajah,
with oriental subtilty was playing a game of his own and fooling
the government. There was an ambassador in a certain capital who
had another ambassador's wife as mistress; there was another who
boldly had had as his hostess his illegitimate daughter.

Then there were the plans for Irish self-government of George
Wyndham, whom he called his Irish cousin. Wyndham was indeed the grandson of the Irish patriot, Lord Edward Fitzgerald.
How unscrupulous some of the Irish Unionists were, he reflected.
Years and years before, he had met Carson somewhere as a young
man and asked him what line in Irish affairs he would take. Carson,
according to him, intimated that he would have more of a career by
going in with the Ulster Unionists and the English Conservatives
than with the Liberals and Nationalists, and so this Cork lawyer became an Ulster leader, probably the first fascist leader in Europe.
The guiding idea openly expressed among these political personages seemed to be based on how one could have a career, be a successful public figure, and be invited by all the political hostesses;
outstanding figures were run after by women for their parties; Parnell had first met Mrs. O'Shea when she called round to the House
of Commons to ask him to dinner. Social affairs were of pivotal importance; for a member of Parliament, an employé of the Foreign
Office, a cabinet minister's secretary to be seen in certain houses
meant they were heading straight to be members of the British ruling classes—a *Herrenvolk*. It is very hard for Americans or perhaps

for any people now to understand what it all mounted up to. Wilfrid Blunt took it as a matter of course, liberal and radical as he was; the importance attached by the English to society and such things, and to good form, was in his bones; if you wanted to talk nastily about anybody you could accuse him of some lapse in social behavior. Asquith, during his first marriage, somebody had informed Wilfrid, before he had married Margot Tennant, had been so socially unsophisticated that at a dinner party he would offer his arm to his own wife. Of course, such a thing could never have happened; no passably educated Englishman could be as innocent as all that. Then he told the story of a member of the royal family who had been so ignorant of the difference between a composer and an instrumentalist that she had asked a famous composer to play the piano at a party and was terribly nonplussed when he answered, "Ma'am, I play the piano very poorly." As aristocrats spend so much of their time entertaining one another, they have naturally developed a special talent in gossip; it was a sort of hereditary habit in courts and courtiers, in ladies in waiting, ladies' maids, and second footmen. Gossip seems to be the very foundation of the social life of that partly closed and yet hospitable society always open to artists and scientists and men of intellect that was known in Europe as the *haut monde*. But in London one might easily get the notion that the whole British Empire, the Foreign Office, the embassies, the House of Commons were run on gossip and the tittle-tattle behind the scenes of political hostesses. Wilfrid Blunt's diaries, like Saint Simon's memoirs, even like Tacitus's Annals, are gossip on a grand scale, the gossip current in the ruling classes.

Then, like every British aristocrat I have ever known, he was very sensitive to other people's looks and appearances. Personal beauty seems to be a sort of fetish in the English upper classes; in no other upper class in Europe have so many men married women for their beauty regardless of their class or occupation. When Wilfrid talked about people he always spoke of their looks with either pleasure or disgust. Richard Burton, who had so much influence on him that he sent him wandering among the Arabs, repelled him by his appearance; he was ugly, he said, and wore terrible clothes. Then Francis Thompson was "a peaked little cockney." W. E. Henley was deformed, had thin legs, and the maliciousness of the hunchback. Shaw was "an ugly fellow with a pasty face and a rusty red beard." I think his irritation was greater at ill looks in men than in women. Yet as he gossiped like Saint Simon or Tacitus, so his diaries, like their works, are a sort of appendage to history; he knew all the people who made the history of his time as well as most of those who made the poetry. He himself, I think, thoroughly enjoyed the roles he played both in politics and in poetry; he was a sort of *enfant terrible* in British public life, afraid of nobody, championing every good cause, militantly anti-imperialistic, condemning the government's wars and attacks on other countries' rights. The photographs he had of himself in his various roles in life were of interest to him, and he exhibited them with pleasure. There was one as a remarkably handsome young man in a romantic cloak, with a Byronic look and the air of one who had dared and done everything a young man could, including bullfighting. Then there was his photograph in manhood in his prison garb in Galway gaol, and a wonderful picture of him in the black gold-bordered robe of an Arab chief. He had indeed lived the interesting and full life that he himself described as proper for a man. "No life," he said, "is perfect that has not been lived, youth in feeling, manhood in battle, old age in meditation."

When I knew him he was at that period of life which he thought should be devoted to meditation, but a snapshot of him that I had for long but have now lost did not show him in meditation. He was in action, breaking in a haughty Arab horse with myself mounted beside him in the light vehicle the Arab was harnessed to. As we tore through the woods, that horse did everything with its four legs that an animal could do—standing at intervals on two of them, climbing a tree with three of them, trying to upset the vehicle with all of them. We were both hilariously happy over all these feats, and I pleased him by making it a Byronic occasion, repeating:

> Bring forth the horse. The horse was brought.
> In truth it was a noble steed,
> A Tartar of the Ukraine breed
> Who looked as tho' the speed of thought
> Were in his limbs.
> On and on and on we dash,
> Torrents less rapid and less rash.

I *tried* to repeat it, I should say, for I had to pause at intervals to keep myself from being flung in the air. Wilfrid, though he was then seventy-two or seventy-three, mastered that horse so that, contrary to all prognostications, we returned safe and sound to New Buildings, the horse peaceably walking on its four legs. He joyfully told the company every detail of our drive, saying I had not shown a tremor, for the Arabs and the Irish, he maintained, were born without fear of a horse.

ౠ CHAPTER 17

Departure

WHEN WE GOT BACK to Dublin we found a letter awaiting us from Padraic's aunt in Pittsburgh, inviting us to come to America on our honeymoon and enclosing us tickets for the trip. She had only heard of our intended marriage, I think, the day before the event. However, we had already taken a house in Donnybrook, and, anyhow, going to America seemed a fantasy. So we wrote to her, returning the tickets. She answered promptly, announcing, in her rather dictatorial way, that when the lease ended she would renew the invitation and send another batch of tickets.

We settled down in a dampish, largish, uncomfortable brick house, and Padraic endeavored to make a living by free-lance writing. Every prospect we had married on disappeared, including my teaching job, for Pearse's girls' school ended for lack of funds. In another country, or in a country with its own government, his educational ideas would have gained financial backing. In the Ireland of those days, too many projects perished for lack of money. That the Abbey Theater survived was really a sort of miracle.

I do not think I would ever advise any young couple to take the sort of risk that we did, though undoubtedly artists of any kind will always take them. My husband was extremely unpractical, and I was ignorant of practical issues, though I was capable of learning more about them than he was. Nobody I knew had any interest in money, and nobody would have thought of spending ány considerable portion of his life trying to make it. We had a great many friends, and we all saw one another almost every day, owing to the Dublin custom of having evening *réunions*, which is also a Paris custom. A.E. and Dr. Sigerson were at home on Sundays, we on Tuesdays; the James Stephenses, the Arnold Baxes, Ella Young, and Maud Gonne had their special evenings. Thus it happened that when any stranger came to Dublin, he or she dropped around to the various houses on at-home evenings and was passed along. I remember one of our first foreign guests was Professor George Pierce Baker, who had initiated the drama class in Harvard. Owing to the peculiar sort of antagonism between literary and academic circles in Dublin, we all thought fit to smile at the notion that a professor could teach anybody how to write, and Professor Baker was a good deal satirized. He was, indeed, somewhat on the pompous line. He had come to see the Abbey Theater in action and was free enough of his criticisms and observations. Our bright young men and women said he only understood the machine-made play, not the grand works of art they were engaged upon. Now, as everybody knows, the Abbey School of Drama was a breed to itself, and its most characteristic plays did not really go well in large metropolitan theaters. Nearly everybody, including certain London dramatic critics, was very superior and condescending about Professor Baker. However, my newly wedded husband asked Professor Baker to read a play of his, and as a result of the criticism given, came to the conclusion that it might do a lot of good if Professor Baker gave his Workshop 47 for a season in Dublin.

II

Dublin then was a sort of Mecca for professors of all kinds, and not alone for those who were Celtic scholars. I remember a number who came to write books on Yeats and the Irish Revival, on co-operation and Horace Plunkett, on J. M. Synge and the folk-drama, on ancient Celtic crosses, and there was one delightful American dreamer who came to hear about the Good People and wrote a book called *The Fairy Faith in Celtic Countries*. He came to our house, appropriately as he thought, on the feast of Samhain, in November, and a great deal of Celtic faith was handed out to him by the group. He had a list of other "sacred places" of the world he was going to visit, and the next on his itinerary was Tibet. These visitors would make the pilgrimage to Coole and spend a day or two with Lady Gregory and her artist son, Robert, later killed in the first World War. There were also a number of American women journalists, well dressed and intellectual, who would come to interview the leading people from time to time. These all had preconceptions about Ireland, based, I think, on an acquaintance with a certain type of Irish immigrant and on old-fashioned Irish stories and plays. It was not always amusing to hear them lecture some of our older women scholars on Irish sociological and religious and political problems. As Lady Gregory didn't care much for women, the ladies did not make the pilgrimage to Coole.

About this time a less excited interest in art and literature and a more excited interest in the national demand for self-government was observable in the Dublin reunions; in fact, in A.E.'s, literature began moving into the background. One of those Home Rule bills that for generations seemed to be before the House of Commons was now up once more. Previous Home Rule bills had been always defeated by the Tory element in England. As against this stodgy group, there was a romantic England, and its interest had been aroused by the new movements in Ireland, by the poetry and the plays which, in the case of many I could name, made more appeal to them than they did to Irish people. With all this fresh interest in Ireland it seemed likely that this time a bill giving autonomy would be passed by the Liberal government under the premiership of Herbert Asquith. And, right enough, to everybody's delight, the Home Rule bill passed its three readings and nothing else was talked about in the houses and on the streets. Plans were excitedly being made for putting into action all sorts of new ideas and for the economic improvement of the country. As usual, America was supposed to be greatly interested in all this; a new hope was emerging.

However, there was a fly in the ointment; the Home Rule bill did not get through the House of Lords, that old stalwart against any conciliation to Ireland. But it happened that the claws of the House of Lords had been recently clipped by Asquith's government, and a veto of the Lords could now hold up a bill for only two years. The Tories had every reason to believe that the bill could somehow be killed in the two years. Nerves were strained, for the Irish are excitable and impulsive and, like all peoples who have been long oppressed, have a tendency towards nervousness. The fight of hundreds of years, the frustrated efforts of various leaders, both English and Irish, to get some measure of self-government operating in Ireland, had worn down all patience. The revolutionary section in Irish politics who always distrusted English intentions began to get more and more influence as the strain increased; the cooler heads counseled calmness. Two years was nothing in the life of a country or even in a generation, and then the Lords' veto would lapse, and this bill, meager as it was acknowledged to be in the powers it offered, was a first installment of self-government.

The Tory hostesses in London began to concoct plans in their drawing rooms to prevent the Home Rule bill from coming into operation. Edward Carson, the Ulster Unionist leader, was their hero, and they set out to back him in his organization of opposition in northeast Ulster. Carson was a good deal of a playboy and he put his considerable histrionic abilities into directing the opposing movement. He brought back the Tory rallying cry raised by Lord Randolph Churchill over a previous Home Rule bill, "Ulster will fight and Ulster will be right," ignoring the fact that in Ulster, the province which historically is the most nationalist in Ireland, nearly as many were for the bill as were against it. Carson proceeded to organize an army which he called the Ulster Volunteers, with the backing of the rich landowners and merchants in the northeast, the section that had been colonized chiefly by Presbyterian Scotch. The English army stationed in the Curragh of Kildare backed Carson's Volunteers, and a retired British officer commanded them. Large quantities of arms and ammunition were imported from Germany. The Tory ladies bought ambulances, made bandages and pajamas, King George was threatened if he signed the Home Rule bill; some of the leaders announced their intention of inviting the Kaiser to take over northeast Ulster. Nobody in Nationalist Ireland took all this very seriously. The Unionists were staging a show to frighten the government, in spite of the fact that some London papers warned the government that Orange Ulster never fights, but that if Nationalist Ireland was roused by these goings on, history and present circumstances made it clear that the Nationalists would fight. Indeed soon a Nationalist army was started. In my own experience the half-English people in Ireland found the situation even more intolerable than the hereditary Irish. They were, perhaps on their English side, the descendants of free men and women who had subscribed to those overestimated overadvertised charters of freedom that popped up now and again in English history.

As the Carson anti-Home Rule Volunteers had imported guns and ammunition, so now the Irish National Volunteers started overt preparations for buying guns on the Continent. It was soon obvious that the British Government was getting uneasy. The constitutional Irish leader in the House of Commons was John Redmond, and, Nationalist as he was as far as Ireland was concerned, he was also loyal to the British Government, or, at least, he did not want to promote anything unconstitutional. It was whispered around that the Asquith government had asked him to get a measure of control over this new aggressive movement. But John Redmond had been long out of touch with young Ireland and made no imaginative appeal at all to it. Still he was the head of a machine, that disastrous political invention common in all countries, and he was able to split the Irish Volunteers into two groups, those who followed him and were more or less constitutional, and those who followed the Sinn Fein leaders who were willing to fight for the control of their country. The whole country was in a ferment.

Meantime the lease on our house in Donnybrook was running out; we had held many enjoyable reunions there, the last I remember being on New Year's Eve, 1913. We walked out in the garden in the moonlight at midnight and sang the New Year in. Arnold Bax, A.E., and Fred Ryan, who was then editor of Wilfrid Blunt's paper, *Egypt*, drank the New Year in on strong tea. We had told them all we were going to America for a couple of months, as the aunt in Pittsburgh had written announcing that in spring she was once again sending us tickets. However, we were advised by everybody that we could not stand the heat of summer months

in America and that, anyhow, as my husband had been asked to
give some lectures, it would be better to spend the autumn instead of the summer in America. It is now over thirty years, more
than half our lifetime, since we drank the New Year of 1914 in
with strong tea in Donnybrook, and we have never since spent a
New Year's Eve or a New Year's Day in Ireland; but on that eve
we did not guess what our future would be.

We fixed on August as the month to make the voyage to America, and after giving up our house, took a small cottage on the
hill of Howth, where it was a Dublin habit to spend some time in
the summer. We did not have much security, but we got along
somehow, and I went in three days a week with a portfolio like a
statesman to work, of course without pay, in the office of the
women's section of the Irish Volunteer movement. A dowdy,
pleasant young woman, somewhat old-maidish and schoolmarmish,
with the heels of her brown stockings showing an elaborate darn
above her low brown shoes, would come in occasionally and work
in the office. She was Mary Spring-Rice, the daughter of Lord
Monteagle and a cousin of the then British ambassador in Washington, Sir Cecil Spring-Rice. I mention her especially as this
young woman was a great yachtswoman and was the commander
of the yacht in the gunrunning that later brought in the guns for
the Irish Volunteers.

Shy as a rabbit, she had the courage and fighting spirit of several
Bengal tigers, and the competency of a few field marshals. The political climate was getting hotter and hotter, but as my line was
literature rather than politics, I was a little puzzled as to who was
going to fight whom, or whether the Irish and Ulster Volunteers
were going to fight each other, or whether both were going to fight
England. People were following some instinctive urge rather than
a logical direction. Some of the ex-British officers in the Irish Volunteers were willing enough to fight Carson and for Home Rule,
but I do not think they would fight England, even Tory England,
and in fact, a couple of them later dropped out. Dublin was full
of European newspaper correspondents at this time, for the city
had long been a center of interest in European capitals, first for
its celebrated literary movement and now because the country was
on the verge of a political revolution.

Then suddenly a dramatic happening knocked everything off balance. As we were sitting one Sunday afternoon in the garden of the cottage we had rented, drinking tea with friends and talking about our approaching visit to America, a newsboy came up the country road shouting, "Stop press." We bought the newspaper and read of the murder of the Austrian archduke in Sarajevo, an unknown place name to us. I think few if any of us had much notion of what this might portend, though I distinctly remember one of our guests, Joseph O'Neill, an educator as well as a writer, both of which he still is, saying, "This may mean that the European war is on us at last." I was struck by his saying this, for, like most people in the world at the time, I barely understood what a war was, and thought he could not be talking sense. We continued speaking about our coming trip to America and about the forthcoming gunrunning which we all expected, though none of us knew when it would take place, or whether the guns would be run into Dublin Bay or into some Munster harbor, or whether there would be more than one gunrunning. That, I think, was our last Sunday in the cottage, because, as we made our final preparations for America, we moved into the village hotel.

On my next visit to the office of the Irish Women's Council (Cumann na mban) the auxiliary of the Volunteers, a request was made that we send in to the men's committee all the money we had collected. Then, a little later, the weekly organ of the Volunteers, the *Irish Volunteer*, announced that the Dublin battalions would make on a certain Sunday a route march from Dublin to Howth. One or two people thought that Howth Harbour might be the scene of one or another of the expected gunrunnings, and a subterranean rumor went among a few people that the fated day had arrived. As the tramp of marching men came nearer to the little fishing village, we stood outside the hotel and waited to see them. Soon the voices of the officers could be heard in a loud, excited command, "On the double!" and the Volunteers came racing down the street towards the harbor. Voices from the ranks called out, "Come along," and my husband who was a member of the Volunteers, and one or two other bystanders joined them. In the harbor a ship was making for the pier. It was, as we knew later, Erskine Childers's yacht, steered by Mary Spring-Rice, and assisted by Mrs.

Erskine Childers, a Boston woman who had been Molly Alden Osgood. The yacht swung to the pier with great swiftness. The guns were unloaded by eager and willing hands, and each Volunteer, drilled and disciplined for the event, shouldered his gun, fell into rank, and the battalion started its march back to the city.

My husband returned to the hotel, bringing to luncheon Professor MacNeill, who was the commander of the Volunteers, and Darrell Figgis, who had purchased the guns on the Continent. As we sat down at table, my husband, to the alarm of the waitress, placed his rifle on the floor, for he had acquired one like the rest of them. The telephone wires had been cut early in the morning, but Professor MacNeill was expecting a messenger to tell him of the progress of the rifle-burdened men into Dublin. In another country it would be difficult to imagine a grave, scholarly professor of history engaging in a gunrunning and with such solid reasoning as to the rightness of his effort. As a historian he knew Jefferson's "Resistance to tyrants is obedience to God." Darrell Figgis, on the other hand, also a scholar and a well-known writer, was a gay adventurer of the Elizabethan type who could write a poem, lead a battle, or make the laws of the country—charming, cultivated, self-important, and one might guess of somewhat wild passions well kept under control. It was he who had actually bought the guns on the Continent—in Belgium, it was said—and loaded them on a ship which met Erskine Childers's yacht in the North Sea. The yacht had to weave in and out of navy patrols in the North Sea, was halted once or twice, but the British Navy found little to suspect about a yacht manned by two women, both belonging to the sacred upper classes, and one the daughter of a peer.

The awaited message about the progress of the Volunteers did not come to Professor MacNeill in our hotel. Later in the day we were to hear that the government, which had done nothing about the Carson gunrunning, had sent a regiment of Scottish soldiers to meet the Volunteers and take the rifles from them. The Volunteers fought to hold their rifles, and many succeeded in doing so, but blood was shed and people were killed. It was a tragic and exciting end to the day, but my experience in life has been that most people prefer excitement, no matter how tragic, to tame security, and nobody I knew seemed in any way downcast. To be sure, there was a European war in the offing; maybe, indeed, it had already begun, but I am not sure of this. Ireland is a tight, strange island with an old strange culture, different from the rest of Europe, and sometimes it would take a surgical operation to make her conscious of events in the rest of the world.

The British Government was somewhat shaken by such events, for once more insurrectionary Ireland figured in the headlines of papers in European capitals. It did not look well, on the verge of a war, to have British soldiery shoot people on the streets of a capital in the British islands because they made preparation to insure the operation of a law already passed by the British House of Commons but objected to by some of the Tories. I half remember that British dignitaries came over to look into things and find out the names of those responsible for the gunrunning. Years afterwards, in America, a woman told me how the British ambassador in Washington, Sir Cecil Spring-Rice, stumbled into her drawing room, mopping his brow, overcome by the news of the doings of his relatives in Ireland.

As I look back on all the people concerned in the gunrunning, so high-spirited, so reckless, some young, gay and daring, I am saddened by the recollection of the fate that befell many of them. A tragic love affair and the death of a sweetheart after an abortion, and the ensuing publicity, brought about the suicide of Darrell Figgis. His wife had previously committed suicide, it was said, because of his affair with the girl. Erskine Childers, who, though an ex-British army officer, had gone out in arms with De Valera and others against the Irish treaty with England, was captured by the troops of the newly born Free State and shot for rebellion against the lawfully created Irish government—something that I think will remain a black mark against the able and distinguished Cosgrave ministry. A general of the Free State army years later told me quite calmly that if they had captured De Valera at the time, they would have shot him also. Certainly Erskine Childers, and perhaps Darrell Figgis, was more English than Irish. Mary Spring-Rice has been dead for years, the only romantic episode in her life being her adventurous gunrunning experience.

While the excitement was still at its height, my husband and I took a steamer at the North Wall for Liverpool, where we were to board the Atlantic liner for our visit to America. A few days before, we had been notified by Cook's Tourist Agency that, owing to the "fortune of war" and the rush of Americans home from Europe, we might not be able to get the accommodations booked for us by our aunt. The agency advised us to get the liner at Liverpool instead of at Queenstown, where there would be little room after the Liverpool passengers had been catered for. Professor Houston, who had founded the *Irish Review*, gave us a farewell party, but we did not think it would be a long farewell. We had stored our clothes and furniture and had lightheartedly made plans for a New Year's Eve party at the end of 1914 such as we had had at the end of 1913. We figured on being back in Ireland for Christmas, but one member of the party, Thomas MacDonagh, who later was executed with Padraic Pearse for rebellion against the British Government, said warningly, "You will not be back. You do not realize it, but you are going to America to live there." And Una O'Connor, now a Hollywood actress, said, "Don't come back with gold teeth and shiny shoes." Somebody else said in a not too serious voice, "Both of us [the speaker and Thomas MacDonagh] are bidding you good-by forever. We are going to fight for Ireland's freedom and we are going to be killed." Not even the mystical note in their voices damped our spirits or changed our plans; we would be back in Dublin in a few months, just as Yeats had come back after a few months.

৩ CHAPTER 18

First Weeks in America

WE LANDED early in the morning in the dismal city of Liverpool after having on the boat the usual breakfast of bacon and eggs and tea. I got a real thrill when a uniformed official of some sort called out, "All for America, this way!" We were directed to an office which dealt with the passengers for New York, or anyhow, with those who already had tickets. It seemed to me that for hours and hours we stood waiting in a hot sun; there were lines and lines of people of almost every race I had ever heard of. It became clear to me now that there was a war of some sort on, and that all those people were trying to escape from it; some were Americans who had been on a vacation in Europe and hurrying to get home; some were simply people trying to get out of Europe. Be it known that at this time nobody—this seems unbelievable now—needed a passport for any country except Russia; to go to America one just bought a ticket and stepped on a liner. The passport idea was one of those limitations on freedom that came in with the first European war.

Very worn out after long standing in line, it was our turn to face the clerk and show him our tickets. He was very snappy. . . . No, it did not matter that we had tickets for months; if we wished to go to America at this time, we would have to take what we could get. However, those with tickets would be given some preference over those who had none. Would we or would we not take a third-class cabin? We must not take up his time, as he had still a long line of people to deal with. I wished like anything that I were back on the Hill of Howth among the rhododendrons and gazing over Dublin Bay. But we hastily took what the clerk offered, and after what seemed a long time got on board the ship and joined another line of weary people and crying children on the third-class deck. I had never before seen people treated in masses and not as individuals, and I was appalled at the procedure. I remember how it struck me intensely that the population of the world was getting too large for human resources to cope with, and that some disaster was imminent. This was the second time in my life that this idea had forced itself on me: the first time was when, as a student, I stood in the railway station of Aachen waiting for somebody to meet me and noted all the time-wasting, nerve-racking formalities that a bureaucracy was inflicting on us.

On board the ship the third-class passengers passed before a snooty English purser who kept repeating to each questioner the phrase, "the fortune of war." I asked him what had become of our original accommodations. He was impatient. They had had to be sold to somebody anxious to get back to America and who apparently could pay a fancy price. Now this was not according to my ideas of democracy, which had mostly a theoretic and idealistic basis. His answer was devastating: "This is an English ship, madam; kindly walk on." A steward took a group of us deep into the bowels of the liner, and we arrived at a small stuffy cabin, one narrow little box berth above another, but we threw ourselves down in utter weariness and slept till morning in the stifling air. In the morning, on deck, we discovered we were among the lucky ones; lots and lots of the third-class passengers were even in a deeper hold of the ship, sleeping in hammocks or on anything that could be found for them; the ship was packed; many, many ships in the wars that have been since must have been packed as that ship was, but I do not think any of them could have been much worse. There was even a more dismal part of the liner than ours—at the other end, below the third class, which was called "the Macedonian deck," and strong mountaineer-looking men, some of them in strange national garb, wandered sadly about it. This deck was a legacy of another war, the first Balkan War, when Macedonian refugees had in some way made their escape to America, packed in the hold of a ship like people on the early emigrant vessels, and apparently given a different treatment from the other passengers.

When the weather was fine we walked around the little bit of deck reserved for the third-class passengers and made a few acquaintances—a German-American family returning to America, some Irish boys and girls who kept themselves happy by singing, playing a melodeon, and dancing whenever a corner of the deck was free. The most interesting and cultivated of the people we encountered were three Negroes—Mrs. Locke, a schoolteacher from Philadelphia, her brilliant son, Alain Leroy Locke, and a girl pianist. Alain Locke had been a Rhodes scholar and was returning from Oxford, where he had been very happy. He had learned a lot about the Irish literary movement and was glad to meet my husband and discuss the Abbey Theater with him. I did not then understand why they never appeared in the dining room but always had a steward bring them something to eat in their cabins. It was only later that I came to realize the extent of the American color prejudice. The three were the first Negroes I ever knew, and they gave me a sense of the artistry of the Negro race such as a long residence in America has added to. I found that one very rarely met cultivated Negroes in America; in New York they were all isolated in Harlem, and it was only in Paris that one could meet people like Countee Cullen, the poet, and the sculptor, Augusta Savage, casually as one met anyone else in the arts.

The voyage, of course, was excessively uncomfortable; on rainy days or rainy hours there was no shelter on deck, not even an awning, so we had to take refuge in our stuffy cabins deep in the hold of the ship; there was no social hall; there were several sittings for meals in the barracklike dining room, so that by the time breakfast was cleared lunch began, and the room could not be used for any lounging or loitering by the passengers. Only a few of the people around us seemed to speak English natively—German and Yiddish were the most common languages, though others were spoken which I did not recognize, perhaps Serbian or Polish. There was an interpreter who must have spoken about a dozen languages; he was a warm kindly man who spent a lot of his time separating the boys and girls: he was floored when an Irish boy and girl, their arms around each other, spoke to him in Gaelic and pretended to know no English. I still remember his words when, at the fall of dark on the deck, he tried to separate the sexes: "Now, my pretty lassies, down to your bunks!"

When I asked anybody what nationality he or she was, I would receive the haughty answer, "I'm an American citizen," and this gave me an idea of what "civis Romanus sum" must have meant to the ear of the barbarian in the days of the Roman Empire. That people could call themselves American so determinedly after being only a few years in the United States, brushing away their European past, was impressive, especially to me, coming from an island the inhabitants of which would only unwillingly admit to being British subjects though governed by Britain for hundreds of years. These Americanized Europeans gave me the first direct notion of the United States democracy. They held meetings on deck protesting about the treatment of the third-class passengers, about the food, about the lack of seats and the lack of shelter from the rain. They drew up a document addressed to the purser, beginning, "We, the undersigned American citizens," but I have to say that they brushed the rest of us aside as people not entitled to any say at all. The haughty purser was unimpressed; the document was not in the best English anyway, having been drawn up by somebody whose native language was Russian or Yiddish. "This is an English ship, gentlemen; you must submit to the fortune of war; we're doing our best to take you where you belong."

II

As we approached the coast of America we were harangued by a ship's officer whose speech was turned by the interpreter into various languages. It announced that all those passengers who were not American citizens would have to go to Ellis Island for examination. What sort of examination? There would be a physical examination, a literacy examination, and a few other researches such as whether we had ever been in gaol or wanted to overthrow the government. Being sent to Ellis evoked a fantastic picture in my mind, an image made up of the stories I had heard about the trials of emigrants, about political prisoners being transported to Australia, Dostoevski to Siberia, and I vaguely wondered whether, at the last moment, the dire sentence to Ellis Island might not be changed as had the order for the execution of Dostoevski. Those third-class passengers who had started from home with first- or second-class tickets made a protest, some angrily, some in a crushed sort of way: why were we, who, to quote the purser, had been forced by the fortune of war to travel third-class, presumed to be lacking in some necessary attributes while those who got our original accommodations were presumed to be virtuous, literate, law-abiding, in good health, and were allowed on American soil unbarred and unhindered? At an early morning hour New York could be seen in the distance; it had then but few skyscrapers in comparison with what it has now, and nothing like the present dazzling sky line with those turreted buildings that Thomas Hardy longed to see before he died. The Statue of Liberty in its large bulk appeared just as we were told it would. I examined it not for its symbolism but for its artistic drawbacks: it obviously affected the crowd on deck; it had all the large commonplaces that can make an appeal like national anthems, hymns, and brass bands.

The non-Americans were steered to a ferry, and after a short time we walked off on Ellis Island. Long lines of people were there before us from some other ship or ships. These were the most remarkable groups I had ever seen, and of seemingly every known nationality in the old Eastern Hemisphere. The day, I remember, was blazing hot, and the costumes of the emigrants, though some were beautiful, must have made the wearers miserable in the strong sun. There were Russians in blouses and furry headgear; there were Greeks and Albanians in kilted mountaineer costumes, the women wearing handkerchiefs on their heads instead of hats; there were Bavarians in short leather breeches and woolly stockings; there were brightly clad men and women who looked like, and probably were, gypsies, their ears weighted with earrings. The motley crowd, the whirl of languages, the sun on my dress of Irish wool made my head ache and whirl. The lines moved with a snail-like slowness into a building where I do not think I heard a word of English spoken. At some point my husband and I were separated, and I found myself walking beside a strangely well-dressed woman in a line past a couple of interpreters. The woman spoke to me in French—she was a Rumanian. As, in those days, no passports were required, the interpreter, I suppose, had no means of knowing the nationality of those he was speaking to. I forget now in what tongue or tongues he addressed myself and the Rumanian, but the gist of his interrogation was to find out what language or languages we spoke or understood. Myself and the Rumanian, first one and then the other, said French, German, Italian—*français, allemand, italien.* For some reason he was exasperated. "Young ladies, I don't want a list of your accomplishments; I want to know if you speak English—the American language." The Rumanian got excited and informed him, first in French and then in English, that she was a gently nourished woman—a common phrase in the journalism of the period—a lady, in fact; that she had been in America before, that she had bought a first-class ticket and that she did not understand the reason of all these humiliating examinations. I backed her up. My eyelids had been twisted up and down in search of eye disease; a doctor, an alienist, I think, had examined me in search of madness or sanity; I had found his questions silly and told him so; still another doctor —all were in uniform, so that I did not understand at the time what they were—had tried to find out if I had tuberculosis. We were backed off to still another doctor, some different sort of psychiatrist, I imagine. He was marvelously gentle as I now look back on him, and he must have been working all night. However, we were the only ones in front of him at the moment. Obviously he was a cultivated man—the handsome Rumanian had a way with men, and she got free in a minute or two with laughter on his side and hers. As for me, I sat silently in a chair under his scrutiny, half in tears.

"Did anybody frighten you on board the ship?"

"No, but this sort of thing frightens me."

"Have you ever had lung trouble?"

"No, I have anemia."

"Are you always so nervous?"

I was really frightened now, because I had heard that nervous people were often held on the island and delicate people returned to the country of their origin. He went on:

"Are you an artist of any kind?" Perhaps he was trying to account for the nerves. "You seem an educated woman. Just what is your education?"

"I'm a university graduate." He smiled pleasantly and said, "It must have been humbling to be asked if you can read or write."

My Dublin flippancy got the better of me, and the Dublin literary snootiness about academic education:

"Many university graduates cannot read or write." He was not amused.

In a relatively short time, however, he let me go, smilingly saying he supposed I would not be a burden to the taxpayers. With a group of other women I was shooed to a waiting room and asked to sit on a bench until my name was called, which would mean my husband had been located. Everything was done with what I now realize to have been amazing efficiency and great consideration, though at the time I was too worn out to understand this.

A middle-aged Irishwoman seated on the bench, who had been in America before, kept instructing the greenhorns on how to set about getting jobs. A furtive-looking man came along, asked us what nationalities we were, and began suggesting the sort of work we might engage in. He suggested chamber work for the Irish girls and asked me if I would not like a job in a hotel. He explained the work—dusting, cleaning, making beds. "You are a nice, smart-look-

ing girl," he commented, "you should do all right in this country."
The middle-aged Irishwoman, annoyed that so much of his conversation was addressed to me, broke in angrily, "Speak this way, mister; that one 's makin' a hare of you; I know her sort; that one
couldn't clean a room; talk to us down here." A woman beside me
with a German accent amiably suggested manicuring. "You'd get
lots of tips," she told me, "especially if you worked in a hotel." To
avoid further instruction I thought it well to say that I was coming
on a short visit to relatives. At length my name was called and I saw
my husband approaching, his suit all chalk-marked with hiero-
glyphics such as were on my dress and a label attached to his buttonhole such as was on the rest of us. Then, first in English and
then in other languages, a uniformed man called out, "Everybody
for Penn Station, this way." A crowd was being herded together by
a few officials. I noticed that both my husband and myself were
labeled "Penn," and the officials tried to make us join the group.

But my ease and courage had, by this time, returned, and I refused to join any more lines or go any place else on orders. I said
we were not going direct to our destination, but were spending a
few days in New York. This caused a slight sensation and a warning: "I'm speaking for your good; don't you go rambling about
New York." We might have been overborne, but the gracious doctor came to our rescue, and he handed us over to somebody who
had the power to liberate us.

My husband had some staggering letters of introduction to con-
spicuous personages, and though, on the whole, they were not of
any more use to us than such letters might have been to Columbus,
they impressed the functionary we now stood before. . . . Theodore
Roosevelt, William Randolph Hearst, David Belasco, Nikola Tesla,
the old Fenian, John Devoy, a number of Irish judges and lawyers,
a variety of college deans and presidents. Still the aforesaid functionary was not really sure that we were competent to struggle
along in New York for a couple of days and advised us to telegraph
our aunt in Pittsburgh. As he spent his days coping with emigrants
from many countries he was not convinced of our mastery of the
English language, especially as the dashing Rumanian on her way
to a ferry, a silver-mounted dressing case in her hand, rushed
towards us with a lengthy discourse in French. But after they had

got through the formalities, the kindness of those officials in Ellis Island was so touching that I really understood how helpful the human race can be and how anxious to co-operate with one another ordinary simple people can be when left to work out their own destiny. Not that I think America is really as free as European countries are or used to be in some matters: freedom of speech and opinion are more easily accepted in old countries; long-inherited intellectual freedoms are difficult for mixed strains and mixed classes in a democracy, but all other freedoms are better understood in America than anywhere else.

Getting off at the Battery and having no notion of the enormous length of Broadway, we got on a streetcar to take us to the Hotel Woodstock, at Broadway and Forty-third Street. After what seemed hours we got to a pleasant bedroom, and I sank between the sheets and sipped the watery liquid with thick cream, such as I had never seen, that the hotel offered as tea. But my elation at the modernness of everything—at the telephone in the room, at the slick effective machine-made furniture—was so great that I got a sense of wonderful renewal. The furniture I was accustomed to had been in use a long time; some of ours was eighteenth-century and was old mahogany or old oak, and what was new had not the wonderful newness of this I saw around me. As we walked on the street, what struck us most was the dazzling sunshine and the newspapers: these had extensive news of the whole world, and we really got the idea that there was a war on in Europe and that lots of countries were engaged in it. The headlines were scarifying; people were setting out deliberately to kill one another; the pleasant wood carvers of Germany, the people who had made the grand French civilization, the sons of the landladies in the boarding-houses of Soho and Pimlico, the men in the Irish regiments who always went out to fight in any old war anyway. Then there were solemn articles in some of the periodicals whose effort was to tell America that she had better get into the struggle to save civilization. It was all bewildering.

Arrived in Pittsburgh, however, we found nobody at all interested in the war at that stage—the last war they knew about was the Civil War, and they did not seem to care much about Europe. I think the relatives did not find us amusing; especially they did not find amusing the young female their nephew had married. Like most people in Pittsburgh they did their own housework, and that ubiquitous person, the Dublin maid of all work who whitened the steps, shined the door knocker, cleaned the shoes, waxed the floors, polished the windows, and handed us our meals, and all for a small pecuniary return, was absent and unknown. But there were all sorts of luxuries: people who did not have maids had automobiles, fur coats, iceboxes, continuous hot water; they had compact houses and wonderful bathrooms; they had marvelous contraptions for cleaning; everybody was well dressed, seemingly well off, and competent to do any work connected with a house. The only meat, apparently, they wanted to eat was steak, roast beef, and chicken—steak in Dublin was tough, and we had roast beef and chicken only occasionally. There were, however, rich people in Pittsburgh who had menservants and maidservants, and the insides of their houses were even more marvelous than the aunt's house. But it was what people threw away that really knocked me over; it seemed that to get things mended was a complex affair, and that to throw out an old chair or an old mattress and buy new ones as the simplest economy was the general idea.

Nobody cared to have old things around unless such as might be classed as professional antiques, and those who had them did not start out by owning them; they bought them at an antique store. Modern American furniture seemed to me so grand I wondered why people hankered after old French or Italian or English things.

The names of the writers of the Irish Revival were pretty well known, and soon we were called on by charmingly dressed women who invited us to various parties. My husband was asked to give drawing-room lectures and poetry readings, but as he had never before been paid for speaking in a private house he declined the first check, much to the hostess's embarrassment. We did not conceive of people being paid for such performances, but Thomas Woods Stevens talked us round to the idea. He was the brilliant teacher of dramatics in the School of Drama in the Carnegie Institute: what he knew about plays and stagecraft would have made him a power in the land in a small country with an experimental theater, but in America centers of culture were so far apart that such men were not publicly known. While we sojourned in Pittsburgh the Carnegie School of Drama did a group of Irish plays: they did Yeats's *The King's Threshold*, Synge's *Shadow of the Glen*, and my husband's *The Betrayal*, all as well done, it seemed to me, as they would have been in the Abbey Theater, but with a difference of emphasis. Some of the players afterwards became Broadway actors and actresses; the girl who played Fedelm in *The King's Threshold* was Mary Blair, who later played several parts in Eugene O'Neill's plays and became the first wife of my friend Edmund Wilson, the critic. In Carnegie, Professor Geoghegan of the English Department was a nephew of our dear old Dublin friend, Sarah Purser, and he helped us to many interesting acquaintances. At a party to which he brought us I first met Willa Cather, and something about her appearance and conversation so struck me that I asked the hostess, who was a little vague about such things, if Miss Cather was not a writer. "I think she has written a book," she informed me, "but teaching is her profession." She talked about the pueblos in New Mexico and the art and lore of the Indians in such a way that I ever afterwards felt she was one of the most interesting people I met in America, and I later read every book she wrote; I met her at intervals in New York and elsewhere and always kept my great admiration and even veneration for her. Oddly enough, Americans in those days appeared not as interested in their own as they were in European writers.

Perhaps because Pittsburgh was the first American city we ever stayed in, my memories of it are romantic and hazy. I was startled by the swiftness of the pace of everything, the lack of that leisurely life of Dublin, where time seemed to go more slowly and people had hours for conversation, the days were so long. Then it was my first encounter with men who were in big business, all of a kind that I had hardly even heard of, such as steel, plate glass, electrical contraptions. Then most people had some Irish blood—in fact, members of my husband's family had emigrated there in another generation, and he himself might have been born in Pittsburgh but for the accident that his father had returned to Ireland. It was there that I first heard the curious designation of Ulster people as "Scotch-Irish"; it was not so much to discriminate them from the Nationalist Irish, for Ulster Presbyterians had been amongst the best-known fighting Nationalists, but from the Catholic Irish, against whom there seemed to be a prejudice which surprised me at the time, for I had been brought up to believe that America had no prejudices of class or religion. The wealthy people in Pittsburgh for the most part called themselves of Scotch or Scotch-Irish descent, even those who had pure Gaelic names. In fact, the prefix "Scotch" seemed to denote some special distinction, and Scotch whisky, Scotch tweeds, the Scottish Freemason Rite, and Scottish visiting preachers were regarded as something very top drawer.

We were not the only ones connected with Irish movements to appear in Pittsburgh at the time; there passed through and spent some days in the city a delegation of the Gaelic League, headed by Nelly O'Brien and Fionan MacCullum. The Gaelic League was half in and half out of the literary revival just as the Sinn Fein group was; they didn't altogether approve of each other, but in America they all seemed to be the same. Many of those in the New Irish movement had lectured in America—Douglas Hyde and Shane Leslie for the Gaelic League, W. B. Yeats and Lady Gregory for the literary movement, Lady Gregory with the kudos of Theodore Roosevelt's approval and his publicly expressed excitement over her versions of the old Irish sagas; Maud Gonne had lectured for the political movement. The interviews in the newspapers showed what seemed to me an undue interest in the social and family connections of the groups. Lady Gregory's title was played up; Nelly O'Brien was featured as a granddaughter of Lord Inchiquin, which she was, and a lineal descendant of the O'Briens, kings of Thomond, which she was also. Her family was, of course, one of the oldest in Europe, but it seemed odd that this rather than her intellectual distinction and patriotism should be emphasized in a democracy, but one of the reporters, of Irish parentage himself, gave me a fancy explanation. "They are so used to Irish servant girls here that it is really news to let them know there are other people in Ireland." I annoyed him by laughing. Just the same I realized that American delight in titles and ancient lineage was a romantic interest like that in ancient ruins, medieval castles, and characters out of legends. In any case it was more imaginative and human than the later interest in crooners, band leaders, and movie queens. Nelly O'Brien, in spite of a certain dumpiness—she and Lady Gregory had a great look of Queen Victoria—did have a princely air, and the picturesque if unfashionable clothes she wore added to the effect. Her dress was that embroidered garment, worn with a brath and silver or copper ornaments, which was supposed to be the lady's attire in Gaelic Ireland, and which was frequently worn in Dublin evenings.

But I must say that I was unfavorably struck by the sort of thing the Gaelic League thought suitable pabulum for American audiences. Nelly O'Brien's fellow organizer was a patient, hard-working, scholarly man who knew every phase of native Irish culture, but his idea of entertaining or informing a mixed American audience was to streamline singing, dancing, storytelling, and history into a half-hour's entertainment. After a few words of explanation he would say, "Now I will sing you a Gaelic song," and would proceed with a stanza or two in a voice that seemed totally lacking in tonality or training; after another explanation he would announce, "I will tell you a story," then he would give us a sort of anecdote. He got himself, if not the audience, roused, and went ahead with samples of dancing: he perpetrated a few steps of a jig or a reel, and then he gallantly whistled a few bars of a traditional air. I was not astonished that part of the audience burst into uncontrollable laughter; they did not understand any Gaelic, for one thing, and it would have taken a lot more than a few whistled bars to make them sympathetic with folk music. Not many in America are interested in folk art; they are interested in culture art, and the valiant attempts of some American writers to claim transplanted Silesian, Bohemian, or Dutch folk tales as native American products make an appeal only to the sophisticated.

The time we had fixed for our return to Dublin was now approaching, but a number of things came in the way. There were other lectures in the offing, and these were mostly for dates after Christmas. Our newly made Pittsburgh friends kept urging us not to return without spending some time in New York, and then from Ireland A.E., Lolly Yeats, and Sarah Purser wrote advising us to stay in America until the war was over, which was supposed to be soon; a young Irish member of Parliament told us that by spring 1915 the British and French armies would be in Berlin and peace dictated from there. It is doubtful if any military man held such notions, but the belief in the might of the British Empire was strong; besides, nobody knew much about wars; the only war we knew of in our lifetime had been in South Africa, and that was out of our latitude, as it were. In addition to all the advice we received we were influenced by the fact that many sources of my husband's income on the other side of the Atlantic had dried up. Most Irish writers made the bulk of their income by writing for English periodicals, and some of these had now ceased publication, and their staffs had gone to war undoubtedly with the idea of restarting when hostilities were over. So, urged by circumstances and by our advisers, we wrote to all the friends we had invited for New Year's Eve 1914 to say that we would not be home until spring and that we would have an Easter party instead of the New Year's Eve party we had planned. In reality, we were never again to spend either New Year or Easter or spring in Ireland.

౩ CHAPTER 19

An Apartment in Dingy Beekman Place

CARNEGIE INSTITUTE gave us a reception, which was a sort of farewell party, a day or two before we left Pittsburgh: the institute was a real intellectual center and gave a focus to the artistic life of the town, a notable thing, considering all the bustle of big business that was around. Our Carnegie friends saw to it that we did not arrive in the wilderness in New York; they wrote to friends they knew would be congenial to us, and we were met at the train by two young writers, James Shelley Hamilton and Wilton Barrett, and a third, Walter Storey, lent us his apartment while we were looking around for a temporary abode. In no other country, I believe, could such kindness, helpfulness, and even honor be shown to two young people, the young man having to his name only a couple of plays produced by the Abbey Theater, a couple of books of prose, and a slim volume of verse.

The Irish literary movement might not have aroused so much sympathy but for the fact that there was also in America at the time a literary and artistic awakening which the first World War did a great deal to smother. It was not only that young men were killed or wounded, but that psychically people were maimed so that burgeoning expression wilted. America can forget quickly, and who now remembers the Sonnets from the Patagonian of Donald Evans or the poetry of George Stirling—both of these poets later took their own lives—or the single distinguished poems of other young men such as "He Whom a Dream Hath Possessed," by Sheamas O'Sheel, or "I Have Loved Helen of Troy and the Blonde Marguerite," by George Sylvester Viereck, or that lovely sonnet, "Tears," by a Baltimore schoolmistress, Lizette Woodworth Reese?

New York in 1914 was not the spectacular city that it is now. A dynamic city it always was, but then it was far from having the distinction it has in these days; it was only when it began to rear its head towards the heavens in towers and turrets that it took on beauty and character. The city then had a sort of scattered look, as if it had been prefabricated. Its show skyscrapers were the Flatiron Building, the Singer Building, and the Woolworth Building; it is hard to believe now that European visitors were taken to the Flatiron Building as one of the sights of the town.

But about the New York of the time the oddest thing was its lack of modernness; all the places we lived in were lighted by gas, for the ordinary apartment house had not yet changed to electricity. The Fire Department was only partly motorized, and the engines tore through the streets drawn by galloping horses, grandlooking creatures that inspired lines of Vachel Lindsay's "Firemen's Ball":

> Give the engines room,
> Give the engines room
> Lest souls be trapped
> In a terrible tomb
> Says the swift white horse
> To the swift black horse . . .
> They are hitched, they are off,
> They are gone in a flash
> As they strain at the driver's iron arm.

Steam heat was not common; the houses that we and most of our friends lived in were heated by hot dusty air, or else by anthracite stoves, in which one saw the coals through a little window in the stove door as they burned. The five-story brown house, either as private residence or apartment house, was all over the place; the well-to-do lived in the private brown houses. In spite of the nostalgic way they have been written about, I found them far from romantic or interesting—the rooms were often too narrow, too long, and too gloomy. I must have been an arrant little provincial, because I compared everybody and everything to what I had known in Dublin and thought all the houses, except those in Washington Square, drab in comparison with the Georgian houses of Dublin, with their large bright rooms and their outlook on spacious squares. The West Side was a fashionable part of town, Riverside Drive being very chic, and the part of 110th Street overlooking Central Park, and now a Negro quarter, was much sought after; the houses in the West Fifties were of the more select residences. In the next decade their owners or tenants had all moved to the East Side.

Thinking that we were only staying a few months, we rapidly gulped down everything that presented itself to us. For the winter until spring we rented a furnished apartment in Beekman Place, then an unfashionable and dingy part of the city, though amazingly characterful. A great beauty was lent to it by the East River, so much more interesting than the written-up Hudson, which, in spite of well-meant efforts to attach to it Dutch and Silesian folklore, is really a boring kind of river. The Beekman Place apartment was owned by an Englishwoman who had brought over her lovely English oak and mahogany furniture, and was very distinctively and pleasantly Old World. For the five-room furnished apartment in a walk-up brown house which is still to the good though now radiant in new paint, we paid the sum of thirty-five dollars a month. All the section east of Third Avenue, around the Fifties and below, was very foreign and like the moldy and run-down part of a European city—like the Bastille section of Paris, for instance—into which drifted men and women of all European nationalities; in the Fifties, Polish and Russian Jews were in the majority. Beekman Place at the time was certainly dingy, but with the bright New York sun shining on the water, the boats and the barges, all the life of the river which we could view from our windows, we felt we had struck the pleasantest living quarters in the city. The owner of our house was a Pole who lived in the basement with his wife and grown family; he had, I seem to remember, been a small tailor and presser who, with what savings he had amassed, had bought this house, which, later, must have brought him a pretty penny when the neighborhood entered on its *Social Register* career. The houses were not well kept, and there was but little janitor service—not only that, but somehow or other our gas was tapped, as an official of the gas company informed me, so that it supplied other sections of the house. Then somebody had the key to our flat, so that when we went out our telephone was used, and once the thirty-five dollars for our rent, which we always placed in a drawer as the first tax on our resources, was removed. This was such a disaster that we walked up and down the street until two or three in the morning pondering on what to do.

Our friends and friendly theater managers saw to it that we were well provided with theater tickets, and we saw plays several times a week, all of which I have forgotten except one which dealt with the life of chorus girls and small actresses dramatized from a novel by Owen Johnson, who was then a coming writer— does anybody remember him? The girls seemed to be perpetually receiving presents of silk underwear and flowers from sundry gentlemen, which they promptly sold to peddlers for ready cash to pay for their rent and food. This was very different theater fare from what we were accustomed to, and I enjoyed it. However, the clothes worn in these plays had a gaudy splendor which was a little too startling for an islander like myself; the stage dressmakers tried to get everything on an actress's dress that they could manage, especially dazzling fur trimmings. Outside the theater the women one met in the street or in houses were exquisitely dressed and groomed, their hair waved, their nails manicured. Both men and women thought a lot about their clothes; to present a good appearance was everybody's aim, and in the main avenues and streets one encountered, I believe, the best-dressed crowd of any city in the world. What struck me not quite pleasantly at first was that the women were all made up, generally discreetly but sometimes otherwise; rouge, lipstick, and powder were to be seen everywhere.

In the islands then known as the British, except for a light film of powder occasionally on faces, nobody in those days made up except ladies who were described mysteriously as "women of a certain class." In Dublin it used to be repeated as if it were very shocking, quite accounting for any wickedness in his poems, that Baudelaire said he preferred women's faces painted to faces *au naturel.*

With all the paint and lipstick there were odd pruderies and old-fashionednesses. When Sarah Purser's nephew at a party offered me a cigarette, the horrified look of my hostess prevented my smoking it; very few women at the time in America smoked. In a restaurant I was tactfully approached by a waiter and requested to put my cigarette down. In the summer at beaches, as I was to discover, women in bathing suits had to keep their legs covered with stockings—women's legs apparently had the impropriety attached to them that St. Paul associated with women's hair.

We must have been sort of pioneers in Beekman Place, for many of the friends who came to see us, though old New Yorkers, had never been in sight of it before—it was, in fact, regarded as a sort of slum. Following the Dublin habit, we had an at-home day, when we dispensed tea and cake before an open fire: this was every Sunday. In 1914 people were easily entertained—the drinking habit only came in with Prohibition—and our guests were quite happy with tea and conversation. We had arrived in America with numerous letters of introduction, and we got to know all sorts and conditions of people. The Irish Literary Renaissance was at that time very much the rage, and as my husband was about the best-known of the younger members of the movement, the great stars of which were Yeats and George Moore, we did a lot of lunching out, dining out, and even breakfasting out. On Sundays and national holidays we sometimes dined out twice, once in the middle of the day and again in the evening. On one such day we dined at midday with a waiter and in the evening with an ex-president and had a much grander meal at the waiter's and far classier wine.

Having at the time the attraction of the strange and the exotic, we were entertained by all sorts of people. As I write I cannot understand how we ever had the time and energy to go to all the places we went to and enjoy everything. We were occasionally invited for week ends to houses in Long Island, and again these were as varied as our acquaintances; some were small and servantless, a couple of others were as large as Norman castles or the houses of Tudor nobles, though they must have been constructed at the end of the nineteenth century or even at the beginning of this. They were built by the father or grandfather of the owners, like the George Pratt house in Glen Cove, which had the appearance and the appurtenances of an establishment that had been there for centuries. But the Nicholas Brady house in Manhasset had been built by the owner, and everything, including the very trees, had a look of rooted ancientness. These trees, Irish yews, had been dug up full-grown and transplanted, and they at least were very old.

After a couple of days' stay the feeling of ancientness and the resemblance to European houses wore off; the walls and rooms had not soaked in the personalities of generations of dead men and women. Nothing could make up for this, neither the old tapestries nor the old portraits nor the old furniture. Even at the time I did not think their owners were much related to these establishments; they were imitation European; indeed the owners themselves or their children later, not very much later, abandoned them for one reason or another. But in their day the owners, especially the women, were the most hospitable people in the world and without, as far as one could see, any snobbery. These houses were furnished with pieces that European palaces and even cathedrals had been ransacked for; there were innumerable bathrooms and closets, and none of those unwieldy furniture pieces that passed for wardrobes in European houses, in all the houses I knew, except Dublin eighteenth-century houses. Indeed there was every comfort in these great houses, but I remember hunting in vain for a bell or a bell rope to ring for a cup of tea in the morning. The mistress of nearly every little house in Britain and Ireland who owned a maid of all work or a kitchen slavey had her cup of tea in bed in the morning like the grandest of the land. But there were no bells in Long Island bedrooms; instead there was a telephone with an array of little buttons and inscriptions under them: "Housekeeper," "Butler," "Valet," etc. In desperation I tried the button marked "Butler," and promptly a respectful English voice asked ingratiatingly,

"Whisky or brandy this morning, sir?" At once I grasped that he was confusing my room with that of another guest, and I asked timidly what button I should press to get a cup of tea. "Personal maid, moddom." Instead of tea a complete breakfast was brought in; one could breakfast in bed in America, but that insular habit of having tea in bed and breakfast when one got up did not seem to be practiced, in spite of the imitation of British habits that one found everywhere among the wealthy and cultivated. My return hospitality was what might be called courageous; I asked my hosts to tea with Irish soda bread or to a meal of boiled chicken and ham or chops and broiled tomatoes, and a dessert bought in a pastry store. But people liked coming to the apartment in Beekman Place, and when the chairs gave out they sat on cushions on the floor.

In addition to ourselves Beekman Place had been discovered by a group of French artists, who, I think, all lived together in a house near us. They had come to America because the reverberations of the great Armory exhibition of 1913 had spread to all the capitals of Europe, and artists thought New York was a place where they could be appreciated and sell their wares. There would come to see us Duchamps, who had painted the sensational "Nude Descending the Stairs," Gleize, Picabia, and others whose names did not fasten themselves on my mind. The French would say that Beekman Place was like Paris, and we would say it was like Dublin; in its present state it is like neither. We were all young and poor, and in spite of the numerous friends we made we were lonely; the roots of the Old World, the culture of the Old World, were in our bones; we were used to places where for centuries people lived and died and were buried, where a long interchange between man and the earth had taken place. We were used to ruins half as old as time; we Irish especially were used to them, for we had lived in a country which before this war had more ruins of abbeys and churches and castles than any other in Europe because of the recurring wars and invasions. In New York everything, comparatively speaking, was new, even those houses that seemed dilapidated and worn. We who would all have been foreigners to one another in Europe were fellow countrymen here, exiles in a century of exile, and somehow we clung together. The bulk of our friends had been born in Europe, and we all met at regular intervals. On Saturdays we would go to Willy Pogany's studio party and there encounter another collection of exiles, all believing themselves to be so only temporarily. Tony Sarg lived next door to Willy, and though half English, being indeed the nephew of a lord mayor of London, was technically a mid-European, as was Pogany, and though both had British wives, they had to betake themselves out of London when the war began. Pogany's studio was haunted by Europeans of every nationality and every shade of political and war opinion; sometimes there was there a strange woman in a high-necked red silk blouse and a fantastic hat, Rosika Schwimmer, a pacifist who induced Henry Ford to send a peace ship to Europe, "to get the boys out of the trenches before Christmas." The simple-mindedness of this was characteristic of the attitude to war at the time; none of us really knew what a war was; some of us hardly realized there was a war on.

Though Pogany's Saturday gatherings were more polyglot than our Sunday ones, I had more difficulty in keeping my guests on good terms with one another. J. B. Yeats, W.B.'s father, who would several days a week be seated in an armchair by the fire, drinking tea, sometimes took a dislike to one or another of our Sunday visitors, a talkative woman or a foreigner he could not get the hang of, and when he got home he would write me a long letter of protest about having such people. He would walk all the way from his French boardinghouse in Twenty-fourth Street, where he had a dingy room with an iron bed, a cheap worn rug, and an easel on which was always erected a portrait at which he tinkered day after day. One of my guests drew from him an extra-vehement protest; this was a slim young Austrian journalist, Rudolf Kommer, whose satiric and disillusioned Viennese tongue as well as his friendship for George Moore ruffled J.B.

Kommer, whom we nicknamed "Anatol" after Schnitzler's character, lived near us in the East Fifties in a German-Jewish boardinghouse, for he himself was of Jewish descent. After our Sunday reunions in Beekman Place we occasionally went back with him to a supper composed of a variety of sausages, cottage cheese, sour cream, *Apfel Strudel*, and beer. When our *gemütlich* Anatol afterwards rose in the world, he became, it seemed to me, a different personality. As a sort of chief of staff to Max Reinhardt he resided with him in the famous castle in Salzburg, where they concocted the idea as a publicity stunt of getting society women to play in the New York production of *The Miracle*, in which, as Kommer sardonically said, real acting was not necessary. So they went about setting the Hudson on fire by getting a duke's daughter, an Italian princess, and a New York society girl to take turns at moving through the part of the Virgin and the Nun. In sequel to this, Kommer seemed to get richer and richer; he exchanged his boardinghouse for the Hotel Ambassador, had a famous table at the Colony Restaurant, and became an essential appanage of high society; indeed, I understand, a sort of upper-circle matchmaker. After he came to cut a figure in the beau monde we saw but little of Rudolf. Once when I had him to dinner to meet Elinor Wylie and some other writers, he left early, saying at the door in disgusted tones, "Why do you have such horrible food and such terrible women?" It being near Christmas, I had had roast turkey, and remembering his suppers of mysterious sausages in the old days, I had thought a few slices of turkey would delight Rudolf. After the Elinor Wylie party I never saw him again, though I occasionally came on his name in the society columns of the newspapers, where he was referred to as the portly Herr Doktor.

If J. B. Yeats took a dislike to Kommer, on his side Kommer took a positive hatred for another of our Sunday guests, a New York lawyer, John Quinn. Quinn in those days was a very important personage, a Standard Oil lawyer who had been a law partner of Bainbridge Colby and who professed a strong interest in the arts. He had had some connection with the famous Armory exhibition of modern painting and had been mixed up in the Irish Revival to the extent of giving commissions to a couple of the painters and arranging lecture tours for Douglas Hyde and W. B. Yeats. He had written an article or two on the chief figures of the movement and had financially backed an Irish literary society in New York. He was a persistent patron of modern art, chiefly French. Years later in Paris I heard a picture dealer refer to him as *le grand Monsieur Kan*. Quinn had stacks of pictures against the wall of his apartment in Central Park West, canvases which he would pull out and exhibit to his guests after dinner. He would also now and again do some poetry reading in an Ohio voice and would make terrible hash of Yeats's most esoteric volume, *The Wind Among the Reeds* (for Yeats and other Irishmen would stay with him when in America). His artist friends were given to insisting that he probably understood literature, but his snooty writing friends thought that it must be painting or sculpture that he understood. I remember only one of the pieces of sculpture in his room, an egg-shaped thing called "Portrait of Mdlle Pogany." The food at his dinner parties was sound middle-western—steak, apple pie or hot baked apple, without wine; there may have been cocktails, though I do not remember, being no cocktail drinker at the time. Now and again, at one of his parties, he would ask considerately, "Shall we be cozy and have coffee with our dinner?" Later he acquired a French couple to do his housekeeping and then went in for soufflés; crêpes Suzette, baba au rhum, and such sophistications. He was very dictatorial, of the type lately depicted in books as Nazi, though he professed a violent dislike for all Germans and said that if, by pressing an electric button—this was during the first World War—he could kill every German baby, he would do so. "I don't like the way the Germans paint; I don't like the way they eat oranges," he announced.

An invitation to one of his parties was a sort of royal command; if one did not answer immediately, as once I did not, he would get a secretary to telephone to say the party was already made up and that we need not bother replying. There was an occasion when he was giving a late party for a visiting celebrity; as my husband was on a lecture trip, I telephoned to say I would come in with a young man with whom I was dining: my would-be host seemed astounded and gave me a lecture to the effect that he did not know why a young married woman was dining with another man in her husband's absence, and that, anyhow, as it was a very intellectual group he was gathering together, it was my husband he wanted, not me. His opinion of me was succinct: "A paintable girl but dumb as they come." With all his dictatorialness he wilted when anybody tackled him in an approach to his own way, as my husband did a few times.

The desire for immortality takes queer shapes, and some of the shapes it took in John Quinn reached a point of comedy. In addition to picture buying, he went in for manuscript buying, sometimes on poor advice; he would visit the author whose manuscripts he had bought and get his photograph taken with him. One of the odd sights of his apartment were pictures of him and Conrad, or him and Yeats, or him and some other author, one sitting down and one standing up like a honeymoon couple, Quinn with his tight-lipped monkish face without a glimmer of temperament beside Conrad's remote melancholy face or Yeats's mysterious and prophetic face. There was nothing mysterious or remote about John Quinn's countenance, though he might have passed for a priest or a bishop, so prelate-like was his appearance. I had a desire to see him photographed with Amy Lowell in the same fashion as he was photographed with Conrad and Yeats—the combination would have been striking and might have interested posterity. I was balked in the plan by his accidental meeting with her during one of her cyclic descents on New York to sell her own or other people's poems or to get them reviewed. Quinn had called to see my husband about something in connection with James Joyce; he had hardly begun what would have amounted to the usual John Quinn allocution when the doorbell furiously rang several times and soon we heard Amy's voice screaming for someone to bring her a chair, as she wanted to rest on the landing before mounting the next flight. Quinn bolted down the stairs, and as I followed and introduced them he looked at the bulk of Amy with fairly open astonishment. "So you are the great John Quinn?" said Amy, rising to the occasion. He should have answered, "So you are the great Amy Lowell?" But he did not. Quinn and Amy had a considerable resemblance to each other in character and dictatorial manner, as they both had with Elizabeth Marbury, who dabbled in play broking and politics and who, like Amy, was very bulky. All three could be the rudest people on earth, but, at the same time, Quinn and Amy were kindhearted and did a lot for other people, but I have no knowledge of Marbury's heart.

John Quinn could not have been so monkish and ascetic as we believed, for when he died a lady whom we occasionally met at his parties claimed more of his estate than he left her, because she had, as she said, been his common-law wife from his youth, and

I have the word of some of his men friends that she was not the only one.

He liked being host to well-known visiting Irishmen; Yeats always stayed with him, and in the summer of 1914 for a short time he had had as guest Sir Roger Casement, but their politics did not match, and Casement moved to another abode. One day my husband and I went down to William Street to see the old Fenian editor of the *Gaelic-American*, John Devoy, a '67 man, which meant he had been in the aborted rebellion of 1867 and had been in gaol as a political prisoner. While waiting in the outer office we saw the tall figure of Casement in earnest conversation with one of the editors, a Captain Freeman. Devoy himself had his own distinction of appearance, a powerful head with thick gray hair that gave him a strong resemblance to Sigmund Freud, but beside the aristocratic figure and face of Roger Casement, all the people in the office except the extraordinary Freeman looked plebeian. In fact Casement was so different in mind, body, and life experience that he roused their suspicions to the extent that some of the Irish organizations had him trailed by a detective, who found everything he did quite aboveboard, as the editor of another Irish paper, the *Irish World*, told us. Indeed he was spied upon by all sides wherever he went.

The only thing Casement and the others in the *Gaelic-American* office could have had in common was their passion for Irish freedom. They all led the lonely lives of revolutionaries, Devoy, without wife or child or home, living in a furnished room, Freeman similarly situated, though he would dine convivially in Petitpas's with J. B. Yeats and could be the most entertaining of company, for he had apparently spent some time in nearly every country in the world, especially those in which some sort of revolution was brewing. The editorials of this curious man published in this obscure Irish-American paper were the best-informed on foreign affairs in New York. Devoy had served in the French Foreign Legion to learn soldiering for the next Irish fight; Freeman had been an officer in the British Army for the same purpose, and with his precise speech, his well-cut clothes, his bearing, he looked an officer and a gentleman, though he had been engaged so long in plots, counterplots, intrigues, and conspiracies that a sort of spylike expression had come into his face. Still he was trusted by all his colleagues in that guarded and oath-bound organization, the Clan-na-Gael. John Devoy, who always declared that he had never met an Englishman whom he had not liked, but that he wanted them all out of Ireland, spent his days and nights editing his ferocious little paper, building, planning, one could not say plotting, for he was candor itself, to bring about the coup that was to lead to Ireland's freedom. England had long ceased to bother about him and his group, had grown indifferent to physical-force movements in Ireland, had ceased to put rebels in gaol, when the day Devoy had spent his youth and manhood planning for suddenly came. Some years later I saw him in Dublin standing on one side of Leinster House, where Dail Eireann met, his hands gripping tightly the bars of the railing, as if he could not trust himself to stand, watching with excited, tearful eyes a detachment of the new Irish Army, in green uniforms, marching by to pay honor to him with bagpipes playing and colors flying, horses prancing. Devoy's day had come, but he must have been about eighty at the time, and he died a year or so after.

Casement, when we saw him in Devoy's office, was staying in a hotel in Brooklyn, and he invited us to tea there the next day. We were sitting in his room; I had poured the tea, and we were talking and munching bread and butter, when Casement with a warning glance said to me in the elementary Irish which was all he or I knew, "*Foscail an dorus* [Open the door]." I rose and swung the door open. There stood outside, silently, a waiter. "What do you want?" Casement asked. "I came to see if you needed more hot water," and the man moved down the corridor slightly confused. "See, I'm being watched," Casement said. My generation in Ireland was a little incredulous of spy stories, and I thought it possible that the man had honestly stated his reason for being outside the door. However, some days later as we sat in a drugstore eating ice cream—a strange treat to us—as Casement was talking of American food and American customs, I saw him start slightly, and, following his glance, noticed the same waiter in everyday clothes standing near us at the counter. "Ah, George," said Casement, "buying stamps, I suppose? In New York one buys stamps in a

drugstore," he remarked to us loudly and pleasantly, "or at a cigar
stand, because there are only three post offices in the whole city,"
and the man soon left. Again I was incredulous of the suggestion
that he was spying. "Who would have you spied on?" I asked Casement. "The British Embassy," he said, and there was an undertone
of hysteria in his voice. The answer surprised me, for the British
ambassador of the time, Sir Cecil Spring-Rice, was an Irishman
with a fair collection of rebel relatives. "They are watching all
Irish Nationalists in America on account of the war." Then he
said gravely, "You must look out; you are attractive young people,
and you will be liked, but you are Irish Nationalists, so be warned,
be warned."

As we parted he gave us a book on Conrad by a man called
Richard Curle. Conrad had once admired him, and in his hard
times in Africa, Casement had been a good friend. But later the
Irish Nationalist became too much for the transplanted Pole who
adopted everything English to an extreme degree, and he turned
against Casement. Nevertheless, when they knew each other in
Africa, Conrad wrote some very fine things about Casement and
about his championship of the downtrodden and his lonely resourceful courage in trying to save the black men from torture and exter-
mination in the rubber plantations. He has related how he watched
Casement walk away for his investigations "into unspeakable wil-
dernesses, swinging a crook-handled stick for all weapons, with two
bulldogs at his heels, and a Loanda boy carrying a bundle for all
company." The Loanda boy cooked what meals Casement ate and
washed his laundry in what running streams they met by the
way. A few months later Conrad saw him come out of the wilderness "a little leaner, a little browner, with his stick, dogs, and
Loanda boy, and quietly serene, as though he had been for a
stroll in the park." For his efforts Casement received conventional
honors, but very little real appreciation or understanding—he was
against the big battalions.

After that ice-cream party in a downtown drugstore, where he
bought me a bottle of lilac perfume, we never saw Roger Casement again, and the rest of his career is public property and even
part of history. He was hanged for treason to the British Empire

in London in the summer of 1916. His countrymen and country-women and many English friends backed him to the last, and knelt outside the prison in prayer at the hour he was hanged.

ह्ब CHAPTER 20

Chicago, 1915

THE FEW MONTHS for which we had taken our apartment ended in March 1915. Luckily the end coincided with some lecture engagements my husband 'had in Chicago and the Middle West. Once more I packed our belongings, stored our clothes, all but what fitted into two suitcases, with one of which Padraic started for Chicago, and with the other I went to Baltimore to stay with old Dublin friends, Ernest and Madeline Boyd, for the two weeks Padraic was supposed to be on his tour. After he came back to New York we thought we might bid good-by to America and return to Ireland. Though I was attached to my new American friends, I was homesick for Dublin and the Hill of Howth and the Bay of Dublin and the long twilights and the air of morning and the Yeats plays at the Abbey Theater and the pleasant evenings round fires where we tired the sun with talking and sent him down the sky.

Ernest Boyd was British vice-consul in Baltimore at the time; I had settled down with them for the two-week interim when a letter came from Padraic saying that more lectures were in the offing which would probably keep him four or five weeks away, and his hostess in Chicago, Mrs. Vaughn Moody, enclosed a note inviting me to join him at her house. I wanted to go back to New York for my clothes, but Padraic telegraphed to come as I was, as Mrs. Moody's household was very informal and nobody bothered about dressing. And so, after the longest railway journey I had ever taken in my life, I was met at an early morning train by Mrs. Moody herself with a very large open car.

Harriet Moody was a remarkable-looking woman with a face

resembling the portrait of the seeress Madame Blavatsky, only handsomer; the resemblance came probably from the spiritual adherences and the transcendentalisms which were in both. I was a little at sea at first about her and even more about her household, but it turned out that she was a businesswoman on a fairly large scale, running a food factory, a catering business, and, later, a restaurant—I had only known of her as the widow of the poet, William Vaughn Moody. She lived in a large house in the South Side of Chicago, and her household was made up of people in various capacities connected with her work—there were her secretary, Edith, a westerner, Bessie, Irish, who ran the house, Catherine, a New Englander who was a sort of bursar and bred Irish setters as a side line, Charlotte, Mrs. Moody's sister-in-law, who did other odds and ends and who was always accompanied by a red setter, pleasant to me, because setters were the dogs of my childhood; in addition there were various servitors—a mysterious Hindoo who used to bring up our breakfast in the morning, and a couple of students from the University of Chicago who were working their way through and who slept on the third floor, away from the rest of the household. The evening meal, marvelously cooked, came from her catering business and was served on little separate tables placed in front of each guest by a handsome Bulgarian student who made an excellent butler, as silent and well trained as any employer could desire. Once during a conversation about Central Europe, when an English guest began to comment on Bulgarian affairs, the young man broke his carefully kept silence to give us the information that his father was that Prime Minister of Bulgaria of whom the guest was speaking. The couple of Europeans present were a little startled, but Mrs. Moody took it all as a matter of course and asked the young man if he had any photographs of his family. As he brought in the coffee he handed around the photos of his father and mother—his mother a beautiful woman in evening dress with handsome jewelry. Altogether Mrs. Moody's was a household impossible in even the most bohemian family in a tightly bound old country. It was very impressive in the way it ignored old-country prepossessions; both employer and employés equally ignored them. Later when I sent some English writer friends to stay there—for Mrs. Moody was always happy to have a writer of any kind on the premises—they could not make head or tail of the household, with its complete absence of social distinctions of any kind.

Mrs. Moody had a passion for poetry and knew a great deal about it, far more indeed than did Harriet Monroe, who came to the house to dinner a few times during our stay. I greatly looked up to Mrs. Moody's feeling for literature as well as her knowledge of it, and remember that when somebody after dinner read the work of one or other of the newer experimental poets of the time, like H.D., she would grasp it immediately, though I have generally to hear or read a poem twice before I really understand it. She had a curious interest in men, emotional but not erotic, and she would get interested in one after another, particularly if they were young poets, so strongly as to obliterate for the time being her other friends. Like many intellectual women I have met in America, she did not take much stock in women, and I think she preferred those who had no intellectual pretensions at all. She herself had a very well trained mind, had graduated from Cornell at a time when few women had gone in for university education, and was at this time one of the governing body of the university. For a time she had taught in a high school in Chicago, the usual outlet for educated women, and many of her pupils in after life became distinguished. All her guests—and she had several dinner guests every evening—were intellectuals or artists of some kind, and as Chicago was heading a midwestern literary movement at the time, we met there and made a fast friendship with Edgar Lee Masters, who read us his unpublished Spoon River Anthology. Carl Sandburg read us verses, the free rhythms of which then seemed strange. Sherwood Anderson read us his curious introverted prose, and Vachel Lindsay, whom we already knew from New York, blew in from Springfield and, as long as anybody listened, would stand before the fire, tirelessly chanting his poetry which had a new note in it, the excitement of a circus or a game—and with a complete lack of self-consciousness. He was a troubadour; he naturally wanted to wander the roads, saying his poetry to all who would give him a hearing. He had indeed done this, and like an Irish ballad singer had handed a printed sheet containing the poem he had chanted to anybody who gave him a meal; he called his sheets "Rhymes to Be Traded for Bread." Harriet Monroe, dressed in navy georgette with a bar pin, a ladylike but at the same time pushing little woman, would read some old-maidish poetry which we were all pleasant about. However, it became borne in on me that I was meant to be seen but not heard, so I said very little, except to Lindsay, who took me to luncheon at little French and Italian restaurants and to wander around the streets at the lake front, where he declaimed his poetry so loudly that once we were accosted by a policeman. At that time I was popular with Harriet Monroe, though in later years I roused in her a touch of venom when I began to get some kind of critical reputation, but during that visit, anyhow, she approved of me. If she misunderstood me I misunderstood her, too, for I am no quick judge of character and am easily fooled. She had a high opinion of the importance of her family and had no objection to expressing it; when somebody mentioned Amy Lowell's interest in poetry, she said snappily that nobody in the Middle West was interested in what the Lowells did; they were a small New England family. Very seriously she related an interview that her sister had with the Dowager Empress of China. "The House of Monroe has always been friendly to the House of Ching," the Empress had said. I do not distinguish Chinese names very precisely, and maybe it was the house of Ming or the house of Chang, but anyhow it was a dynastic house.

Harriet Monroe could not have been much over fifty at the time, though to my youth she seemed an old lady, for to those under thirty everybody over fifty is old, even everyone who is not a contemporary. As we grow older our contemporaries still remain young to us. Harriet Monroe had done quite a remarkable thing for the poetic revival of the period—how remarkable I was to realize only later. She succeeded in collecting from businessmen in Chicago enough money to endow a magazine devoted entirely to poetry which she edited herself with the assistance of Alice Corbin Henderson, a real poet. But Harriet was the executive energy which pulled everything together, and between the two they got in touch with all the important poets in the English-speaking world and elsewhere. Ezra Pound became the European editor on his own suggestion and helped them considerably with advice and with obtaining contributions. The little Chicago magazine soon got an international reputation and was eagerly read by everybody interested in poetry.

There was another little magazine at the time in Chicago which the indefatigable Ezra also helped on its way; this was the *Little Review,* founded by two young women, Margaret Anderson and Jane Heap. These two editors would publish anything they believed to be good, even if it brought them in conflict with the law and the Comstock society, and so it happened that some of the most advanced experimental prose writers were first published in America in their pages. The first Sherwood Anderson I ever read was in the *Little Review,* and, later, when the two young women moved their magazine to New York, they published some of James Joyce's *Ulysses;* this came through the help of John Quinn, who paid for the contribution. The Joyce piece was considered obscene, and Margaret Anderson and Jane Heap were haled into court. But they had powerful helpers, and if people are powerful enough it is my experience they can generally beat the law. It was years afterwards before *Ulysses* was permitted publication in America, but it has never been published in London or Dublin; this suppression, however, did not prevent the book's getting in and having plenty of readers in these cities. The two young editors were courageous and had a good time with their *Little Review,* and when they came to see us at Mrs. Moody's they reminded me, in their eagerness, of the young people I knew who were trying to run literary movements, and though Jane and Margaret did not have much experience of literature they had a sharp sense of what was new or novel. When they moved themselves and their review to New York I do not think they stood out so remarkably as they did in Chicago; New York can swallow people up who would blossom healthily in a less cosmopolitan center and add greatly to its life. Artistic movements that remain perpetually amateurish in New York because of the scattered nature of their audience can become professional in a smaller place where competition does not crowd them.

Anyhow, in that spring of 1915 Chicago seemed mentally more exciting than New York, though it was not intellectually so sophisticated, but neither Chicago nor New York understood literature with the complex reactions of cities in old countries.

It always seemed to me a great pity that so many Chicago intellectuals moved to New York, for Chicago was then heading for its own place in the sun and was developing its own brand of middle-western culture. It had splendid and interesting foundations, including an opera company, a little theater, and a wonderful museum and art gallery, but what it lacked was a couple of first-rate book-publishing houses, for it is publishing houses that mysteriously cause a city to be regarded as an intellectual center. Publishing was becoming more and more monopolized by New York. What a pity that some New York houses which have branches in cities in Canada did not have publishing branches in Chicago and other American cities instead of just sales offices. Chicago, like all industrial towns, had many patrons of music, and the concerts would be crowded. I have seen the overflow at a Kreisler performance accommodated on the stage, and the audience packed around him must have really been disconcerting to the virtuoso, for he seemed to have hardly enough elbow room for the swing of his bow. Music makes more of an appeal to the tired businessman than does literature, I have often observed.

In Harriet Moody's music room of an evening there would be some quite wonderful pianists, and the sounds they could draw from the piano brought back to my mind with nostalgia the first time I heard great music on the day I entered boarding school. Actually all the players who performed for us after dinner were of professional status and seemed technically to be far superior to some of the much advertised European players who made concert tours, though these had nuances of emotion and imagination that electrified their finger tips. Except for this, I think the Chicago pianists—Viola Cole and Beatrice Faggi (Mrs. Alfeo Faggi, wife of the sculptor) were finer than some European virtuosos like Ely Ney, who sometimes played at Mrs. Moody's.

Though the memories of the Chicago of that period have stuck in my mind as intellectually and artistically one of the most alive cities I had ever been in, yet at the same time people, especially those who regarded themselves as upper-class, were full of prejudices and were less gracious and less sure of themselves than the same class in New York, though they observed carefully enough most of the rules of the books of etiquette. "Westward the course of

empire takes its way," said the Irish philosopher Berkeley, and to
some extent also does the course of human prejudice. The most
coolly unprejudiced and disinterested people I have ever encountered have been Orientals of one kind or another, and the
most prejudiced, Aryans or Anglo-Saxons of one kind or another.
The guest preceding us at Mrs. Moody's had been Rabindranath
Tagore, then fresh from his European triumphs, but because he was
a dark oriental man it had not been easy in Chicago to get hospitality for him until Alice Henderson thought of asking Mrs. Moody
to put him up. His son in a western college had been a trifle looked
down upon because of his dark skin. I think this was only partly a
color prejudice and partly because people of English and New
England descent were inclined to believe that countries belonging
to English vassal states must be inferior. Conquered peoples were
looked down upon. There was quite a number of Americans who
felt English rather than American and who did not mind criticism
of America, but who were offended by any criticism of Britain or
the British Government, and this whether made by English people
or by others. Then, equally strangely, there was an irrational anti-
English prejudice, the more unaccountable as America had long
been free from the domination of England. Perhaps this was due
to incompatibility of manners; I remember hearing a person who
seemed aloof described as being "upstage like a tea-drinking Englishman."

II

Harriet Monroe asked us to a party at her sister's house. "My
sister and her husband were United States representatives in
China," she told us. By this time, after seeing her several evenings
at Mrs. Moody's, a wicked conviction began to grow in me that to
Miss Monroe all writing, but especially poetry, was a form of
vagrancy, but she had adopted poetry and the publishing of poetry
as a means of filling her life, so that owing to this official connection she always did something to entertain visiting poets. Yeats
when on a lecture trip had stayed with her, and she had introduced
him to the conveniences of the innovation trunk with its various
compartments, so that he bought one and delightedly, as she said,

put his shirts in one drawer and his papers in another. George Moore, I remembered, had mocked at that trunk, a sort of receptacle unknown in Dublin until Yeats brought his back. The day of the party, when Mrs. Moody came home from her business and found me with my hair in curling pins, she said, "I don't think you will like this party." "You will meet all the lake-front snobs," said Bessie warningly. But at that time I liked every party, and I enjoyed talking to new people, though I was puzzled as to why in Chicago the flow of conversation was so often dammed by the tremendous care everyone took to talk only commonplaces and avoid offense of any kind. I thought people took offense easily, which rendered it impossible to have any of those violent discussions and expressions of opinion which made conversation so lively in Dublin and Paris. At Dr. Sigerson's people could get violent as to whether the Celts were a red-haired or black-haired people; at Commissioner Bailey's they could get wrought up about the end of Flaubert's *L'education Sentimentale,* and in A.E.'s about the proper pronunciation of "Concobar" in poetry in English, but in polite society in Chicago nobody liked to disagree with anybody.

Dressed up in my second-best evening dress—my best being in storage in New York—a garment made by an artistic seamstress in Rathmines, of plain mauve Liberty satin combined with flowered Liberty chiffon, designed to make me look somewhat like a figure in a stained-glass window or the Blessed Damosel, I started for Mrs. Moody's car. "Miss Monroe's sister's husband was minister to China, remember," Edith, Mrs. Moody's secretary called after us as we were going down the steps. Anton the chauffeur fixed the rug around us, as it was an open car. "Miss Monroe's brother-in-law was ambassador to China," said he.

We arrived; the rooms seemed small after the large rooms of Dublin's eighteenth-century houses, but they were attractively and carefully furnished as rooms in Dublin seldom were, and without that suggestion of professional interior decoration so common in New York which made one hesitate to move a chair for fear of upsetting the decoration scheme. Miss Monroe's sister was very pleasant, and long residence in the East deprived her, if she ever had them, of the gushing manners that some middle westerners overwhelm a foreigner with. I stood looking at a piece of Chinese embroidery, but I thought it was not any more gorgeous than the William Morris embroidery done by Lily Yeats on my arty dress. But Harriet proceeded to explain the wonders of it with romantic expressions like, "the waves of eternity," which she said were presented in the stitches. "My sister was given it by the Dowager Empress of China." A man who kept beside me most of the evening, observing me closely, broke in, "Miss Monroe's brother-in-law was minister to China."

Everyone was drinking out of little glass cups some mixture of strong liquor, a punch. At that time, being only a winebibber, I did not care for strong drink, so my husband and myself asked for tea. A tea tray was brought in, and a woman guest proceeded to pour out a pale watery fluid. "I should like it stronger. In a few minutes it will be stronger," I explained to the puzzled woman sitting in front of the tea tray. I looked around for that inevitable appurtenance of an Irish or English tea table, a slop bowl in which to pour away the pale liquid and get a stronger brew.

"What are you looking for?" asked the observant male who kept close to me.

"I'm looking for the slop bowl," said I cheerfully.

"The what?" said he.

"The slop bowl," said I.

"Get this lady something for slops," he requested the maid. An Irish voice that seemed softly and mysteriously to come out of the air breathed in my ear.

"Put down your cup, madam, and I'll bring you a cup of tea from the kitchen."

An impassive maid handed me later a good cup of strong tea, and I was proceeding to enjoy it when Harriet came over with a few women guests.

"I do love the Irish," said a nasal feminine voice. "All our maids at home were Irish when I was a child."

"Really?" said I.

"My darling old nurse was Irish," said the other. "She nursed us all. She's living with us still. I'm going to give her your husband's poems."

"Going to live in America, Mrs. Colum?" said a brisk masculine voice.

"No, we're returning after my husband gives a few more lectures."

A square-faced woman, large-boned, plain-featured, in a fantastically expensive-looking dress and stiffly waved hair, fastened her eyes on me.

"You came here to make money, did you? How much do you expect to make?"

"About two hundred pounds," said I.

"I always think," she said slowly, and carefully measuring her words, "that it is a pity that people in European countries cannot find enough outlet for their talents at home without being obliged to cross the Atlantic. Don't you think so, Mrs. Colum?"

I took a draught of the strong tea and meditated a minute. "Wouldn't that mean," I asked, "that this country would be entirely inhabited by Red Indians? That would be very interesting."

"She didn't get it," said the man beside me as she walked away. "She's slow."

Harriet Monroe's sister presented a hearty large male; he turned out to be the husband of the lady who had just walked away. "Are you the guest of honor?" he asked.

"Oh, I don't think so," said I.

"Were you born in Ireland, Mrs. Colum?" he asked.

"Yes."

We talked agreeably for a few minutes. "Why," said he admiringly, "anybody would think you were as well educated as an American girl. Are you visiting in Chicago?"

"My husband is here lecturing on the Irish Literary Revival."

"Oh yes, that's about Singe, isn't it?"

"Synge," I corrected determinedly. "Like 'Sing,' you know. No, he is mostly lecturing on Irish poetry."

"My, now, he must be very intelligent. Poetry is Harriet's line. Very intelligent woman, Harriet. She got a prize for writing poetry once. She was so young then that she was called the pig-tailed poet of the prairies. So your husband is lecturing here? It's a pity, I say, that the English prevent the Irish getting educated, they're such a bright people."

"They don't prevent us getting educated, and most of the Irish aren't so bright as you think."

Harriet kept courteously hopping over, presenting people.

"There are a lot of interesting people here," she said. "My sister is really a very interesting woman. Her husband was minister to China, and there are several college women here."

She took me over to a very tall woman in a black dress, though, in fact, they all wore black dresses except myself.

"This is a valedictorian," said Harriet. I obviously showed that I did not know the meaning of the word.

"She graduated from her college highest in her class," said Harriet impressively. "And this is a graduate of Cornell." The Cornell graduate was engaging, and she was dressed carelessly, without the hard finish of some of the women in the room.

"It must be a surprise for you to find so many women in this country college-educated."

"Do you mean university-educated?" I asked, for we use the term "college" in Ireland for secondary schools.

"Yes, indeed, I mean university-educated. We have a lot of university-educated women in America." The hearty male who was the husband of the square-faced lady was listening.

"That will come in Ireland, too," he said, nodding his head as if he were promising something. "The English just can't keep a bright people down forever. No, sir!"

"Illiteracy is not so common there as it used to be," said Harriet.

"Well," said the man, "as I was saying awhile ago, Mrs. Colum is just as well educated as an American girl."

"Are you real Irish, Mrs. Colum?" somebody inquired.

"Oh, the realest," said I. "Is nobody else here Irish?"

"Well, I'm English myself on both sides. The first of my name in this country came over on the *Mayflower*."

"One of my ancestors came over on the *Mayflower*, too," said Harriet.

"Have you ever heard of the *Mayflower*?" asked the observant man beside me who stuck to me most of the evening.

"Yes, I've heard of it," said I. "But it came over some time ago, didn't it? I think I'm too young to remember it."

"I think," said Harriet, "I'm more Scotch than anything."

"Then you must be a Celt," I remarked.

"Oh no, not at all—not at all."

I had always thought that since Matthew Arnold's discourse on the Celts everybody was flattered to have some Celticism ascribed to him. Everybody I knew in London always was, anyhow.

Then there entered a man to whom everybody began to pay enormous attention. He seemed to be somebody so important that I thought he was nothing less than the minister to China. I walked towards him, with the observant man following. The newcomer was called Hobart—Hobart Chatfield Taylor. I was struck by his first name because everybody was calling him by it, and I had never known anybody called Hobart before, though I had known Huberts.

"Are you by chance the minister to China?" I asked him.

"Are you expecting the minister to China?"

"Oh yes. I came here especially to see him."

"Oh, you want to see a minister, do you? Now if you were only in Washington you would see them by the cartload. Have you never seen an ambassador?" He was smiling and kindly.

"Yes, I think so," said I. "They wear stars on their bosoms, don't they?"

"Stars?" he said in astonishment.

"Yes. Stars, garters, ribbons, medals."

"Look here, little girl, are you pulling my leg?"

"She might be," said the man beside me. "She's quite smart. She was scratched by Mrs. X a few minutes ago, and she was quite good."

"Mrs. X is feline," said the man called Hobart, smiling, "the eternal feline."

"*Das ewige kätzliche.*"

"Where did you learn that?"

"Out of Goethe, I think. It's a paraphrase of Goethe's line, isn't it?"

"Where did you learn Goethe?"

"In Dublin," said I.

"Do they speak German in Dublin?" he asked suspiciously.

"They speak everything in Dublin."

The observant man beside me was beginning to look inimical. A little later I overheard him say in an exasperated tone to Harriet, "I don't like this young Dubliner. That dame knows her way around."

ಓ CHAPTER 21

A French Boardinghouse: Irish Revolt

THE FALL OF 1915, just about a year after our arrival, found us in New York once more, and as far from returning to Dublin as ever. We had various problems in front of us, the principal of which was the problem of making a living, and this, somehow, by writing; the next was the problem of where to live. We decided, like some of our friends, to simplify life by living in a boarding-house. The boardinghouse was in that era a characteristic feature of New York life, and I wonder so few ingenious fiction writers found material in them. They were generally, though not always, run by foreigners, who seemed to have the knack and the training to make them pay. Our friend Rudolf Kommer lived in a German-Jewish boardinghouse; J. B. Yeats lived in a French one. We once tried an Italian, or maybe it was a Sicilian, pension, but after the first few days we found it so little to our liking that we decided to pay for our few days in it and get out. The place was as strange as a house in a murder-mystery story, every room, somehow, managed to be dark and gloomy, the windows were hung with heavy, dusty drapery, and the house had guests whose faces we never saw more than once in the dining room. This room in the basement was decorated with knives of various shapes and sizes—stilettos hung from the wall, knives were laid out in rows on the sideboard, and when I looked into the kitchen I saw other knives of even stranger patterns. When my husband notified the patron that we were leaving in a few days and asked for our bill, he made no reply, but a few minutes afterwards he came up to our room, a long knife in his hand, and said his terms were monthly and that he would not permit us to go. The scene ended by our calling in a policeman, who steered us out of the house after he stood by while we paid an extra week's rent. Then, feeling it his duty to give us advice, he told us to try the boardinghouses off the park uptown and leave these downtown places to the more experienced. In a daily paper we saw an advertisement for M. Froissard's boarding-house in the West Eighties, and on calling at the address we found the proprietor to be an elderly and old-fashioned Frenchman for whom Germany and England—perfide *Albion*—were equally un-desirable nations, and we had to convince him that we were neither English nor German before he would agree to take us in. For the sum of seven dollars a week each we were provided with a large room up four flights and two meals a day. As there were no other boarders on the top floor at the time, we had the exclusive use of a large bathroom which had been constructed out of the bedroom between the front and back rooms. This was large enough for my husband to erect a table and his typewriter, and, secure in solitude, he did his writing there.

We had a fair French breakfast and a very good French dinner with which, for fifteen cents extra when we had it to spare, we could get a half bottle of California wine. As we find the French easy to get on with and not alien in any way but generally considerate, we were happy in M. Froissard's in spite of the economic uncer-tainty of our occupation. Sometimes we did not pay the fourteen dollars a week punctually, but as we always did pay it, the patron had no fault to find with us. We had, however, no luncheon, since it would have cost about three dollars a week each extra; conse-quently my husband grew thinner and thinner, and my anemia grew worse and worse. I tried to do some writing and did manage to sell a couple of short stories, but I had as yet no American back-ground, and the magazines did not care much for foreign material. My husband had a slender market for children's stories and books al-most immediately, a series of them being run in the Metropolitan Life Insurance Company magazine. At the time, however, no editor would give me a book to review, though I now and again did a little ghost reviewing for friends who, for one reason or another, got books that I was better able to cope with.

Some of the boarders had special interests connected with the war in Europe. There were a French munitions buyer and his wife, sad people, whose native city, Lille, had fallen into the hands of the Germans; there were a Russian revolutionary and his wife, both intellectuals, and both had been gaoled by the Czarist government in the 1905 uprising. This they told us as a secret, because they firmly believed that if it were known in America that they had ever been in gaol even for holding lofty political ideas, they would be discriminated against or even deported. Like other Russian revolutionaries, they had been living in London, where their small son was born, and M. Lebedeff, who was a journalist, knew some English journalist friends of ours. Madame Lebedeff was a charming and highly intellectual woman, in every way kindhearted but that she had a horror of cats and would fly when she saw one. Once, coming upstairs after breakfast, she saw prowling in her room the house cat to which M. Froissard and his wife were devoted. In terror she shooed the cat out of the open window, where he fell the four flights to the basement and was killed; in rage, M. Froissard climbed to each room to make an inquisition as to who was the murderer of his cat. Finding that it was Madame Lebedeff who was the guilty party, he asked her tearfully, "What would Madame say if I threw Platon [her little son] out of the window?" Madame threw up her hands in horror and apprehension. However, M. Froissard was reasonable. "I only say it for the purposes of the comparison; I throw neither child nor animal out of the window; I am a civilized man. But you other Russians [vous autres russes], you are different." And, muttering angrily, he walked downstairs.

There was a French journalist in the house whose voice was never heard until one day a German band appeared in the street, the common German band of those days, four uniformed middle-aged men efficiently playing gemütlich German airs on a variety of instruments. The sound so infuriated him that he jumped to his feet from the table, where he was drinking coffee, shook his fists at them, then rushed out the basement door and in violent French ordered them away. They obediently collected their instruments and left. M. Froissard, who didn't like anybody giving orders from his house, explained that they were Alsatians, not Germans, and the irate journalist proceeded to orate against Alsatians, who he said were a nondescript people like the Irish—a mélange.

There were several South Americans in the house; one couple had a whole floor, and they had their meals upstairs, as the gentleman did not want to expose his pretty young wife to the gaze of other males in the dining room. She seldom was on view, but occasionally, when she encountered any of the men boarders on the stairs, she would with a flashing smile say, at no matter what hour of the day, "Good morning, sir." Then, besides the regular boarders, there were a group of what were known in those days as "table boarders" who did not live in the house but who came in for meals. These, however, had such nondescript personalities that I recall only one of them, a tall, handsome man who on account of his peculiarly Anglo-Saxon appearance, I at first thought was an Englishman, but he turned out to be an American, Frank Moore Colby. He had a mania for talking French, of which he knew hardly any, and came generally late for breakfast so as to have the opportunity of practicing the language by talking to the patron, who himself served breakfast. As I was nearly always late I would overhear the accounts of himself that he would give to M. Froissard, who at first had a great curiosity about him, a curiosity which, however, was soon satisfied. In answer to a question as to what his profession or business was, Mr. Colby described himself hesitatingly as a *philosophe* and said that he was engaged in writing an important work, for which reason he had temporarily left his home in Washington Heights and taken a room in the neighborhood, as he had found it impossible to finish a book in a household with three children.

Inadvertently and incuriously I got to know a lot about him; the reserve he would, no doubt, have had in English disappeared when he talked his broken French, which he had acquired so recently and with such toil that he did not realize that any other English-speaking person could possibly know any at all—an attitude I have found in people who have acquired knowledge of any kind late in life. Mr. Colby explained that he had saved or had got some money and was devoting the remainder of his life, he hoped, to writing. M. Froissard could not always follow what he related, and would afterwards shake his head over him. "*Il a quitté le domicile conjugal! C'est terrible!*" I did not then realize what it meant to a French person to "*quitter le domicile conjugal*," for I had never thought of the French as taking marriage with undue seriousness. I was interested in Mr. Colby; he was frustrated and puzzled in a way European men seldom are, and he had not achieved any great height or depth of consciousness, but he looked as if he might have a pondering mind which could evolve odd brilliancies. I was not too surprised later to hear his name from time to time and to discover that he had an enthusiastic if small following for his essays. Once when I called to see Francis Hackett and his wife when he was still on the *New Republic* and they had an apartment in Tudor Village, Francis, showing us down the stairs, talked for a minute to a man who opened the door of another apartment: I recognized the *philosophe*; a sort of contentment had come on his puzzled and emotionless face. Francis introduced us, but the *philosophe* did not recognize me—in fact I doubt if he had ever in his life much noticed me. I, however, was so struck at this second encounter that I later made him part of a composite I was building up out of several characters I knew—Stuart Sherman and others— for a story which I later published in the *New Republic* and which I called "Portrait of a Philosopher." I thought I was writing of a typical American intellectual, but later an Englishman told me he was sure I had written about him.

The boarders at M. Froissard's had the privilege of occasionally asking a guest to dinner if one told the patron some days ahead. The Lebedeffs, who had the next table to ours, would have occasionally a wiry-looking, bright, intent little man with a sort of goatee beard, one M. Leon Bronstein, or Braunstein, who worked on an East Side Jewish paper. I remember him chiefly because he would bring the London *Nation* to M. Lebedeff, who would lend it to us, and because of the ease with which he could drop from one language into another. The Lebedeffs whispered that he was, like themselves, a Russian revolutionary. All of them later went back to Russia, but the only one whose later history I know anything of is M. Bronstein. He became Leon Trotsky, and of all things, the head of an army. Years later, in Passy, I thought I saw him again. In the apartment house where we were living I once encountered three men in conversation with the concierge in the loge; the one who was making inquiries, though older, grayer, and somewhat changed, was amazingly like the M. Bronstein of M. Froissard's—in fact, I verily believe it was he. He was calling on someone living in the apartment house, "What is that gentleman's name?" I asked the concierge, who replied impatiently, "Ah, je ne sais pas. Il est russe ou juif; ils sont tous russes ou juifs; il y a trop de russes ici en France." At this time, years after the Russian revolution, all sorts of sequels to it were taking place in Paris, including the kidnapping and complete disappearance of a czarist general.

II

But to get back to M. Froissard's, with its odd collection of non-Americans, all of them memorable and a few of them tragic, we passed the winter of 1915 and most of the spring of 1916 there somewhat uneventfully. Then, one morning, we went down to breakfast and, picking up the newspaper laid at our place, saw that what we knew was going to happen had happened—the Irish once more had taken up arms in a fight for independence; the leaders had seized government buildings and railway stations; the fight was on, the fight that Pearse and others had so often spoken of, similar to those our ancestors had vainly engaged in. The names of the leaders stared out at us from the paper, the young men I had worked with, had danced with, had read poetry with—Padraic Pearse, Thomas MacDonagh, Willie Pearse, Joseph Plunkett; older people we knew well—Countess Markievicz, Roger Casement, The O'Rahilly, Eamon De Valera. I felt the eyes of the room on us. Tremblingly I looked up; everybody seemed to be talking of the happening; the Lebedeffs alone were sympathetic; the French were disapproving if not entirely inimical; the South Americans, all from countries in a perpetual state of revolution, were angrily hostile, and a Señor Savaadra expressed himself in violent language; M. Froissard delivered himself of an oration—while France was fighting for her life, why should the Irish, who had fought for her at Fontenoy, now go into rebellion and play into the hands of her enemies? What horrified him above all was that some of the people revolting were gens de titre. His sense of the fitting was outraged—le peuple revolted, but not la noblesse—les gens de titre. Hearing the inimical voices around me, I had difficulty in restraining my tears. "Do you know these people?" someone asked. "They are our friends." "But how imprudent they are!" said the French munitions buyer gravely. "How imprudent! For England will either shoot them or give them life imprisonment." I thought of how Pearse used to say laughingly, "Prudence is the only vice." Caution, self-preservation, timidity, fear—they are all vices. M. Froissard's telephone began to ring; the newspapers were asking my husband questions about the leaders of the revolt. We went out and walked the streets and bought other papers, of which New York had then many more than now. The accounts were frequently inimical during the week the leaders held out, and even contemptuous. One correspondent described the insurrection as an *opéra bouffe* affair in which schoolmasters got themselves up in high decorated boots and fancy uniforms. Without being sympathetic the correspondents could have been disinterested, but some of them seemed to be either unwilling or unable to get the facts. Many of the reports showed a grave concern, for though America was not yet in it, the war was supposed to be fought for the freedom of small nationalities. However much in theory people believe in fighting for freedom, when it comes to action a great many can find reasons for not allowing one or another nationality to have its own way.

I paid but little attention to the friends who kept saying to us, "It is all foolish and reckless, for of course they cannot win." I knew perfectly well the leaders did not believe they could win against the might of England, but I knew also that they thought of their action as symbolic and that it would in the end have a psychic victory. "This country will be one entire slum unless we get into action," MacDonagh had said, "in spite of our literary movements and Gaelic Leagues it is going down and down. There's no life or heart in the country." The sequel to the rebellion came soon. British battleships bombarded Dublin, British forces went into action, and the leaders surrendered. Boatloads of their followers were sent to prison in England. On a May morning, a fair sunny day, as I got off the subway at Grand Central on my way to see Mrs. Moody, who had come to New York, I saw the headlines of the early afternoon papers. Pearse, MacDonagh, and Clarke executed. I must have sat for long in the waiting room in a dream or a semicoma, for when I looked at the station clock it was late in the afternoon and I saw my husband standing in front of me. Day by day the roll of the executed continued, a few each day—Joseph

Plunkett, Count Plunkett's son, a delicate idealistic poet boy, John MacBride, Maud Gonne's husband, who had been in so many fights that when they wanted to bandage his eyes before he faced the firing squad he waved them aside with the remark, "I have looked down the barrel of a gun too often to bother about one now." There was the strong labor leader and organizer, James Connolly, who was shot seated because he could not stand on account of his wounds; there were the others, all those who had signed the proclamation or who had led battalions.

One, Roger Casement, was not taken in arms but captured after he came off a German submarine, for he had gone to Germany to get aid for the rebellion, as other Irish leaders had gone to other countries for aid in other rebellions. He was held in prison in London, and his trial was so dramatic that the war news seemed secondary. The lawyer who defended him, fittingly enough, was George Gavan Duffy, the brother of my friend Louise, who had taught with me in Pearse's school, and the son of the famous leader, Sir Charles Gavan Duffy. Dramatic were the accounts of Casement's standing in the dock, on trial for treason. "It is impossible for a man to commit treason against a country to which he does not belong. I am an Irishman; not an Englishman. If I am to be tried for treason it should be by my own countrymen." The New York *Evening Post*, commenting on the tragic dignity of his utterance, said that both the language and the trial was Shakespearean; it quoted a line Casement said in defense of one who was captured with him, as Elizabethan in its drama, "The indictment is wrongly drawn, my lords; the man is innocent." The trial dragged on. Then one August morning early a newspaper telephoned us, "Casement was hanged this morning." That was the last of the executions, and with it some part of our youth ended. Our generation in Ireland, or what remained of it, seemed to be like survivals of a past after this. The work they had set for themselves was by no means completed, but it was well on the way, and there could be no going back on it.

The effect of the revolt and the executions on American Irish and even on other Americans was activating: they started to organize; formidable associations and leagues came into being; at that time there were many more outstanding Irish-Americans than now in public life—Dr. Emmett, Judge Goff, Judge Cohalan, Frank P. Walsh, John D. Ryan, Nicholas Brady, and a great many Irish journalists in many American cities. There was a national organization called the Friends of Irish Freedom, headed by the composer, Victor Herbert, the grandson of the Irish novelist, Samuel Lover; there was the young people's association called the Irish Progressive League; there were other societies with strange names— the Protestant Friends of Irish Freedom, which included a clergyman who became an archimandrite in the Russian Orthodox Church. The present head of the Iranian Institute, Dr. Upham Pope, was also one of the Protestant Friends. There were other organizations with figures more comic than useful, stage Irishmen and Irishwomen; then there were idealists of the purest kind who in the interest of freedom worked themselves to death. There were politicians whose chief interest in the cause was to catch votes. Up high on the roll of idealistic workers were such men as Oswald Garrison Villard, William Allen White, Norman Thomas. When the war was over they organized a deputation to the Peace Conference, they interviewed President Wilson, they got Congress to pass a resolution, and not only in America but all over the world people helped. Long as it takes to upset the policy of an empire, it was only about five years after the young men revolted before old men and women, lining the street at O'Connell Bridge, saw the British army of occupation march away to the boats at Kingstown, then become Dunleary. They saw the Union Jack taken down from government buildings and, miracle of miracles, the flag of the Irish revolution hoisted over the oldest English stronghold in Ireland, Dublin Castle, where so many Irishmen had rotted away in captivity. The long fight was almost over. There was a setback during the civil war: for England still held six Ulster counties as a foothold; but the old hatreds were dying. Irishmen began the job of governing themselves, and with this, for all the setbacks, a fresh epoch in Irish history began. That they withdrew from the rest of the world to work out their problems was, I believe, right. Yeats had prophesied that, in the struggle he saw approaching, Ireland would be saved. But he bade the poets to be mindful of their heritage and write of their country:

> Cast your mind on other days
> That we in coming days may be
> Still the indomitable Irishry.

ಶಿ CHAPTER 22

Earning a Living

THE FALL OF 1916 found us once more in New York, two years after our first arrival. This time we took an unfurnished apartment and furnished it with odds and ends, some bought and some contributed by our friends—the Louis Ledoux and an older friend, Thomas Hughes Kelly, who had lived in Ireland for part of the Revival in a large house in Kildare—in fact, it was supposed to be the largest in Ireland. He had given certain scholarships in Dublin, one of which my husband got after he had written his first play. At this period our friend had lost a great deal of his money and did not live in New York, but in a small town in the state, coming up to town occasionally where socially he was very well known. As his wife was of French parentage, he later went to live in France, where, like many Americans, he lived well and pleasantly on an income which would have been insufficient for their tastes in New York. It was curious about Americans in France: they fitted wonderfully into French civilization without ever becoming part of French life; their usual friends were an international set where English-speaking people with a mixture of South Americans dominated and where French people did not figure much.

In this year I took a job which was to amuse very much my friend Clarence Day. I walked into the office of the editor of a daily called *Women's Wear* which dealt with every form of women's dress and undress and had a large circulation, and after a few minutes' conversation with the editor got this particular job. It included translating into English articles of their Paris correspondents, doing odds and ends of editing, and interviewing dress manufacturers, modistes, couturiers; it included also the not unpleasant chore of having tea now and again at a fashionable hotel or restaurant and writing notes on attire worn by the female sex, old and young. In my case it also included an occasional report on the French plays then being produced in New York.

Of the French couturiers I remember one in particular, Paul Poiret, because of a diverting interview with him. Having looked me all over in a very *de haut en bas* manner, he approved of my pleated gray silk dress and jade green beads as being exactly right for my hair. Contrary to Clarence Day's opinion I could be a clever judge of clothes when I put my mind on it as now I did steadily in this job. And Poiret, in addition, complimented me on my shape: for a woman I was well shaped, he said, with a *joli corps*. Notoriously, Poiret had a poor opinion of women's figures; he was always giving out that they had to be improved with artificial contraptions—corsets, pads, elastic, and so on. "Women have to be shaped," was his obiter dictum. He had been so accustomed to giving women advice on their clothes that the apparition of any woman in his presence aroused his instructive instincts.

Then, as I was going away, he informed me that although my dress was a charming get-up for the hour of the apéritif, he would recommend a black dress with a white guimpe as a more suitable office attire for an employé of a journal. When, sometime afterwards, another employé of the fashion department interviewed him about a project a manufacturer had for getting him to design dresses for the business girl, he examined the interviewer haughtily, advised her to go home, take off all her rouge, and wash her face, for, as he told her, no *femme chic* ever rouged in the daytime or adorned her face with anything except a little powder. She returned to the office in tears. Poiret did, I think, travel through America and did make designs for the business girl, but I doubt if they or any other of his ideas were adopted. The American business girl will wear what she pleases and look all the better for it.

With another French couturier I had an equally diverting interview: I forget his name now, but I seem to remember that he was killed towards the end of the last war. He was a chic young man, Vicomte something or another, and he talked about fashions and dressmaking in almost exactly the same terms I was used to hearing literature spoken of. Such and such a couturier or couturière would have great fame in his or her own time, but their creations would not have enough personality or imagination to be mentioned in the literature of the time as Worth or Redfern had been; they would never appeal to *gens de lettres*. Women dressmakers, he believed, would eventually cut out the men. I had some difficulty in persuading my colleagues to let an article the vicomte wrote go in "as was," in his irregular but imaginative English. "What will the Russian-Jewish manufacturers make of such language?" one of the editors asked me dubiously, for *Women's Wear* was a daily paper read, among others, by dress manufacturers large and small whose native language was not English. Right enough, some of them telephoned later exasperatedly demanding the meaning of such phraseology as "Madame will wear for the footing," "Madame will wear for the flirting," "Madame will wear for the rendezvous," for the vicomte had written about the clothes day in the life of a *femme du monde* or demi-monde who lived for clothes and amusement and men, a rather Proust-like female indeed, and the article was much more suitable for a paper like the present-day *New Yorker* than a staid trade publication.

As part of my duties I occasionally reported the French theater though the paper was fully furnished with a dramatic critic, Kelcey Allen, still to the fore and now a member of the Critics' Circle, but French drama was not exactly his line. The French company then prominent in New York was the troupe of the Vieux Colombier from Paris with their director, Jacques Copeau, who had been brought over by Otto Kahn and housed in the theater which after the last war became the first home of the Theatre Guild. The theater and its leading actress became the rage of fashionable New York, and Copeau himself cut quite a figure among the intellectuals, especially the young men who were then running the *Seven Arts* magazine. As for myself, I did not especially care for the performances—they were too careful with the details, too studied and deliberate, and when they played the French classics the atmosphere was far too academic; they had none of the dash and ease of the performances of the Comédie Française which I had known in my student days, with Coquelin's vital playing apparently so unstudied that it seemed to be life itself and one forgot that he was a man in a play.

On Sundays when the regular plays were not on there were sometimes other performers, Yvette Guilbert among them. The account that I wrote of her was unsigned, but a friend of mine and of hers sent it to her and brought me to see her. Later I interviewed her on clothes, as every visiting Frenchwoman was supposed to have something to say about clothes. Yvette delivered me a lecture on American waste and extravagance; the subject was fresh in her mind because she had been in Thirty-fourth Street the day before when a young office girl, carrying a tray from a restaurant, with a meal—for her boss maybe—slipped on the pavement and fell; it was a windy day, and her skirts blew up. "What," asked Madame Guilbert indignantly, "was revealed? Silk petticoats, silk pantaloons, silk stockings, silk garters—such extravagance for a girl of the people earning her living! . . . Then the waste of food! You have all too much of everything! And what good does this extravagant food do you? . . . A good onion soup now—more healthful—but none of you know the use of onions or of cheese!"

Yvette herself was a vigorous daughter of the people, who had started her career, it was reported, in cheap cafés, and she must have experienced hard and dangerous times, but she never lost her good sense; she was a solid woman of the people on one side and on another a great artist.

"You want my views on clothes? I consider them only for my art. For my daily clothes I wear what is useful." And she gazed snappily at the pleated gray silk and the green beads which Paul Poiret had approved of and which I now wore steadily when calling on anyone of importance.

She was pleased, however, with what I had written about her performance, and especially about my description of the use she had made of ecclesiastical colors in one of her medieval pieces (purples and black and virgin blue).

"Why all this babble about clothes?" she asked me.

"But, madame, I earn my living by writing about clothes."

"And I earn my living by art, not by clothes," she said. "Come now, I will talk to you about my art." And she did.

It was a peculiarly French art or peculiarly Parisian art, and one could until this war hear a travesty of it or a poor relation of it in the smaller cafés in the avenues that branch off the Etoile.

These interviews were the high lights of the job: for the rest, the work was dull and tiring, employing but few of the mental faculties. The articles of the French correspondents that I translated were dreary and rambling in the extreme; the fashion articles from various resorts in the United States—in the winter from Florida and California about the costumes of the idle rich—were mostly written by semiliterate women. They were paid by the word, and if I cut out their verbiage too extensively they wrote letters of complaint to the head editor or the proprietor of the paper.

Among other jobs I rewrote advertisements that appeared in the newspapers into snappy little news paragraphs which read like this: "Saks are having for the next five days a sale of women's suits, such and such a price." This chore was the dreariest of all; in fact I think it lowered my mental capacity temporarily. Very few of my colleagues were people of education or culture, but their kindliness and consideration perpetually surprised me. Though many of them had foreign-born parents, I was to them a foreigner —the only one, I think, except an Austrian, a man, who wrote about laces and sometimes about women's lingerie, for, inside and out, women's clothing here was taken with real seriousness.

The employés had a resourcefulness and initiative unknown to me: when they considered they had done anything well they asked for a raise; when they thought they had any ideas they put themselves forward before the heads of the place; there was a lot of competition among them with odd frictions. My training had led me to believe that nobody should put himself or herself forward or try to get the better of anybody, but some in the office were hampered by no such inhibitions; in fact they prided themselves on the smartness with which they could step over the heads of others. For all I know, this may be true of commercial offices all over the world; but, as I had never been in an office before, it was novel to me. Still, with all its dreariness I liked the office and I liked my fellow workers: no one could be kinder than the editor in chief or the proprietor. One of my colleagues was always giving me counsel; he would say, "You don't have to do this kind of work; you are so smart you could be a buyer." A buyer! That was the ambition of quite a few in the office: in their minds being a buyer stood for real success. For a while indeed I played with the idea as well as with the suggestion of the editor in chief that I might become their Paris correspondent after the war. If this had eventuated, my lot might have been fairly pleasant and one that might have given me plenty of spare time. But the daily work was beginning to play havoc with my then delicate health, and having fainted one cold snowy day in the office of a rude shoe manufacturer I was trying to interview on shoe fashions, I ended up in St. Vincent's Hospital. When I recovered, though the kind editor kept my job for me, I did not go back to *Women's Wear*.

II

I took another job, this time as tutor to two boys, Hugh and Peter Paine, for only three hours a day, and this paid me as well as, if not better than, the eight hours in an office and was something I knew how to do well, and so I liked it much better. But I was always so tired that sometimes to get up in the morning and go out was impossible without a glass of port.

We were in considerable demand at parties, and as I was young I loved dressing up in the evenings and going out. Though there were more fashionable parties in New York than theirs, the most entertaining were those given by the Samuel Untermeyers, who had a large house off Fifth Avenue and a larger country house, Greystone, with wonderful gardens within easy reach of New York. The Untermeyers had every quality that made for attractive hosts: they had no prejudices that anybody could feel, but they were committed to distinction of every kind. Mrs. Untermeyer was a South German of the type Hitler would have called a true Aryan, and she sympathized with every art and every form of artistry. In my journey through life I have found the most delightful and understanding hosts to be those of whom one partner was Jewish and the other non-Jewish, for they seemed to complement each other. Mrs. Untermeyer admired her entourage so much that her friend J. B. Yeats said of her, "She loves us all; all her geese are swans." The Untermeyers' hospitality and artistry were an outstanding part of the New York of that period, and in their house everything moved in an atmosphere of spontaneity and happiness. Unearned distinction of any kind—maybe, especially, unearned in-

tellectual distinction—irks me, but one felt that Samuel Untermeyer had really earned his wealth and his distinction. He was
a remarkable-looking man; his handsome face full of intellect,
proud and strange, the face of a man of a very old race with the
sense of responsibility to others that is said to be the mark of an
aristocracy, but which so often is absent from them. I recall his
daughter Irene once saying to me, "I am grateful for one thing that
I got from my father—not money, but a mind I can use." But
minds don't so often make people happy, though they do advance
humanity a little bit.

I remember so many world-famous people coming to the Untermeyers' house then and later—Richard Strauss playing indifferently an accompaniment on the piano for a singer; Einstein, when
he was still a fabulous person, smoking an empty pipe on the
terrace at Greystone because he had had no tobacco during the
war and had become absent-mindedly accustomed to drawing on
a tobaccoless pipe; I remember European statesmen and lawyers
and authors and composers, with a dash of the British peerage
now and again. Oddly enough I do not remember any painters,
though Mrs. Untermeyer as a young married woman had bought
that nocturne of Whistler's which had later caused the famous
lawsuit between him and Ruskin. Having, at that time, considerable fluency in babbling German on account of my not being so
long out of college, and as during the last war German became a
war casualty and few people, even born Germans, would claim to
know the language, I found myself at a dinner party once beside
Einstein and a couple of times beside Richard Strauss. As I had
never heard Einstein's name until my hostess, Mrs. Untermeyer,
mentioned it in the invitation, I was puzzled for topics of conversation, and proceeded to ask him pleasantly what he had invented.
He countered, "Do you know enough mathematics to understand
if I told you?" As I had retained in my memory some notions of
the binomial theorem, a little trigonometry, with a smattering of
physics, and had so informed my hostess, she warmly declared to
Einstein that I could, and we both pressed him to explain his invention, or theory, or whatever it was. He did actually tell us
something about it, and we understood the *unds*, the *seins*, the
habens and a few nouns—there weren't many adjectives in Ein-

stein's discourse—and as he went on he threw back his head and laughed, and said *"Meine schönen damen! . . . Ach, meine schönen damen!"* However, on my next visit to Dublin, when Yeats started talking about the theory of relativity, which he thought was in some way related to his book, *A Vision,* I put a brake on his eloquence by telling him that Einstein had explained it all to me at a dinner party.

Richard Strauss, who was very Teutonic-looking, was unexpectedly witty—as witty as his opera, *Tyl Eulenspiegel;* but his front appearance was not so impressive as was his back. He wore expensive and elegantly fitting clothes, and his back—the expressive conductor's back which a concert audience always has in view—was really imposing. At dinner he would turn the place plate upside down—it was to see what was the mark on the back, for he, it turned out, was a china collector. When the salad was passed, a typical American salad of lettuce and fruit, he asked loudly in German, "How can people eat such stuff?" When someone across the table asked from what country I came, Strauss answered for me, "From the country of Isolde."

III

In those years New York was intellectually very lively; the literary meeting place was the Poetry Society of America, then not long founded and coming into being as the result of the new literary movement, and its meetings were not only diverting poetically but in every other way. The membership was not limited to poets, but included poetry lovers also—that is, the society was for poetry and its readers—and the meetings were enlivened by debates and squabbles not always relevant to literature. At the very first meeting we attended we heard Robert Frost's poems read by the then president, Edward Wheeler. Robert, who later became a great friend of ours, was not present, as he was still in England, where he had been living for a number of years and where his two books, *A Boy's Will* and *North of Boston,* had been published. However, in 1914 and 1915 he was still but slightly known in America. Rumors about his poetry had reached us in Dublin, chiefly because of Edward Thomas's reviews. At the time Thomas was about the most distinguished poetry reviewer in England, and it was with excerpts from him that Edward Wheeler now prefaced his reading, his rather dull reading, of poems from *North of Boston*. What struck me then was the emphasis that Wheeler laid on English approval of Frost; he quoted no American critic at all and didn't seem to think American approval counted. I think that the beginning of the twentieth century and the end of the nineteenth were intellectually America's most colonial periods. On the eastern seaboard one could meet people who hardly ever read an American book; in fact I myself was more familiar with American literature than many of my American friends. In those days, certainly, praise from London was the badge American authors sought. When they could afford it, they took the boat over and called on London editors, publishers, reviewers, and authors. Between the period of Emerson, Poe, Whitman, and the second decade of the twentieth century there had been little poetry that was not an imitation of the well-known English poets; in fact the American poetry that reached Europe for a long time was without any particular character, as a lot of Irish poetry before Yeats was. It seemed as if both American and Irish writers were, for the most part, not conscious enough, not critical enough, at the end of the nineteenth century, to know that they were imitation English. I remember I was once given for review by a London paper some books of American verse which included a heavy volume of Henry Van Dyke's. It was very long-winded and hard to keep one's mind on, and I was at a loss as to what to say about it. I communicated my difficulties to one of my poet friends, and he suggested that I take a bold attitude towards it, ask the neighboring grocer to weigh it, giving, along with the avoirdupois, a smashing account of its emotional, imaginative, and artistic weightlessness and meagerness. But as it was considered the thing to be friendly and even fulsome to America in print, and as Americans were supposed to be easily offended by any criticism, the editor very properly demurred at publishing my youthfully condescending review. Henry Van Dyke's, however, was a fair specimen of the sort of American poetry that reached us on the other side of the Atlantic in my young days. Our elders like Professor Dowden and John Butler Yeats had had Whitman and were valiant fighters for him; in my own childhood we had wonderful Californian magazines that published verse which still sticks in my memory. Does anyone now remember the *Californian* and the *Cosmopolitan?*—not in the least like the *Cosmopolitan* of our time. Dozens of back numbers were piled up in our house, sent over by a relative in San Francisco who had some connection with one of them. But at the Poetry Society the poetry we heard was now definitely American—so American that I was a little surprised at the enthusiasm for Frost evidenced in the English reviews; for in spite of its touch of Wordsworth, both content and rhythm were non-English, non-European; even single lines gave an insight into shapes of life that were distinct from Europe's. In such a line as, "Something there is that does not love a wall," Frost was revealing a state of things that was characteristic of America: walls in old countries somehow kept together and lasted, walls of all kinds indeed were one of the central facts of old countries. In America a wall of no matter what shape, physical, psychological, social, was a temporary affair and was meant to crumble away after a while. Frost's poetry did not make an appeal to all the audience on that first evening; some were unprepared for poetry of this kind with its pure speech rhythm, and a couple of them could be heard asking each other if it was poetry at all. The rhythms of Longfellow, Tennyson, Wordsworth at his dullest, the German rhythms of Emerson dominated their minds.

The favorite, the most widely known poet at this time in the United States, was Vachel—or as he then signed himself, Nicholas Vachel—Lindsay. He had a most memorable way of reciting his poetry, a real personal style, and I shall never forget his first delivery of "The Chinese Nightingale" or "The Santa Fe Trail." It had a magical effect on us all. I never could see a Chinese laundry afterwards without thinking of Lindsay's nightingale—that is, if I looked at it only from the outside—or a big engine or an automobile without thinking of the Santa Fe Trail. Lindsay had done what poets had done everywhere since the beginning, made glamorous the lands they wrote in, and countries are never interesting until they have an art and a literature that do this. The other poets, E. A. Robinson and Robert Frost, had made the New England scene interesting. Some of Frost's poems, such as "Home Burial" and "The Death of the Hired Man," were short stories in verse; a great deal of Robinson's best were also stories or, as in "Flamonde" or "Miniver Cheevey," character studies. So, indeed, is Masters's *Spoon River Anthology*. Character studies, interpretations of human actions, figure a great deal in American verse, whereas the pure lyric seldom does.

Occasionally at the Poetry Society's evenings Amy Lowell presented herself like a whirlwind and harangued the audience, sometimes angrily, sometimes with an insinuating amiability. She was a combination of an aristocrat and a salesman—frank, fearless, noisy, aggressive, sure of herself in private life, but unsure of herself intellectually or in literature, and this though she wrote some fine poetry and cannot be left out of future histories of American literature. She had a handsome face but a rather misshapen body, caused perhaps by some thyroid trouble; she had immense nervous energy even though she was physically somewhat incapacitated through illnesses and surgical operations. But she fought with fury for poetry, for her own and everybody else's. I have heard Percy MacKaye and others say that until Amy stumped the country in a campaign for poetry, few Americans knew what it was or what its value to a country was supposed to be. Amy Lowell was attached to a movement called Imagism which, I think, she partly brought into being; it was really more of an English than an American movement, for the chief stars were D. H. Lawrence, Richard Aldington, H. D. and Ezra Pound—the last two, though American, had shaken the dust of America off their feet. Like a lot of such movements it was little more than the transportation of a French movement into English, for it took over most of the ideas that Theophile Gautier and the Parnassians had propounded more than half a century before.

The Imagists brought out occasional anthologies with pompous introductions, and for a year or two they were the excitement of literary New York and London. The best of the group, I think, was H.D. Just before we came to America, Amy had sojourned in London, and we used to get startled letters from some of our London friends about her—about her parties, her dictatorialness, her odd appearance, her cigar smoking, her assurances that in lineage and intellectuality she was every bit as good as anybody in England. The condescension of some English towards Americans that had previously annoyed another Lowell infuriated her. For a while we saw a great deal of her, and she would frequently unburthen herself on the subject of English snootiness and tell us how glad she was to lecture on Keats at Oxford just to show them over there that Americans knew something. Later her book on Keats received a bad press in England: Middleton Murry, who had himself written a book on Keats, reviewed it in a way that particularly exacerbated her and gave her another grievance against the English. However, apart from the fact that women writing books about great poets are often mauled by men who write the same kind of books, actually Amy's, in spite of her flashes of understanding, had the amateurishness of one who came late in life to scholarship and meditation. The easy familiarity with literature and ideas that comes from long and steady association with them was not always hers. Her *Keats* as well as her *Seven French Poets* and her studies of American poets were long-winded in a way that people sometimes are when talking about something that is not quite part of them. She regretted herself that she had just received the education of a young lady of fashion instead of the college or university education the male Lowells were given. Still a university training, although it might have given her an easier familiarity with matters connected with literature, would not have equipped her for writing books exemplifying ideas: essentially she had not a critical mind, nor was she by nature scholarly as Elinor Wylie was. She may have shortened her life writing books of the kind, for, to have the necessary tranquillity for work that put so much strain on her, she sat up all night writing and slept during the day, getting up in time for dinner, at which meal she saw her friends.

A much more widely known woman writer than Amy Lowell used to appear at the Poetry Society in those days. This was Ella Wheeler Wilcox. Her *Poems of Passion* was read all over the English-speaking world, and she had the appeal in verse that the author of *Uncle Tom's Cabin* or *East Lynne* had in the novel. She wrote the sort of verse that was meant to comfort and console —utilitarian verse, as I have called it elsewhere—with a simple emotional or moral appeal, though it sometimes made a demand on the intellect, too, for she was far from being a contemptible writer in spite of all the mockery of her that was current, and, though not a poet, a few times she very nearly achieved a poem. She wrote a lot better than many women then and now whose work is treated more respectfully. Queen Victoria, who had received her at court, was said to be a great admirer of hers, and there was a photo of Ella that used to be published in her court-presentation dress with the three feathers in her hair. However, sophisticated poetry reviewers treated her work as a joke, and Edward Thomas, who had greeted Robert Frost's work so enthusiastically, wrote a fearsomely satirical review of her, saying that, as she had now reached such a wide audience, as wide as Keats's or Shelley's, she ought to be known by her last name, plain Wilcox, and her books called The Poems of Wilcox. It was said that her incensed husband, supposed to have been the inspirer of *Poems of Passion*, challenged Edward Thomas to a duel. I have always thought she was a little overattacked, for actually, like many popular writers, she was an interesting and kindhearted woman, intelligent if intellectually unsophisticated, not unlike the majority of men and women turned out by colleges and universites. As for myself, I have never understood this nonsense about art appealing to the people in general: the people have no leisure to learn much about it, and if they like their art and science to be utilitarian, if in science they prefer gadgets like toasters and washing machines to the Theory of Relativity, and if in poetry they prefer "I Dreamt I Dwelt in Marble Halls" to "Kublai Khan," it is because of some needs and desires that civilization has not supplied in any other way. There is no point in attacking popular utilitarian verse with high-powered criticism unless it is by poets who could have gone beyond it like Longfellow in "Lives of great men all remind us," or Kipling in "If," or Burns in "A man's a man for a' that," and then with some explanations.

It has to be recognized that rhyme in itself has always consoled people, especially when there are attached to it some little musings on the commonplace happenings of life, musings which do not make too much demand on the mind of the reader. This made the appeal of Ella's verse, and a real feeling for people came through her lines; if she had no distinguished emotions she at least had warm ones. She had an engaging love for small children, and she could sometimes be seen in Central Park—Clarence Day once pointed her out to me there—scribbling in a notebook and at intervals gazing delightedly at bald, bullet-headed babies, or shaking hands with toddlers engaged in digging up the park with tablespoons. The last time I saw her she looked like a pleasant schoolmistress, though I imagine she thought of herself as a great poet, as did all the other lady versifiers of the period, including Harriet Monroe, who thought of herself as one of the first six American poets of her time. Ella might have asked herself why else Queen Victoria should have received her at the Court of St. James's. And such reflection would have settled everything, for the opinions of queens, kings, czars, emperors had a sort of divine sanction for many people in the world.

ৡ CHAPTER 23

Poets and Their Conflicts

As it became evident that our stay in America was not going to be just a honeymoon visit but might last a long time, I settled down to take stock of our surroundings and of the people in our milieu. I have changed many of my first impressions, naturally enough, but a few have remained unchanged, and one especially—of the amazing kindness of Americans, the amazing kindness of most of the people we knew. The kindness of Americans when on a large scale towards other peoples has been consistently abused and their philanthropy satirized, but it is a magnificent thing, a trusting of men in the mass that the older countries do not know and maybe will never know. On the other hand, in old civilizations people, I think, have stronger personal emotions; their emotions towards individuals seem to be far intenser and more lasting than in America. The emotional conditioning is different, but this I slowly realized only after living in America for a decade.

As well as taking stock of my new milieu I began to look backward and take stock of the sort of life I had lived and the people

I had known. It was to an old, narrow, long-settled world I looked back, a world of passionate nationalisms, impassioned intellectualities, and intense private feelings—the two latter, as a matter of fact, I think generally go together. I had known nobody engaged in large business of any kind; I had not, to my knowledge, ever encountered a banker, a stockbroker, or a manufacturer until I came to America. A large proportion of the people I had known were what are called professional people, belonging to what is described in old countries as the learned professions. I had also known small traders, farmers, horse breeders, farm-stock breeders of every kind; I had known wealthy people, but they had not made their wealth; they had inherited it. Now I was to know individuals who had made large fortunes in a generation, and people whose fathers, from being poor, had become millionaires in romantic ventures like gold mining, drilling oil wells, making railroads.

If social differences were rarely emphasized in American conversation, yet there were strong distinctions made between educated and uneducated people, and some I knew had fallen into the way of using terms common in a class-stratified society such as "well-bred," "wellborn," "lady," "gentleman," and even the expression "blue-blooded" was not uncommon. But such nomenclature seemed to be used exclusively to define the descendants of the early settlers, so that I came to understand why I heard so much about the *Mayflower*. Precedence of arrival in America, if it was attached to a recognizable amount of wealth and education, denoted a sort of aristocracy. Frequently I heard words that had been debased in meaning in England and Ireland, or else were old-fashioned—words like "genteel," "refined," "urbane," "gracious," and I encountered these expressions in the writing of the girl reporters in *Women's Wear*. A hat was described as "refined," a woman's appearance as "genteel," a French dressmaker as "not urbane."

I began to see that the whole idea of education was on a different plane from that of Europe. In America it was pragmatic, a preparation for active living, whereas the education I had been subjected to was very far from pragmatic. For the people who educated me, education was "to know"; for Americans, education was "to do." My education was the European humanistic training, an education of the intellect, imagination, and emotions, whereas in this new country education appeared to be largely a training of the practical intelligence and the will to achieve. I was greatly impressed by the inventive and organizing ability of the young people around me and at the number of things they could carry out. Almost any American woman could do a lot more things than I could, but yet I flattered myself that I could do some few better than she could do any single one. I discovered that the European immigrants who adapted themselves most easily to American ways and who materially advanced themselves were those who had escaped the classical and humanistic education with its emphasis on art, literature, and tradition. I was surprised at the innocence of foreign languages even in college graduates; there was often an assumption that familiarity with a language other than English marked a recent immigrant, a greenhorn; generally the second generation prided themselves on not knowing the language of their forefathers.

There was quite a different attitude towards money from that I had been accustomed to. Here everybody, or nearly everybody, I knew wanted to make money and as quickly as possible. One of the main reasons nobody I knew in Dublin was out to make money was that it was almost impossible to make it. But in America it was possible for practically anybody who had any equipment and put his mind on the business. Even artists and writers, a class notoriously indifferent to money-making in old countries, nearly all wanted to make it here. They were anxious to strike on a vein that could bring them money, and lots of it—that is, all except a few poets like Robinson, Torrence, and Lindsay. The trade of writing was extensively practiced in terms of markets just like any other industry—like the coat-and-suit business or the dress-manufacturing business. Writing in my native land was still looked on as an art and did not come much under the money sign; anyhow, but little income could be made by writing in Ireland.

The writers we gravitated towards or who gravitated towards us were those who regarded writing as an art and who took no interest in the fabulously paid magazine writers of the period. There were some quite young and inexperienced people who knew well— and God knows how they came to know it—the difference between the art of literature and the trade of writing. One of these was a raw western boy first sent to us by Harriet Moody—a gangling, semiliterate youth of about seventeen, he seemed. In the first few minutes after entering our apartment he pulled some verses out of his pocket and began to read them in a dull voice and in an embarrassed way. His name was then Harold Crane, but later, when he became a craze of the intelligentsia, he changed it to Hart Crane. How a boy brought up in totally unliterary surroundings could have real artistic talent might be comprehensible enough, but that such a one could have a subtle sense of the art of poetry and be so determined to become a poet, to be willing to sacrifice so much and with such little encouragement to write poetry, was very surprising.

Later, of course, he got a great deal of encouragement, but at the time I speak of the obstacles in his way were hard to face. His father was a manufacturer who produced a delicacy called Crane's Chocolates, and this had brought him in touch with Mrs. Moody as a businesswoman. The young son was thrilled, first to hear of, and then to meet, the widow of a well-known poet, and she on her side was greatly intrigued by the boy's determination to write poetry. But apparently nothing could be more staggering to the manufacturing father than to have a son announce that he was going to be a poet and had no intention of entering the business; in fact, I think, instead he asked for an allowance to enable him to settle down to writing. The account of the interview with his father on this matter, Harold gave us with puzzled emotion. To his mind, fed on literature, being a poet was a distinction to any family. To his father, poetry writing was a sissy game, and he lectured the boy in contemptuous words. "Do you see that girl out there?"—pointing through the glass partition to a secretary in an outside office. "She has more real manliness and independence than you have." I remember Harold pronounced the word with a long western a, so that it sounded "mainliness," and I had to ask him to repeat it before I understood.

He would come round to see us about twice a week and talk about poetry, never getting over his excitement at how much we seemed to know about it. "How do you know all this?" he would ask gravely as he helped me with household chores and to make tea and scones. If he seemed to dislike his father, he was psychologically, though perhaps not emotionally, so involved with his mother that he doubted if he could ever pull himself free of her. Once he made a special trip round late at night to ask about Yeats's friend, Arthur Symons, and he listened to the stories we told him about young Dubliners' interest in Symons's book on symbolism, culminating in a public debate in University College attended by Yeats and all the writers, who listened patiently to a lot of nonsense from some of the students who took it on themselves to make ridiculous Stéphane Mallarmé, Villiers de l'Isle-Adam, and the rest of the symbolists. A sprightly youth on the way to become a "chronic" student, a species common in European university towns, challenged Yeats as to whether he knew that when Gérard de Nerval, who in Rome had led a lobster around with a ribbon, died, a geometrical proof of the Immaculate Conception was found in his pocket. The incident impressed Harold, not with its preposterousness, but with the fact that such an affair could be staged with so much public notice in a city. The comedy which for us was its main feature did not get over to him at all, for he seemed to have no sense of humor. The effect of this story on him was to make him go to the Forty-second Street Library and immerse himself in Symons's book. Afterwards he would put me through my paces regarding some French poet he had learned about. "Have you read Boddelaire or Rimbodd?" he would ask me with his queer pronunciation. "Verlaine?" That anyone could say off by heart a French poem staggered him. But then he was almost equally surprised that anyone could say any poem by heart. Memorizing poetry, it appeared, was not part of American education.

Of course I know that Harold or Hart Crane is now considered by certain literary groups to be one of the great American poets, but in spite of his rich vocabulary, his interesting technique, his strange intellectual lyricism, I could not get, at any time, enthusiastic about his poetry because of his lack of power to give an emotional significance to words or perhaps an emotional significance to his mind or to his life. At this time his verse was being published in small magazines and by Scofield Thayer in his distinguished monthly the *Dial*, which had had its previous incarnation as a Chicago periodical. Scofield had an intense interest in modern art and literature, and the *Dial* had a select audience all over the English-speaking world. Its intellectual distinction, its adventurousness and hospitality, as long as Thayer was able to take an interest in it himself, made it the outstanding American magazine. But there befell him what I have known to befall so many sensitive Americans, a sort of mental and nervous trouble which took him out of life and into a sanitarium. He was a remarkable young man, and my husband and I were very much attached to him. The last time we were with him he told us he was going to Vienna for a while—later we found it was to get himself psycho-analysed by Freud—and beneath the careful self-control we saw that he was distracted and lonely. Loneliness can seize Americans in a way that I have never seen happen in old countries, and there is here far less of that simple joy in life that is or used to be fairly common in Europe even among people in the poorest economic circumstances.

As Hart Crane advanced in his twenties he made new literary friends, and we saw him only at long intervals, and then by accident. Some time before he went to Mexico on a Guggenheim Fellowship I met him in the Brevoort Hotel but did not recognize him until he came up to speak to me. The raw western boy had grown into an interesting-looking man with the head and face of an intellectual, but there was none of that undercurrent of emotional fire in his personality that I have never found lacking in a first-rate artist. With all the admiration that was given him by certain literary cliques, he never really found any assurance about himself or his work. "Do you think I will be remembered?" he would occasionally ask his friends. I have known many writers, both great and small, but never another who for any reason asked that question. He had a habit of turning on the gramophone while composing, and then one day on the boat, returning from Mexico, he turned on the gramophone, pulled a coat over his pajamas, and plunged into the sea—the Caribbean, that he had written of often. I doubt if he got much satisfaction out of his puzzled life.

I, who during my life before I came to America had only known one person who committed suicide, now was to know several. They were nearly all connected in some way with the arts, some of them well known in those days—George Sterling, Donald Evans, Vachel Lindsay, Sara Teasdale—others less well known, many of them women. That strange loneliness that I have spoken of above overwhelmed them. The suicides which gave me greatest grief were those of Gladys and Dorothea Cromwell, twin sisters of great beauty and personality. Gladys wrote poetry, and a couple of her poems are, I am certain, as good as those of any American woman poet. I dislike the word "woman" used before poet, for literary and artistic talent cannot be segregated in sexes, but I use it here because American women poets have more in common with one another than any of them have with men poets; they write a sharp, gemlike lyric which gives a similar character to the work of many of them, so that it is sometimes difficult to guess which one is the author of a particular poem; the high intelligence, the careful language, the undercurrent of suffering and frustration and even of neurosis are similar in a great many of them. Elinor Wylie's, whose work came a few years later, had a resemblance to that of Gladys Cromwell's, and Gladys Cromwell's had a resemblance to Emily Dickinson's, and many contemporary women poets have a resemblance to all of them. This poem of Gladys Cromwell's will show what I mean:

CONFLICT

Divided by the dark,
Our foils converge. A spark
You kindled not, My Enemy,
A spark I never drew
From bitter fires that sear me through and through,
Gleams fitfully.

That spark, that little light,
Is lit where foils unite.
It lives in spite of us, My Foe;
In intervening space,
The little eye that darts from place to place
So clear, I know.

Opinions are not one,
And man's criterion
Is not in us. Between, above,
The cross that weapons frame,
My Adversary, gleams a truth whose name
Might still be Love.

The Cromwell twins had been brought up in a wealthy family, guarded like princesses, knowing but little of the world and somewhat fearful of it. They were born when their parents were middle-aged, long after the previous child, and Gladys, the highly articulate one, once said to us ruefully, "We were an afterthought." Like many American children of wealthy families of the period they were, as they said, dragged around Europe by traveling parents, and they used to tell us of lonely days and weeping nights spent in hotels in Constantinople, Vienna, Venice, and such places. When they made their debut in New York, their beauty and strangeness had made a sensation, their brother told us; they had the high distinction that the daughters of old aristocracies are supposed to have but rarely do have. But the twins had no relish for society, and they informed the members of their family that the people they really wanted to know were writers and artists. Gladys told us hilariously that the family's idea of a writer was Robert Chambers, and he and his wife were invited to luncheon to meet them. Later when she announced that what Robert Chambers produced was not writing at all and that she and her sister were not interested in him or his work, her statement caused angry bewilderment. If Robert Chambers was not a writer, then what was he? Cultivated American families who know a great deal about music or painting often know very little about literature. When Gladys proceeded to publish her first poems and her name began to appear in magazines, the family were alarmed by what they called the "publicity." One of them indeed expressed surprise that she had broken loose to the extent of permitting some poems with her photograph to be published in an anthology. It was hard to explain to her family the difference between budding fame and raw newspaper publicity.

Just after America entered the first World War we spent some time at their house in the White Mountains. They expressed their belief then that it would be their duty to go to Europe as war workers, since no male member of the family was acceptable for military service. I was from the beginning discouraging about their going, knowing how unprepared they were to face what they would have to experience as nurses and canteen workers. They were rather nervous of men and had no notion at all of what war conditions or soldiers were like; they had lived such a sheltered life that they had never been in the subway or a public conveyance of any kind until just before they left for France. When they came to bid us good-by they told us with excited interest that they had come on the subway, having got rid of their car. Gladys lent me her typewriter and some of her French books to keep until she returned. But we were never to see the Cromwell twins again. From the crowded boat on which they were returning, they jumped into the ocean. They were then about thirty, beautiful, talented, wealthy, and it must be that they saw no life before them, and that what they had seen of war was too troubling.

ౘ CHAPTER 24

A French Writer in America

IN THOSE DAYS the one among us newcomers from Europe who had the richest and most varied background, the most complex personality, and the warmest temperament, was a French writer, Jules Bois. In the nineties and in the first decade of the twentieth century he had been, not only a well-known dramatist and novelist, but a semipublic figure, a personage, as he would say himself, in French public life, one whom the government sent on missions to foreign countries or as an emissary to state functions, almost a cabinet minister, as he told us. He had been sent to French Africa, to Syria, to India, Greece, Turkey, and Egypt—why, anybody who knew Jules Bois well might have wondered, for he seemed incapable of learning anything about any country except France. Of some state function in India when Curzon was viceroy—perhaps it was the Durbar —what he best remembered was his riding a caparisoned elephant in a state procession and how, from this eminence, he could look into people's houses and see the domestic life of simple India— women nursing babies in crowded rooms, preparing meals, or dressing. He had been the honored guest of maharajahs, had visited Hindoo monasteries, had studied Indian religions and customs with remarkable superficiality. He had beheld the Himalayas, and he imagined the sight had made a great impression on him.

At the period of the first World War he was sent, first to Spain and then to America, on some sort of propaganda mission. But the French are very poor in the propaganda line, and Jules Bois was no exception. He almost immediately got into difficulties through associating with compatriots who, before America entered the war, were intriguing for an early peace with Germany. Among these was a colorful gentleman named Bolo Pasha, who later was executed in France for his activities in this line, although there appear to have been other Frenchmen in the intrigue who lived to intrigue another day. Jules Bois himself never directly mentioned these matters to us, but we had learned from the newspapers that he had received money from Bolo to further the French propaganda. The money could not have been a great deal; it was said to have been to pay for hire of halls, but his taking it put him under a cloud with some of his countrymen though not with others, certainly not with Paul Claudel, who, when ambassador to Washington, gave him a decoration for his services to France, for of course he was a fervidly patriotic Frenchman. But he never got it into his mind that a Frenchman was called upon to be a partisan for France's allies in the war. He really did not know much about them; he had no interest whatever in the Anglo-Saxon brand of democracy or in Anglo-Saxon institutions; *liberté, fraternité, égalité* transcended such simple-minded notions of freedom as had evolved in England or were invented in America. France, French literature, the Catholic tradition were the only things that really mattered, France always first and the others a little lower down. There was something about Jules Bois that reminded one of every figure in French literature or history—he was Bouvard and Pecuchet, he was M. Jourdain of *Le Bourgeois Gentilhomme*, he was Harpagon in *L'Avare*, he was quite a bit of Tartuffe, but he was also Balzac's saintly curé, and one of those historical French cardinals with a touch of the Chevalier Bayard and the saintly King Louis.

On his lecture folders he described himself as *délégué de l'idée française à l'étranger*—how Molierian the title! And from time to time, if not continuously, he received a small stipend from the French embassy. He worked hard for France and *l'idée française*, lecturing everywhere he could get a hearing and writing in obscure French-American papers. But that there might be any other ideas in the world he either ignored or was completely innocent of. It was hard to know how people followed his lectures, because his English was fantastic and always remained so. He had learned it from a study of the English classics—Chaucer and Spenser and Shakespeare—and while his vocabulary was copious, it was peculiar, as was likewise his English construction. He couldn't always recall nouns or the names of things, and so he frequently substituted a paraphrase. When talking about Pascal, for example, he informed his hearers that he had "invented the little chariot propelled by the hands of man"—the wheelbarrow. Apples became "what brought perdition to Eva." He would use such words as "pejorative" and "apodictic" as if they were so customary that they could be brought out at any old time.

But the fantasy of his vocabulary did not prevent the exercise of his wit—a Voltairian wit. I remember his speaking of Pope Leo XIII, who had received him in private audience and whom he venerated, as "a great aristocrat, a great diplomat, a great scholar, a great poet, and . . . they say . . . he died converted." He could assume a very grand air, as became a celebrity who had had his plays produced in the French national theaters, acted by Bernhardt, and who had been decorated by various potentates, who had figured in the salons of duchesses, had his books censored by the Index Expurgatorius, and had fought a notable duel. Eleonora Duse was his great admiration; he was her devoted friend, but the woman he had been most in love with was the singer, Emma Calvé. Until his death he carried with him everywhere her photograph and that of his father, both placed inside a copy of the *Imitation of Christ* which he always had with him. He gave us accounts of other affairs of the heart or of the senses that had engaged him, some of which I suspect took place only in his own mind, to quote my childhood friend, Bartley, concerning his own love affair. But that Jules Bois had once been gloriously and magically in love as perhaps only a Frenchman can be was evident from the exuding warmth of his personality and from his belief in and attachment to women, especially to women of genius. When he talked of Duse or Bernhardt or Calvé he made one realize their genius, their sensibility, their deep communication with life. An emotional upset, a quarrel with a lover, could paralyze them, unfit them for all work, make them ill for days, or even, in Duse's case, for years. "Life is more difficult for women of genius than for men," he often said. "My dear, dear friends! How I have loved them!" He never tired talking of Paris, of his friends, of his past—such a rich past that one marveled how he could spend the last of his life so indigently in New York West Side rooming houses, generally up four flights of stairs, in a room littered with papers, clothes, shoes, pictures with their faces to the wall, and encompassed with books, the closet containing a gas burner, a few pieces of cracked crockery, and an old saucepan or two in which he occasionally cooked something. However, he always had at hand a good supply of red wine and a bottle of fine cognac.

From the time of the first World War, except for one return visit to France, he lived the remainder of his life in America, a genuinely displaced person. On this visit he did not seem to have renewed many of the friendships of his early manhood—perhaps it was impossible, so many of those he had known were dead. And whom had he not known in French public life—statesmen and generals, Briand, Poincaré, Pétain, Foch—but especially he knew the men of letters; he had worked with the great Provencal poet, Mistral; as a young man he had been secretary to Catulle Mendès; he had been intimate with Villiers de l'Isle-Adam and Verlaine; he had known that strange South American Frenchman, Jules Laforgue, whose influence on all modern poetry, French and English, has been so amazing—notably so in the case of T. S. Eliot, and in the work of all those younger poets we call modern. Jules Bois appears to have known him during that period when Laforgue was reader to the Empress Augusta in Berlin, where he caught tuberculosis. With his head thrown back in laughter he would gaily chant lines of Laforgue:

Oh, les pianos, les pianos dans les quartiers aises!

and then with a sudden change of humor:

Les cors, les cors, les cors . . . mélancoliques!

Changeant de ton et de musique,
Ton ton, ton taine, ton ton!
Les cors, les cors, les cors!
S'en sont allés au vent du nord.

And with a mixture of gaiety, melancholy, and memories that La-forgue's poems always aroused in him, he would say, "But after all, my friend Jules Laforgue died in Paris. It would be sad not to die in Paris! Think of dying here and being buried in Brooklyn!" I recall what another displaced person said to Henry James: *"Mourir à Londres, c'est être bien mort!"* For Jules Bois, to die in New York was *"être bien mort."* "What about being buried in Woodlawn?" I would ask facetiously. "For me, Père Lachaise," he would say. And as I thought of the French cult of the dead and the little edifices built for them and the ribbons and flowers attached to the grilles on All Souls' Day, I would say, "I think I prefer Montparnasse where there's Baudelaire and Sainte-Beuve for company—that's my favored cemetery." But in spite of his admiration for Laforgue, he had but little interest in other French modernists and would relate with satisfaction how, as a member of a jury, he had passed over the first volume of Proust and given the award to Marcel Schwob, who, with Paul Bourget, remained his great admiration among the novelists. It was hard to know how he got to be on any literary jury, for intellectual integrity was not a noticeable part of his character.

He had known well that Flemish Frenchman, Huysmans, and most of the symbolists; he knew Mallarmé, but he remained unconverted to his ideas, explaining Mallarmé's use of language as the result of a fall which injured his head, causing him to forget French rhythms and take up English rhythms. When I asked him if he had known George Moore in Paris, he said simply, "Yes, through his mistress; we had the same mistress." Some time in the nineties his interest in magic and esoteric studies generally had been both extensive and intensive. He belonged to the group who studied the works of that curious Frenchman who built up a strange reputation for himself under the name of Eliphas Levi and wrote books on Transcendental Magic. This brought Jules Bois in touch with the initiates of MacGregor Matthews's Order of the Golden Dawn, among whom were Yeats and Maud Gonne. Then he became involved in psychic research and was made president of the Society for Psychical Research in Paris. He made a study of those underground religions which flourished in Paris of which the devotees are like members of strange religious orders, sometimes making a stately ceremony out of their vices and their counterreligious rituals like the Black Mass. His book *Little Religions of Paris* brought down on Jules Bois the censure of the Church.

Maybe it was through his association with Maud Gonne and Yeats that he got his interest in Ireland. He had a notion of it such as I have encountered sometimes among French people—that it was a land of mysterious Celts who had in the past been magicians and some of whom yet could exercise magical powers. Maud Gonne and Yeats emphasized this aspect in his mind. But, too, he was fascinated by Maud Gonne's beauty and her fame and her enigmatic relation to French politics. She had founded in France the Society of Saint Patrice, composed of French people of Irish ancestry, the descendants of the Wild Geese or the soldiers of Napoleon. It was through his Irish friendships that we came to know him in America, meeting him first at the house of John Quinn.

At this time, the period of the first World War, Jules Bois had ceased to write books, or, as far as I know, anything except articles on France, the saints, and derivative poems in the Lamartine tradition. In spite of his great endowments he never gave me the impression of being a man of much intellectual power; writing gifts he certainly had, and the sound French literary culture, but instead of intellect he had what might be called the wisdom of the heart and a profound inner life that shed a radiance around him. One could say about him that he shared nothing he had, except his rich personality, the psychic abundance that was essentially Jules Bois, and this he did unconsciously.

In a peculiarly French way he was deeply religious, but with him religious experience and ethics seemed to be separate affairs, and sex altogether a private matter. He would go to Mass diligently and piously every Sunday, write eloquently about saints and mystics, make pronouncements about God and eternity that had all the knowledgeableness of a doctor of the Church. Then, almost in the same breath, he would talk of an affair he was having with a married woman and would add, "It is not an adultery, because her husband knows about it." His life, if one could credit all he said, was punctuated with affairs of this nature. Certainly nothing to do with sex gave him any sense of sin; it was always simply a question of *amour* and did not displace his mystical communications with God or interfere with his pious telling of his rosary every evening. Religion and sex were to him the great experiences, and neither interfered with the other, and, in fact, neither in his mind seemed to have any connection with ethics. His ethics came out of the civilization to which he belonged and were not a religious matter.

Jules Bois was perpetually engaged in some abstruse intellectual labors that took up hours of his days but showed little results. "This will be the year of achievement," I have heard him more than once announce at the beginning of a new year. But the truth was that his once immensely strong constitution had become undermined in America by casual meals, with nobody to alleviate the discomforts of his existence, so that he had but little energy for his tasks. Yet he tried hard to complete one or two ambitious works which he was always fiddling with and which, to add to his handicaps, he insisted on writing in laborious English. His last couple of years he spent in a dreary apartment in the upper West Side which was furnished with odds and ends contributed by his friends— devoted friends he always had, both men and women, and from almost every walk of life. He had a sort of mania which I have also observed in a couple of other people, notably Elinor Wylie, for keeping his intimate friends apart from one another, never letting them meet if he could help it. One was often surprised to encounter here and there people never mentioned by him who were his intimates, his helpers and even co-workers in some of his activities—esoteric Catholicism, or that subject about which he had a lifelong curiosity and an immense knowledge, psychic manifestations of every kind. It seemed as if he wanted to have separate compartments of his life, his affections, and his interests; he segregated them. This came undoubtedly from a touch of neurosis which might be accounted for by something in his history, perhaps the Bolo connection or some love affair, or his dabbling in magic. The inner circles of his intimates were to meet at his deathbed and funeral and gaze at one another in astonishment, they represented such different activities in the world: he had kept his friendship with each of them so secret from the others.

Towards the end of his life, the latter ten or fifteen years, he began to show many eccentricities, and these became marked after the visit he made to France in the twenties. On his return he gave a triumphant interview to the newspapers in New York in which he claimed to have discovered the psychology of the "superconscious" which could irradiate a wider circle of life. As Freud had sunk down to the subconscious, he, Jules Bois, was soaring upward. He delivered a lecture on this before some learned body in Paris, and, according to himself, there had been an instant conversion to his ideas. I was a little puzzled myself and crudely inquired if it mattered what that which lay outside consciousness was named, whether sub or super. He was very angry and reproached me with being a materialistic follower of Freud. Yet I did not really disbelieve in his psychological discoveries, for I knew that he was immensely intuitive and had a great range of perceptions. Occasionally after some childish outbreak on his part I would decide that he was quite irresponsible; then, casually, a few moments later, he would make a remark of such profound wisdom and originality that it seemed as if it had come from a distance beyond ordinary thought.

After his return from the fateful visit to France a somewhat new sort of personality emerged, and he who had once been so proud of his well-known name decided to alter it. So from this period on he appeared on his cards as "Dr. H. A. Jules-Bois" with a hyphen between the two last names. He was vague about where the "Dr." came from, but as a matter of fact, it is almost impossible in America to keep people from calling a public lecturer or a well-known writer "Doctor" or "Professor," the respect for academic titles is so great. I have heard Maurice Maeterlinck introduced on a lecture platform as "Professor Maeterlinck" in San Francisco, and I suppose the author of the *Divine Comedy* could have found himself addressed as "Professor Dante," so perhaps in the case of Jules Bois he was using a title that had been spontaneously bestowed on him, a courtesy title, like one of those attached to the children of peers in England.

About this time there seemed to grow up in him—or perhaps it was there always but we had not noticed it—a craze for the highly placed in society. It seemed to come on him especially after he had received the rosette of the Legion of Honor, when he would go to some evening party handsomely attired, his face beaming, the red rosette in his buttonhole. Once when he was not invited to a certain party at Mrs. Cornelius Vanderbilt's he kept our telephone ringing all day in a state of extreme agitation, telling us that it was an affront to France and to the *idée française* which he in person represented that he was left out. Finally, in the course of the afternoon, he prevailed upon my husband to telephone Colonel Creighton Webb, who he said was a friend of France and would see to it that this dire happening was averted. The colonel laughed hilariously but gave a solemn undertaking that he would induce the hostess to invite Jules Bois. Then came the suffering for me. On the day of the reception, which was, I think, next day, he telephoned me that his laundry had not come back and that he had no *chemise de cérémonie* suitable for the occasion, and appealed to me to provide him with one and have it delivered immediately. He gave me all his measurements, but by this time his agitation had reached such a point that my husband thought it safer to deliver the *chemise de cérémonie* himself and to stay with Jules Bois until he was dressed; this took up the whole afternoon. Then another disaster impended. Halfway in the taxi, Jules Bois discovered that he had not affixed his rosette in his buttonhole. My husband tried to persuade him to go on to Mrs. Vanderbilt's without it; distractedly he refused. "The company will not well regard me without my order." So back the taxi had to turn to allow him to attach the order to his coat lapel. After a strenuous time my husband finally deposited him at his destination.

In his last years, as he was no longer in a position to make money either by writing or by lecturing, his intimate friends thought of him as penniless, and he would ask all of us for anything he felt he needed—clothes, food, money, help in cleaning up his apartment or in typing his generally fantastic correspondence, which would include wily letters to the President or other personages in power, designed to give the impression that H. A. Jules-Bois was the most representative Frenchman in America and that France was the most important country in the world and so deserved great consideration from America. Sometimes it would happen that when one section of his friends got together a little money for him they would discover that another section had been secretly asked by him to do the same. But he had such power of attracting affection and holding it that his deceptions were regarded with amused tolerance. He was a few years older than he admitted, and at last he got so ill with a complication of ailments that he could no longer wash or dress himself unaided. My husband, who went several times a week to bring him food and to help him with his toilet and his correspondence, tried for long in vain to induce him to go to the hospital, where he could be taken care of. He would burst out indignantly "But that is a cemetery!" Then one day my husband, going into his apartment at an unaccustomed hour, found him being expertly taken care of by a strange young man, a Greek, obviously an intimate of long standing whose existence Jules Bois had kept secret. This young man, it turned out, had devoted himself to him whom he called *le maître*, for many years, and had been concerned in a great many of his activities; the two agreed to meet again at the apartment, and one day they wore down Jules Bois's resistance to going to the hospital enough to get him dressed and installed in a taxi, his rosette in place, his *Imitation of Christ*, inside of which were the photos of his father and Emma Calvé in a dispatch case, not forgetting his rosary and his typewriter, and he was put in bed in a gloomy little room.

Jules Bois was a difficult patient, and it happened that he was waited on by unsympathetic attendants, none of whom suspected or cared that a really gorgeously endowed human being full of power and passion, who had lived profoundly in close connection with other human beings of greatness and power, was dying miserably among them. He lay for weeks in this gloomy room, receiving the friends who visited him. Then, somehow, it became known that his often mentioned poverty was not a fact: when one of his women friends told me she had heard he had savings of a few thousand dollars, I was incredulous, but this devoted friend of his tried to induce him, while his faculties were still all working, to make a will, disposing of his money in the way he wanted, or else to leave it in trust to some of his friends who would know his wishes. Finally his Greek friend had a will drawn up: Jules Bois signed it; none of us thought much about it; we believed that if he had sufficient to arrange for a decent burial and a tombstone, it would be the height of it. His Greek friend and my husband were those designated to put his wishes into effect. Some weeks later, in the early morning hours, he died without any of his friends beside him but only the hospital attendants whom he hated, and his savings, through his being declared incompetent—wrongly, I am sure—at the time he made his will, are about to be taken over, as I write this, by the state of New York. It was thought by his friends that whatever he had over his burial expenses would go partly towards getting his manuscripts published and to the war-starved children of his native Marseilles. No one knew what he had left in savings, for they were distributed over several banks. Later his intimates were staggered to learn that they amounted to nine thousand dollars, a modest sum, no doubt, in the estimation of some people, but remarkable for any writer not a popular novelist or playwright, and even more remarkable for one in Jules Bois's situation. No doubt he had held onto his savings to provide for his last days in Paris or in a monastery as an oblate, like his friend Huysmans. But alas for human dreams! He died in New York and was buried in Brooklyn.

৪৯ CHAPTER 25

Return to Ireland

WE HAD BEEN in America about eight years before we managed to get together enough funds for a return to Dublin. My husband was slowly making a place for his work in America, and now he got a good advance on a novel, *Castle Conquer*, in addition to having steady royalties from his stories, his retelling of old tales, and his children's books. In fact he had acquired, almost by accident, such a reputation in this field that just before we bought our tickets for Ireland he was given a commission by the Hawaiian legislature to go to the islands, make a survey of their traditional stories, and put them into shape for children. And so our stay in Ireland would be limited to a couple of months.

We were longing to see our friends and the new government that had been set up and to gain which so many of our group had suffered death. This time we had to get a passport to travel, for that freedom of movement which had existed before the first World War had come to an end; the governments of the world had fastened on another way of keeping people bound and tethered. We gave up our apartment, once more stored our furniture—we always seemed to be putting things into storage—and bought our tickets. We left with a great deal of good wishes, seen off by a group of our intimates, for we had many friends—also some few enemies, but these were really not personal; they were either due to the literary jealousies common in large cities or to the fact that we were Irish Nationalists, belonging to the party in Ireland that had put an army in the field against Britain. The American Irish had helped the Irish in Ireland with all their might and all their extensive influence, a fact which, I think, the Irish at home have never quite understood or appreciated.

For the American Irish had, oftener than was realized, to struggle against a prejudice of strongly pro-English sections of American opinion. Supporters of Irish nationalism were frequently penalized in their jobs, attacked in the newspapers. As a matter of fact this pro-English feeling is always strong in what might be called the ruling classes in America, the wealthy people of every stock, including German. The one live American foreign policy, consequently, is to support England in every war if not in peace. If European peoples had realized this it might have prevented their plunging into two wars.

Naturally we knew that the Ireland we were on our way back to was a different country from the Ireland we had left. The Irish had not got all they wanted out of their struggle, but an Irish Free State had come into being and an Irish government was functioning in Dublin. In bright sunshine we left New York, and in summer clothes. But after a few sunny days at sea we sailed into the dim, foggy northern ocean and the cool damp weather we had been born to. The liner as it approached the Irish coast suddenly drew down the flag it was flying and ran up the new Irish tricolor, green, white, and orange, and we turned to each other with emotion. We were sorry it was not the old one, the harp on a green ground, which had been the only cultural emblem on a national flag in Europe. But just the same, the new colors were immensely thrilling, and we saw a tender coming towards us flying the same tricolor, the flag of the revolution. When we got off the tender the young men at the customs who examined our baggage wore Irish uniforms, the two or three odd policemen called by the new Irish name Gardai also wore Irish uniforms; there was not a Union Jack in sight—that flag which had dominated not only the country but the minds of the inhabitants for so long. I saw men and women who had spent long years in America weeping as they stepped off the tender and beheld the change, weeping because of some overwhelming emotion that must have included joy, but which was also mixed with sad memories of history.

We stepped into the softest air and onto the greenest grass in the world, towards a group who came to meet us, tall, slender people with every shade of red in their hair. As we entered the third-class carriage of the Dublin train there also got on some sailors in British uniform, for a couple of the ports were temporarily in British hands. The rest of the passengers were the Irish country type of my childhood, happy, simple people with their market baskets who had been to some fair, all very articulate and sociable with one another, singing to enjoy themselves or to pass the time. An old man with an ashplant for a walking stick started a song in Irish that he rendered in the peculiar traditional style; he was a gay old fellow, happy to be on a train and delighted with the company. Everybody bantered everybody else and laughed in good spirits. In turn each person sang or recited—reciting was called "wording a song"—a poem was a song, and that was that, and this may account for the Irish way of saying poetry, always in a chanting voice. In stepping off the tender and onto the train we had come into another civilization, the old civilization of my youth.

The English sailors were in the same carriage but in a compartment separated from ours by the back of the long seat. I had been in the habit of saying in America that a lot of the English were exactly like Irish people, and my English friends in America had said so, too. But these sailors represented a different race; they and the people on the other side of the partition were incomprehensible to one another. I had known many English sailors—I had, indeed, a brother-in-law who was in the British Navy, and he had once brought me to tea on a battleship among a pleasing set of comradely young men. Our fellow travelers, however, were the dourest English I had ever come across; they sat silently, inimically, playing cards. To break down their aloofness a pleasant country woman drew a bottle of poteen out of her market basket and, leaning across the back of the long seat, invited the sailors to have a thimbleful. They shook their heads morosely without a word, as if they had been instructed, "No fraternization." She then offered it to the old man who kept on singing, and he partook of it enthusiastically. After his next performance, this time a song half in English and half in Irish, a dialogue between a fox and a man whose goose the creature had made off with, "Good morrow, fox, Good morrow, sir, pray tell me what you're atin'." "A fine fat goose I stole from you, and won't you come and taste it?" the old man, energetically applauded for his effort, invited my husband either to sing a song or to word one. My husband repeated a poem which, he explained to the admiring audience, he had composed himself, and everyone expressed delight. Then the old man in his patched clothes, after another draught of the poteen out of the neck of the bottle, felt he had to do the honors and be a sort of host. He rose to his feet and spoke first in Irish, which was obviously native to him; he then turned to English. "These are officiated gentlemen," he said, referring to the sailors, who, I think, were petty officers, "and it is only right they should be asked to join our pleasures." He leaned across the seat and, addressing the only sailor who had the curiosity to look up at him—the others kept their eyes on the cards—"Mister," he said, "you have a harmonious face—will you rise us a harmony?" No answer. Then he turned courteously to the others. "Let yez not be shy, gentlemen," he said, "we're sort of amatures ourselves." No answer. "If yez can't sing, yez can word it like the young man here." No answer. Still the old man was not dashed. "Sure we'll be vexed if yez don't join our pleasures," he said. Never a word. This time he gave it up and sank back on his own seat. At the next stop he and the rest of the country folk got out, with a courteous salute to us all. These simple people were not the fighting Irish; they showed no sign they had been through any fight, and I doubt if they were very conscious of a change of government.

But when we got to Dublin we were right in the middle of the fighting Irish. As we drove across the city whose landmarks had so excited me when I came up from the West to become a university student, we saw the scars of battle. The most memorable of the old buildings had fronts and sides broken and roofs gone; men with rifles guarded the streets; here and there were barbed-wire fences. The uniform of the armed soldiers was the new Irish one, the flag over the buildings was the revolutionary tricolor, but the city seemed a city in wartime; it was borne in on us that a civil war was really on.

The treaty that had ended the years of insurrection had been accepted by but a small majority of the national assembly, so there was a large minority set in anger and disappointment over the fact that the republic they had fought for had not come into being and that partition left under another flag six Ulster counties. De Valera and his republican forces stood aloof from the new Irish government. Brother was fighting brother, sons were fighting fathers, wives and husbands were on opposite sides. Arthur Griffith, who had been such an influence on our youth and who indeed had created the new Irish polity, was dead—dead, it was said, of a combination of overwork and a broken heart at the enmity of the people who had once been his devoted followers. The military genius the revolution had thrown up, Michael Collins, had been killed in an engagement between the new Free State troops and the irregular army. The new ministry had executed several leaders of the anti-treaty forces, some of whom had sacrificed everything they owned in a fight against the British. Such executions by a conquering party after a struggle is over are always a blunder. Feelings were extremely bitter, we discovered, for the bulk of the Irish have little power of compromise, and the compromise settlement aroused some of the fiercest emotions I had known among the people. Even the gentlest had grown bitter: a kindly person like Jack Yeats was so against the settlement that he was against his poet brother, W.B., who, later, was made a Free State senator.

In addition to a natural despondency because so many of our friends were gone, the young men I had worked with, danced with, who used to read their new poems to me, the disunion around me added another despondency. The thrill I had experienced on stepping onto a soil that had over it its own flag, and whose public servants wore the national uniform, diminished. The widespread anger against the settlement had not everywhere the same basis; for some it was not so much that it fell short of the national aspiration as that the old secret romance with Kathleen ni Houlihan was over—with the Little Dark Rose, the Poor Old Woman, the Silk of the Kine, all the symbolisms through which a romantic passion for the country had been expressed for generations. Now that the romantic symbol was taken from them, or partly taken from them, there was a sad bitterness as over a lost love. The less romantic, unacknowledged psychological reasons produced the bitterest hatreds of all: inner frustrations, disappointments, jealousies long repressed now came up in the guise of a fanatical patriotism and even among people who had been anti-national while the struggle was on. Then, as in every country, there was jealousy of the men who from humble beginnings had made their way to the top and who were now the rulers, a jealousy that had not existed against the unknown British rulers. And there were the really heartbroken people who could not get over the partition of Ireland that had left the territory of the Ulster princes who fought the last fight for Gaelic ways, the territory that was the scene of the national epic, of St. Patrick's foundation, under another flag. Against all these were the remarkable men of high courage and integrity who, having accepted the treaty, were determined to make it work, and who believed that it was a large and developing installment of Irish freedom.

Of course, with all the quarrels about partition, the character of the old city of Dublin, with the stamp of the Celt, the Norse, the Saxon, the Norman, could not change, but the atmosphere was very changed from my student days when poetry and a sort of mystic romance filled the air. Of the places of reunion only A.E.'s and Dr. Sigerson's were almost the same. A.E.'s Sunday evenings, crowded with young men and women as well as the older habitués, seemed a continuation of the old days; people were sitting around, drinking tea and coffee, talking about literature and construction of plays and novels and assonance in poetry. Somebody made the old remark I had so often heard in my student days about Yeats's creative period being at an end. I could not resist laughing in the face of the young writer who delivered himself of it with such conviction. Professor Rudmose Browne, of Trinity College, was talking French as of old, to foreign journalists; somebody else was speaking in a language I was told was Russian; the usual traditional liberal visiting Englishman was scoring British imperialism, especially as it had been exercised in Ireland. Another was giving an account of George Moore, who was now settled in London with his Aubusson carpet. Mrs. Russell was handing round tea and coffee, and A.E. was talking of pictures he had painted in Donegal.

But strangest, and at the same time most familiar, sight of all was Constance Markievicz sitting in her usual place on the couch in the corner, a brown dog lying at her feet. It could not have been the same brown dog she used to have, but he looked exactly the same. There she sat, she who had fought side by side with men in the insurrection of 1916, had been condemned to death with other leaders, had her death sentence commuted to imprisonment, and had recently been released after serving part of her term. Yeats, who had known her in her youth as the daughter of the great landowner of his native Sligo, Sir Henry Gore-Booth, had described her in a poem riding to hounds, "the beauty of her countryside." But now, as she sat there, she whom I remembered as a beautiful woman, only second in beauty to Maud Gonne, was haggard and old, dressed in ancient demoded clothes; the outline of her face was the same, but the expression was different; the familiar eyes that blinked at me from behind glasses were bereft of the old fire and eagerness; she gave me a limp hand and barely spoke to me. The last time I had seen her, before the Howth gun-running and a little while before we left for America, she had been most interesting, telling me of her stay at Oscar Wilde's house in London shortly before the great scandal broke. His wife, a friend of Constance's, was then very happy that his affair with Lilly Langtry was finished and was looking forward to a tranquil domestic life with their two children.

I had known Constance Markievicz in her vibrant maturity, at the height of her beauty and her courage, when she was engaged in masculine activities, the training and drilling of boys in a national youth movement she had founded. At that time she had not been devoid of feminine coquetries or unconscious of her looks, though her ordinary attire, then, was a tweed suit and a mannish felt hat, but she would on occasions get herself up in a Paris frock and, when few others in Dublin used cosmetics, put powder and rouge on her face. A remark of hers to me, when I was a young girl, I always remembered, for it had a real feminine vanity: "I am not interested in men, for I have had the pick of too many men." But now no trace of beauty remained; she was like an extinct volcano, her former violent self reduced to something burnt out. She had lived strongly and passionately several different kinds of lives; as Constance Gore-Booth, Sir Henry's daughter, she had been a great rider of horses, a follower of hounds and a hunter of foxes; she had been a society beauty who had frequented fashionable gatherings and the balls of the viceroy. Then she had been an art student in Paris at the great ateliers, where she had married a Polish painter, Count Casimir Markievicz. Then, when the Irish Renaissance began, she had returned to Dublin, bringing her Slav husband with her. Her sister, Eva Gore-Booth, was one of the new Irish writers, and in my student days we all knew her verse, especially her "Little waves of Breffni":

> The little waves of Breffni have drenched my heart in spray,
> And the little waves of Breffni go stumbling through my soul.

When they came to Dublin she and her husband made an interesting social circle and ran a theater, one of the numerous rivals to the Abbey Theater that sprang up in the city. But Constance was an Irishwoman who found the call of Kathleen ni Houlihan stronger than anything else. Her husband had first helped her in her Nationalist activities, but as these more and more absorbed her, they separated, and he returned to Poland. As a Polish Nationalist, Casimir Markievicz—"Cassie," as he was affectionately known in Dublin—had fitted marvelously into the Irish life of the time and had easily understood the Nationalist movements. His singing of the "Wearin' of the Green" in a pronunciation of his own was a remembered feature of Dublin gatherings.

The movement Constance had founded must have been the first national youth movement in the world. Baden-Powell had founded the Boy Scouts, but they were international in design, whereas Constance's was purely Irish Nationalist and militant; she called her boys the Fianna after the old Irish legendary warriors. Her tremendous energy, her nationalism, and her hatred of injustice brought her into the Irish labor movement, and she worked with the transport workers' leaders, Jim Larkin and James Connolly, during the famous strike of 1913. It is hard to realize now that this strike was international news. Afterwards she went into the Sinn Fein independence movement and fought as a leader in the rebellion of 1916 with the young men of her Fianna.

In the tradition of the old Gaelic queens she had taught the young men the use of weapons and how to wage war. I remember her saying to Padraic Pearse, then headmaster of St. Enda's and St. Ita's schools, "If you will supply the officers I will supply the men," and his reply, "We may have to devote ourselves to our own destruction so that Ireland can be free." After her release from prison she had been elected to Dail Eireann while it was still an underground body, the first woman parliamentary representative either in England or Ireland. Now as I saw her she was obviously a dying woman, sunk in dejection, a dejection resulting either from her imprisonment or from the loss of her hopes. What she had fought for had not really come into being; maybe nothing on earth could have brought it into being, so romantic and heroic was it.

What she talked about now struck me as very strange, considering what she had just come through. She was writing a play, and she held forth about it as if it were her one interest in life. After the life she had lived she was now thinking of how she might dramatize or symbolize some of those ardors and endurances of hers. But her vitality was too low to do anything more; her fight, her imprisonment, the prison fare had depleted her and dimmed her personality. She had been a fighting Irishwoman, a woman of high aristocratic courage, who was afraid of nothing—that, at least, the aristocratic training at its best really can give, moral and physical fearlessness—but how rarely is it at its best! It made me sad to see how little attention was paid to Constance Gore-Booth by those in the room; perhaps the habitués of A.E.'s had become accustomed to seeing her sitting exhausted there in the corner, the brown poodle at her feet. Their indifference did not bother her; her name would pass into the history of her country as she well knew.

II

America, of course, was the topic in A.E.'s; the Nationalists had an idea that she had been none too friendly to the Irish struggle for independence, while a Unionist present demanded why America had come so belatedly into the war against Germany. No one seemed to have any conception of how hard friends of Ireland in America had worked for the Irish cause, or what they had stood up to in personal attacks. The pert young wife of the Trinity College professor asked me if there were any cultivated people in the States. I answered, "I can hardly tell you how often a similar question has been put to me about Ireland in America." It was one or two of the younger writers who had sprung up since we had left Ireland who really exasperated me. There are but few writers in Ireland, and those who are recognized have an importance and a self-importance out of all proportion to their production. The ones present were, naturally enough, doing their best to get published in America and to get a public there. Yet they talked about American literature and American readers in the most *de haut en bas* manner. The usual European attitude that America and Americans existed to do something for them was not entirely absent from Dublin. Only A.E. and James Stephens knew enough about American literature to be really interested in it, and both were anxious to pay a visit and meet American writers.

In the house that was lent us by friends for our stay we returned to the old Dublin habit of being at home one evening a week when our friends would be sure to find us, and everybody came who used to frequent our Tuesday evenings in Donnybrook when we were first married. Not all the friends amongst our contemporaries were alive; as well as those who had been killed during the years of rebellion there were others who had fallen in the first World War. But the older ones, who to my generation and even to the generation before had seemed the pillars of Dublin, were still all alive, and they arrived every at-home evening. The oldest in years was Sarah Purser, whose wit was still far ahead of anybody else's, and her description of the two gentlemen who were both trying to be the President's right-hand man in the new social life of the new state as the Old and Young Pretender had a double-edged wit. She was the only one who kept her head at an official function arranged by both Pretenders when it was discovered that the least prepossessing woman in Dublin had accidentally been seated beside Augustus John: instead of being left gasping she had calmly remarked, "Well, unless they had given him two gypsy girls they couldn't have done any better."

When Alice Stopford Green entered the room, Sarah would stiffen up a little. These two distinguished women did not care much for each other; they represented opposite types of the brilliant woman, of the *femme savante.* Mrs. Green, generally known as the Widow Green, was a historian and the widow of the historian, John Richard Green, who wrote *A Short History of the English People.* She had been a friend of my husband's since he first began to write, and though she liked me well enough she did not take me seriously—in fact she seldom took women seriously at all and often had a whole dinner party composed exclusively of men. In London, where she had lived all her married life, she had been a great figure, had held a famous salon, hobnobbed with cabinet ministers, editors, poets, and peers. Despite her Irishness, her rebel Irishness, she had unconsciously through her long residence in London adopted many English points of view. However, all the friends she had in high places, including prominent statesmen, did not prevent the British Government from ordering her out of London and back to Ireland. It was probably her intense efforts to save her friend Roger Casement from the gallows that finally led to the order for her banishment from London. But here in Dublin, away from her lovely house in Westminster, away from her disciples and her distinguished guests from every European country, she must have felt like Madame de Staël exiled from Paris and the Rue du Bac.

Politely but remotely she greeted the women present, directing her serious attention to the men. She was very different indeed from the other women, even from the women writers, for she had been through a more severe intellectual discipline; her historical books, *Irish Nationality* and *The Making of Ireland and Its Undoing*, were important and original contributions to history and had a great influence on the changing English attitude towards Ireland. At this time she was a Senator of the new Irish state, taking her responsibilities very earnestly, and she was a public figure in the way a political man is a public figure. Making an effort to continue her London salon, she valiantly entertained the young ministers of the Free State and the leaders generally, but the apprenticeship of most of them to affairs and to life in general had been served, not in salons, but behind barricades, on the run, and in gaols; they were the type of the new leaders springing up in Europe, and she and they did not really understand one another. Her life in London had, I think, also made her incapable of understanding the Dublin type of intellectual of which Sarah Purser was the outstanding exemplar—women who substituted wit and gaiety, as do Frenchwomen, for the traditional solemnity of the *femme savante*. Little as the Widow Green could understand Sarah, she understood even less the delightful Susan Mitchell, Sarah's rival as a wit, who worked with A.E. on his weekly and helped him in the Agricultural Organization Society.

There was a glitter of female intellect in the room, but when Maud Gonne, still the most beautiful woman I had ever seen, arrived with her friend, Mrs. Despard, the show stopped, as they say in America. As these two beautiful old women entered the drawing room I could not help feeling a thrill; they had been heroines of my girlhood; it was nearly a decade since I had last seen them. Beauty is not as common in Ireland as is personality, but these two were not only beautiful; they were incredibly distinguished and full of almost everything that makes a rousing personality. Both had been inspiring leaders; Maud Gonne had been known all over Europe and even in America as "Ireland's Joan of Arc"; she had in Yeats's poems passed into literature. Then Mrs. Despard had been one of the outstanding figures in the woman-suffrage movement and the head of an organization called the Women's Freedom League. I recall the difference I felt between her speeches and the Pankhursts'; the Pankhursts fought magnificently, but when they made speeches they talked like lawyers and politicians. Mrs. Despard's speeches had warmth and poetry and that intellectual reality mixed with emotional intensity which I have always thought is a Celtic quality. Intellectual reality, however, is a different thing from practicality, and the Pankhursts' speeches and policies took in a wider range of practical life; they thought in terms of the British Empire; they thought imperially, as Joseph Chamberlain would say. I felt about them as I often felt about ambitious people—that they were as much devoted to their work for the cause as to the cause itself. But for Mrs. Despard, the cause was the thing, and she was willing to be its handmaiden. When woman suffrage was won, she joined with her friend Maud Gonne in the Irish national effort, where at one time she must have been a great thorn in the side of her brother, Lord French (Field Marshal French of Ypres) when he was viceroy in Ireland. Making an Irishman viceroy was an effort towards appeasement by the English Liberal government, but it did not work.

Except for Mrs. Green, who, like Lady Gregory, had personal ambitions, none of our other women guests had any personal ambition that I ever could discover. The two Yeats sisters, Lilly and Lolly, were, like all members of that amazing family, full of personality and artistry: they worked hard at printing, painting, and embroidery in their workshop, the Cuala Industries, but this was not as a means to any personal ends: it was a sort of patriotic endeavor. Evelyn Gleeson and Sarah Purser, also artists who ran art industries, one weaving, the other, stained glass, seemed to work entirely for the country, for the cause as it were. One quality was common to all of them—they would work for their country without counting the cost.

III

Few of the men had as rich personalities as the women; of course A.E. and James Stephens could dominate any assembly, but none of the other men in the room came near these two. Because of childhood's allegiances, the greatest disappointment of all was my writing uncle who had first initiated me into literature. He was now a civil servant in Dublin; he looked handsome and well groomed as of old, but he whom I once thought the most brilliant of men, so learned in literature, now seemed old-fashioned and conventional. He had five or six books to his name which, except for the opening pages, I had never read, and he had published some verse in the periodicals; the literature, and especially the Irish literature, he knew, was anterior to Yeats and the Abbey Theater, and though he and Yeats were contemporaries, Yeats's writing was strange to him and Joyce's intolerable. He was still capable of offering me sixpence or even a new hat as he used to if I could explain what certain poems of Yeats's meant. There was but little room in modern Ireland for the taste of the generation he adhered to, and he entirely disapproved of me and of my associates, so that he could hardly speak of them without exasperation. Though he did not know it, the Irish literature he liked—Carleton, Gerald Griffin, Aubrey de Vere, Lever, Lover, and his beloved Thomas Moore—was the kind that reflected English taste, and Moore's songs were mostly made for London drawing rooms. "That is the trouble," Arthur Power, one of the new authors, wrote, "of the literature of a conquered country; by force of circumstance it must pander to the taste of the conqueror. Ireland never produced any literature worth while until it was free of English taste."

Over the people who came to see us every Tuesday evening, people so interesting, so vital, so formed by a warm experience of life, there hung a heavy cloud of disagreement. One group in the room was at enmity with the others; some openly spoke of others as traitors to their country. All those who came to see us were the people I had been lonely for during my years in America; theirs were the voices, theirs the conversation I had longed to hear, and yet at every one of our At Home evenings I was depressed by the insistence on and the dramatization of political differences, for I had not foreseen so much ill will. To add to my depression, the Dublin rain which I had partly forgotten in the bright sunshine of New York came down in pours, but in the rainless hours I would wander over the old city, so like a French city, and stroll down the misty quays, so like the Paris quays with their old bookstalls, their old furniture shops, their queer hotels and houses. In Grafton Street there were the familiar tearooms, in one of which was, what seemed to me, the same little orchestra playing wailing

Irish airs. I knew none of the present habitués, but the young students drinking tea and eating cakes, carrying their books in straps, practicing their French or German on a foreign student across the table, behaved very much as my generation did, but they really had, as I was soon to discover, a different outlook and different interests. Then I could cross O'Connell Bridge many times a day without meeting a single individual I knew where once I knew so many. But like those whom Horace used to meet on the Appian Way, the crowd was always of the same age.

The atmosphere of the city was greatly changed; it was not now the city Joyce celebrated in *Ulysses*, or the city that had made the Abbey Theater and the Gaelic League, or the city that once worked itself into a frenzy over the plays of John Synge. And where were the famous Victorian survivals that one used to encounter several days a week strolling between Trinity College and O'Connell Bridge? There used to be Professor Mahaffy, all tied up in black gaiters, with his queer plebeian Irish face that now one sees only in caricatures. Mahaffy could talk of Sophocles and Socrates as if he had met them at dinner the night before, where, like Dublin gentlemen, they drank a little too much. Yeats had taught us to writhe when Greek was translated into the Swinburnian meters that Mahaffy quoted, his body seeming to keep time to them as if they were jig tunes. The Gaelic League had taught us to smile when Mahaffy talked of the kings he had dined with. Once when he had returned from a visit to Greek royalty bearing as a gift a strange-looking little dog, Oliver Gogarty, one of the wits of the town, wrote verses on it in the very sort of meter in which Mahaffy was accustomed to quote translations from the Greek:

> He was given the hound
> By the seed of a king
> For the wisdom profound
> Of his wide wandering—
> But was it the owner, or donor, or dog that was
> led by the string?

and stately Professor Dowden, very genteel and New Englandish, repeating over and over again what he had written in his youth about Shelley and Shakespeare. It was always said of Dowden that

something withered in him and died after Matthew Arnold wrote
that essay on his Shelley book, for Arnold convicted him with his
most terrible urbanity, not of being a sublime fool, but merely of
being a foolish fool. And where was the gentleman with the monocle and carrying two swords who used to walk so purposefully every
afternoon up O'Connell Street and whom Joyce has in *Ulysses?*
Lacking these figures, the eighteenth-century streets seemed less
lively. George Moore had been off the scene for years, now living
in London. Lady Gregory was now too old to walk around in the
rain, her skirts turned up over her flowered silk petticoat to save
them from becoming bedraggled. And I missed those young men
who, when they approached me in the street, would draw their
latest poem from a pocket and read it with appropriate gesticula-
tions. Writing a poem as a day's work was no longer the spectacular thing it once was. Some public figure remarked that the young
men were all writing constitutions because it was easier than writing sonnets.

It was beyond O'Connell Bridge that the ruins began, the destruction wrought by British cannon during the insurrection or
by opposing factions in the Irish civil war. Sad for the disappearance of historic buildings as well as for the missing faces, I walked
off the quays and into the side streets where were the old churches,
Christ Church and Swift's St. Patrick's, old streets where in another century had walked men who, too, in their day had made
literature and passionate thought seem the most glorious thing in
life. Their ghosts were in the air around me—Swift, the most beloved of them all, so beloved in his day that an old history of Dublin tells us weeping crowds surrounded the Deanery where he lay
dead and begged for a hair of his head to hand down to their children. Goldsmith, also beloved, slipping in among the crowd to
listen to a ballad singer trolling out something that Oliver himself
had written. Burke and Sheridan appeared amongst the ghosts,
they, too, lords of language, as well as Sterne and Farquahar, and
Thomas Moore, belittled by my generation, and also the ghosts of
those Yeats had ordered us to admire—Davis, Mangan, and Ferguson. Yet, considering them all, I was mindful that the greatest
of Dublin's literary figures, Yeats, was still treading its streets, now
actually a greater poet than he had been in my admiring youth.

But he, too, was changed—in some ways the most changed of all. In his fifties he who seemed to be born for celibacy had married and was now a paterfamilias, a senator, and a Nobel Prize winner, world-famous and filled with honors. He was calmed down, with a home, a son, and a daughter to write poems to, and a young wife to hand him his slippers and the decanter of sherry he liked to sip. He had indeed become more human, more related to ordinary humanity, than in the days when he lectured the young people, harangued the town, and fiercely fought his intellectual campaigns.

IV

After some weeks we left the city and went to the country. All over the countryside historic houses had been burned down for no reason that one could see except that it may have been the revenge of the have-nots against the haves that was later to blaze out all over Europe, that indeed had already begun in Russia. Lord and Lady Dunsany asked us to stay with them in County Meath for a few days, and it was pleasant to find almost nothing changed here. The castle and its old rooms were the same; I slept in a room where I had slept before, with the same portrait over the mantlepiece, the same eighteenth-century ewer and basin, no longer used, settled on its old mahogany stand. A cup of tea was brought up to me in bed in the morning by the same maid grown a little older. There came also to stay a haughty American youth who clearly did not see why peers should consort with poets even when the peer was himself a poet. The Dunsanys were certainly not wholeheartedly for the new Irish order, but their main interests and allegiances were, as always, for things of the mind. I doubt if fundamentally they ever cared greatly for any other sort of distinction in spite of Dunsany's pride in his ancient Norman-Irish ancestry and in his relationship with the great Hugh O'Neill, the Tyrone of the Elizabethan wars, whose portrait, resembling that of a French symbolist poet, hung on the dining-room wall.

Lord Dunsany could talk with equal enthusiasm about the castle of Trim, built for King John, which he owned, and about a poet he had discovered in a village. They drove us around to see the

burnt remains of stately old houses which had been destroyed, and
I asked myself why all this had to be. Why, especially, had the
houses of well-known Irishmen like Maurice Moore, George's
brother, and Sir Henry Grattan-Esmonde, men of known patriotism
and strong nationalism, been sent up in smoke? They and the
families of their owners had long been landmarks in Irish history,
and what could the Irishmen who had destroyed their houses have
against them? On the other hand, I was not particularly troubled
to hear from our hosts that the house in Kerry belonging to the
Marquis of Landsdowne had been burned down. He was the descendant of a dubious if able personage named Petty, sent over a
couple of hundred years before by an English sovereign to survey
confiscated Irish lands and who had managed to survey himself
into a large stretch of property in Kerry which his descendants still
held. The grandson-in-law of the Marquis, Harold Macmillan, of
the London publishing house, later in London told me that his
grandfather-in-law, after the burning of the house, had come over
to England as a martyr, but not being able to endure living in
England had gone back to his native Kerry and was living in rooms
over the village pub.

From Dunsany's we went to stay at the house of another friend
who was a squireen and a horse breeder. The great entertainment
for any of the guests in the square nine- or ten-roomed house was
to be taken to the row of stables at the back to see the sprightly,
handsome young horses, some of which our host hopefully regarded as material for winning one or other of the great races in
England, Ireland, or France. If people called in the evening they
were taken out to the stables by our host with a lantern, where the
horses' eyes flashing in the semidark and their nervous stamping
feet were sometimes a startling experience to non-stablegoers. Our
host specialized in hunters rather than in thoroughbreds, though
the great admiration of his life was an American, Harry Worcester
Smith, who had arrived from America with a shipload of thoroughbreds which he announced would show the Irish that these, and not
the half-and-half horses which they favored, made the best hunters.

Revolution or literature was not the topic in this establishment;
horses were the great reality, the means by which our host made
his living; they were also the means of his enjoyment of life, his

sport, his recreation; without them he could hardly imagine existence. I can think of no better fate than this—that the means of earning a living should not only produce an adequate income, but also give a zest to life. "Hunting," said our host, as he sat at the head of the table, carving a fowl from his own back yard, "is the best sport in the world—the only sport." I thought of the French king who wrote in his diary "Ennui, ennui" on the days when there was no hunting. Everybody to his own trade, and the only thing that was wrong with the world, according to our host, was that not enough of its inhabitants understood the delight of companionship with horses. I understood it myself to some extent, and in spite of the unrest and fighting in the country I enjoyed myself at the horse breeder's.

In his house our meals were stupendous: in the morning, after tea and biscuits in bed, we descended to a breakfast of the best ham and eggs, the best sausages, the best toasted bread anywhere in the world. At about one o'clock we sat down to a meal composed of two roasts, one of which was always ham, after which there was pudding, cheese, and all the whisky anybody could drink. In the late afternoon we had tea and hot scones; at night we had cold meats, salad, and Guinness's stout, after which we took our last look at the horses.

However, it happened that our host or his brother, or maybe his brother-in-law, had some connection with the new Irish government or was a member of the Dail or something of the kind, and for that reason, on the fourth night of our stay, our host received a confidential missive to the effect that the Republican Army would burn down his house, and that he, his family, his guests, his horses, had better move out. What to do with the horses was the main concern. "But the house?" I asked, for his little eighteenth-century house had great charm. But he was indifferent to history. "If they burn the house, I'll get compensation and build something up-to-date," which later was exactly what happened. We all moved out, as our host thought it best, thankful for the consideration shown in the warning given, whereas other houseowners had had their houses, household treasures, and everything, set fire to without a moment's notice.

Before leaving my old world to go back to America and from that to the Pacific islands, I thought I should like a little tranquil or even amusing time, so I decided to accept a gay invitation to spend a few days in London, and incidentally to see a publisher who wanted information about new American books. My husband, however, preferred to roam through revolutionary Ireland. I started out from the horse breeder's in my sport clothes, just as I was, with a few things in a bag, to get the mail boat from Dunleary.

ह∽ CHAPTER 26

Bohemia in London

THE JOURNEY between Dublin and London can be the most uncomfortable on the globe; between Dunleary and Holyhead the sea is notoriously agitated, and one starts being seasick a few minutes after the boat pulls out and continues being so for the approximate three hours of the voyage.

The boat was filled with men who looked like our late host— strongly built, red-faced, horsy-looking, courteous men clad in tweeds and leggings. Though it was early in the morning, about eight, and the sea was extremely choppy, these men at once sat down in the dining room and ordered whisky and cold ham. The women, some equally horsy-looking, however, retired to berths, ministered to by a stewardess, to appear on deck just before the boat reached Holyhead. There was for the first time in my experience a customs examination in Holyhead, and everybody's belongings were minutely searched. Almost more than anything else I had seen, this showed that there was a separate government in Ireland. Some of my traveling companions pretended to know no English and turned on a torrent of good or bad Irish at the sailors and customs examiners, with the result that they were humorously answered back in Welsh, for the sailors on the Holyhead boat are Welshmen and have never given up talking Welsh. The young man who requested me to open my bag asked if it contained guns, dynamite, or explosives of any kind. "They have a lot of explosives over there now, haven't they?" he asked.

Six hours later I descended at Euston from the Irish mail train, and the publisher who met me undertook to entertain me for the evening and offered me a choice of diversions. We might dine with his partner; there were theaters and clubs; there were celebrities we might call on; and finally—his voice sounded yearning but slightly hesitating—we might go to a well-known public house, where there would be gathered a collection of artists, musicians, professional men, hack writers—the men mostly young, the women mostly pretty, some of them respectable, some of them not. The writers, he said, a few of them, anyway, were likely to become well known; some of the less frequent habitués were even internationally famous. Augustus John occasionally visited the club, and in his train came a couple of beautiful models. This all sounded very much like the average camp following of the arts everywhere, but Bohemia in London has a long tradition, and there still exist successors of the Mermaid Tavern.

The publisher's wistfulness about the pub allured me, whereas the proposition as to the celebrities bored me. I dislike celebrities unless they are men or women of genius, because in the process of becoming celebrated they so frequently lose all life and eagerness, unless, as I say, they happen to be people of genius, when, as a rule, the older they grow, the more life and eagerness seem to radiate from them. To the publisher's relief I settled for the pub. We dined, after which he marched me through a number of little streets contiguous to the British Museum, then through a side door we entered the Select Bar of the pub. Nobody knows England at all who does not know her pubs, those clubs of men and women of every status. The room we entered was large and seemed at first sight to be composed chiefly of mirrors and a number of men and women in a more or less intoxicated state. When I got used to the mirrors, the smoke, the people, and the dazzling bar full of bottles of all shapes, sizes, and colors—the America I had left was in the clutch of Prohibition—I perceived that almost none of the men was intoxicated and only one or two of the women; the others were sober enough and were sipping very harmless-looking drinks. We were an immediate object of interest, the publisher rather than myself, because in the course of life many of the young men present had tried to sell him something, and one or two had succeeded. As we sat down a number of them came to our table in the middle of the floor, the publisher proving a greater attraction than the five or six highly decorated ladies who sat at tables against the wall. As I threw an eye on the gentlemen around me I caught in a roving moment a glimpse of myself in one of the numerous mirrors: the reflection was not flattering in the bright greenish light, and I perceived it would doubtless have been better if I had imitated the ladies in the corner and applied some rouge diligently to my face. Here indeed I was very far from revolutionary Ireland, and my immediate experiences there receded from my mind. Taking my eyes from my reflection, I again surveyed my companions. Strangely enough, every one of the men had a curious distinction, the distinction that intellect or imagination, or perhaps merely suffering, gives to a face.

"Dearest," began the semi-intoxicated fair-haired man who took the seat next me, "what will you drink?"

"Cut that out, Tommy," said my protecting publisher, "and brush up your brains a little."

A young gentleman opposite me who had got himself up to look like Aubrey Beardsley, or perhaps it was Dowson, in a sort of bright blue braided jacket, fastened his eyes on me. "Benedictine, lady," said he, "or a brandy and soda?"

He had a very striking face, dark, eager, imaginative, with a sort of weak defiance and a muddled spirituality, like an angel who had been too much influenced by a defying Lucifer. He was indeed a traditional English artist type, the kind who might, in a drunken lifetime, write one immortal poem, or maybe only an immortal line—"A rose-red city, half as old as time"—and have his name forever enrolled among the great names in English anthologies. But he would undoubtedly end his days in a garret and probably die of tuberculosis.

"What do you do for a living?" I asked him interestedly.

Without hesitation he produced a small crumpled paper from his pocket and handed it to me. It was called the *Union Jack*, price twopence.

"I write stories in that," he said. "They publish me every week because I always put the right words in the right places."

"The right words in their right places?"

"Yes. Don't you understand? I always say, 'She had a queer wistful desire,' or, 'He felled him to earth with an unerring aim.' Do you understand? That's me," and he pointed to a name on the cover. "Not really me. My real name is—I write poetry, damn good poetry."

"Say a poem for me." The table urged him on, and he recited some verses. They were of average magazine quality, with all the words in their right places, as he had said about his stories, and I was surprised that the owner of such a head and face could perpetrate such a piece of commonplace verse. I made no comment. And then my attention was distracted by another offer of a drink, this time from the owner of a dark, middle-aged, humorless face—very handsome, as indeed all the men were handsome.

"What do you do?" I asked, accepting the glass offered me.

"I write little manuals, nothing arty at all. Now I'm engaged on a series called *Sex and the Sane.Life*."

I was so surprised that I spilled some of my glass. "You are not Havelock Ellis or Marie Stopes in disguise?"

"No," he said seriously, "my name is ———. Of course I use their works for reference."

"He means," said the poet of the *Union Jack*, "that he did not invent sex; he only tries to prove that it was not the invention of a god gone mad."

By this time the waiter was handing me a tray containing a selection of drinks. I picked out what I conceived to be a green chartreuse. The blue-coated poet bowed. "From me, lady," said he.

I had begun to sip the liqueur when I perceived in the mirror a good-looking young woman watching me angrily. She rose from the corner where she sat and walked towards our table, placing herself behind the chair of the poet. She put her hand on his shoulder and, glaring at me, said:

"Let her swell friend pay for her drinks. You can't afford to. Do you know," she demanded from me, "that you are drinking his breakfast?"

I had sufficient aplomb to finish the glass, and then the publisher assured me that I was not drinking the poet's breakfast, or anybody's breakfast, for, no matter who seemed to be standing the drinks, he was footing the bill.

I watched the young woman interestedly. She was faintly intoxicated, but only faintly, and her pale face, slight figure, and long nervous hands expressed an extreme sensitiveness and strong feeling that gave a tenseness to the atmosphere. I tried to throw an expression of sympathy into the glance with which I met her nervous, angry, honest eyes, stripped of everything except her profound interest in the young man in the blue jacket. In a sudden flash of intuition I understood her: she had thought I had not appreciated the poem he had recited; she thought I was not appreciating him—that I was taking him and his poem and his drink altogether too lightly. She was deeply impressed by his talents, for she belonged to that type of woman who loves genius in a man more than she loves anything else and who will nourish it with her heart's blood.

The poet remonstrated with her and tried to induce her to go back to her seat, and as her eyes turned on him pleadingly I knew that, though in time he might cast her aside and she would pass to another and briefly tend another's hearth and fire and briefly share another love or woe, all her powerful stock of emotion was forever exhausted in her feeling for this blue-coated young man who might, because of it, leave a poem that would be preserved in the anthologies. I tried to make a place for her at the table, and for a moment her sensitive face trembled with a smile. During the altercation a man whom I had not noticed before appeared from somewhere and stood by her. He spoke to her in a low tone, and she moved away. He sat down on the place I had made for her, and the waiter poured out for him a large glass of whisky which he tossed off easily. This newcomer was patently so sober that nothing could ever intoxicate him, neither life nor love, nor art nor drink.

"What are you?" I asked him.

"Irish, and not proud of it," said he, motioning the waiter to pour him another.

"I don't mean that, I mean what do you do?"

"I am a sculptor."

"A damn bad one," said the fair-haired man opposite who, for long, had been sunk in a sort of drunken silence. The newcomer cast an appraising and critical eye on me. I thought his glance was somewhat inimical.

"Do you hunt?" he asked.

"Hunt what?" I demanded, irritated.

"Hunt! Foxes, otters, rabbits, anything."

"Yes," asked the blue-coated poet, "don't you hunt?"

There was nothing but frank curiosity in the question. I was bewildered for a moment, and I involuntarily turned to the publisher. He touched my sleeve. "You know you do look a little like a lady deer stalker in these tweeds," he said.

I caught sight of myself once more in the mirror that advertised Bass's Ale, and light flooded my brain. I had been under the illusion until that moment that I had been accepted by this gathering as a person like themselves, somewhat related to the arts, a writer, I was sure. But my reflection in the glass was the least like that of a lady author that anybody's could be. I had just arrived in London from the horsiest part of the most horsy country in the world, and here I was clad in what was the smart costume of the sporting countryside from which I had come—hand-woven tweeds of an elegant cut, a soft felt hat with a feather, leather gloves, and that sort of walking stick peculiar to Ireland, an ashplant. I suddenly perceived the inwardness of the gibes which had at one moment met my ears from some of the ladies in the corner. I really looked a shocking outsider. Almost anything else in the world—sky-blue taffeta trimmed with spangles, or even the skirts of a ballet dancer, would have been more in keeping with my surroundings than the garments I was attired in. My embarrassment was relieved by a skirl of pipes at the door, which was shoved open, and a number of people appeared. A piper in tartan violently pumped a reel out of his pipes, two or three men and a woman danced around him for a moment, and then they walked in, leaving the piper still there playing away.

The piper ordered a drink to be sent out to him, for apparently he was not allowed inside the room. One of the men and a woman came and stood by our table. The publisher told me who she was —a well-known model—and her face and figure gave a sort of lyrical lift to the atmosphere similar to that given by the intensity of feeling of the other woman who had stood by the blue-coated poet's side a few minutes before. The newcomer knew everybody, and a chair was vacated for her immediately. She was no longer very young—certainly in the middle thirties—and her eyes and face lacked intensity, but they were of a surprising and whimsical beauty. "How lovely you are!" I found myself saying.

"Yes, isn't she?" the sober Irish sculptor suddenly flamed up. "But you should have seen her ten years ago. Hold up your chin!"

She raised her little chin like a child and sat silent while he passed his fingers over her lovely neck and indicated her points. The whole scene was almost incredibly English—the drinking writers drinking in a tavern as their like had always done from the days of Kit Marlowe and Ben Jonson, talking as their like had always done about art and life and beauty and the best ways of transmuting them into words or clay or paint; and the beautiful model was so English, the English of the painters, as she sat there laughing and drinking, her face so like that lovely reckless laughing face that Romney never tired of painting.

Two of the men who had come in stood at the bar, and the third, a heavily built, eager-faced man, approached us and spoke to one of those at the table in Welsh. "A fellow Celt," said the Irish sculptor, "a great Welsh bard, the bard of the Eisteddfod." I did not know whether the sculptor was serious or not. The Welshman shook my hand. "Isn't that music awful?" said he, waving his hand towards the Highland piper who was tuning up again. "These Gaels know nothing about music—nothing, nothing." He placed his hand in a pained manner on his brow. "But maybe they know about poetry," said he suddenly. "Maybe you know about poetry. I wish you could tell us what these Irish poets mean. Can anybody understand them? They are as bad as the Scots and their music."

The large man standing at the bar who had come in with the Welsh bard advanced impressively towards us, holding a glass in his hand. "Stop," he said in a strong western American accent. "The greatest thing that ever happened will be the American Legion Convention in Paris." We gazed blankly at him. "The greatest thing that ever happened. You'll see them marching through the Arch of Triumph—that will be a sight!" He unsteadily raised his glass. "To the American Legion!" he said in a severe loud voice.

He had a round, full, bespectacled, middle-aged face, a large, stout figure, and a childishness of expression that gave his face a flabby immaturity like that of a baby that some magician's wand had suddenly turned into a grown man with all the intervening experiences of a grown man non-existent. "Ah, you won the war, didn't you, Uncle Sam?" said the fair-haired man at our table. "What did you do in the war, sir?" asked the American. "Saved my skin, Uncle Sam," said the fair-haired man. "Ran away to Ireland when they passed conscription—taught catechism there."

"Shut up, Uncle Sam," said the Welshman good-humoredly, "and give us all a drink. I want to hear about these Irish writers." He turned to me again. "Do you know what any of them means? Yeats and his red-rose-bordered hem. What does that fellow Joyce mean? Did you ever read such stuff? What does Shaw mean with his Methuselah stuff? Why did they give them the Nobel Prize? 'Drink to me only with thine eyes'—that's something to have written. Here's to Ben Jonson." The American handed him a glass, and they both drank.

"I do know about poetry," said I solemnly. "I know everything about poetry, and if you listen to me I'll tell you."

"Lady fox hunter," said the blue-coated poet, "we don't want to know *everything* about poetry, but I should like to know what all that mystic Irish stuff means. Pity a poor Saxon. What do any of these fellows mean? I understand one line of A.E.'s: 'There's a lonely road through bogland,' but not another—not one other."

"Ah," said I, "but A.E. becomes a poet only when he stops being mystical."

"Hear, hear!" said the sculptor.

The Welshman had another long drink. "Say two consecutive lines of any Irish poet that a man can understand."

"I will," said I. I thought I was choosing the poem with some subtilty. "Here goes," said I. "This is A.E.:"

> Be not so desolate
> Because thy dreams have flown,
> And the hall of the heart is empty
> And silent as stone,
> As age left by children
> Sad and alone.

Those delicate children,
Thy dreams, still endure:
All pure and lovely things
Wend to the pure.
Sign not: unto the fold
Their way was sure.

Thy gentlest dreams, thy frailest,
Even those that were
Born and lost in a heartbeat,
Shall meet thee there.
They are become immortal
In shining air.

The unattainable beauty,
The thought of which was pain,
That flickered in eyes and on lips
And vanished again:
That fugitive beauty
Thou shalt attain.

As I said that lovely lament for all lost dreams, for all unrealized desires, for all unattainable beauties, the faces around me seemed to change; some softened into a drunken self-pity, some grew grave and troubled, some eyes glowed with the thought that their dreams had really been an immortal mood that had taken an immortal mold.

The bartender waited attentively for the end of the poem. "Beautiful," he said, "beautiful." The gramophone began to play something from *Samson and Delilah*. "Ah, the fatal music," he said. "Eleven of the clock, ladies and gentlemen. Time, time." "More poetry," said the Welshman. "Time, ladies and gentlemen," shouted the bartender, now becoming urgent. He rang a bell. "Eleven of the clock. All those who 'ave 'omes, go 'ome. Off the premises, ladies and gentlemen. Time. Time."

ह्~ CHAPTER 27

Changed Europe

MY HUSBAND joined me in London and we looked up our old
friends. First, of course, the Meynells, who had lent us a cottage for
our honeymoon, the most interesting as well as the kindest literary
family in London, the center of hospitality for all visitors and
known to countless poetry-loving Americans. Francis Thompson
had been the laureate of the family; his poems had been dedicated
to Wilfrid and Alice. Alice now—alas!—was dead. Of their children,
Monica was not there, Monica of whom Thompson had written:

> I am but, my sweet, your foster lover,
> Knowing well when certain years are over
> You vanish from me to another.

Thompson's godchild, since Sir Francis, of the Nonesuch Press,
was absent also, but there was there beautiful Viola, of whom
Thompson wrote:

> Wheeling angels, past espial,
> Danced her down with sound of viol;
> Wheeling angels, past espial,
> Descanting on "Viola."

Now she was a writer, and after charming many men finally married a simple Sussex farmer; there were Sylvia Lucas and her lovely
daughters, Sylvia of whom Francis Thompson had written:

> O Spring's little children, more loud your lauds upraise,
> For this is even Sylvia with her sweet, feat ways!

And Wilfrid, center of all, kind, gay, humorous as of old, welcom-
ing every comer: how the Meynells had time for all their callers
and guests I never could make out.

Then we saw Dr. Sigerson's oriental-looking son-in-law, Clement Shorter, editor of the *Sphere*, and the persistent tracker down of Brontë lore, the Pruntys, as he called them; John Drinkwater and his violinist wife, Daisy Kennedy, who kept the stateliest house I have ever seen an author in; Emily Grigsby, an American who lived in an old, old cottage about an hour from London; she seemed to be straight out of the pages of a later Henry James novel. She had been well known in New York in the first decade or so of this century as a great enchantress; like all enchantresses she was kind and charming, and maybe she had been beautiful. She had many friends in London among intellectuals who were devoted to her. Her malapropisms were delightful—lovely fantasies. "My mother insisted on calling me Emily," she told us, "on account of my grandmother knowing Chaucer." Evidently she had heard some of her literary friends speak of Palamon and Arcite and Emelye. "You know," she said, "Oscar Wilde read to me his 'Ballad of Reading Goal.' " "Gaol," with my mania for correcting people, I said. She did not notice the correction, but poured out another glass of Bollinger champagne. "I ordered this at the vineyard," she said. "They called it Emily after me." Then her wonderful necklace, she said, was given her by an "Indian chief" from East India—a real, ruling chief, she said. Emily Grisby was one of the most attractive women I have ever met, and I am sure that anybody who knew her can never forget that kind, simple, charming woman with her puzzled love for "the things of the mind" and her instinctive if not intellectual understanding of them.

Then we saw our musical friends, chief of all our old friend Arnold Bax, the composer who is now, as I write, Sir Arnold. He had lived in Dublin during our early married life and his; he liked to spend months of every year in Ireland and had really two personalities and two names: as Arnold Bax he was a well-known composer, as Dermot O'Byrne he wrote Irish short stories, poems, and plays, some of them extraordinarily good; the idiom he employed was that made famous by Synge and Lady Gregory, a sort of literal translation from the Irish somewhat heightened. Some prosy purists objected to the style and would have preferred a flatter English, but actually it was the only medium for expressing a certain extravagant and fantastic Irish character, the type that Arnold gloried in as did Synge and, to a less extent, Lady Gregory. While in Ireland he spent some time in Irish-speaking districts and would come back with an extravagant vocabulary which he turned off on all his friends or in his short stories. The country and the people never lost their fascination for him, for there are some English to whom Ireland is like the romantic continuation of a fair, unfinished dream, as Sorrento was for Sainte-Beuve—"*Sorrente m'a rendu mon beau rêve infini.*"

I do not remember whether it was on this or an occasion later that we first met T. S. Eliot. His office was not far from the Thackeray Hotel, opposite the British Museum, where we used to stay, and we dropped in to see him. Though he was born in St. Louis and was really very American, I do not think he could have spent his life in America. He was not in the least like any Englishman I ever knew, yet that he was of clear English descent one could not but realize; one felt that England was his homeland; he needed it, not for his happiness, but to fulfill whatever dream of life he had. He must have been twenty-five or over when he settled in England, and that is really a rather late age for anybody educated in one continent to settle easily in another; that was my own age when I came to America, and I realize that it was a little too late for actual identification with American ways. However, I think it is probably different with expatriate Americans whom the longings for old cultures, long-developed civilizations, and the warm life of humanly fertilized soils drew to Europe. Nevertheless, Eliot looked a little alien in London; he was very carefully dressed, not in the *dégagé* British manner, but in the deliberate American way; his handsome face and figure had not at all the British look; he seemed to be aware of his own alienness, for he told us of the remark of a French writer of immediate American-Spanish ancestry, "All of us born in North or South America feel more at home with each other than we do with anybody in Europe." He seemed to quote this with approval and assent.

We dined with him in a typical English restaurant, where in true British fashion we drank sherry before dinner and port after it—he loved the whole English civilization as did Elinor Wylie, and every custom belonging to it. His poetry, of course, puzzled the life out of some of the natives of the land he had adopted, but others were its warm admirers, particularly that great friend of all poets and writers, Lady Ottoline Morrell, who had a house near the British Museum and who also was one of our warm friends. She had been the intimate of many writers, especially of D. H. Lawrence. Snobbish as England is, or used to be, I have never been aware of any snobbery where art or artists are concerned. Generally the higher the social circles, the less snobbery there was to be found, though sometimes pride of descent can make a man as much of a bounder as can snobbery. Lady Ottoline, a Cavendish-Bentinck and the sister of a duke, had no snobbery at all, but she had an unprecedented humility before the practitioners of every art which made some of her less scrupulous novelist acquaintances write of her with mockery. "These fellows," remarked James Stephens, also a friend and admirer of hers, "don't often get the chance of patronizing a member of the ducal families; it is a sort of inverted snobbery on their part." Once when I told her in a puzzled way of how badly I had been treated by people for whose welfare I had exerted myself to the utmost, she exclaimed, "I thought I alone had such experiences." And her husband, Philip Morrell, broke in, "You couldn't have had such experiences as Ottoline. Ottoline is like a little dog that runs after a carriage and, trying to keep up with it, gets entangled in the wheels." He said this sadly, for he did not approve of all of Ottoline's friends, some of whom could be quite patronizing to him and did not realize that the beautiful country house that several of them described in their books was his and not an inheritance of Ottoline's.

Certainly Philip was overshadowed by his fascinating and sympathetic wife, but in his own right he was a distinguished person. He had been a well-known member of the House of Commons; he was one of those Englishmen whose thoughts and activities are deeply concerned with freedom and belonged to that group whose mouthpiece was the old London *Nation* under the editorship of Massingham, with Henry Nevinson as his right-hand man. They are all dead as I write this, both the *Nation* group and the Morrells, and there are none to take their places: they were part of the delight of visiting London. Philip was a fine political historian, and it is a great pity he has not left more books behind him. Perhaps he was too much the Englishman not to be impressed by the

Cavendish-Bentinck connection and by William of Orange, a hero of Ottoline's. The Bentincks had come over from Holland with William of Orange, who had given a great estate to the founder of the English branch of the family, and the two branches still kept close connections.

The last time we were ever to see the Morrells together was on a later visit of ours to Paris—some years later—when Ottoline wrote from the Bentinck place in Holland to tell us they would be in Paris and at a hotel near us. They arrived very gay and full of entertaining stories. The Dutch Bentincks had given shelter to Kaiser Wilhelm the Second after the first World War, and at this period he was living near them in Doorn. The Morrells had been traveling around Europe with suitcases, staying in simple hotels, and on arriving at the Bentincks' were sartorially unprepared for the announcement that the former Kaiser was coming to dinner. I suppose they managed to borrow some garments for the occasion. They were bowled over when the old gentleman arrived in state like a ruling monarch, with gentlemen in waiting, outriders, and trumpeters who announced his arrival. He must have known the Morrells before from the account they gave of his greeting them. At dinner they were discussing English politics, and at mention of one incident the Kaiser exclaimed, "Ha! What would Grandmama think of that?" The tone must have been faintly satiric, or the remark a family joke, for Philip told us that he didn't at first grasp that the Kaiser meant his own grandmother, Queen Victoria. The Morrells recalled that Wilhelm was just as much English as Edward the Seventh and that in speaking English he had less of a German accent. One gathered that the loss of his throne had not depressed him too greatly, and he played happily at the king-emperor business in Doorn without the appurtenances of empire and palaces. The Morrells' amused account gave me, more than anything I heard or read could have done, the sense that kings and courts were really fantasies translated into action. The Kaiser could go on with the fantasy without the responsibility or the labor of being a ruler, the only thing lacking being public interest in the spectacle which in the time we had entered was better done by the cinema. The old popular delight in royal personages and their doings was becoming transferred to movie actors and actresses. I was never to see the Morrells together again, for, a few years later, just as we arrived in London from America, looking forward to seeing her, Ottoline died. I think she will live in memoirs because she had the personality, appearance, and interests that make a character for the memoir writers, and she knew very many of the writing trade.

II

On this first return to Europe from America, although we went to Paris partly to see James Joyce, my husband's old Dublin friend, it happened that we missed him; he was, as his French friends said, *en voyage*. His *Ulysses*, circulated widely in some countries, kept out of others by censorship, was just then a world sensation. This work was so new in concept, in technique, in matter, in everything, that few readers at the time really comprehended it. It was, among other things, an application in fiction of all the new ideas concerning the subconscious. Mrs. Bloom's monologue at the end of the book follows the technique of an actual psychoanalysis where the patient lies on a couch and lets his or her mind flow out in words without any inhibitions or logical direction. About this monologue the psychoanalyst, C. G. Jung, wrote to him in very Teutonic English, "I think the devil's grandmother knows as much about the psychology of a woman—I don't. . . . It is a string of psychological peaches."

Ulysses was without any guideposts for the reader, and to this day I find it difficult to convince myself that anyone unfamiliar with the life and topography of Dublin can really understand it. Joyce himself doubted if any such person could, though he might get a good deal of it. It is one of the most local books in the world, with all sorts of local and topical references and local and topical jokes familiar to Joyce's generation of Dubliners. Most of the English reviewers and some of the American ones had no notion of what it was all about. In America the reviews of three bright young critics of the period that Joyce liked were Edmund Wilson's in the *New Republic*, then edited by Herbert Croly, Gilbert Seldes's in the *Nation*, edited by Oswald Garrison Villard, and mine in the *Freeman*, edited by Albert Jay Nock, with Van

Wyck Brooks as literary editor. Brooks was absent at the time of publication, so my review went in to Nock. He bogged at printing the opening lines, a harmless enough sentence to the effect that in the next couple of decades from that time (1922), many books would be published on Joyce and *Ulysses*. He wrote me an annoyed letter saying that he was deleting these lines, as they would be an exaggeration if applied to Cervantes or Tolstoy on the publication of any of their work. But later he was fond of publicly quoting a version of my opening sentence and of saying how right I had been.

I had known Joyce only by sight in Dublin, but he sent me a cable on the publication of my review. Now, as we arrived in Paris, hearing from Miss Beach, he telegraphed from Italy asking us to wait for his return, but as we were due in the Hawaiian Islands in a few weeks we could not stay. There was in Paris the one who might be regarded as the greatest promoter of Joyce's work, and indeed of all modern work, that fantastic and remarkable man, Ezra Pound. Before anybody else, and when Joyce could not find a publisher, Pound gauged correctly the value and uniqueness of his work. He had fought tooth and nail for the publication of *Portrait of the Artist as a Young Man;* he fought equally hard, but in vain, for a publisher for *Ulysses*, which finally was brought out by two Paris women booksellers, Sylvia Beach and Adrienne Monnier, both brilliant and accomplished and the friends of every important writer in Paris, native or foreign. Their bookshops in the Rue de l'Odéon were opposite each other, and if one crossed from one to the other a few times a week one encountered nearly every well-known figure in the literary world, such as Joyce or Paul Valéry in deep conversation with Sylvia Beach, the Frenchman more talkative than the Irishman. André Gide in Adrienne Monnier's, talking gravely of the dedication of Joyce to his work. For many years both women worked steadfastly for Joyce and his renown; they organized a French translation of *Ulysses* worked on by several collaborators. I was present in the spring of 1931 at a reading of this before a literary gathering in Adrienne's bookshop, but in spite of the efforts expended on it, the translation did not seem to me to be very satisfactory.

Ezra Pound was a longer-time expatriate from America than T.

S. Eliot, and a far more convinced one. He had by this time likewise expatriated himself from England, where he had become a
trifle unpopular, and was now on the verge of expatriating himself
from France. "One has to keep going east," he said to us, "to keep
one's mind alive," and at the same time he announced that there
was not a soul on the banks of the Thames who knew anything
about anything. Unlike Eliot, he had a pronounced American
accent of the middle-western provenance, and in spite of the ducal
Renaissance beard would have passed anywhere as a slightly eccentric middle-western professor. In London at the beginning of
his career he had attached himself to the Irish Literary Society or
to its meeting rooms and became such an intimate friend and
helper of Yeats that he conducted a portion of Yeats's correspondence and business affairs. The connection between them was
not easy to understand, but Yeats dedicated a book to him, *A
Packet for Ezra Pound*, and to his dying day was attached to him
in spite of an impatient characterization of him in a letter to Lady
Gerald Wellesley (Dorothy Wellesley) as an American professor.

At this period, Pound and his young wife, an Englishwoman,
the daughter of Yeats's great friend, Mrs. Shakespeare, were living
on the left bank and seemed to be the center of a group of American writers and journalists. Ezra insisted on taking us to a lecture
by Lincoln Steffens on Soviet Russia, the Russia of Lenin, in the
apartment of one of his friends. The lecture seemed to me of an
appalling dreariness, and I hated being dragged to it, with all the
interesting things in Paris one could go to. But Ezra listened to
it with rapt attention, his eyes glued to the speaker's face, the very
type of a young man in search of an ideology, except that he was
not so very young. He seemed to have an intense interest in new
political and economic ideas, and after Steffens was finished he rose
to his feet and started talking about the Douglas plan, to which
he had tried to convert Arthur Griffith and through him the new
Irish state. He had begun the writing of those letters of his to every
prime minister in Europe on this subject. Maybe if they had listened
to him it might have done something for Europe; at least it couldn't
have done as much harm as the ideas that the prime ministers themselves cherished. A little later he was to interest Yeats, who liked
everything that had the appearance of intellectual disciplines, in

aspects of the fascist state which, in spite of everything, had a romantic attraction for some people, especially a certain type of artist. Later I was not surprised to hear of Ezra's attachment of Italian fascism, though he was strongly anti-German. He liked to be mixed up in everything that was going on around him, and some time before this, when there was an Irish race convention in Paris, he got into that, too.

The comedy side of this convention seemed to have impressed the French more than its serious side, which represented an attempt to bring together divergent Irish opinions so as to make use of the fruits of the revolution. With all their humor, the people of my race can, in assembly, behave more humorlessly and absurdly than any other race in the wide world. The organizers had the idea of fishing up well-known Continentals of Irish ancestry, descendants of the princely families banished, or that had fled from Ireland after one or another of the disastrous fights for freedom. This resulted in the assembly being presided over by a Spanish grandee, the Duke of Tetuan, a descendant of the O'Donnells of Tirconnel. His grandeeship had barely concealed his boredom with the whole business; it was said that he sank into a state of somnolence from time to time, to wake up when a pretty woman rose to say something. Ezra, of course, was present, escorting Yeats, who knew only English. There were speeches in indifferent French, and one of the delegates delivered an address in that language concocted for him, it was reported, by Ezra. This had happened some time before, but it was still the talk of various circles in Paris. The audience, particularly the French portion thereof, had been sometimes a bit uncertain as to what tongue they were being addressed in, thinking it might be the very best Spanish of Tetuan.

After hearing the Steffens lecture about the new world that was being made for us, I promptly accepted an invitation from another guest "to view one of the ancient monuments of Paris," to wit— Sarah Bernhardt in a new play. It was not much more than a decade since I had seen Sarah in Dublin in Maeterlinck's *Pelléas and Mélisande*, playing the role of Pelléas to Mrs. Pat Campbell's Mélisande, but in the meantime there had been wars, the overthrow of kings and emperors, political revolutions, artistic revolutions, Proust, Joyce—and Bernhardt did indeed seem to be from a long way back, from the horse-drawn carriage and gaslit-street period. I was so forcibly impressed by the fact that she was a figure out of another world, another sort of civilization, with another ideal of art, that the play itself, which was certainly not good, almost failed to register. As a student I had seen her as Hamlet in a few scenes without thinking it in the least preposterous that she should play a male role, because in my youth we accepted with faith everything that Sarah did on the stage, but now seeing this old woman with an artificial leg essay the part of a young man gave me a sort of psychic shock, and I cannot remember any other figure in the cast or even much about the play. It was a piece called *La Gloire*, by the younger Rostand, and was all about a young man overshadowed by his father's greatness. I suppose it was really *L'Aiglon* at three or four removes.

Sarah's movements, when she did move, had, naturally, no spontaneity or agility; she kept seated a good deal, though for one lengthy scene I remember she stood before the portrait of the young man's father delivering a long-winded speech with great fervor and much gesture, sinking at the end of it with a sob to the ground. It added to all the other impressions I was receiving on this visit to Europe that the world we had known was passing away—the dingy little theater, Sarah's head and profile as she faced the portrait speaking the conventional French verse. In a long entr'acte I took stock of the audience, listening to their remarks, and noting that it was composed of people of a generation or even of two generations back; they were all out of Sarah's past, and they eagerly discussed the performance, comparing it with other performances of hers. As often since, I was struck by the fact that the French expect artifice and what we might call unreality in the theater, and so could forget that a woman was playing the role of a man, an old crippled woman playing the role of a young man; it was a role like any other, and what they watched was the art with which it was played. Bernhardt was really part of their lives and of that wonderful French memory in which a place is kept for everyone who expresses the spirit of France, of what our friend Jules Bois called *l'idée française*, as Sarah over and over again had expressed it.

When we saw the French people we had known before the war, a few of whom had been students in Dublin in my time, we found the French of our own age disillusioned, somewhat distraught people, disillusioned with the war, not very hopeful about their own future. Men who had been distinguished officers, holding important army posts, were turned back into civilian life and to prosy ill-paying jobs such as insurance clerks, small civil servants, workers in offices. Some had been wounded and had lost the zest for life; in the streets one met more frequently than in London *les grands blessés*, men who had lost a leg or an arm; most pitiful of all were the war-blinded, sad-faced men led around usually by a devoted woman; the scars, the memories of war were recent. There was even then a general disgust with the Third Republic; in some way it did not seem to represent the people but to be a kind of imposition that they barely tolerated. Gay Paris was not so gay for the natives; the franc had been devaluated, savings were worth almost nothing; the money the people had put into Russian bonds had vanished with Imperial Russia. But foreigners were gaily romping around Montmartre or Montparnasse, getting astronomical francs for their dollars or pounds. In the apartment of a Sorbonne professor we met a couple of Germans, and they told us of the wild fantastic gaiety that was reigning in Berlin, which was also full of foreigners, getting even more astronomical marks for their various moneys. One of the Germans was going to America to teach in a college; I told him about Ezra Pound's saying, "One has to keep going east." "No," said the Sorbonne professor, "one has to keep going west; as a start I'm going to Ireland myself, then to South America." The exodus from Europe was beginning. I found myself leaving without tears, looking forward to America and my American friends. But the journey ahead of us was long; after crossing the Atlantic and a hasty meeting with our friends in New York, we would have to cross the American continent and half the Pacific to Hawaii, and whether this was going west or east, I really did not know.

३∾ CHAPTER 28

Hawaiian Interlude

FOR THE SECOND TIME in our lives we disembarked in New York, this time with something of a sense of home-returning. We were met at the boat by our friend Lloyd Morris and his delightful mother, who later gathered together many of our friends to give us what they called a welcome-home party—Elinor Wylie, Bill Benét, Edwin Arlington Robinson, Jules Bois, Herbert and Jean Gorman. Then there was a send-off party given us by Edgar and Leonora Speyer.

Once more we bade our friends good-by and started across the continent for San Francisco to get the boat for Honolulu. As we stepped on the Pacific liner the Orient confronted us; the deck hands, the stewards, were all Chinese, so numerous that we each seemed to have a personal attendant: evidently they were all of the coolie class and seemed starved and undersized. The boat, like a Europe-bound boat, had among the passengers a multitude of buyers who talked continuously about the goods and products of the Orient; Tokyo and Peking in their minds had the place that Paris and Vienna had for those on the Atlantic ships. The women buyers had gorgeous jade necklaces and bracelets and occasionally wore as wraps on deck wonderfully embroidered mandarin coats. On New Year's Day we were midway across the Pacific, and at the special dinner a United States senator on board made a speech about Abraham Lincoln. For the first time I came up against the southern die-hard enmity to the Yankee. The handsome southern woman at our table who was making a voyage round the world bridled up and then burst out in passionate indignation: "A little less about Abe Lincoln and something more about Jefferson Davis would be a help. Abe Lincoln was the worst American that ever was." I was astounded at the conviction she showed; she followed it up by speaking of her son in these terms, "If Ed ever marries a Yankee, I'll die." An incident of another kind on the boat has always remained in my memory. A relative of Robert Louis Stevenson's wife talked to us about the Stevensons' living in Hawaii. "She treated her first husband badly," this woman told us. "He tried to do everything for her; she was crazy to be an artist, and he saved up and sent her to Paris to study. But all that led to was that she met Stevenson and dropped her husband. There was no poetic justice in it at all," she went on, "for she and Stevenson were very happy and had the admiration of the world. The other poor man just sank out of sight."

The voyage from San Francisco was about as long as that from New York to a European port, and the queer roll of the Pacific was really more sickening than the wild Atlantic waves, because there seemed to be no letup in the physical malaise. The oriental staff waiting on us with ceremony were silent and remote, very unlike the chatty fellows on Atlantic liners, and this made the trip seem longer. At last, one bright morning when we came on deck we saw the islands rise out of the sea, mountains, lovely, gilt with sunshine, exotic, yet vaguely disappointing, as all things looked forward to are when reached. Later, on the pilot boat there came to meet us a deputation who, entering the dining room where we were at breakfast, greeted us in Hawaiian and English and placed *leis* round our necks with a grave "*Aloha*," which can mean so many things from "welcome" to "farewell," as we were to discover.

We were escorted to our temporary abode, a small cottage on the grounds of a school outside Honolulu, not far from the famous Bishop Museum, where my husband was to work on the legends. Here we were greeted by another deputation and driven around to see the sights. Worn out by weeks of traveling and my usual chronic anemia, I nearly succumbed to exhaustion and must have seemed morose and stupid to our kind hostess. What struck me almost immediately was that Hawaiian patriotism and pride of birthright were not limited to the Polynesian population, but were quite widespread among those Americans and Europeans whose families had been about a century on the islands. The next thing that struck me was a sort of anti-Americanism, an antagonism not unlike the feeling against the British in Ireland. This varied in strength from a mild resentment to downright hatred, and this was not lessened by the presence of the American army and navy, some members of which, especially on Saturday nights after potations of *oklehao*, could be as recklessly unpleasant as military anywhere. We were told right away more than our minds could take in of the grievances of Polynesians and of the frightfulness of some *haoles* or white people, and about the descendants of the missionaries grabbing the wealth of the islands. We, as people born in Ireland under the domination of England, were supposed to have an inside understanding of such matters. But we soon found that certain of the descendants of the missionaries were passionately Hawaiian, had been against the annexation by America and had favored the continuation of the native monarchy, and were devoted to what members of the royal family who remained. In spite of the fact that some of their descendants became exploiteering industrialists, the first missionaries were men and women of very high character. Their descendants with whom we became friends, like the Judds and the Emersons, had the same high character and the same devotion to duty.

The native Hawaiian population were dusky-skinned, with a complexion like some Hindoos I have known; they were often, especially the high-caste men and women, very tall, very large people, quite the largest members of the human race I have ever seen. They had intermarried a good deal with the whites, or Caucasians, as they were called, and some of those of mixed stock had the outstanding missionary names.

Some days after our arrival the governor of the islands, Governor Farrington, gave a reception for us in the official palace, one of the residences of the native royal family. This as a democratic function could hardly be surpassed, for there were no invitations, there being simply a proclamation by the governor to the effect that there would be a reception for the poet who had come to put Hawaiian legends into shape and for his wife—so that anybody who felt like putting on his or her best clothes proceeded to the palace to take a look at us. As we stood in line with the governor and his wife, an impressive company of various national descents, eastern and western, entered. Among the firstcomers were tall old Hawaiian ladies in the long nightdress-like garment called a *holoku* in which the

first missionaries insisted on clothing the native women who were
not by nature much inclined to cover their nakedness. As the tall
women entered, those who had been court ladies in King Kalakaua's palace, who were descended from the high chiefs and were
themselves known as high chiefesses, began to chant the *meles*,
the name songs of their ancestors, giving salutation to the portrait
of the King. In comparison with these women in their straight long
garments, with the whale- or shark-tooth necklaces that were the
badge of their high descent, most of the whites present looked
small, colorless, and insignificant. They stirred in me some racial
memories of Irish chiefs who had had their own bards and harpers
and chants not so unlike the name songs that now overwhelmed
me with their strangeness and their poignancy.

II

The last king had been named Kalakaua, but the earlier kings
had been called Kamehameha, from the first warrior Hawaiian
chief who had made himself king of the eight islands and imposed
government and laws on the people. This first Kamehameha was a
great general and a great person; the story of his rise, his reign, and
how he made a kingdom of the islands is very much of the same
pattern as that of the early European conquerors and rulers. He
knew that the marauding whites were more advanced than the
Hawaiians in material equipment, and he determined to learn
everything he could from them—how to build ships, use guns, and
make tools. When it suited him he made a couple of whites from
an expeditionary ship members of his council. The Kamehameha
dynasty were real rulers, able, intelligent, liberal, and receptive in
spite of the belief in their divine ancestry on which their power
was based.

The missionaries who arrived at the time of the rise of the
Kamehameha dynasty did a great deal for the native people in
many ways. However, even after a hundred years of Christianity,
I noticed that some of those I met had a lingering devotion to
Madame Pele, the volcano goddess, and to some of her traditional
rites. The Hawaiians did not seem to me very different from

Europeans of the same social grades: the rich were like the rich, the poor like the poor Europeans, except that they had somewhat different habits of living. The missionaries who found them living in grass huts showed them how to build timber houses on the New England model; they tried to improve their health, which had broken down under the impact of the white sailors with different diseases—in fact the whole story of the New England missionaries is one of great self-sacrifice, hard work, exhausting pioneering labors, and much responsibility. They got the language into written form, opened schools, built churches, created with their limited resources medical centers. Soon their descendants became a Hawaiian aristocracy, some of them with the highest qualities of a functioning aristocracy. Frankly, I do not know how this could have been helped. The missionaries must have been of a very vigorous stock, and it is probably true that their vigorous descendants who had no taste for missioneering could not very well help becoming rich in such a naturally rich country. All they had to do, their apologizers told us, was to organize the growing business of Hawaii, and for a naturally pioneering people this was in the day's work. As for myself, I thought of the history of the country I was born in and how easily some such explanation could have been made for the invaders and exploiters who grabbed the richest lands.

We were called on by a great many people, Hawaiians, half Hawaiians, *haoles*, and even Chinese and Japanese. There were so many Japanese that one might easily imagine the islands to be Japanese; they had been admitted in large numbers to work in the sugar-cane and pineapple plantations because the native Hawaiians, small farmers and fishermen by tradition, could not be got to work in gangs. There were a great many Chinese also, and though they were less assertive than the Japanese, neither race seemed to have any of that subservience so common among poorer Europeans before their "superiors." Though the Japanese were employed to do the domestic work in the houses of the well-to-do, they had little of the domestic-servant mentality: in fact the women were on a very easy footing with their mistresses.

The whites occupied the dominant position in the islands, and some of them, male and female, were like the soldier in Kipling's poem who liked to be "where there ain't no ten commandments."

The dazzling sun, the tropical flowers, fruits, and trees, banjoes, ukuleles, and hulas, the moon over the Pali, went to their heads; they went in for what they called "having a good time," which for the whites in tropical countries means having a reckless time. Although it was during Prohibition, there was in profusion a Japanese liquor, sake, distilled from rice, and another, *oklehao*, distilled from the ti plant. At the time I was no alcohol drinker, so I cannot experimentally describe these drinks, but from their visible effects on Saturday nights on members of the American forces I should say they had considerable potency. As for ourselves, we never went into a Hawaiian house in search of native lore without being offered one of them.

My husband worked at the Bishop Museum, where he had access to the collections of native literature which had been assembled and translated by scholars both of pure native descent and of *haole* descent. In the mornings we took lessons in Hawaiian, and while we did not spend long enough in the islands to acquire much proficiency in the language, we got to know enough to be able to make out what was said to us and to read some of the poetry. The very fact of being able to do this, even in an elementary way, gave us an insight into the character of this strange and isolated people such as we could have got in no other way. This was true of my husband more than of myself, because he kept working at the native literature with native scholars beside him all the time.

In these warm islands it was surprising how much of the poetry was about the rain and cold, and surprising how much of it was romantic. I had often heard that romantic love was a comparatively recent European development, but in Hawaiian we found touching romantic love poetry. The very first piece of Hawaiian I found myself able to read was an enchanting love poem made up of the tiniest words put together with a mixture of shyness and artfulness by some lovelorn girl. Each stanza had a refrain, "*I ku anu e*," meaning "from the cold":

> I call on you, O dear one,
> Breast so cold, so cold.
> Oh, how cold the nightfall!
> *I ku anu e.*

> How very cold the wind is,
> The raindrops and the dew,
> Bodies have to shiver—
> *I ku anu e!*

and then there is this insinuating last stanza:

> What if we two clasp
> Arms around each other,
> So we may not feel
> Wind or rain or dew?

What I reproduce in English is ponderous in comparison with the Hawaiian, with words like the notes of a bird. That we understood the language to some extent, and so could make out part of what people were saying to us, made the Hawaiians more friendly to us. Though a suspicion grew on me that many of the real natives long since had ceased to be really friendly with the newcomers or the visitors to the islands.

I visited only the larger islands like Oahu, Hawaii, Maui, Kauai, but my husband went to nearly all the others, including the leper island, Molokai—though he did not go to the settlement—being indefatigable in digging into native lore and native life. As a young man in Ireland he had been conditioned into just such studies, loved them, and developed a strong admiration for the Hawaiian race and its historical characters. While he was on other islands I stayed in Honolulu with Mrs. Julie Judd Swanzy, a missionary descendant whose family had held high office under the native rulers; some of her family had married Hawaiians; the services of her family and their connections gave her a special place in Hawaiian life. I have seldom met a more intellectually gifted woman or one with more of a sense of responsibility to her native land, which, of course, to her was Hawaii. She had married an Irishman from Dublin, and we knew some of his family. She had such a place and was of such a type as were the grand duchesses in European countries. I cannot imagine a more delightful way of living than was hers, but I doubt if anyone will be in such a position again anywhere in the world.

Her chief residence was in the hills just above Honolulu, quite

near the town, a house surrounded by porches and wonderful
tropical gardens with a pool of the bluest water I ever saw. Her
house was furnished mostly with oriental pieces—Chinese, Japanese,
Indian, with some Filipino—and for sheer comfort and delightful-
ness it could not be surpassed by any house in the world. The large
bedrooms opened on *lanais* on which one could stroll in the mild
air at any hour of the night or day; the softly walking, attentive
oriental servants who had their own quarters in a sort of compound
outside the house were not in the least servile, but quite chummy
and very anxious to tell me all about themselves; at least the women
were. Every morning the Japanese maid who brought me up my
breakfast told me the latest developments in her troubles with her
husband, her common-law husband he would be designated in the
U.S. for, as she explained, she had not been united with him in
court. He had now taken on a concubine, but that, actually, was
not what she objected to; it was that he had possession of their
joint savings, and she was invoking the law to get her share out of
him. How alike the human race is all over! For I encountered exactly similar situations in France, where, though the marriage tie
among working people is generally lasting, it is frequently sancti-
fied by neither law nor religion; it is a private matter between them
as it was with the Japanese maid and her husband. Her marriage or
union or whatever it might be called had been a friendly arrangement with no grand emotions involved, and what she was concerned with was a business arrangement about possessions. She was
a little inclined to call the new female in her place a hussy or some
Japanese equivalent, but she was free from any devastating feelings
about her. She asked for everybody's advice as to what she should
do to get her savings back. Under exactly the same circumstances
in France, several times I have tried to give advice—*mes économies,
madame—il a pris mes économies.* In France before the latest
World War, even with a legal standing a wife had no right to her
own savings.

In addition to her spacious house in Honolulu, Mrs. Swanzy had,
as was fairly customary, a mountain house and a beach house. The
mountain house, to which one drove slowly up the side of a mountain, was something like a hunting lodge, which, when Honolulu
became too warm, she or her family inhabited. It was simply and

picturesquely furnished like a Swiss chalet except that it had a loneliness that no house in Europe could have; it had the loneliness inherent in new or comparatively newly inhabited countries. The same could be said of her beautiful beach house by the blue waters of the Pacific, in spite of the fact that everything around it was tranquil, tropical, colorful and gay, and, on first acquaintance, enchanting. But the dust of dead men had not for thousands of years enriched the earth as it had Europe's, nor had the emotions of men about it during long generations been put into verse or paint and canvas or into symphonies—the chronicle of human emotions and dreams had not been ample enough.

This strange loneliness or emptiness was even greater when we stayed in a real Polynesian village on the large island, Hawaii. The capital of this lovely island is Hilo; I remember it rained there every day, a mild rain called in the native poetry "the little rain of Hilo . . . where the rain walks softly through the lehua trees." Shortly after our arrival at the hotel in Hilo we were called upon by a Hawaiian dignitary, a very large man even for a Hawaiian, carrying a huge shiny paper umbrella. My husband, known already in the native language as the *haku-mele mai Ilelani*, the poet from Ireland, had wandered out to see some storytellers whose addresses had been given him, so he was not present at the conversation between myself and the visitor, though I think he would have enjoyed it. The visitor was learned in native lore, but not in that of other countries, though his English was good and fluent. He told me that when he heard the name of the *haku-mele* as one who could make the Hawaiian tales into English, he went to the library and asked for some of his books. One in particular he liked, *The Adventures of Odysseus and the Tale of Troy*, because the stories in it of great chiefs and warriors and voyagers so much resembled the traditional Hawaiian legends. So he advised everybody to the effect that the man who knew all that was the very man Hawaii needed for its tales, and he was sure his advice had influenced the legislature. Unnecessarily perhaps I entered into a lengthy explanation that the Odyssey was really written by a Greek *haku-mele* by the name of Homer who had lived long ago on islands not perhaps so unlike these Pacific islands, and that the present *haku-mele* had simply made a version of Homer's *moolelo*. He put me a question:

would the Hawaiian book produced by the *haku-mele* be as good as Homer's? I dodged the question, but said it might inspire some future Kanaka *haku-mele* to wander from island to island the way Homer did and put down in one great *mele* the high deeds of the gods and great chiefs of his race. He nodded, for his mind was quick and artistic.

When the *haku-mele* finally turned up, flushed and enthusiastic after his visit to old Hawaiians who had recited poems, our caller greeted him a little distantly, his mind perhaps alienated on discovering that he had not really composed the *Iliad* and the *Odyssey*. We asked our caller's advice about living in a native village, and he thought our choice of the remote village of Kalapana a good one; there were no whites, and nobody, he believed, was Americanized or knew any English, except the children. On this account he advised us to take with us someone who knew both English and Hawaiian to act as interpreter, but we had already arranged for this and were taking with us a man of American descent who knew the Hawaiian language and lore better than any except the most learned of the scholars.

III

Some days later we set out for Kalapana early in the morning in the usual softly falling rain of Hilo. Just outside Hilo the inevitable sugar cane came into view, but there were long stretches of land which the lava flow had rendered incapable of cultivation. As we went along we dropped into some of the Hawaiian houses, and the people, gladly enough, chanted *meles* and danced hulas very different from the stage hula familiar in the United States. Where the smaller houses near Hilo had all a New England look no matter who lived in them, the larger ones had a British atmosphere; a great many were doubtless inhabited by British plantation managers. The humbler plantation workers were mostly Japanese who occupied tiny, dismal-looking shacks, all clustered together. After a couple of hours we reached, not our destination, but a sort of encampment village called Pahoa, which in itself and its environment seemed to be entirely inhabited by oriental plantation workers. It was of a surpassing ugliness, as almost all ephemeral and makeshift things are. This village looked as if it had grown up over-night in the midst of cane fields, and though, perhaps, it was no worse than some of the coal-mining towns of Wales or Pennsyl-vania, the contrast with the bright sunshine and the exotic beauty of the islands made it look simply outrageous.

We had brought no provisions of any kind with us, and this was a great mistake, because even a thermos flask of coffee would have made our subsequent experiences easier. It was lunchtime when we got to this plantation village, and finding that one of the dingy oriental stores had "Restaurant" written in English on the window, we went in. Inside were several bare wooden tables, and in the center of each was a bowl of brown plantation sugar, a bottle of sauce, and a salt shaker, signs that *haole* civilization had penetrated this far. In a room off the main room we could see a large stove on which a Chinese was frying chunks of beef. A Japanese with a khaki helmet, heavy shoes, and leggings entered after us and called out in English to the Chinese, "What is there to eat?" "Rice, steak, ham, and eggs." He ordered steak and rice; evidently the sinister-looking chunks of beef were called steak. We perceived by the sartorial getup of the Japanese that he was no mere plantation worker but an overseer of some kind. We spoke to him about the village and the neighborhood around. He answered shortly and assertively, and though we did not ask the question, he informed us that the Japanese represented more than half the population of Hawaii. The Japanese assertiveness may have been dislikable to an extent, yet I accorded it an unwilling admiration. Some of their newspapers expressed their minds on all matters relating to the American government of Hawaii, in which the Japanese had no voice, with, to some people, revolting boldness. The overseer tossed a sentence at us now and again as he ate an enormous plate of the fried beef, which he covered with a sauce from the bottle; then he swallowed almost whole a small pie, followed by a lump of cheese. "Very Americanized, truly," observed our companion. The beef we eschewed and ordered ham and eggs. The two men of our party ate it to a finish, but I, after watching the Chinese pre-pare the food and cut the bread, wandered forth in search of oranges and found in a store a pineapple, which was just handed to me for the asking without pay. Until you eat a pineapple in Hawaii you don't know what a fresh pineapple is.

We drove out of the village and into the most mysterious kind of country along a road of hardened lava, with seas of hardened lava each side of us stretching from the mountains to the sea. We had in our notebook the names of two well-to-do Hawaiian families of mixed missionary descent whom we called on in this wilderness. The first we found unresponsive, but the second greeted us with charming hospitality and gave us excellent tea and sandwiches. The house was not unlike that of an Irish squireen, with the same sort of furniture and the same sort of family heirlooms, even to the spinet against the wall. The man of the house had a pride in both races from which he sprang, pride in his Hawaiian relics and in his New England furniture which, a hundred years before, had been brought by his missionary ancestors in a sailing ship around the Horn. Our hostess, who was either British or American, wondered why we wanted to go for a stay in Kalapana; to drive there, look around, was one thing, but to stay . . . She did not believe that anybody there had any beds or bed linen, and she, personally, had never heard of any *haole* woman who had spent even one night in Kalapana. Our hostess was a cultivated and intellectual woman, and I did not know how she was able to stand the isolation. After we left this house, the road and the land we traveled through became more eerie than any we had yet seen—a black land with an odd brave lehua tree forcing its way through the lava and showing scarlet blossoms. What enormous boiling over of the mountains made this lava stream flow unhindered to the sea! There were huge lava rocks on the ocean's edge against which the waves dashed— not loudly, like the Atlantic waves, but with a sort of smothered echo. I thought with sympathy of the terror of the Hawaiians of old who had believed that their goddess Pele lived in the volcano and when she was angry made her mountain vomit to destroy the lands and people. Once when the lava flow was so terrific that it almost covered the whole land on one side of this island and continued so long that the people thought the burning liquid would even dry up the sea, for all the pigs sacrificed to the goddess were of no avail, the king, Kamehameha, cut off a lock of his hair and threw it into the lava stream. This action of his was effective; he was able to mollify the goddess because, like all Pacific rulers, he was a descendant of the gods himself and so related to Pele. Many times this legend was told to us.

We might have been the first people who ever burst into the silent sea of lava, and the emptiness of the place was made more eerie by the occasional signs against trespassing, boards on which was written simply "Kapu," which is the same word as "taboo"— it brought us back to another age. Finally, as night was almost upon us we met a man and a child on the road, a tall man nearly seven feet high, handsomely built, and looking like a god in the dimness. The friend with us addressed him in Hawaiian and asked how far it was to Kalapana; it was yet a few miles off. Continuing in the darkness, we came on the usual little New England painted house, and thinking we had arrived, got off. Inside the open door stood a woman of mixed Hawaiian and oriental blood with a group of almost naked children around her. She said in moderately good English that she was a schoolmistress, that she herself had once taught in Kalapana, which was still a little way ahead of us. We started off again, and soon, on the lava edge of the sea, we reached the line of little board houses that was described in the tourist guides as a real remnant of Hawaiian life, the village of Kalapana.

We had the name of a woman whose son we had met in Hilo, and a boy pointed out her house to us at the end of the village. There were actually three houses, roughly built and raised above the ground on logs stuck deep in the earth: two of the houses were joined by the same veranda or *lanai*. After a lengthy conversation joined in by numerous members of the family, the woman of the house, who was surprised by our appearance in the village, especially at such a late hour, agreed to take us in. She was a beautiful middle-aged woman who had in early life acquired some English; it seemed to me that her *haole* education had made her a little suspicious and subtracted somewhat from her native Hawaiian dignity; she was not quite so much at her ease as were her aunt and uncle, who offered us the whole hospitality of their house at once. It was sometimes difficult to understand the relations of people in a native household, but we gathered that the two elders were husband and wife and uncle and aunt of the first woman we spoke to, whom I shall call our junior hostess. Her children, too, were there—a tall young boy in his teens and a graceful girl; smaller children appeared who seemed to be the grandchildren of our senior hosts; they had learned English at school and talked easily to us as we sat on the *lanai*. Two of the women withdrew to one of the houses to prepare food for us, and soon the children followed them. After quite a long time, during which the older people's supply of English and our supply of Hawaiian were well exercised, the boy came out and said, in offhand American manner and in the tone of one who had learned the sentence from a phrase book, "Will you folks come in to dinner?"

We went into the middle one of the three houses and entered a bare but not unlovely room with a table in the center, some seating arrangements, and a piece of Hawaiian matting on the floor. The meal was laid on the table and consisted of rice, poi, the native dish of pounded taro root which looked for all the world like billsticker's paste; there were, in addition, canned herrings, and we knew our hosts had put their best foot forward, for anything out of a can is a great delicacy. The family did not sit down with us, but instead had their meal in Polynesian fashion, crouched on the floor around a large common dish of poi, each having a little bit of fish on a plate beside him. Our junior hostess sat and talked with us very politely, without, however, eating herself. She explained that though the old people, like her uncle and aunt, all found it uncomfortable to sit on a chair at a table, she had brought up her children to eat with knives and forks at a table, and that they could very well do so when occasion required.

After this meal we all sat on the *lanai* and were entertained with music and singing accompanied by the steel guitar and ukulele. Hawaiian songs as sung in theaters in the United States are rather quick and jazzy, but the singing here was slow and mournful. I have never heard Hawaiians sing in any other way in their own country; the truth is that with primitive people music or song or dancing is not an expression of gaiety but of the incomprehensiveness of the universe and the mournfulness of their lot. The soft language with its numerous *l*'s and *m*'s and barking *k*'s was wonderfully suited to the music, which is not, however, really native, but is mostly founded on the hymn tunes taught by the early missionaries. As we sat on the *lanai* a gorgeous moon shone through the faint rain, coconut trees leaned over at an angle with the ground, their roots half torn up by storms or by the wash of the sea. In the distance we could see an outrigger canoe drawn up on the black sands; the moon shone down on a black land, black mountains, a dark sea, and the dark faces of my hosts—the most mysterious land and the most mysterious people in the whole world, it seemed to me then. In this black land by the sea, in this remote island village, this race was still living in its old way except for the imitation white man's dwelling, for a grass hut was now a rare sight. "We are a dying race," our senior host said a few times during the evening. He said it without sadness or bitterness, and just as if making a statement. They had made but little resistance to the inroads of whites and Orientals with their sugar and pine-apple plantations; they were not made for resistances; they were intended to live on their warm islands with little labor. The climate was enervating, and it was especially damp and warm on this side of the island of Hawaii. Like all really attractive persons and peoples, their sense of self-preservation was not strong.

After the singing we were shown our sleeping quarters in one of the houses. The Hawaiian was at all times inclined to have a number of separate houses rather than a single commodious one. Our hostess had proudly informed us that she had beds, which, I gathered, few of the other villagers had. The room she showed us into as well as the one allotted to our companion was spot-lessly clean, the bed linen was even dainty, the pillowcases had the royal Hawaiian motto embroidered in red and little rows of tucks. The four-posted wooden bed, however, had no mattress, no springs, nothing but a flat board on which was a *lahala* mat; over this was placed a sheet and a patchwork quilt such as the missionaries had taught the islanders to make. The natives sleep easily on a hard surface, but sleep was difficult for a *haole* woman accustomed to mattresses and feather pillows. As I lay awake I heard all night the suppressed beat of the sea against the lava rock. At early dawn I got up, dressed, and walked down a few paces to the sea, the Pacific Ocean. It had none of the fierceness or the tragedy of the Atlantic in it; the Polynesians had never been afraid of it—they were used to it almost from the moment they were washed in it after they were born. I have seen little children whose center of gravity was as yet undecided, and who stumbled at every effort to walk, swimming like fishes in the sea. In the past the Hawaiians had gone long distances in their outrigger canoes; indeed they must have voyaged for thousands of miles in them; they are known to have swum enormous distances. The sea could only have been kind to them, or such confidence in it could not have been engendered; one never hears of anybody being drowned.

On the *lanai* again in the early morning we all sat, all except our senior hostess, who was busy at household duties. Some of the neighbors gathered, the women very fat in their loose *holokus*, the nightdress-like garment in which the New England missionaries had clothed the Hawaiian women a hundred years before. Thinking I could not understand their language, they asked our traveling companion various questions concerning the *haku-mele*, who was still asleep on his hard board. What was his religion, his race, was he rich, what did he do for a living? This little I gathered, but much of the conversation, of course, escaped me, as my Hawaiian was limited. Our junior hostess put a question with a long string of words that puzzled even our learned companion; then she explained some of it in English—the United States Geological Survey: did we belong to the United States Geological Survey? The members of the Survey were the only white strangers she had known who had spent any time in the village. Our companion tried to explain us; the *haku-mele* had been hired by the Hawaiian legislature to write their stories and legends in English so that the English-speaking children of the territory could know them. The older man declared vigorously that the young people were ashamed of their old lore, that not one of them knew a *mele kahiko*, and that the descendants of the generals of the great king, Kamehameha, did not care to know the name songs of their ancestors. The stripling interrupted the old man and said in English, "But we are American citizens." Some of the native Hawaiians were proud of being Americans, but in others the rage against the whole white world and against the Americans who had overthrown their sovereignty was bitter indeed. The old man spoke with the same passion about the decay of their native life as I have heard expressed by old people in the West of Ireland.

After a long conversation we were called in to breakfast in the same room in which we had had supper the evening before. For breakfast we had exactly the same dishes as before, with the addition of boiled salt beef and Chinese cabbage. This latter our senior hostess had prepared as a special delicacy for the stranger, and it wrung my heart that I was incapable of beginning the day on salt beef; I was indeed incapable of beginning the day on anything except tea or coffee and toast, and such was entirely unheard of here. Without the toast I could have done, but not without the tea or coffee. But as my hostess was beginning to look disappointed and to feel that the food she had so plentifully supplied was unpleasing, I manfully attacked the herrings, the poi, and the cold rice. I had always imagined that in a desert place or during a famine I could live on a few articles of diet. In a remote village in the West of Ireland I had lived for a long stretch on bread and butter, potatoes, milk, and tea; not one of these necessities was of the fare of our hosts, though in some respects they were less primitive in their mode of living than people in remote parts of Scotland or Ireland.

After breakfast the smaller children went to school; the two older people, the uncle and his wife, sat on the floor and went on with their weaving of mats; my junior hostess placed herself in a chair on the *lanai* and proceeded to embroider something with red cotton; my sex all over the world seem to enjoy employing themselves with needle and thread in a way that gives them much satisfaction. I had more latitude to observe my hosts than on the previous night: they were all handsome and intelligent and belonged, it seemed to me, to what is called the Aryan race, in spite of their darker skin. I am inclined to think that they were superior, in all forms of intelligence except the practical intelligence, to Europeans of similar status. Their practical intelligence was probably as good as that of most of the artists I have known and as that of the *haku-mele* they were entertaining. It was not great enough to enable them to cope successfully with the exploiting whites, the Caucasians, as some of our Hawaiian friends called them, who now owned the choice spots of their islands. In a way it was their thirst for progress that was their undoing; the white man came with his religion, his inventions, his new forms of civilization while theirs had remained stationary for long on account of their isolated position. The kings and chiefs welcomed the white man and his new ideas and new customs, and, naturally enough, the newcomers quickly gained the upper hand.

Like Hawaiians of the towns, my hosts lived in an imitation-American dwelling; they wore American clothes, but they had not the white man's comforts or food. They rarely ate cooked food, and though there was generally some sort of cooking arrangement outside, there were no fires or fireplaces in the houses, so that when people got rained on they had no way of drying their clothes until the sun shone again. I was not surprised that so many had colds and tuberculosis. I have seen them go round shivering in wet clothes, and I began to understand why so much of their poetry was about the cold and the rain. They had forgotten or discarded their own native lore for the treatment of disease; the *kahuna*, the native medicine man, had long been out of favor, and survival for the Hawaiians was becoming a struggle. My younger hostess told me sadly she feared that soon there would be no more pure Hawaiians, for so many of the girls wanted to marry outside their own race, the whites being the favorites, and after them the Chinese; there were also marriages with the other races on the islands, the Japanese, Koreans, and Malays.

Later in the morning we went out in the car and wandered all over the village and the neighborhood; we went to see a cave of refuge where, in time of war, the women and children were taken for shelter. Wars all over the islands in old times had been frequent until the great Kamehameha fought a series of battles and placed all the islands under his sovereignty. Then there was peace, and he proclaimed as a sort of rule of peace that an old man could lie undisturbed on the roadway. In the houses we were shown what relics of the past the people had: because they were poor they had not much, and I imagine that, like Europeans, they succumbed to the temptation to sell inherited treasures to seekers after such things. The wonderful royal capes of gold and black feathers had been sold and were in European museums. Some of the villagers, however, had still old hardwood spears, calabashes, and wooden platters, and the descendants of the nobles had their whale-tooth necklaces.

We were offered hospitality in the shape of *okelhao* which we declined. I would almost have given my soul for a cup of coffee, for after some nights on a hard board and days of a diet of salt fish, cabbage, and poi, I had acquired a raging headache that not all the aspirin I had brought with me could alleviate, in addition to a cold, an earache, and a variety of stomach ailments. Besides, the sensation of loneliness in this black backland weighed on me so that I was in a continual depression; so the *haku-mele* decided to dispatch me back to the civilization of the town before I acquired any more ailments. As for himself, he was delighted with everything—hard-board beds, salt viands, coffeeless breakfasts had no terrors for him. After tramping around all day in the open listening to stories, songs, and watching hulas, he could eat anything and sleep anywhere. As the car drove out of the village with me, I looked back and saw him standing in a group waving to me —a smallish white man surrounded by very large, very tall, dark-skinned men. I wondered when I should hear from him again, for in this remote village there was neither telegraph, telephone, nor much communication of any kind with the outside world. After what seemed interminable hours we—that is, the driver of the car and myself—got out of the black lands and off the lava roads and onto gray roads once more. At last we got back to the town of Hilo with its hotel, its banyan trees, its strange fruit trees. In the hotel I sank into a bed and stayed there for a few days, ministered to by a kind Japanese maid who kept recommending a cup of sake from time to time.

When I felt my vigor return and was deciding to go back to Kalapana to search for the *haku-mele*, a car drove up to the hotel and he, very gay and chippery, descended. Having spent all the money he had brought with him, having been charged twice from time to time for various things, he had left; otherwise he might be in Kalapana still. Now he informed me that as soon as I was ready we were to set out again, first to the volcano, and then all over the rest of the island of Hawaii.

IV

We started out for the volcano, Kilauea, which was then in eruption but without any overflow of lava. Though I brought a thermos flask of coffee, it was not really necessary this time, for there was no reason to fear board beds or meals of poi and cabbage; there was a modern tourist hotel near the volcano. We set out in the afternoon so as to view the volcano by night; as we drove up the mountain we saw in the distance a red glow overhanging in the sky like a pillar of fire. On each side of the road upward there were enormous tree ferns and thick tropical growths of nameless plants in the damp mountain forests. There were strange movements among the growths; one felt that slimy animals were everywhere in the wet thickets, for "the little rain of Hilo" was falling as always. Then we came once more on the black lava, the black land that we had been familiar with at Kalapana. The watchers of the volcano, those scientists who lived near it all the year, had announced that though the fire in the pit was higher than usual, there would be no boiling over; everyone would be safe, people and houses and villages.

Suddenly we arrived and saw an enormous open amphitheater; people were standing and sitting all around, some on what seemed to be campstools, all gazing intently downwards. We got out of the car and walked towards the groups and looked into an immense burning pit; it was like a combination of Saint Teresa's Vision of Hell and Dante's Inferno. The tumbling waves of fire, the rivers of fire, the fountains of fire, the sound of lava waves beating against one another, the rivers flowing through these waves, were like the realization of the hell I had heard of at every convent-school retreat. Involuntarily my eyes kept searching the liquid fires for lost souls, and it seemed to me as if I saw limbs tossing in the fiery rivers that flowed through the black molten lava, and the sound, the groanings, the noises that came up out of the pit were like the plaints and wailings, the thunderous rumblings that came to Dante through the starless air. Here was the "dolorous valley of the abyss which gathered thunder from endless wailings," and here was the great river on the shore of which were those persons who had committed the sins that in spite of my theological upbringing I believed to be the greatest sins of all, greater than all the seven deadly sins. Here, it seemed to me, that I saw those who made the great refusals, those who were neither good nor bad, those who were never alive, those who were neither rebellious nor faithful but only out for themselves. The tumbling of the lava waves never stopped, but sometimes, as if for a moment, their moaning and lamentations ceased, and then there would arise from the pit a smell as of brimstone, for there arose smells as well as sounds. But with it all it seemed a vision; it did not seem real as, for instance, the Grand Canyon had seemed real to me. The Grand Canyon had not been in any literature I knew, and when I saw it, I saw it for the first time, my mind clear of the visions of others, for I had never read a single description of it. But the volcano of Kilauea was quite familiar; if Dante hadn't seen it, he had dreamt it sufficiently clearly to have reported it exactly; Saint Teresa must have seen it in a vision; John Milton also, somehow, had a view of it, and, fearful as was this huge pit of fire, my mind is not really certain that it is still there, a mountain in Hawaii for any traveler to behold with his eyes: for me it is a kind of dream and not a geographical entity.

That night I stayed alone in the hotel; the rest of the party went to a cabin that had been loaned to them. In the morning an incident happened which made me learn something about myself that I had not realized before: it was the beginning of a bright sunny day, and one could look right down the mountain to the valleys and the ocean. One piece of land out in the sea I took to be an island, and I asked the Japanese waiter what island it was. I could not understand his reply on account of his pronunciation of *l* as *r*, but at the table by the window next to me were the only other people in the dining room, a man and a woman, the man obviously a professor of some kind and, I think, German. He heard my question. "That is not an island," he said, "it is a *halbinsel*— a half island—a peninsula," and then he quoted:

Paeninsularum, Sirmio, insularumque

from Catullus's poem to Sirmio. A thrill passed through me as I heard the familiar line, and I realized to what an extent I saw places through a haze of literature, especially poetry. For many others as well as myself, much of the glamour of places must come from what has been expressed about them in literature. That peninsula down below me jutting into the Pacific, no matter how lovely it was, could never have the appeal of "Sweet Catul-

lus's all-but-island, olive-cinctured Sirmio." Perhaps people who
were never possessed by a poem have this great advantage over the
literary-minded—they can see and feel things for the first time.
But as for me, I am really lonely in places which have not been
recorded in art or literature.

We spent days driving around the island of Hawaii, staying
nights in odd houses, or once in a way in little hotels. At the other
side from Hilo was the lovely sunny land of Kona; I never could
understand how it always rained in Hilo but was clear and sunny in
Kona. In one place by the sea we came suddenly on a deserted château, an exact reproduction of a French château, that one of the
native royalties had had built. It was lovely, lonely, desolate, de-
caying, entirely out of place in these volcano-made islands, but
all the more striking for that: it was so European. The Hawaiian
royal family had visited European royalties and had known their
castles and courts. Every trace of them I came upon, every story
I heard about them, made the Hawaiian royal family seem people
out of a romance. The stepson of Robert Louis Stevenson, Austin
Strong, as a little boy had known King Kalakaua, and from his
stories about him, as well as from Stevenson's own poem, I felt
that he really had been a king out of the kingly days.

We came to know one of the remaining members of the royal
family, Princess Kalanianaole, the widow of Prince Jonah Kalanianaole who was the nephew of King Kalakaua's wife, a prince
who himself was descended from Kawelo, one of the great figures
of Hawaiian history, one equivalent to Charlemagne in European
history. One of the last things I remember before leaving the
islands was a reception she gave for us in Honolulu, indeed a farewell party. She was so tall and large as to be truly majestic, with
that gravity of face and demeanor and resonance of voice in which
royalties had been trained. As I stood in the receiving line beside
her, in her gorgeous French dress with, across her bosom, a line
of decorations from European rulers—most of them and their
empires had vanished at that time—she seemed to me one of the
two or three most magnificent-looking people I had ever seen.
But as for her conversation, I do not remember a word of it. Some
of the guests curtsied to her, some merely bowed; though I had
learned an elegant court curtsy at a convent school and this might

be the only chance I was likely to have for using it, I was not able to go through it properly on account of a bandaged ankle which was just recovering from a break. When, after what seemed to me hours of standing and handshaking, my royal hostess moved to a sofa and motioned to me to sit beside her, I could have cried with relief.

However, before this reception, which took place on the eve of our departure, we went to visit some of the other islands; my husband went to all of them except the smallest, Lanai, I to a few only. One quite large one was Maui, where we stayed in a hotel which seemed to exist for the use and benefit of salesmen, for drummers are always wandering over the islands selling things. "You could sell a Hawaiian anything," one of them in the hotel told us. "He would buy a railway train if you gave him a sales talk." There were a good many people of American stock on this island, all learned in old Hawaiian lore, and some of them brought us to see one of the last of the classical hula masters who lived in an old-style grass hut. Hawaiians often live to a great age, and this man was old even for a Hawaiian; his memory went back to the native sovereigns, for he had been a celebrated hula master and doubtless had staged some of those great ballets that were the glory of the court. He now for us put two young dancers through a hula form we had not seen before, giving the rhythm of the dance by shaking a gourd that had in it either pebbles or fruit stones. The old hula master gave the impression of being a great artist who had fallen from high estate. I had a feeling that he was utterly unconnected with the world around him and with the *haole* civilization that was spreading over his islands. He seemed sad and lonely, but proud in his memories: he had once served in the court of a descendant of the Heavenly Ones. The Hawaiians must have been supreme in the ballet. What a loss that that long-developed, religious art—for it was dedicated to a goddess—should have been eradicated through a prejudice and survive only in a stage grass-skirt hula.

Between this and our return to Honolulu a fantastic incident befell us. A small steamer on which we were tramping around stopped for a few hours in some out-of-the-way harbor, and we were literally dragged off the boat by some isolated American residents. We were the only members of the white race from the outside world to strike that part for some time; the residents were avid for new faces and voices, and the fancy stories that featured us in the islands' newspapers made us seem sort of mythological beings.

At length the end of our stay came; we departed as we had arrived, *leis* round our necks, the strain of *aloha oe* in our ears; and a photographer snapping his camera at us. We left indeed in triumph, for the evening before my husband had given a reading of the versions of the stories he had made before a group of Hawaiian scholars, and they had been given a warm reception.

ঔ CHAPTER 29

Elinor Wylie

BEING ROAMERS AND RAMBLERS, after Hawaii we made another trip to Ireland and thence to France and Italy, where at the time everyone was strong for the Mussolini regime—so strong, in fact, that other countries were beginning to think they should take that pattern up. Some of the most impressed of the visitors were Americans, and I remember one American painter saying, "If this is tyranny, give me more of it." He even stuck to this opinion through World War II, and was not thrown into gaol or anything. However, I had no particular emotions about it myself, as, on the whole, I am a believer in the dictum *plus ça change, plus c'est la même.* When we got back to New York we found that many of our friends had retreated to the country because New York rents had soared to such a point.

Elinor Wylie invited us to look for a house in the Connecticut neighborhood she had retreated to; the Van Wyck Brookses did the same; some Westchester friends drove us around their neighborhood to look at houses and apartments. In the end it was Elinor who found a place that suited us in a continuation of the street in which she lived, and we quickly moved into it, settling down there at the beginning of 1925. The house was pleasant and roomy, a happy, sunny house, though during the residence of a later tenant a murder was committed in it, and we saw what had once been our home figuring in the picture papers with photographs of all in the case. Elinor Wylie had, a year or two before, married William Rose Benét and was settled down writing novels and poetry and helping to look after three stepchildren. She worked hard at her writing and bothered as little as possible with the trivia of housekeeping, having an expert Swiss housekeeper.

As for myself, I was deep in household tasks, and though I managed them with more ease than some of my friends and had a maid of sorts, housekeeping took up too much of my mind and absorbed a deal of what energy I had. Though I had set out for the country with the intention of working steadily on a book, I did little on it except take some notes, for running a house was more of a chore than I had foreseen. In the afternoons, when her work was finished, Elinor would come round to tea, for she liked to talk and eat the hot scones and jam which she had been used to in her years of living in England. In the evening there often came Louise and Maxwell Perkins, he the editor of Scribner's publishing house, and Michael Monahan and Bliss Carman, who lived round the corner, and sometimes the Van Wyck Brookses, who lived some miles away. We had many good literary evenings, though it was by no means a literary neighborhood.

Eugene O'Neill and his wife, Agnes, had lived for years near Ridgefield without having a single local caller, though at the time he was the most famous dramatist in America. Spending the week end with them once, we returned from a walk with Eugene and his huge Irish wolfhound, to be greeted by his wife with the excited information, "We've had our first caller—the Episcopal clergyman." The American countryside was a far cry from Europe, where any well-known writer was very important and sought after. I was astounded at the attitude to writers unconsciously revealed by people we met, even by people connected with publishing. Once at a picnic, while discussing the mental breakdown of a friend, a publisher present said seriously, "Well, he was always going around with writers, and that upset his balance." As nearly all the writers and artists I had ever known were amongst the most balanced of humankind, I pondered on this statement for long. Of course I had known exceptions from whom the troubles of life had taken their toll, but who could have been better balanced than Yeats, Robert Frost, Alice Meynell, A.E., Arnold Bennett, or Willa Cather?

I must say that I never thought my friend Elinor Wylie was in the same category; her life had been a troubled one, and, as she wrote in a poem, she had lived "under a sky reversed and evil-starred." To everybody in that neighborhood her history was known, and she was an exciting, even a momentous, figure. Elinor had left her first husband and her infant son and had eloped with a man whose name she, as a writer, always bore, Horace Wylie. For years she and he had lived in England remote from all their friends and under an assumed name. From what I have heard of him from others, Horace Wylie was neither so interesting, so brilliant, nor such a man of the world as Elinor believed him to be: she was highly impressed by people, men or women, whom she believed to be *du monde* and delighted in the phrase "persons of quality." However, he must have been a cultivated man, of distinctly literary and philosophic temperament, because, as she often told us, he really opened the world of poetry and literature to her. In the house in which they had lived in the New Forest he scheduled part of the day for her instruction and took delight in furnishing her mind. In addition he must have had a romantic temperament, because he decided that while living in exile they should call themselves "Mr. and Mrs. Waring" from Browning's Waring, and she told me how he often imagined his friends in Washington saying of him in Browning's words, "What's become of Waring since he gave us all the slip?" She spoke of him as being like Swift, and this was his own idea, too, a Swift to whom she played the role of Stella and Vanessa, for she was several years his junior.

From her conversation I gathered that they lived in a pleasant house in comparative luxury, for Horace Wylie was then well-to-do, and before the first World War an income anywhere in Europe of about five or six thousand dollars a year assured one of easy living. They had a few servants, and Elinor had, what highly delighted her, her lady's maid. She liked all this and their occasional runs to the Continent, staying at the Ritz in Paris, as well as the intellectual life she and Horace had together. They had not many acquaintances, and once in a way they ran into people from home who snubbed them, for, in Victorian parlance, they were a mystery couple living in sin and had of course to make other concealments than the concealment of their real names. Like many Americans, Elinor regarded the life of the English upper classes as very fascinating and liked every contact with it. Once when they were invited to a country house, and Elinor, looking forward to her visit, had got her wardrobe together with great care, the first fellow guest she encountered was a woman who had known Horace Wylie in Washington. They had frequently been able to elude old acquaintants because communications were then not so quick nor so numerous as they became later. But now, here in this house she had felt so happy to be invited to, she came against the potential enemy, the woman who thought it her duty to tell her hostess that a fellow guest was not what she seemed to be, that she bore an assumed name, that the man with her was not her husband but a lover. When, some time after dinner, her hostess approached Elinor and said she wanted to speak to her privately in her room, Elinor felt herself quaking, and something in her mind snapped; I think it never really came together again. It was characteristic of Elinor that when relating this she described the dress she herself was wearing, the marcel wave in her hair, and the new dressing gown she had brought with her. The hostess informed her of the tale she had just heard from the American guest and inquired if it were all true. Elinor acknowledged everything and suggested that it might be well if she and Horace left early the next morning. I do not remember if they actually left or not, but the hostess had the not uncommon English romantic attitude to love and lovers and became a friend of Elinor's in such a way that it increased her warm feeling for the English and for England. However, this incident seems to have been the forerunner of others of their kind which left their scars.

Then, to add to her tribulations, the news reached her that her husband, Philip Hichborn, had committed suicide. During the years I knew her she spent many moments trying to convince herself that her leaving him was in no way responsible for the suicide, because, as she was wont to say, it did not take place until a couple of years after her elopement. She did not realize, or did not want to realize, that an emotion or an agony can keep on growing in some natures until it becomes overwhelming. During these years in England she had a couple of children who were either dead-born or died soon after birth. On the occasion of one of these childbirths the hostess whom I have mentioned above was her warm friend and helper.

The next incident of importance that befell the Warings changed their lives completely. Shortly after the war began, a British government office issued an order that everybody in England living under an assumed name should report to the police. This, for some reason, was too much for the Warings, so they decided to return to America, that Horace should try to get a divorce, and that he and Elinor should marry. When I first met her around 1921, Elinor for some years had been legally Mrs. Horace Wylie; she and Horace were then living apart, though not actually separated; he was doing some work in Washington, and she was in New York living in the society of writers and artists, which was her natural milieu, and working on Condé Nast's magazine, *Vanity Fair*, of which Edmund Wilson was managing editor at the time. At this period her poetry was known only to a limited group, for she had not yet published *Nets to Catch the Wind*. At William Rose Benét's suggestion I asked her to read some of her poems at a poetry reading I was getting up in the MacDowell Club for the benefit of the MacDowell Colony. Though her voice was somewhat harsh and lacking in resonance, her poems and her appearance made a very great impression on the audience. It was at this meeting that Amy Lowell insisted on being put in what she called "the place of honor," the last on the programme; but when her turn came it was late and some of the audience started to leave the hall. Amy never forgave me for allowing the programme to drag out to such a length or for permitting a dancer with colored spotlights to make the experiment of dancing to the words of poems—said poems being read by their authors, John Farrar and John Weaver. Amy never wrote to me or came to see us again. It was on this occasion, too, that J. B. Yeats, the painter, father of W.B., made his first and last appearance on a platform as a poet, for a very short time afterwards he died. But if Amy fell out with me, from that reading dated my friendship with Elinor.

A good many of her friends have mentioned her mental or nervous instability when writing of her. She was certainly unstable, but considering the tragedies she had endured, the beatings she took from life, she held herself together extremely well and with immense courage. Like many women who have suffered, she had her moments of serious unbalance, but what really stood to her was her industry at her work and the discipline that came with it. She had made herself an artist, which few women either take the trouble or have the leisure to do. Then, like all the real writers I have ever known, she was an intellectual and a scholar. What disturbed me far more than her neuroticism was her vanity, for, though I had known women as vain who had far less to be vain of than Elinor, at times they could conceal their vanity, but Elinor never could conceal or camouflage hers. If she was not overtly considered the most important and beautiful person in every gathering, she suffered and showed her suffering openly. I have seen her more than once walk out of a room in indignation, real indignation, when she thought someone else received more attention than she did.

In London in her last years, when she became well known and saw a great many literary people, her vanity became legendary, and stories centering around it were related for years after her death. The most widely publicized story was about a week-end visit to the country house of a titled hostess who had something to do with the Poetry Society of London. Elinor, it appears, was placed at dinner beside somebody who had never heard of her, and, besides, in the English manner, she had not been previously introduced to all the guests in the drawing room. Sometime during dinner she conveyed to her hostess the information that she was not feeling very well and she feared she would have to return to London that very night. She was wearing her famous Paul Poiret dress of cloth of silver which she had got a little while before in Paris, and she was annoyed that nobody present noticed this triumph of the couturier's art, which, incidentally, later became her shroud. The resourceful hostess, however, in that interval after dinner when the women left the dining room, collected some of her female guests in her dressing room, explaining the situation, and suggested that they devote the time before being joined by the men in the drawing room to flattering Elinor as hard as they could. They made her the center of her group and fell to praising her silver dress, her looks, her poetry. After repeating some of her poetry she told her hostess that she would not leave that night as she had intended, because her feeling of illness was passing away. No doubt this vanity of hers was pathological, but it was also, I am sure, due to something in her childhood training; Elinor often told me of her mother's admiration for her and her sister; she would tell them that they were the most beautiful girls in Washington and refer to Elinor as "my lion child." I have heard American mothers in their daughters' presence directing attention to their beauty and talents in a way that would horrify a European mother. I do not think that vanity, basically, is more common among Americans than among others, but when it occurs it is more unrepressed and consequently attracts more attention from Europeans.

There was a good deal of the spoiled child about Elinor, and this made her wayward and unpredictable; at one moment she would be a miracle of deep penetration and sound judgment and at another go all awry. Often she was remarkably shrewd in her estimates of people, but would have unaccountable hostilities and equally unaccountable likings. She would solemnly warn me that somebody I knew was fiendish, and the next thing I would hear was that she had that very person to dinner, and often for some practical reason in connection with reviewing or publishing. Though, when with her, I had to preserve the convention that I did not do any writing myself and never once spoke of anything I was doing, she would frequently speak of me to others as one who knew about literature. However, I never could make out how much she cared about anybody in her environment; but, for all this, the impression of Elinor that remains with me is not one of self-centeredness. Certainly self-pity was not one of her weaknesses: that, unlike most women writers, she could transcend. She was a proud, brave woman in spite of her childishness, her changeableness, her waywardness. Though she had had three hus-

bands and wrote beautiful love poetry to a fourth man, she was
not at all an erotic or amorous woman, and I never thought she
had much sentimental interest in men: if she sought admiration
for her talents or looks, it was from both sexes. For her first husband, Philip Hichborn, the father of her son, I think she cared
little, but Horace Wylie had fascinated her; she talked about him
a great deal—about his clothes, his habits, his mind, his "princely
air"; in her novel *Jennifer Lorne* he appears as an eighteenth-century man of fashion, and in her poem "Peregrine" as a defiant outcast; she said of the character in this poem that it was a combination of his character and hers, some lines being true of him and
some of her. In a little privately printed book of immature verse,
there is some authentic love poetry which must have been inspired by him.

When she eloped with Horace Wylie she was an inexperienced,
almost raw girl, and his influence on her must have molded her
intellectually into what she became. Her beliefs about him, romantic as they certainly were, were probably nearer the truth than other
estimates of him I have heard from friends and acquaintances of
his who were given to describing him as dull and uninteresting;
one indeed who knew him well said he had the mind of a suburban realtor. But a man who could throw his life away for love,
flinging prudence to the wind, is rare anywhere, and almost impossible to imagine in that period in America, so I am inclined to
credit Elinor's vision of him. Then her very last words to me, two
days before she died, were about the man she wrote the sonnets to,
and as she showed me his photograph she said, "I think he is like
Horace Wylie—you would have liked Horace."

The neighborhood we all lived in in Connecticut bored her;
she had loved the English country, especially the New Forest section where she had lived with Horace Wylie, but the Connecticut
country seemed empty to her, as it did to some Americans and
Europeans. Her occasional remarks about it reminded me of that
comment that Henry James made to Somerset Maugham about
the wide, empty streets of Boston. She had imagined that she
would like the American country as she had liked the English
country, but in about a year she tired of it, sold the house she had
bought, and went back to live in her entertaining and agitating

New York. Of course she was very restless, and there was no one in the neighborhood who had any particular appeal for her; some few she actively, if temporarily, disliked. But on their side it could be said that she was a somewhat disturbing person with a neurotic temperament and occasional obsessions.

There lived fairly near us writers of different grades of achievement: Bliss Carman, the poet, really a Canadian, and Michael Monahan, who had been the editor of a couple of lively magazines and had written a couple of books that should have been better because of his vigorous personality: he had written a book on Heine without knowing a word of German and had got it published. Of our own generation there were Van Wyck Brooks, Henry Longan Stuart, and, oddly enough, Hendrik Van Loon, who looked years older than the rest of us but was of the same period. Brooks we had known previously, my husband knew him when he was one of the editors of the *Seven Arts* magazine, which had on its staff other young men of promise, including Randolph Bourne, whose ideas meant a great deal to the young men of his generation. We knew Van Wyck Brooks also when he was literary editor of that brilliant weekly the *Freeman*, edited by Albert Jay Nock.

Nock must have been one of the most discerning and accomplished editors that this country has ever had, a man who, though of fairly recent English descent, exhibited typical Yankee traits and was slightly eccentric in his independence. He kept off band wagons, and slogans did not fool him: like many another independent mind of his generation, he was a follower of Henry George's, and the paper was single-tax. He was fond of quoting Rabelais and would end an argument with, "No sooner than then and not otherwise than thus." A man of great cultivation himself, he was always saddened by the lack of knowledge among the younger writers and the lack of sane and accomplished elders to give them any guidance. I had done considerable writing for the *Freeman*, as had Constance Rourke, Lewis Mumford, Llewellyn Powys, and many others who became well known afterwards, though they were practically beginners in those days. The paper had a small enough circulation, but it was read by nearly every intellectual in this country and in England, and while it lasted exercised great influence, but its subsidy was suddenly withdrawn and it ended just when everybody was prophesying its brilliant future.

The end of the *Freeman* brought Van Wyck Brooks's journalistic life to a close. At this time he was not the successful and bemedaled man of letters that he later became, and when we all lived in Connecticut he was not producing very much. As a young man he had come greatly under the influence of John Butler Yeats and had lived at the same French boardinghouse, Petitpas's, listening night after night to the old man's conversation, which he never forgot and which he sometimes brought echoes of into his literary work. Brooks had made a good deal of a reputation while still a young man and had written at least one excellent book, *Letters and Leadership*. I thought that his books on Mark Twain and Henry James were very illuminating, for they were a bit of American social history even if his conclusions and interpretations were biased. He had an odd though, perhaps, not so unusual way of reading into his subjects his own characteristics and problems, and he was sometimes aware of this, especially as regards Henry James. He thought actually that he was attacking Henry James for the things he had wanted to do himself, such as living abroad on an independent income, and he got so worried about this at one time that he withdrew the manuscript, though later he sent it back to be published as it stood. Brooks's interest in literature was continuous and intense; he was devoted to the literary life, and has stated in print more than once that writing with him is a natural function like eating or sleeping. Yet with it all I never thought that from the artistic or aesthetic point of view he could be described as a literary critic: his later successful works about New England were social history based on literature. The critics who attacked these books because they were not bona fide literary history or literary criticism were, I believe, all wrong—such was not their import. They gave Americans, especially New England Americans, a consciousness of a past, both historical and literary, what he himself called "a usable past."

At this period in Connecticut, Brooks was depressed about himself, suffering from melancholia and prone to think of himself as a failure. Money and success were frequently the topics of his conversation, and though I believe that intellectually he was opposed to them—I think it was he who invented the term "the acquisitive life" as opposed to the creative one—yet I could not help coming to the conclusion that he would never be happy unless he acquired both: they represented the pattern of life that he had an inherited comprehension of, and it is doubtful if he could have fitted painlessly into any other. He would often talk longingly about Europe, and I think his dedication to the American past was in part a sort of compensation for not living there. At this time his great friend was an Englishman of Irish parentage, Henry Longan Stuart, a striking-looking man whose ascetic appearance attracted Elinor Wylie, who was always interested in the ascetic, and who if she had been brought up in a Catholic country would probably have been inclined to the conventual life. Henry Stuart was one of those wandering European men who in America make a living by desultory literary work, translations, and a little lecturing. These men are generally of some British mixture, seldom pure English, but Irish-English, Scotch-English, Welsh-English, and they never seem to be able to settle down to domestic life. Henry was attached in some editorial capacity to the Catholic weekly, the *Commonweal*, and diligently wrote reviews of somewhat indifferent quality for other periodicals. He was said to have written one striking novel called *Weeping Cross* and some verse. Elinor was one of those who was greatly impressed by the novel, but she never understood how it could have been written by the man we then knew; he had probably been greatly changed by the war, in which he had fought and been injured by his horse falling on him. He had no such distinguished or stimulating mentality as Brooks, but he was an interesting and appealing figure, as such lonely kind of men are, and his conversation, especially on literature, though by no means profound or witty, was knowledgeable and entertaining. His mind, if it was not distinguished, was discriminating, and like all educated Britishers he knew literature well and could say innumerable poems by heart; there was no Babbittry about him, and consequently he did not have to prove to himself that he was not a Babbitt by going on the numerous platforms that writers were just then beginning to mount. He was a Catholic of the English kind, something different from the Irish and French, the kinds I know most about: it was more mellow than the Irish and more puritanical than the

French, but like everything English, it had a great deal of elasticity and compromise about it. It was not surprising that he held Elinor's interest more than any of the other writers we met in Connecticut.

II

It would be hard to find a greater contrast in character, temperament, and appearance than between Henry Longan Stuart and Hendrik Van Loon. Hendrik was tall, fat, unascetic-looking, and with an embarrassing lack of reserve which seemed to himself and some of his friends as rather "cute." He had a sort of engaging schoolboy face of the Teutonic type, yet at times he looked as if he had a nervous structure that might go off in fears and terrors or *crise de nerfs* or something of the kind. He went in vociferously for a variety of radicalisms and freedoms—free speech, liberty of opinion, and other items that we were supposed to have, anyway, and in addition a selection of up-to-date proletarian and party-line views. But like many such people he was intolerant, though not too much so; he had not the Ku Klux Klan temperament so characteristic of the vociferous radical and the vociferous reactionary, and on the whole he believed in the same freedom for other people as for himself—to some extent, anyhow. When he was not being rude, which appeared to be seldom, he could be pleasant and engaging. His rudeness, bewildering to Elinor Wylie, was, I think, part of the general ponderous waggishness he went in for, and was a sort of by-product of his odd Teutonic humor, which was often hard for my uncomplex Celtic wits to follow.

It was generally at the Brookses' that we saw him. He was a great friend of Van Wyck's, and Mrs. Brooks was quite maternal about him. "Hendrik is just a great big boy," she would say. "It is very easy to manage him—feed him well, flatter him a little, and he is yours." He would come in suddenly and dramatically, entering into the conversation with great verve. "Unclean, unclean!" he called out once, coming into the Brookses' garden, where we were all at our ease under a tree, raising his hands like an approaching leper.

"Let's talk Irish," he said waggishly. "The language I have been listening to for four days was Irish."

He had been at some political meeting or convention and gave what apparently was an ironic and amusing account of the affair, because Van Wyck laughed heartily, but I could not follow it. Van Wyck had simple admirations, but one never knew when they would suddenly change and go round and round; however, I don't think his admiration for Van Loon ever did change.

"He is a modern Erasmus," he would say of Van Loon. I was, I am afraid, indignant at the comparison.

"Are you mad, to say such a thing, Van Wyck?" I asked.

When Van Loon talked quickly, the traces of a foreign accent that lingered in his speech became stronger.

"Ven ve vent into the World Var, ve thought ve vere fighting for . . ." Something or another, I forget now what, because I've never been able to get the hang of what wars are about, anyway. But when Van Loon would use "we" or "our," as if he were a typical American, I would marvel a little, because the sense of ownership in America seemed to me to be the privilege of born Americans or what Van Wyck called in one of his books "hereditary Americans." Though I find myself saying "we" or "our" when I am abroad, and though I have been over half of my life in America, I make an effort to reserve these "we's" and "our's" for special occasions, partly because I feel an exile always, everywhere, including the land in which I was born.

But to return to Hendrik Van Loon. One day I was in the Brookses' sitting room when he came in accompanied by a young man, a writer, obviously. Van Loon threw an inimical glance at me, for by this time I had acquired a taste for puncturing his statements and for gazing interrogatively at him in an innocent manner.

"Are you Mary Colum?" asked the young man. "I like your mind so much; it's a free mind."

"How could it be a free mind?" Van Loon butted in. "She's afraid of the little Pope. She asks the little Pope in Rome what to think about everything."

"Ah," said I, "I now see what's wrong with your histories. You know no Roman history. You ought to know Roman history—it's quite important."

"You don't understand her," Van Wyck would say nervously when a disagreement like this occurred. When Van Loon wanted

to be contemptuous of a person or thing, he prefixed "little" to
the name.

"I don't like these secretaries with their gush and artificial smiles,"
I remarked of the young lady employees of a certain publisher.

"Ah," said Van Loon, looking at me wickedly, "you're afraid
they will catch your little husband."

"The word 'afraid' is too common in your vocabulary," said I.
"It does not exist in mine."

I did not really feel I was being very smart, and I think I was
annoyed.

"Why does he always want to be so ponderously rude?" I asked
Van Wyck.

"Ah, you don't understand him," said Van Wyck earnestly as he
was handing me into a bus at Westport. "Hendrik has a complex,"
he went on. "It's through having lived with a bowitch. He got an
inferiority complex."

The bus went off before I could get an explanation of this weird
statement. But during the next few days I tried to get one. My
English friend Gladys always knows everything about America,
for she had a relative connected with the American past who was
a colonial governor or some such functionary. I talked to Gladys
on the telephone.

"Van Wyck says Van Loon got an inferiority complex through
living with a bowitch. Do you know what a bowitch is?"

Gladys thought for a minute. Then her answer was fairly convincing. "Yes," she said, "it's one of those things they call antiques
in New England. They call it a cobbler's bench."

I had never seen a cobbler's bench at the time, but knowing the
tendency of anything New England to give an inferiority complex
to some people, I was ready to believe that a cobbler's bench might
bring on that state.

"What is it like? Could one get an inferiority complex from it?"

"If you were that sort, you could get it from a Cape Cod fire
lighter. A cobbler's bench is something like what we put the baby
on at home," Gladys informingly added. "They use it as a coffee
table."

The next time Van Loon figured in my life was at a luncheon
which Benjamin Huebsch, the publisher, gave for his author, Sher-

wood Anderson. I happened to be placed beside Sherwood, having written what was supposed to be an understanding review of his work. A speech or two followed the luncheon, which was at the Brevoort Hotel. As we were all feeling very pleasant, Van Loon rose ponderously to his feet. I knew from his expression that he had the idea of being humorous.

"I vant to say a vord," he opened up. "I should like to ask Sherwood Anderson why he publishes with Ben Huebsch?" Then he sat down. This must have been considered funny by some present, because a certain amount of giggling followed it. But Huebsch looked grave, and Anderson in a puzzled tone said to me, "Maybe I ought to look into that." Ill-advisedly afterwards he did leave Huebsch and wandered from one publisher to another. I felt like slapping Van Loon good and hard.

I forgot about the bowitch conversation with Van Wyck for several years. Then it happened that when I was living in Paris on a Guggenheim Fellowship I met in Bernard Faÿ's a German professor who, after spending a year or so at Harvard, got so overcome with attachment to New England antiques that he took a few of them back to Europe with him.

"You haven't got a bowitch among the pieces?" I asked him.

"I don't think so," said he. "What is that?"

I didn't like to say it was something that gave an inferiority complex, for the professor seemed to be infected with a bad form of that and was fawning nervously on a Sorbonne don who claimed to be such a strong Germanophile that he had decided Germany was not so guilty of the war as was generally supposed.

It happened that our friend, Arthur Johnson, of Boston, had been staying in Bective House in County Meath a couple of months before, when we were there, and was now in Paris. At dinner that evening with him at Foyot's I told him about the German professor. He, curiously enough, had known him the year he was at Harvard and had had him to dinner at his house in Louisburgh Square, for Arthur always had everybody to dinner.

"Arthur," I asked when we were eating duck with orange, "what is a bowitch?"

"A what?" said he.

"A b-o-w-i-t-c-h," said I, spelling it. "It's some sort of New England furniture. But what? Brooks says that Van Loon got an inferiority complex through living with a bowitch."

"My God!" boomed Arthur in his deep voice. "It sounds like something out of Krafft-Ebbing."

We went on eating and drinking Vouvray. Suddenly Arthur exclaimed: "Why, you dumbbell! You've dropped a *d* out of the word. I know what it means. Van Loon's first wife was a Bowditch."

"A what?" I asked weakly.

"Will you never learn New England history?" Arthur demanded. "Don't you know 'the Cabots speak to the Lowells'?"

"Yes," I finished, " 'and the Lowells speak only to God.' "

"Well," said Arthur, "when they're all through speaking to God, they speak to the Bowditchs. They are our first families. Now do you understand?"

৯‍ CHAPTER 30

Sojourn in Connecticut

I HAD NEVER LIVED in a small town anywhere before, but only in the country or in a city. However, this was not a characteristic small town; actually it was a distant suburb of New York, and in addition to its own native and immigrant population, it had a large commuting group representing what might be called the well-to-do American middle classes; the men went to the city every morning on the commuters' train and came back in the evening in time for dinner; the women stayed at home and looked after their households and children. I had never come in touch with a group of this kind before. Here I was greatly struck by the difference between domestic life and domestic arrangements and those with which I had been familiar in old countries. The women were amazingly efficient in running households and caring for children with the minimum of domestic help, or sometimes none at all. They were far more tied to domestic duties than women of similar education or economic standing in Europe and had, it seemed to me, a far narrower life. Even those who had spent their youth undergoing academic training and who had college and university distinctions could cook and do housework efficiently, run furnaces, wash and iron the children's clothes; generally they did all this very well whether they liked it or not. I remember once reading a scarifying article in an English paper called "Servantless America," warning Englishmen, professors, teachers, professional people, against taking jobs in America where their wives would have to wear out their youth in menial work—cooking, cleaning, and scrubbing. The English writer, Vera Brittain, who for a while had lived in a midwestern college town where her husband had held a professorial job, tells us in her autobiography, with something like horror, of the life in a university town where the faculty wives spent their days in a steady round of deadening domestic chores. She herself got a dislike of callers because, having no maid, she had to get tea for them and wash the dishes afterwards. It certainly seemed a waste of material to have university-educated women, or trained musicians or artists spending the best part of their days in household routine. But Providence or tradition has occasionally instilled a liking for household chores even in the minds of the most intellectual women, and nearly every woman likes looking after a baby. However, after the first glow of marriage, some of the women I got to know were inclined to become resentful and discontented enough.

For the first time since my boarding-school days I was thrown a great deal among my own sex; now that I reflect upon it, I realize that the women I had known intimately before this period were not engaged in the ordinary affairs of life at all, but were in special avocations. The group I came into in Connecticut were young married women with husbands and children and households to look after. Most of them, undoubtedly, were of a type that one would find in the suburbs of any large city in any country in the world and would certainly have their replicas in London or Paris or Berlin. Their level of both health and good looks was higher than among European women, and perhaps their general intelligence also. But they were less saturated in the intellectual, artistic, and historic experience of the race; the old disciplines had not marked them for good or bad, and so they had the charm that Europeans noticed in American women. At the same time, among some of them, there was a lack of spontaneity and a sort of studied manner with a dependence on rules of behavior out of etiquette books that made them sort of unknown quantities: one never knew whether they meant a word they said or whether what they did represented anything real in them; it simply was their interpretation of well-bred behavior. Even the busiest of the women I had come to know, even those who had to do the bulk of their own housework, were very careful of their appearance and regularly patronized the beauty parlor. The discontent of a few was noticeable, but what I think made for the discontent in most cases was thwarted ambition of some sort: some few wanted renown, some wanted lovers and admiration, some wanted larger incomes, some higher social status. Like most of the human race, they had more natural gifts of all sorts—talents, emotions—than they had outlets for in the pattern of their lives. I noticed here something I had often noticed in life before—the least gifted had the most ambition; they would exaggerate a small aptitude for one of the arts and believe that, if they only had the opportunity, they could be professionals. Even if they had the talent, they had little notion of the labor and discipline involved in becoming a professional in any art, and no inclination to undergo it. Some of them even thought that those carefully wrought poems of Elinor Wylie's were things that she dashed off on the back of an envelope before breakfast.

Some of the women I met had an ostentatious intellectuality; occasionally there was a bluestockingism that was overwhelming. In men, learning which is beyond their intellectual means can become a humorless and stodgy pedantry, but in women it goes off into forms of absurdity that has been satirized in many literatures. Having a sharp memory for the spoken word, certain of the highbrow conversations fastened themselves on my mind. Molière or Sheridan could not have thought up more fantastic dialogue than was current from time to time at parties. One woman used to deliver herself of such odd pieces of learning and in such a rehearsed way that Elinor Wylie was of the opinion that she had boned up on them the evening before. "I was reading Plato yesterday," she once remarked to Elinor and myself, "and I came to the conclusion that the only thing that can be reached in philosophy is the periphery." We knitted our brows in the effort to find out what this could mean. The same woman gave Elinor an account of how at college she had acquired an intense faculty for concentration which was now all dissipated in domesticity. "A faculty for concentration on what?" icily asked Elinor. "On the things of the mind," was the reply, given with a glance that implied that such things were very remote from the pair before her. But to Elinor, whose faculty of concentration was intense and won at a great cost, her claims had a total irrelevancy.

Then there was the time when this lady perused Unamuno's *Tragic Sense of Life* while she was brushing her hair, which she told us was the only time she had for reading, and lectured us for the rest of the year on the tragedy that was life which she thought we ought to get some conception of. She had also a malapropian faculty for misquotation in English and Latin, which latter tongue she flung around in her letters. She was addicted to letter writing, and she thought nobody in the neighborhood was familiar with Latin. Once she remarked about her husband, "His mind is mortised and termined by Plato's philosophy of beauty and angelic manifestations." There was another lady who never went to New York to do her shopping without bringing Blake's *Prophetic Books* to read in the train. The only person I knew who had carefully gone into these works, Yeats, had to retreat to monastic seclusion for some months to read them and then made no claim to having mastered them. But this lady, all the way to Grand Central, would turn page after page, munching chocolates the while. Bluestocking-ism can be contagious, and we found ourselves working up some in self-defense, but I'm afraid we did not take the right line; we were left with a feeling that we were not convincing. Certainly the lady who claimed that she read French every day, but who actually never mastered an irregular verb, was openly skeptical about my ability to read any of the French volumes I had in the bookshelves.

One of the bluestockings was of a type I had met before and have met since in other countries—a woman of prosy mentality with a rationalistic outlook, sensual and devoid of spirituality, who imagined that she had communications with spirits, saw visions, foresaw the future, and did automatic writing. Such women are invariably able to keep their husbands in a state of awe and fear of their powers. They followed the same pattern everywhere I knew them—were given to opening their husbands' mail, cautiously re-sealing it, and later informing them of its contents which had ap-peared to them in writing on the wall or in the throes of a trance. They would read your hand or your horoscope and privately give the neighbors an account of the awful things they had discovered about you. I think this kind of thing represented some recompense for a feeling of inferiority, or an escape from their own common-place lives and minds. Then, too, there was another international type here, the *femme fatale*. These, likewise, were given to what I believe to be fantasies: they were intelligent, romantic women with a taste for poetry, and they imagined lovelorn men addressing them lines from the poetry they had read, such as "A pardlike spirit, beautiful and swift," or "The good stars met in your horoscope, made you of spirit and fire and dew." Once I was called upon by two of the *femmes fatales* on the same day; they each wanted to talk to me about a man I knew who, each wanted to tell me, had been so much in love with her that she unwittingly had ruined his life and absorbed all his power of emotion. The first one puzzled me, for the man she talked about, an Irishman, was barely known to me. She had been misinformed, maybe by the man himself, whom she had just met again after a lapse of years, because she as-sumed that I had had some sentimental friendship with him, and she wished to squash any importance it might have had for me. She told me how he used to address to her those lines from Meredith's "Love in the Valley":

> When her mother tends her before the laughing mirror,
> Tying up her laces, looping up her hair,
> Often she thinks, were this wild thing wedded,
> More love should I have, and much less care.
> When her mother tends her before the lighted mirror,
> Loosening her laces, combing down her curls,
> Often she thinks, were this wild thing wedded,
> I should miss but one for many boys and girls.

How phony it was I did not realize until the second *femme fatale* called on me in the afternoon to reveal her piece of sentiment about somebody's unrequited love for her. The man she talked about I knew well in a friendly way, but what amazed me was that the role she had cast for herself was the same as that of the first lady—the second man had addressed her:

When her mother tends her before the laughing mirror. . . .

Skepticism began to enter my mind, because I was sure of one thing, the second man had never read Meredith's poetry, and the only verse he could say by heart were some stanzas from the *Lays of Ancient Rome*. Talking over my callers with an artist who was then staying with us, I received what was the key to the incident. "They have been reading that play of Barrie's," he said. "They are identifying themselves with the actress, the enchantress, in the play. Those lines are quoted to her." I often wonder why in books more is not made of the fantasies men and women concoct about themselves, for they reveal, if not the complete personality, some key part of it. Many people's effort is to make their whole lives correspond to the fantasy, and this is sometimes disastrous, sometimes not disastrous at all. James Stephens has written a delightful book about feminine fantasies in *Mary Makebelieve, the Charwoman's Daughter*. But, on the whole, literature has taken too little stock in such things, although, the moment we think about it, we perceive that they are a great part of the lives of some people.

Though it was the absurd ones who stood out and were talked about, the charming, intelligent, and useful women were in the majority, and, in most cases, these were more interesting than their husbands who commuted to the city every day, mowed the lawn on Saturday afternoon, went to a dinner party on Saturday evening, spent Sundays around the country club, and hardly ever read a book. What impressed me a good deal in the family life was the position of some of the husbands: they were dominated by their wives in a way that, in old countries, wives are supposed to be dominated by husbands, who, not uncommonly, are a great deal older. The men had a sort of filial relation to their wives, the wives seemed often to be the husbands' as well as the children's mothers. I would not go as far as Sinclair Lewis in his novel of marriage, *Cass Timberlane*, who declared that America was the only country where men lived in continuous fear of their own wives, but some of

the men I knew certainly were afraid of their wives and to a degree
that no woman I ever knew was afraid of her husband—perhaps
because a woman's agility in fooling a man when she abandons her
mind to the idea is far greater than any man's in fooling a woman.
Some of the men would never say or do anything without their
wives' acquiescence, and occasionally when at a party a man, made
daring by a cocktail, gave free rein to some of his opinions or talked
flirtatiously to a woman, he would receive a surreptitious glance
from his wife such as I have seen naughty children get from their
mothers implying, "Wait till I get you home!"

The trouble, I think, was that many of the men married too
young, before they had any real sense of what they were doing, and
passed from their mothers to their wives without enough intervening experience of life or of other people, and so they got the relationships confused. All their lives they knew too little of other men
and women. As children they were very close to their mothers, who
gave them the care that in good economic circumstances hired
help did in other countries, and which in poorer economic circumstances children either do without altogether or somehow give
one another. Henry Stuart used to say that he believed American
children, owing to the care given them by their mothers, grew up
into far healthier and stronger men and women than Europeans.
But my own opinion is that many of the children would have been
far better off, psychically, anyway, if they had been pried earlier
from the maternal bosom. I shall never forget the amazement of
an Englishwoman when I read her a paragraph from a letter I
received from an American friend. Owing to some family upset
the American woman had to send her youngest son, a husky youth
of about eleven, to a boarding school. "He is so little," she wrote,
"and he did not want to go. He cried all the night before." My
English friend's little sons had been packed off to boarding school
at the age of eight without being asked whether they wanted to go
or not, and had gone without a whimper. Early boarding school
was a common British pattern in the economic class to which they
belonged, the same economic class approximately to which my
American friend belonged. Without approving of either habit,
I am less inclined to the American pattern where the children are
tied to their mothers for so long. A great deal is to be said for

trained care of children outside the family: Tom Wolfe once remarked that a woman who serves her family too much is likely to enslave them in return.

I am not certain how much of my observations were especially true of American suburban life; it may be that I was, in general, simply beginning to understand more of life and of ordinary human relationships, for up to this time a good proportion of my life had been spent among a special kind of people. I was now among a group of men and women endeavoring to get along together in family life without much help from religion or tradition, which in European countries can hold them to their duties. Here they were held by the law, by family habits and dependencies, by the social organization, and all the duties consequently had an exaggerated hold on their loyalties. A passing infidelity and a man was promptly divorced. It was almost a crime for a man to invite a woman not his wife to tea or luncheon. Once during Prohibition I had dinner with a friend's husband in a speakeasy in New York, and some of his male acquaintances at another table thought it such a good joke that they sent us over a bottle of French burgundy to celebrate. I could not understand why my companion was so embarrassed, as having luncheon or dinner with men was no rarity and practically no treat in my life. I have often thought that the frequency of divorce in America is due partly to the fact that any sort of simple friendship between men and women is almost impossible except in the case of people in the arts. "To know a man in this country," a Connecticut friend of mine is in the habit of saying, "you have to marry him."

The people who were freest and had the best time of all, it seemed to me, were the working people: they had more pleasures, more interests, and at this period, in the good years before the depression, there was well-paid work for all. Many of those in Connecticut were either immigrants or of recent European ancestry, and owing to the fact that European emigrants tend to go to places where their kin already are, the simple people around had scores of relations and lived in close touch with their neighbors, the elders indeed having a sort of patriarchal life.

The commuting class seemed to have no such roots and no such close relationships with one another. What passed for friendship and friendly intercourse was often merely the effect of propinquity and common membership of a country club or traveling in and out on the same train. Their seeming rootlessness was perhaps a necessary factor in a new country with a roving population; hardly any of them were related to anyone else in the neighborhood, as they necessarily would be in an old country or even in parts of America at distances from metropolises. Here it seemed actually true that the immigrants and their families were less strangers in the country of their adoption than were the commuting class whose ancestors had been long in America. The immigrant people were so satisfied with what they had reached here that they had little ambition to raise themselves further in the world; with them there was something stabilized; the daughter of a woman who had been a domestic servant became a domestic servant, the son of a stonemason, a stonemason, and so on.

The Italians made their surroundings as much like Italy as possible, built their houses on heights, surrounded them with flowers; they grew grapes and made wine, and one could behold an Italian family any evening during the Prohibition period sitting down to spaghetti or macaroni and the red wine they made themselves. The Hungarians could make from peaches and dandelions more potent drinks than red wine, and on Sundays they had gay hilarious parties with colors in the girls' dresses that would take the sight out of your eyes. Most of the Hungarians and Italians could do almost anything with their hands; to watch an Italian family building their own home, big and little helping, was a memorable sight. The foundations were laid with great care amid a babble of conversations, scoldings, and orders from paterfamilias: the house finished, a stone wall would rise in strength and distinctiveness as a fortification for the garden. Every Italian in the neighborhood seemed to be always building something, and one realized that the common illustration in a Latin grammar of simple sentence construction, "Balbus was building a wall," had a real psychological basis; these descendants of the Romans, whatever else they were, were builders, and when the financial crash came and some of these immigrant families had to go on home relief, their poverty did not reduce them to despondency as it sometimes did those of native descent. They all helped one another; they had their own churches, their own social life, their own habits and customs, so that they never really could feel themselves bankrupt.

ॐ CHAPTER 31

Death of Elinor Wylie

SOME YEARS OF LIFE in Connecticut, although broken by a few visits to Europe, made me anxious for a change to the city again. We missed our friends, for we had seen but little of some of them during those years, and when a couple of them suggested that we should spend some part of the winter in New York we thought the idea a good one. Accordingly we took a furnished apartment in the Fifties for some months in a house on the site of the present Barbizon-Plaza Hotel. We moved in towards the middle of December, and a day or so later I was startled to hear Elinor Wylie's voice on the telephone. She had come back from England, where she had been for several months; she had been in the habit of spending her summers in England since she left Connecticut. What startled me was that not only did her voice seem to come from a long way off; it had a different, more assertive note as it gave me the information that she did not intend to stay long in New York, that she had in England written some new poems which she would like to read to us, that she had had a number of sonnets privately printed by the village printer near where she had been living, that one side of her face was temporarily paralyzed through her catching cold from sitting by an open window in a railway carriage. The English doctor had called it Bell's paralysis and told her it would not last long, but meanwhile one side of her face was immovable, not noticeably so unless she tried to smile. As soon as she had arranged a few matters and saw her new book of poems through the press, she was returning to England.

Thereupon I asked her to dinner for a day or two later, to be exact, for Thursday, December 13, 1928 to hear the sonnets; characteristically she made a stipulation as to who else should be present;

she did not want to see many people, and she would like me to invite some friends of ours whom she had not previously met. But she wanted Ridgely and Olivia Torrence; Ridgely was then poetry editor of the *New Republic* and had published much of her work. I invited also Nathalie Sedgwick Colby, our old friend Thomas Hughes Kelly, then living in Paris but over in New York for a few weeks, and Joe Kerrigan, the Irish actor. When Elinor arrived with her husband, Bill, I found her facial paralysis hardly noticeable, but though carefully groomed and beautifully dressed as always, she seemed to have lost some vitality, to be more fragile. She gave us to understand that we were in for something special in her new poems, that she believed they were her best. She was pleased with the company, which she seemed to think was select; however, Kerrigan, who sang some Irish folk songs, had to leave before the recitation. But Elinor was so delighted with him that she insisted upon his coming to see her before she returned to England.

After dinner, which we had in a restaurant around the corner, I placed her in a large armchair in the middle of the group, and she began, not to read, but to repeat from memory, eighteen poems, prefacing some of them with, "Bill likes this one." I had expected to hear some kind of philosophical poetry, because she had written from England that she had been reading philosophy and that it was getting into her work. But what she began to repeat to us now was love poetry, ardent sonnets, intellectual and spiritual, as was all her work, into which she had put a part of herself I had not known was there, which perhaps had not existed or awakened to existence before. Still, as she recited, I thought they were purely dramatic sonnets about some ideal personage that her imagination had constructed, a "created being," as Yeats would say, and I had little curiosity as to what dim facts of experience lay behind the ardent language of the sonnets. I thought they expressed a potentiality of her mind, some part of her that she had never used in life, for it was a common meditation of mine and sometimes the subject of conversation with her that often the most alive part of us is something we have never been able to translate into living or into factual experience. Ridgely Torrence pleased her by asking her for the sonnets, which he wanted to publish as a group in the *New*

Republic. Nobody who was present ever forgot the reading of those poems, and the undercurrent of tragedy in them and in herself came over to us—a tragedy of which she was completely unconscious.

Fairly early the next morning she came round and sat on a sofa talking about her future plans; the way we had received her sonnets the evening before seemed a lucky augury for her book, which was then in the hands of her publishers—in fact, that very day she was going to have a consultation with them. The book later was given the title of *Angels and Earthly Creatures,* but I think she had a number of other titles in her mind. After a conversation about the poems she opened her little satchel and, characteristically, took out one of those little bottles of bromo seltzer which she always carried for that headache of hers. I gave her a glass of water, and she swallowed the contents of the little bottle. When my husband left and went back to his own room to work, she drew from a notebook a snapshot of a tallish-looking, obviously middle-aged man. "I became very attached to somebody in England —this is he. I wrote the sonnets about him." I was at first a little startled, but as she went on talking about him I began to think that, maybe, it was all somehow the continuation of the thread of her life with Horace Wylie; her remark that the original of the snapshot was like Horace, her life in the English country once more, the New Forest, the visits to London, the dropping over to shop in Paris—it seemed to me the old life she had once told me about, relived again almost as in a dream. That she was really in love with this man I believed to be true and real as far as romantic love is reality; she felt she had to live somewhere near him, and so was leaving America behind. It may be that she did not tell me all of it, but I have never been able to swallow some of the accounts of her relationship with him given by others. "I am not taking anything on this time," she said, and these are her words precisely. "He calls to see me once a week, and we talk and sometimes walk together." What they talked about she told me—a great deal about philosophy—and he would repeat to her Scots ballads in dialect which from childhood she had liked and recollections of which had gone into her poetry. As she spoke to me of it, it seemed a simple and rather pathetic relationship where two people with obligations to others were attracted to each other in a romantic and intellectual way. Elinor seemed to be attached also to his family and spoke about them with affection. It was amusing to find a sort of schoolgirl infatuation connected with the things she told me: her friend had referred to the legs of American women as contrasted with the sturdy ones of his countrywomen as "spindle-shanks." She exhibited her own legs to me. "Look how they have filled out!" she said. "That is from walking; I have walked and walked." She joined with me in laughter over this because she used to be so proud of her slim legs and ankles. Then she had got her facial paralysis a day or two before her friend's weekly visit; she sent her maid downstairs first to warn him, to prepare him for the change in her looks.

Although she was going back to England after Christmas, her intention was to see her husband frequently. She was determined, she told me, never to get back into the crowd in New York that she had been in. This surprised me, for she had seemed to enjoy every New York party, so much in fact that one evening when she was giving a party herself, suddenly remembering there was another party in a house near, she left her guests and went off to it. There was a side of her that could never resist a crowd, but now I was to find that many of the people who used to be always in her conversation seemed to be fading out of her mind.

We were to be in Ireland the following summer, 1929, and she planned to join us there when her husband came over to see her from America and to induce her brother-in-law and sister-in-law, Stephen and Rosemary Benét, to come, too. We made some more plans of this kind, and then she rose to go to lunch with her publishers and to talk over the publication of her new book. At the door I half promised to go and see her two evenings later, Sunday evening, when, she told me, she and Bill would be alone in the apartment. I could not get there; I had intended telephoning her the next morning to make another arrangement. Very early I was awakened by the persistent ringing of the telephone; it was our friend, Douglas Moore, telling us that Elinor was dead. She had died suddenly the night before of a stroke. Her husband had left the room for a minute and was getting her a glass of water when he heard her voice saying, "My God!" She had fallen from her chair and was lying on the floor when he went to her; she never spoke again; she was dead. We now realized that this last had been the third stroke, the facial paralysis the second, and a previous happening, when she had fallen downstairs, the first. Her death happened almost as she had written of it in a poem that was to come out in her book.

> If a little vein within me broke,
> The blood would frighten your pillow;
> But there's brave red earth beneath the oak,
> And water beneath the willow,
>
> At the little noise our death will make
> No red deer need stand still;
> Get up, get up, for Heaven's sake,
> And climb to the top of the hill!

II

A day or so later there was a funeral service at her apartment, and a few of her intimate friends were invited. Her body had not been removed to a mortuary chapel, but lay in the bedroom of the apartment. My husband had spent the night with her husband, William Rose Benét, for it is forlorn for anybody to be alone in an apartment with the dead, and especially with the beloved dead. As she lay there she seemed like a figure in marble. She was in her beloved silver brocade dress; she had loved all silver things, and even the word "silver" had a special appeal for her. Her beautiful hair that she always had shampooed with a reddish rinse was bright about her still features. All the marks of small irritations, little vanities, little sulkinesses, were completely smoothed away; only what was eternally herself was now revealed. Maybe there is some nobility of character beyond goodness, beyond kindness or unselfishness and devotion to others—she had not these—and of that this nobility is what we see in certain people's faces after death.

For the first time I met her mother. Elinor had once told me laughingly that in a sudden outburst, when informed of some new, untoward happening in the family—and there were many such happenings—her mother exclaimed, "I have given birth to a generation of vipers." Now at Elinor's death she was averse to any funeral service in a public place; she wanted no publicity, for Elinor's elopement and matrimonial affairs had figured in the papers too often; I doubt if she liked the purely literary publicity her daughter had got as a poet—the reviews, the interviews, the fame.

I could not look at Elinor's dead body without giving way; I wept openly as I knelt beside her, for something had passed away from the earth, spirit and fire, and a sort of emotional power hard to qualify. As I rose from my feet a hand was held out to me: I gazed into a boyish, Celtic-looking face, Scottish or Irish or some mixture of the kind. As he pronounced his name I caught only the last name, "Hichborn," and I realized strangely that this freckled-faced boy of nineteen or twenty was Elinor's son, the son of her first husband, the child and husband she had eloped from. As far as I knew, except for one meeting, unfriendly on his side, she had never seen her son since she had left him. My mind was con-fused for a few minutes as it ran over Elinor's past, and I found myself speaking to the boy as if he were Horace Wylie's son. Elinor had told me that Horace was what is called in this country Scotch-Irish, and I was subconsciously accounting for the Gaelic appearance of the boy before me. We stood side by side for a minute or two looking down at the wonderful dead face of her who had been his mother but to whom he had meant so little. My mind, I recall, had difficulty in taking it all in, but kept itself fastened on the man, Horace Wylie, who had flung his life away for her, to be abandoned also by her. Now penniless, I knew, he was making a living in Chicago teaching society women to play bridge. I had never seen him, this man who had been so recklessly in love with Elinor, laying flesh and spirit in her hands. It seemed odd that he was not there. "Is your father here?" I asked the boy in my confusion. How would Horace feel when he heard of her death? Her to whom he had taught so much, whom he had helped to make a poet on her own admittance. With what they had ex-perienced together, suffered together, could he ever really feel apart from her? His absence from that room seemed the strangest absence of all.

Very few people were present: there were members of both families, Elinor's and Bill's; the young sister-in-law to whom she was so attached, Rosemary Benét, was away in France with her husband, Stephen Vincent Benét; there was Elinor's publisher, Blanche Knopf; there was Edna St. Vincent Millay, whom I saw for the first time, Douglas and Emily Moore. As we all collected in another room after the service, the group gave me the impression I have often had at funeral services held in a private house, as if it were all a sort of party, with conventional chatter, conventional greetings, conventional good-bys. Edna Millay was talking of planting trees in her place in the country. "The first tree will be for her," she said. "It shall be called her tree." Among many incongruous things said, this seemed the most incongruous: perhaps it was because I knew Elinor had no liking for trees.

None of us attended her actual burial: it was in Pennsylvania, the home of her fathers.

III

A few months after her death the book whose publication she had arranged for came out—in May, to be precise. It was her fourth volume of poetry. Elinor Wylie knew that death was dogging her footsteps and would soon overtake her, and this knowledge colors almost every poem and makes still more tragic an almost intolerably tragic vision of life.

It is not often that the last work of a poet is his or her best; the power of growth of all but a very small number of writers is not very great. They may acquire a more accomplished technique, but they rarely surpass themselves in profundity of thought or depth of emotion: it is exactly in these two qualities that Elinor Wylie's last book surpasses all the others. The emotion, for all its intellectual statement, is so intense that one pauses to consider what made a human being feel so deeply and suffer so greatly. That she did not feel greatly for anyone would have been the opinion of most people who knew Elinor; in a way, but with many afterthoughts and overthoughts, I subscribed to the same verdict. The emotion I believe to have been there, but the people who could rouse it were not there, and there was always that neuroticism that turned the emotion in on herself. She had got up a passion for Shelley that seemed to me more real than many passions between people in the flesh. And with all her independence of thought and mind, she always seemed to be seeking protection; that Shelley was her guardian angel was something she really believed, and she wrote about him:

A subtle spirit has my path attended,
In likeness not a lion but a pard;
And when the arrows flew like hail, and hard,
He licked my wounds, and all my wounds were mended;
And happy I, who walked so well-defended,
With that translucid presence for a guard,
Under a sky reversed and evil-starred;
A woman by an archangel befriended.

No Catholic could have a more fervent belief in the protection of a guardian angel or a patron saint than Elinor had in the guardianship of Shelley. It gave her a real confidence to have this belief. Maybe it helped her towards that splendid courage, physical as well as spiritual, that impressed me and, as I know, impressed many others. She had an instinctive recoil from anything that seemed like cowering or cowardice. Once we were talking about a friend, a man who had got a nervous or mental breakdown for what appeared to be slight reasons. "That's craven," she said meditatively. "No one need let themselves get like that—I know that." She added in complete good faith, "Shelley helped me over many a bump."

She seemed to write little out of a mood or out of a passing emotion, as many poets do, but nearly always out of complex thought that was entangled in the roots of her experiences, and this has made some of her poetry, in spite of its directness, so difficult that it reveals its secret only after many readings. Clarity of diction and directness of expression were always characteristic of her, but these things cannot of themselves make a profound thought or idea easy of comprehension. Than the language of a poem called "O Virtuous Light," nothing could be clearer:

Mysterious as steel and flint
The birth of this destructive spark
Whose inward growth has power to print
Strange suns upon the natural dark.

O break the walls of sense in half
And make the spirit fugitive!

> The light begotten of itself
> Is not a light by which to live!
>
> O virtuous light, if thou be man's
> Or matter of the meteor stone,
> Prevail against this radiance
> Which is engendered of its own!

In its expression this is luminous, but it remains a very difficult poem, for it states, with an elimination of all unnecessary explanation, a truth long pondered over. It is a statement of a conclusion that emerged from her own conflicts: that those who live in the world of the creative mind, by the light of the intellect, are living too dangerous a life for human beings.

In sheer intellectual power I do not think I have ever met a writer who surpassed her, though, like most women, she had never worked out a way of using all her intellect; she used it in flashes. Her vocabulary is very remarkable because, while so alive and fresh, while she stamped her own mind on every syllable, it is so thoroughly, so completely in the tradition of English poetry that we can almost tell where every word was used before: we recognize a phrase, a turn of speech, as the twin of something Shakespeare, or Donne, or Milton used. Inside this mold of form, this mold of language, used and re-used by a long line of poets, she designed new patterns of emotion, wove new webs of thought. She who so loved opposed things must have greatly loved expressing her free mind inside such solid, unshaking boundaries. There was always something in her that delighted in contrasts and antitheses; her types were the Eagle and the Mole, her nets, Nets to Catch the Wind; she did not care for halfway houses, half loaves, "the middle mind" or "the moderated soul":

> The worst and best are both inclined
> To snap like vixens at the truth,
> But, O, beware the middle mind
> That purrs and never shows a tooth.
>
> A pinch of fair, a pinch of foul,
> And bad and good make best of all.
> Beware the moderated soul
> That climbs no fractional inch to fall.

I knew it was a high compliment from her when she once said of me, "She has not the middle mind." Elinor must have been grateful to old John Donne that he gave her the title of her last book, *Angels and Earthly Creatures*, so sharply antithetical in her own daring fashion. I never cared for her novels, but I believe that her four thin volumes of poetry place her among the eight or nine important poets in American literature, and one of the few important women poets in any literature. But the cost of producing high poetry can be great. She learned a great deal from living, but though she could be gay at moments her life was unhappy, and she wrote down as the essence of the wisdom she had extracted from the years:

> Mortality has wearied us who wear it,
> And they are wiser creatures who have shunned
> This miry world, this slough of man's despond,
> To fortify the skies we shall inherit.

One hopes that that archangel who, as she said, "befriended her in knightly servitude," "under a sky reversed and evil-starred," will still befriend her throughout "the Uranian years," under a fair sky where all the good stars meet.

ॐ CHAPTER 32

Literary Critic

AFTER ELINOR'S DEATH we returned to Connecticut, though we never again spent a whole winter in it; summers there were lovely, but winters were rather dreary, and everything around recalled Elinor, whose loss hit all her friends very hard: something rare and strange had gone out of the world, some brightness had fallen from the air. I think she was attached to me, or, anyhow, attached to my affection for her and interest in her work. I do not get over people's deaths easily, and not only the loss of Elinor Wylie but the loss of another couple of friends made me unsettled. We began to go more often into New York than we used to; Elinor, when living in Connecticut, always stayed one night a week in the city, two whole days in fact, when she visited a beauty parlor and saw numbers of her friends. Then she would return and settle down to work until the next week. But at the time I had far less physical energy than she had, no such powers of concentration, and my mind got scattered easily.

We went in occasionally to stay with Mrs. Murray Crane, one of our earliest American friends, the most intellectual of the New York hostesses, whose interest in art, literature, and philosophy was intense, and who ran the nearest thing to a French salon in New York. She always had people of intellectual distinction around her and guests from all over the world, including politicians, ex-chiefs of cabinets, generals, and these gave diversity to the conversation. It was fun to talk politics with men who had run a government and of the wickedness of war with generals who had won a few campaigns.

And, of course, we went now and again to some of those parties characteristic of that era of beautiful nonsense and bathtub gin. The maddest, merriest of those parties, which at the same time managed to be discriminating, were those given by a handsome, wealthy connoisseur of the arts, George Gordon Moore, who lived in an exotically furnished house in the East Fifties, with rooms called by names such as the Persian Room, the Roman Room, and so on. He owned coal mines and ranches and everything, and bought whole libraries now and again so as to have something to read when he went to live in a shack by a coal mine or in an adobe hut on a ranch. He was gay, ready-minded, brilliant, and at his lavish parties nothing so vulgar as gin was served; there were bottles of champagne handed out by lackeys who seemed to enjoy the parties no less than their master. In addition, there was in corners of the room champagne in buckets of ice from which the guests could help themselves. The host had a way of his own of arranging his entertainments: he would say to his butler, "Let's have a beauty night," or, "Let's have an intellectual night," or he might, on consultation with this major-domo, mix them. The host seldom if ever knew all his guests, and some of them had never been invited at all, or were invited at second or third remove; but they all had to have some distinction. I think that if the butler had not all the names of the guests who presented themselves on the list given him, he would, after some tactful inquiries, get rid of the unqualified.

My husband, seated one night beside a beautiful young woman, inquired from the host who she was. "I don't know," said he. "It's up to you to find out." My husband got her name: she was a movie actress of the period, and she remarked she did not know anybody present. "Tommy Hitchcock brought me here," she explained. "Do you mean the polo player?" asked my husband. "I don't know who he is," she said. "I met him on the train coming from California, and he invited me to the party he was going to."

But it has to be said that the guests who thus casually invited other guests to this house never forgot the host's demand for distinction of some sort—beauty, or talent, or fame, or, maybe, wealth, and I must say the parties never degenerated: they kept alive and eager up to the early morning hours. The women guests, society women, cinema actresses, debutantes, celebrities of some sort, were lovely to look at, or distinguished, and sometimes dazzlingly dressed; the men were most entertaining and appeared to be of every nationality and every shade of opinion. Our host reminded me of a Roman emperor—maybe it was Hadrian—who gave entertaining parties, knew everybody, had been everywhere, including to the wars and the provinces, and wrote a little himself. If a woman present was particularly picked out for his attentions he armed himself with a few cushions and reclined gracefully at her feet, pouring out champagne for her to the accompaniment of subtle compliments, and if she was in the bluestocking line—and provided she was gay, or witty, or good to look at, he had no objection—he would toss off a few lines from a Roman poet about love and the good Falernian wine or similar Bacchic potion. A good deal of verse of one kind or another was recited. I have a memory of an elderly literary gentleman, Michael Monahan, holding a glass in each hand and reciting tearfully and endlessly:

The Bells of Shandon
That sound so grand on
The pleasant waters of the River Lee.

In this era of prohibition many fantastic things happened, and Americans got to be almost as expert at breaking their own laws as the Irish were at breaking English laws, and likewise thought it some sort of virtue. Speakeasies were run, as everybody knows, under protection of the agents of the law; the restaurant speakeasies often served very good food and liquor, imported wines, excellent scotch whisky. It seemed as if every country in the world were engaged in a conspiracy to make America defeat its own laws. In a speakeasy restaurant in the Fifties I saw a big official of a federal government office and a state judge so drunk that the proprietor kept pouring strong black coffee down their throats in an effort to sober them up before letting them out on the street. Publishers had special speakeasies to which they took their authors to arrange their contracts. I had in France got used to the idea of the Third Republic not representing the people, and now I got used to the idea that the legislature in our great republic could pass a law that few people wanted.

Bootleggers with good liquor to sell were cultivated by smart society. Once we went to a dinner party given by the daughter of an ex-member of Wilson's Cabinet, an intellectual and artistic party. In the middle of the excellent cocktails the host, a recent bridegroom, brought in a well-dressed, well-groomed young man in dinner clothes; he wore what was then an innovation introduced by the Prince of Wales, a shirt delicately flecked—at that period the last word in smartness in male attire. The host presented him to everybody, but in spite of his expensive clothes he seemed ill at ease, though less so after our host had given him several cocktails. "Don't speak unless you are spoken to," I overheard the youthful host instruct him in a low tone. We were seated in groups at different tables, and the stranger was at the table of the host's mother-in-law, a beautiful and witty woman. The guest raised a glass to her. "Oh, lady," he exclaimed, "you look like my mother!" Then he proceeded to talk about the city government until somebody at the table changed the conversation to Lytton Strachey's *Elizabeth and Essex*, then just out. My husband started to discuss the role of the Prince of Tyrone, Hugh O'Neill, in the book. He was interrupted by the guest with the assertion, "O'Neill is a good guy. Don't any of you say anything against him!" After

this things got a bit out of hand, though the guest was far from
being insensitive; in fact he had a rather sensitive face. Soon he
asked permission to telephone, which he did from the hostess's
bedroom in an audible tone to somebody called Mary whom he
asked to expect him in half an hour. He bade us a graceful enough
adieu, but to our surprise the host led him through the kitchen to
depart by the kitchen entrance. When, after a delay, our host returned, he was asked by his wife, "Who is your friend?" he replied,
"He is a bootlegger, a celebrated one."

"Who invited him here?" his wife asked.

"I did," said our host. "He has given me cases of wine and scotch,
and when I asked him what I could do for him in return, he told
me, 'You can ask me to a refined home where folks sit round to
dinner in evening dress, where there are real oil paintings and
pianos, and where they talk about music and things between bites.'
He's a very fine fellow," our host continued, "but his legitimate
business was stopped, and he has to carry on as best he can. The
Mary he telephoned to is his girl, and you know," he said to his
mother-in-law, "he paid you a compliment when he said you were
like his mother—he just adores her."

"Why did you take him through the kitchen?"

"He couldn't go through the front way; he might be caught; his
guards are in the back hall—three or four of them. When in the
kitchen he slipped off his shoe, took a twenty-dollar bill out, and
offered it to the cook. She refused and was very rude to him. I don't
want a cook around who is rude to my guests."

The bootlegger, we got to know, later was killed while putting
up a fight against police officers who surrounded him in a house
somewhere in the environs of New York.

II

Years before in Dublin, Yeats, speaking to me about things I
had published in the *Irish Review* and elsewhere, advised me to
become a critic, and though the advice made no particular appeal
to me at the time, as I had sold some short stories in London and
was bent on writing a novel, I always kept it in mind. "I believe

you have a genuine talent for criticism," he said. And then he set to gravely considering my prospects. "Of course," he said, "there would be a prejudice against women in such an occupation; custom has by now permitted them to be poets, novelists, even dramatists, although," he continued, "a really important dramatist like Lady Gregory would not have had a chance but for the Abbey Theater." And but for his own support of her, I think he even said. Men, however, he went on, still regarded criticism and philosophy as their own province, and would be sure to resent a woman's pushing in. Then he did some real thinking about it and suggested that I tentatively adopt a man's name until I made some headway and reputation. He recommended that I make myself an authority on some kind of literature—French literature, for example, as I was already deeply interested in it—so that I would have to be consulted about it, and from that I could go ahead to all branches of literary criticism. If I began by translating Paul Claudel's plays, he told me, he would put them on at the Abbey Theater, and if I turned them into verse, he himself would help with the verse.

I might have literally followed his advice if I had stayed in Dublin, but not long afterwards I married, and not long after that again I came to America and dropped all notions of writing for a while. Writing I believe to be a very risky occupation, not only as a means of earning a living but because, when well done, its demands on the whole person are so exhausting that it can become psychically risky, and writers as a class, unless they are able to take it, are liable to nervous strains and even breakdowns. Then, as writing is a publicity-promoting profession, it can arouse a great deal of enmity. As for criticism, it is about the riskiest of all branches of the writing profession; it is very difficult; it demands a complicated equipment, a great deal of experience, not only of literature, but of life; it is none too well paid, and not so many readers know when it is first-rate. Then, in authors whose books they handle, reviewers are bound to arouse antagonism, for some authors are very touchy, particularly those who are natural amateurs; actually, however, all writers tend to overestimate their own products, even those who are outwardly modest.

As for myself, naturally I got accustomed to being clawed around occasionally and attacked frequently, if not always, for the wrong things—a lack of knowledge of something in which I was proficient, such as literary history or French literature or even English literature, by people who thought either that I had been exclusively educated on the Continent or hadn't got any formal education at all. Then there were young men who supposed I had not read Marx or Freud—I could have passed an examination in their works—or Goethe, in whose work I did pass many examinations. Some of the letters I received really made me hilarious, as when a gentleman, claiming to be an authority on Shakespeare, wrote to ask me why I had palmed off on my readers a line like, "Keep up your bright swords, for the dews will rust them," as Shakespeare, when it was obviously a little thing of my own. Then there was a professor who wrote to ask me where I got some lines of a translation of Homer I used, as they were in no version in his college library— they were the most familiar of the translated lines of the *Iliad*, I should say. And it was not always those whose books I reviewed I stirred up: there were some of the male sex who simply regarded me as a sort of intellectual rival and whom every line I wrote reduced to a state of spluttering exasperation. Though the warmest praise I have ever got in both America and England came from men, when it comes to real clawing, scratching, biting, the male of the species can be more ferocious than the female. It has a long history, this male objection to female intellectual pretensions, and the vocabulary of the phraseology of denigration has been centuries in the making, and some of it is very effective. Variations of Samuel Johnson's "A woman preaching is like a dog walking on its hind legs; you are surprised, not that it is not well done, but that it is done at all" are used all the time, when a woman does anything unusual. Now the effectiveness of this remark consists in the fact that it is true of all amateurs, male and female, of all half-baked and half-equipped practitioners of any kind of work—you are surprised that they can do it at all. But as the female amateur in the arts is more common than the male, its general truth is more applicable to women.

However, I never minded being hit if I were allowed to hit back, for, having undertaken what had been considered a man's occupation, criticism, I had to learn how to be an expert fighter. I have a racial talent in that line, anyhow, and can use both the rapier and the bludgeon with fair skill, so that sometimes even a strong fighting male has expressed regret that he got into "a muss with that woman." One of the first things a woman philosopher will have to do, when there is one, a female Berkeley, say, or a Bergson, is to learn to hit back with effectiveness. But I think there should be rules for intellectual combat as well as for physical combat, a sort of Queensberry rules—no lying about your opponent, no hitting below the belt, no ganging up, no dragging in of references to anybody's personal life.

I flattered myself that I kept the rules, but once Edwin Arlington Robinson mildly remonstrated with me after I had had a run-in with somebody in his presence, and I have never forgotten it. Somehow or another I had got myself into Harriet Monroe's bad books, and Harriet, when she abandoned her mind to it, could be very malicious. How or when her unfriendliness to me began, I am not quite sure, but I traced its beginning to an incident which is worth mentioning because it throws a light on the amateurishness of women in the fighting line. I did not know Harriet very well, having, as she lived in Chicago and we in the East, rarely seen her; in the beginning, when I had been supposedly a passing visitor in this country, she had been friendly enough—in fact the very first book I reviewed in America was for her magazine, *Poetry*. On one of her frequent visits to New York we encountered her at Leonora Speyer's. Leonora, after dinner, began to consult us about poets in an anthology of American poetry she was preparing for a German publisher. I think she was including about a dozen in all, and I thought her choice of poets so good that I expressed hearty approval. Suddenly I saw Harriet glaring at me with angry eyes; then she turned in a rage to Leonora. "Why have you omitted me from that anthology?" she demanded. None of us had noticed that Harriet was not included; in fact none of us would have thought of including her among important American poets. I have to admit that I did not think of her as a poet at all, or even as a writer, but she was an extremely good editor, and her services to poetry were very great; her magazine, for which she had laboriously collected funds so that she could pay her contributors a fair sum, was known all over the English-speaking world. And here she was, unmistakably being overlooked. Nobody present knew what to say or how to handle the situation. Harriet rose to her feet and without a word walked out of the room, pulling her cloak from where it was hanging, and proceeded to open the hall door. I had jumped up and, following her, tried some appeasement. But Harriet was not one to be appeased in a matter of this kind. She turned to me as she stepped across the threshold. "Who gave you the right," she demanded, "to lay down the law about poetry?" and she went down the steps, dragging her cloak after her. Now I wonder would a man have behaved like that! Would anyone except an amateur have cared so much about not being included in an anthology?

I had practically forgotten the episode until Harriet came on a visit to the MacDowell Colony when I happened to be there while my husband was in Ireland. She arrived in a sort of state to have a look at the creative minds. As it happened, there were some very good ones there at the time—they included Willa Cather, who was finishing *Death Comes to the Archbishop*, and Edwin Arlington Robinson. Harriet, of course, was seated at Robinson's table, for he always had the same seat at the same table in the dining room, as he always had the same studio, for he was the dean of the Colony and had been one of the earliest Colonists. Nobody ever took possession of Robinson's chair until once Maxwell Bodenheim seated himself on it defiantly, by way of letting all present know he was against privilege. We had known Edwin Arlington Robinson and Ridgely Torrence since a few weeks after we arrived in America, and used to meet them at the home of Louis Ledoux, a devotee of poetry who had published a couple of volumes himself. I sometimes sat at Robinson's table in the Colony, for I knew he liked me and I could amuse him.

At this particular time, for a week or two, he had been unable to write—his muse was taking a rest. With what is called the dry Yankee humor he told me he was in such a low state that he felt he would have to take a course in poetry. I undertook to give it to him, and we had been proceeding gaily with reading assignments and studies of French verse, and were having a good deal of fun until Harriet's advent. As I entered the dining room he and Harriet were already seated at the table, and he threw me a signal with his eyes, jerking his head in the direction of a chair opposite, which I took. I think he was terrified of being asked what he was working at, which was exactly what happened. Mildly he informed Harriet that he was working at nothing, that he was suffering from accidie, and that he had to take a course in poetry to waken his mind. "I'm giving the course," I announced. "She's very good at it," said Robinson with a chuckle. Though Harriet giggled slightly, her eyes said as plain as anything, "We are not amused." A little later he asked me to say the last stanza of Verlaine's *"Art Poetique"* which delighted him, especially on account of its last contemptuous line, *"Et tout le reste est littérature."* "Wouldn't it be terrible," said I, "if after this course you began to write 'literature'?" "I'm afraid of it," said Robinson, putting his fingers to his forehead with a characteristic gesture and a characteristic slight laugh. Harriet remarked that the Irish, having been so long deprived of literacy by the penal laws, were apt to let their brains go off in conversation. Another man at the table, turning to me, said, "I wonder you do not write poetry, you know so much about it." "Perhaps she knows she could not write it," said Harriet. "Not everybody who knows about poetry can write it." "Of course not," said I, "I always knew enough about poetry to know I could not write it." Robinson looked at Harriet nervously, and after dinner took me aside. "I wish you had not said that," he protested deprecatingly. "It was a hard one on the old girl—she had no comeback."

But Harriet, I guessed, would have some comeback, in spite of the fact that, as I knew, she liked me personally. The next day was cold; it was late August or September, and I was wearing a knitted woolly dress. "How fashionable you are!" remarked Harriet. "I always believe fine feathers make fine birds." Now nobody in Peterboro ever wore fashionable clothes, and mine was a very rural garment indeed; I had bought it a few years before in Paddy Gallagher's little factory in Dunloe, in the wilds of Donegal. But Harriet later described me as flaunting around in fashionable clothes and a fashionable wave, both of which I affect at times but certainly not in Peterboro. Her next item had more malice, and I think some people believed her. When she told a story that was later found out to be inaccurate, she always blamed her poor memory, but it was too bad that her inaccurate stories were always malicious. Now she spread a yarn that we had "escaped" from Ireland in 1916, dodging submarines, or, maybe, on one, and had arrived at Mrs. Moody's in Chicago all bedraggled by crossing in such difficult circumstances.

ह्ल CHAPTER 33

Life in Paris

WHILE LIVING IN PARIS in March 1930 I received news of my first Guggenheim Fellowship. We had to return to vacate the house in Connecticut which I had subrented to a New York real estate agent who paid us one month's rent, broke everything breakable, and left us to pay the arrears of rent, for we did not own, we had only rented the house.

We had been spending some months in Paris from time to time and got to know a few French people. Foreigners very seldom know them, for of all races in the world that I have ever encountered the French have the least interest in knowing strangers. Still we got to know more than most foreigners, first of all because we were writers and got to know other writers, and, more importantly, because a certain number of people had a romantic interest in Ireland because of an Irish ancestry or because they had learned Daniel O'Connell's speeches at school. Then T. S. Eliot had given us letters of introduction to some of his friends among the neo-Thomists, to Jacques Maritain, whose work I later introduced to Scribner's in New York, and to Charles du Bos, who, in addition to being a very distinguished critic, was the romantic aristocrat, quite in the Chateaubriand tradition. We first met him in his apartment in an old house on the left bank, but later he held a sort of salon in Versailles where foreign visitors to Paris collected. He spoke several languages, and as he had some English blood, he spoke wonderful English, but wrote it less well. At this period he was very sad that his great friend, André Gide, had fallen out with him over something he had written about him: the usual fate of critics. He was one of the few hospitable Frenchmen I ever knew, and I think it was the English in his ancestry that made him so. I understood he had inherited quite a fortune, that his father had been a member of the Jockey Club like Proust's Charles Swann, and had been a friend of Edward VII, but that somehow he had got rid of all he owned. He had a handy knowledge of all European literatures, and one met writers and artists from every country at his house; also some of those witty and intellectual Frenchwomen of the salon tradition whose *esprit* dazzled one. One woman, I remember, could recite so much of Dante and of Aquinas's *Summa* that I wondered her name was not famous.

Among other hospitable Frenchmen we met was Abel Chevalley, also a critic. He was a French Protestant, a very different type I should say from either the French Catholic or the French Jew. Abel Chevalley had made an admirable translation of some of James Stephens's books into French; he had been minister plenipotentiary to the Balkans, and in connection with this mission he told us a very funny story about a woman journalist, Odette Kuhn, a friend of H. G. Wells. He had given an official dinner when minister plenipotentiary, and Madame Kuhn, one of the guests, in describing him had recorded that he had scraped the dirt out of his fingernails with a penknife under the tablecloth. This had delighted him, because, as he said, he was of lowly origin, his wife having the only ancestry in the family, these being the Flauberts. A little later H. G. Wells had lectured at the Sorbonne and, while being driven there by Chevalley, had asked him, as one having connections with the Quai d'Orsay, to make sure that Odette Kuhn was made a French citizen.

M. Chevalley took a certain pleasure in escorting me around, even bringing me to a football match—which sport, to his astonishment, I had never attended before. He had been one of the first Frenchmen to introduce football to France. "In Maupassant's time," he said, "the young men were only interested in girls; I don't think there's a single sport mentioned in French literature except hunting and tennis." He was out to change all that, and described to me the first football match that had ever been in Paris when a chalk mark was put on everybody's coat to show he had been at something unusual. The game we went to was well enough attended, but I knew nothing about it, and when he asked me, "Isn't that a grand scrimmage?" I had to inquire, "What is a scrimmage?" In disgust he took me away to a literary café, where he presented me jocosely as the only woman critic since Madame de Staël, and he was delighted with the stir my non-French appearance caused— *ʼair étranger,* he said.

A sinister-looking, middle-aged man who, I heard, had spent his time mourning an unhappy love affair, as Paul Valéry was supposed to have done, kept trying to trip me up by repeating some school-book poetry which he pretended to be by Valéry. French people, like the British people, learn a lot of poetry by heart, and their minds are furnished with it. Despite the cool, businesslike arrangement of their marriages and sometimes their love affairs, and their reasoning minds, I was often struck by what seemed to be their sentimentality: they would repeat with gusto mushy sentimental verses by Lamartine or De Musset or Leconte de Lisle: on the other hand, it is possible that my taste in English love poetry was equally mushy. I never heard as much talk about sex in France as in America, but more about romantic love. However, with most of them, love seemed to be one thing and marriage another, the latter a social arrangement for the family. The sinister-looking gentleman talked about a French writer—was it Mérimée—whom his father had known during the Second Empire, and who had been a friend or tutor of the Empress Eugénie, as having been so disastrously in love that his life was forever marked by it. "I wonder he didn't die of it," said I, slightly satirically. "Ah, madame," he replied, "one can die for love—that is easy—but to live without requited love— that is hard; that is what tries the courage; he did that." I could not imagine a conversation of this nature in a New York café or cock-tail room, or even a group of men repeating poetry: in fact, as Joel Spingarn once pointed out, it is very hard to find a love poem in American literature at all. As we came away Abel Chevalley re-marked, "You behold in me the only Frenchman who has never had more than one love affair." He had never been in love with any-body except the woman he had married, whereas the group we left, provided it was requited, seemed to be able to fall in love multi-fariously.

There were still survivals of the old literary salons in Paris, but to all intents and purposes, among writers, anyway, café gatherings had taken their place. The literary people and the university groups —*les savants*—held what they called *réunions*, not unlike the old Dublin literary gatherings, except that somebody would read a paper and a discussion would follow. I suppose this was the classical French salon procedure. The Chevalleys had a house in Montparnasse with a large room occupying, I recall, the whole third floor, which Abel used as a study and where he received his guests. After a paper on some subject was read, the host would lead the discussion, wine and sweet cakes would be handed round, and everyone, native and foreign, showed they were delighted to be there; invitations to a French home were so out of the way. The host, a very patriotic Frenchman, liked foreigners, and I think he understood he was doing a service for France by inviting Americans and British to his house. He and André Siegfried, and, of course, André Gide, were French Protestants, and they seemed as different from other Frenchmen as Northeast Ulster Presbyterians are from other Irishmen. I never could make out whether the difference came from religious upbringing or whether actually they did not have a different racial blend, perhaps something Anglo-Saxon or Teutonic or Swiss.

The *réunions* at the house of Jacques Maritain and his beautiful wife in Meudon had a different character altogether: they seemed to me to have much more of a Latin stamp and were very Catholic. Once after a paper on Baudelaire had been read there was a vigorous discussion as to the poet's Catholicism, and I was struck anew by the way Frenchmen can separate religion and sex morality. It would not have occurred to me to regard a man who led the sort of life Baudelaire did and celebrated in his poems, as a Catholic, in spite of his prayers, but when somebody else present agreed with me and ventured a few remarks to this effect, Jacques Maritain settled the matter by declaring with authority, "The intellectual structure of his mind was Catholic." I have often since been struck with the fact that this statement could be applied to many Frenchmen, even the most atheistic. Pierre Janet, lecturing at the Collège de France to a mixed audience from many countries, would, when speaking of early psychological influences, talk about first confession and first communion as if they were universal experiences.

When I told James Joyce of Maritain's statement about Baude-laire, he was very satirical and made considerable fun of anyone having a Catholic structure for his mind. Actually, I have never known anyone with a mind so fundamentally Catholic in structure as Joyce's own, or one on whom the Church, its ceremonies, symbols, and theological declarations had made such an impress, though I have reason to doubt that he had ever entered a church except to look at the architecture since he had left Dublin: the Scholastic was the only philosophy he had ever considered seriously. It was too bad that when Joyce died and some of his friends in New York wanted to have the customary Mass said for him, every priest approached, even the Jesuits whose pupil he was and for whom he preserved a great respect, refused on the grounds of Joyce's alienation from the Church. But Father George Ford, the chaplain of Columbia, had the customary prayers said. It is remarkable that people far less Catholic than James Joyce, like Paderewski and George Cohan, were given all the rites, and in the Cathedral, and that they should have been denied to him. But Joyce had done the unforgivable thing in English-speaking Catholicism: written freely of sex.

Joyce, my husband's old Dublin friend, and his family were the people we saw most of in Paris. At this time Joyce was the most famous writer in the world, and when he appeared in a café or restaurant people took tables near to have a look at him; he always had a table facing the wall so that all anybody could see of him was the back of his head; his guests sat facing him. There may have been some Frenchmen in whom the life of Paris soaked into their veins and pores as that of Dublin had done in Joyce's case, but I doubt it. Nobody has ever written of the life of a city, so identified himself with that city and its history, as Joyce has with Dublin. The fact that he left it early and became a Berlitz teacher in Trieste, far from diminishing his impressions, clarified them, far from clouding his memory, made it more exact. *Ulysses* and *Finnegans Wake* are the epics of a city, the histories of a city, the memories of a city, and of all the languages somebody there might have understood and spoken. And as cities grew up by rivers, Joyce's *Finnegans Wake* is a history of rivers, a history of the city's civilization and population, with everybody, from kings to washerwomen, whom his imagination could conjure up as moving in its streets and environs. His two big books must be the most local in any literature, and I doubt if he really cared much for anybody who was not familiar with Dublin's streets and ways.

Until the end of his life I think he was waiting patiently for the signal of an Irish government to invite him back, to place bay leaves on his brow. But governments seldom approve of great writers, and I think the Irish are peculiarly indifferent to what the writers have done for them. Everybody who was out in revolution, everybody who did a little fighting in 1916, every post-office official, every policeman or soldier receives a pension, but the government of Ireland had nothing to give their great poet, W. B. Yeats, who gave them more prestige than all their little or even their big officials. I am convinced that all governments should pension a number of practitioners of the arts, a number in proportion to their population, and have a Minister of Fine Arts, or in America, a Secretary of Fine Arts, independent of the party in power, of public opinion, of religion, or any extraneous interest, one who would devote himself solely to getting the best possible assistants who would find out as nearly as possible the most worth-while people for an income, a not too large income, not one above the general level of moderate comfort. This is really one of the most essential things for a government to consider. For art, the most lasting product of a civilization, has no value that can be assessed in money: any such value would be accidental or arbitrary or even connected with factors that would have little or no relation to art. If some readers of these lines wrote a good or amusing novel, or an amusing play, they might make considerable money, or if they wrote *War and Peace* or *Arms and the Man* they would have steady royalties. But if they wrote the *Divine Comedy* they might have the privilege of walking up and down another's stairs, or if they composed a Mozart Mass, of being buried in a pauper's grave, or they might get five pounds for *Paradise Lost*.

Now the problem with Joyce was that he was engaged in literary experimentation, a sort of experimentation which, at the time, few publishers could feel interested in, and which while doing he had to spend the major part of his time earning a living at something else. He had left Dublin as a young man, some time after graduating, with the woman he married, to become a Berlitz teacher in Trieste. He labored hard, teaching English to all sorts of people—waiters, businessmen, and fashionables—and in what poor leisure he had, he worked first at *Portrait of the Artist as a Young Man* and later at *Ulysses*. It was hard enough to get a publisher for *Portrait of the Artist*, though Ezra Pound, with that remarkable critical insight he has always shown, tried unwearyingly to get a publisher, and eventually succeeded, really starting him on his career as an experimental writer. Joyce said of him later, "Pound took me out of the gutter."

When the war of 1914 started, Joyce, his wife, son, and daughter, being officially British subjects, had to leave Trieste and go to a neutral country; they were allowed to depart without difficulty on the promise from Joyce that he would not engage in war activities. They left with sadness, for Joyce loved the old Austrian Empire, and he and his family had their happiest days in Trieste. "They called the Austrian Empire a ramshackle empire," he said to us later in Paris. "I wish to God there were more such empires." He worked hard enough to make sure his family lived in comfort, and I remember his telling us of the music he and Nora, his wife, heard, of the restaurants they dined at, and their enjoyment of life in general for quite little expenditure. These old European countries had almost discovered the secret of being happy in life which had eluded the Anglo-Saxons.

Troubles, however, began when they got to Switzerland during the war. To support his family, teaching English was not enough: too many in Switzerland at the time were doing that; his eyes were steadily failing; he had to look to something else. Joyce started a theater in Zurich to produce English plays. Eventually he had some sort of run-in with the British consul which upset his nervous temperament to a considerable degree; money difficulties ensued; he wrote to the publisher of *Portrait of the Artist*, Benjamin Huebsch, and to my husband that he was in dire need of a thousand dollars. To get a sum like that in America for a writer nobody knew much about at the time seemed an impossibility. Benjamin Huebsch, then a young man and not the great publisher he is today, had somehow got together a couple of hundred dollars, but my husband and myself had **no talent** for asking money. After hard thinking, one day as I came home from my work of tutoring I had a brain wave. I decided to ring up Scofield Thayer, the editor of the *Dial*, who had written about the parts of *Ulysses* that had appeared in the *Little Review*. I was very brave at the start, but as his voice answered, I weakened and could not put over the request. I simply said, "I have something to talk to you about." I remember his prompt answer: "I'll be round in twenty minutes." At the time we lived in West Seventy-ninth Street, and nervously I began drinking cup after cup of tea until his arrival. When he came in, his appearance, his interesting face as he sat in our sitting room up four flights of stairs, gave me courage, and my husband began to tell him about Joyce's case. At my husband's request I read aloud Joyce's letter, rather nervously, I think, for I was a nervous girl. I can never forget Scofield Thayer's sympathy. "Don't try to collect anything yourselves," he told us. "It will only harass you. I will give whatever is necessary." He had kept a taxi waiting outside, for, as I heard long afterwards, he had come round as a friend of ours, thinking we might be in some difficulties ourselves. I found myself weeping as he left, not only because of his generosity, but because I knew that very few people understood what he was trying to do for art and literature, and what a rare spirit he was. Sad to say, some years later he fell a victim to that dread ailment of the sensitive American, a nervous and mental breakdown.

Joyce always said very earnestly that this sum saved him at the moment, for he was not making much on the theater venture; the troubles connected with it would have harassed a more equable temperament than his. Then one day, while he was away at rehearsal, a letter arrived from England informing him he was being sent by an anonymous donor either five thousand dollars or five thousand pounds—I am now a little uncertain which. Nora, all excitement, put on her hat, went over to the theater, and, before all the company rehearsing, informed him of their luck. Joyce was so overcome that he said little, but he always remembered that in the midst of the conventional congratulations the wife of an actor in the company turned to Nora and said with an edge to her voice, "And so, Mrs. Joyce, you open your husband's letters."

The money was from Miss Weaver, who had once backed the feminist weekly, the *New Freewoman*, and later the *Egoist*, in which some of Joyce's work had appeared. Later she gave him a much larger sum on which, if he had been careful, he could have lived the rest of his life at ease. What a pity that the kind friend did not divide the money into a yearly income which he could not exceed: the lump sum had a bad effect on the whole family: they had no notion of money, and though they had a not too expensive apartment, they were extravagant on things like clothes, hotels, restaurants, and vacations: they simply thought the money would last forever. Now I think this is the great temptation of the writer whose mind is taken up with his work—in off hours he wants comforts and recreation, often of an extravagant kind. Joyce loved restaurants, liked being among the crowd in them, and would go for long stretches to the same restaurant every evening for dinner, entertaining his friends lavishly. For years he frequented the Trianons, near the Montparnasse station, where he had a favorite table and a favorite waiter, Norbert, who frequently, when he was alone and drank too much, escorted him home. Once, in the absence of his wife on a vacation, he invited a number of friends to dinner, where everybody drank a great deal of champagne, and Joyce, departing in an expansive mood, presented an array of bowing waiters, who had not been attached to his table, with a hundred francs each. I, backed by either the proprietor or the headwaiter, collected the hundred-franc bills from the waiters, giving them ten francs instead. As they had performed no service, even this might be called extravagant. We all escorted Joyce, whose continuous smile showed how happy he was over the whole proceedings, home in a couple of taxicabs. One of us put him to bed. I fished up an envelope, put in it the hundred-franc bills I had retrieved from the waiters, placing the whole under a clock on the mantelpiece for him to find in the morning.

II

The last time we were in Paris, in 1938, he had exchanged his old restaurant, Trianons, for Fouquet's in the Champs Elysées, which had the clientele of a New York night club and was filled by the world of fashion, of art, of the theater and the cinema. When any visitors came over from Dublin he would invite them to dinner at a restaurant: he was so happy when any Dubliner understood his work and liked it, especially if he was a non-literary personage. Once when we were in a café in Montmartre, a Dubliner who recognized my husband came over and spoke to him. He was over in Paris to attend a football match between an Irish and a French team, one of those teams that our friend Abel Chevalley had fostered: like many simple Dubliners he was soaked in *Ulysses* though he made no pretense of literary sophistication. Immediately we knew he was the very type Joyce would like, and I telephoned to ask if we might bring him round. Joyce was alone in his apartment; it was Sunday, and the family had gone somewhere. He answered enthusiastically, "Bring him right over." The Dublin citizen was a little dazzled, but he was delighted to come. What particularly fascinated Joyce was that this guest belonged to a family of old Dublin glassmakers, the Pughs, and represented an item he wanted for *Finnegans Wake*; the careful reader can find it there. He handed a copy of *Ulysses* to the guest and asked him to read a chapter aloud in the accent of a lower quarter of the city, the Coombe. The visitor produced something that enchanted Joyce and showed that he must have read parts of *Ulysses* aloud many times and could reproduce the exact low-down Dublin accent necessary for this particular episode. Joyce, obviously delighted, felt that here was a simple citizen for whom *Ulysses* was a national masterpiece. Once, I remember, when asked where he would like best to live, he said slyly, "In a city of about half a million population, an old city built on a river with a woman's name." "And with a castle inside a courtyard," I suggested, "a villainous castle with a villainous history." He nodded.

But any hopes he had that Dublin would give him some official recognition were vain: no Irish writer except Bernard Shaw received official recognition in our time, and he only when a very old man, after he had written a letter flattering to the government. Yeats was made a senator, but that was because he had been associated with the Nationalist movement all his life.

Joyce was a very lonely man who paid dearly for his fame, though, maybe, if he had not had the fame, things might have been even more desolate for him: he did actually enjoy the attention that his fame brought him. Like all outstanding figures, he aroused jealousy and malevolence, and a prying into his private affairs with a misinterpretation of them. One to whom he had been kind and hospitable wrote the most poisonous attack on him that I have ever read on anybody: it not only concerned itself with Joyce, but with his family and friends, his father and his wife. How it ever got published I cannot understand. We kept it out of his way for years, but, eventually hearing of it, he insisted on procuring it; he was deeply hurt because of its effect of humiliating his family. Then he would receive the most violently insulting letters in answer to a simple request. No doubt he had what might be called a persecution complex, but really this was not surprising, for he was actually persecuted. Against all this, he had the most attached friends, for he was a reliable friend himself and would help one with any old thing—to find an apartment or a maid or a doctor, how to plan a journey or pick out a hotel. He gave a great deal of consideration to such things, and if any of his friends were ill he would shower them with attentions and gifts of wine. When we lived in Paris he would telephone every day to find out how we were and how things were going with us. On his side he expected a lot of attention and help of all kinds from his friends: he really was not very far from blindness, and consequently he had to have a great deal of help for *Finnegans Wake*, not only help in putting it together, but for the reading of the necessary obscure references, books of every kind from the *Arabian Nights* to old-time Dublin directories, from the works of Vico to that of some romantic lady author like E. Barrington, who dealt with picturesque historical figures: one volume of hers which particularly interested him I remember because it was about some collateral connections of my own; he examined me minutely concerning what the family traditions about them were, for it was such items that he worked into his scheme of *Finnegans Wake*.

Finnegans Wake, as his friend Eugene Jolas has pointed out, seemed in the end to be almost a collective work, so many friends helped him with the minutiae of it, though of course, the molding of the material, the whole creative energy in it, the pattern, was Joyce's own. Stuart Gilbert, who wrote so much on his work, helped him regularly and tirelessly; my husband helped him whenever he was in Paris, and of his help he was very demanding because of the Dublin connection and because of a native knowledge of the history, the personages, the topography that Joyce was putting into the work. In Joyce's study in his apartment in Square Robiac, he would have a bottle of white chianti on the table, a medley of books and notebooks, a gramophone somewhere near: surrounded by such items, he and his helper set to work. The amount of reading done by his helpers was librarious, as he might have written himself, as were the notebooks filled with the results of their reading which generally boiled down to only a line or a paragraph. His great helper outside the literary people was Sylvia Beach, who, with her friend, Adrienne Monnier, had been the original publisher of *Ulysses*, an undertaking of great financial risk. They were certainly sound critics, because they knew what the book was about, and in the end they had a share in the author's fame.

I think Joyce was very demanding on both of them, especially on his great friend, Miss Beach: he never knew when his demands were too onerous, and then there were always a few people who tried to make a breach between them. Joyce had undertaken in his family life more than other men, because he was not only a genius but the one member of his family who had much practical sense. It was he who arranged every family detail, wrote every letter, engaged apartments, arranged for vacations, treatment of illnesses, and everything else, for he had a particularly helpless family. I am not sure that any of them ever read a thing he wrote—he told me once with amusement that he asked them where one could find samples of Irish humor, expecting that they might have found some specimens in *Ulysses*, but he found them innocent of the whole work. For all that, he loved them devotedly and had a united family life until the late 1920s. His son had married a beautiful American girl, who not only had an independent income, but produced what Joyce wanted, a grandson who was named after the hero of *Portrait of the Artist*, Stephen, with the addition of his own name, James. His son, Giorgio, had no religious affiliations, and neither had his daughter-in-law, an American of Jewish descent, yet when their son was born they fell into the pattern of the

French life around them and had the child baptized in a Catholic church.

It was a curious ceremony, with neither the father nor the mother showing any familiarity with religious ritual; my husband and I had been picked as godparents, but the grandfather was to be kept in ignorance of the whole proceedings, as it was felt he might disapprove of this recognition of a sacrament of the Church. Though I carefully schooled my husband in the questions and answers of the ritual, his French like Yeats's, being somewhat hazy, yet he got so mixed up in the *"Je renonce's,"* the *"J'accepte's,"* the *"oui's"* and the *"non's"* that when the priest put the routine questions as to whether, on behalf of the child, he renounced the devil and all his works and pomps, he promptly answered *"Non,"* so that to this day I am not certain whether Stephen James is a Christian, a pagan, or a Manichaean heretic. Also, at a strategic moment, my mind slipped on a sentence in the Apostles' Creed, and, to crown all, the officiating priest wound up by asking graciously, *"Est-ce que l'enfant est le petit fils de M. James Joyce, le célèbre écrivain?"* We were all panic-stricken for fear the news of the ceremony would get into the papers and we would all be put on the carpet by Joyce, for at this period he believed all religion to be a sort of elegant traditional symbolism or else a sort of black magic. However, he did not hear of it until some years later, when I accidentally revealed it to him, but then it made no difference one way or another, for his mind had marched in another direction.

The birth of the child gave Joyce a great uplift; he had a descendant to replace the ancestor, his father, who had just died. At the moment of the birth we were in New York for a couple of weeks, early in 1932, where my husband had crossed to give some lectures: a cable came announcing the coming into the world of Stephen James Joyce. Joyce's father had died towards the end of 1931, and he wrote a poem celebrating the birth of the grandchild and mourning the death of his father. He mailed the poem to us in New York; my husband placed it in the *New Republic* after, surprisingly enough, having had it declined in other places. The lay person often imagines that famous writers have no trouble in getting anything published, but, as a matter of fact, they often receive refusal after refusal. Once when on behalf of Joyce I wrote to an American publishing firm I knew well, offering an anthology of his work which certainly should have a considerable and continuing sale, I received the astonishing answer that no anthology of Joyce could be complete without the risky passages, and that they could not publish those for fear of a lawsuit. Now the risky passages might have been omitted, and they were not so risky, anyway, in comparison with what has since been produced on this side of the Atlantic without any question of censorship. The next publisher I approached offered an advance of two hundred and fifty dollars, saying such an anthology would not sell, but he would risk it. Joyce was even more furious about the second than the first reply and cabled a refusal right away. A third publisher wrote, "It is too late for us to get on the Joyce band wagon." I sometimes think the stupidity of publishers with regard to literature could not be surpassed by a dame schoolmistress. Random House, a couple of years later, published and made a great success of *Ulysses* after a court action in which the judge decided that the book was not pornographic.

Although the success of *Ulysses* in America must have helped the sales of *Finnegans Wake* later, a few years before this Joyce received what were, considering the multiple difficulties of the text and the fact that no publisher's editor could have had time, even if he had the knowledge, to clear up what it was all about, really extraordinary offers for the book. As far back as the summer of 1931, several years before the work was finished and when he was spending the summer in London, he had offers from American publishers which included advances of upwards of three thousand dollars, which covered payment for some signed copies of the book when published; in London he was offered four hundred pounds; he wrote all this in letters to my husband and myself at the time we were in Paris; however, in these letters he expressed the belief that none of the publishers interested knew "anything about the book." It was in the beginning of the next year that he received offers from New York for the publication of *Ulysses*, which, as we all remember, was procurable only in bootlegged or pirated copies. The pirated copies—they were copied or photographed from the

Sylvia Beach edition—so incensed Joyce that he got a number of well-known writers to sign a protest, and this, I think, prevented their further sale.

III

On the St. Patrick's Day of that year, Sylvia Beach and Adrienne Monnier collected all Joyce's friends to give him a dinner at a restaurant. I have always thought that something in Joyce's behavior on that occasion hurt these two friends of his and led up to the later breach between them all. Each guest was contributing to the expense, and all ordered a grand meal with Lanson and Pommery champagne. But as for Joyce, no approaches could get out of him what dish he would like us to order for him beforehand. He said he would order it himself, and when we all sat down we perceived that the waiter handed him a dish of lentils. Now I had never seen Joyce, who was quite a gourmet, eating even lentil soup before, and the most amiable conclusion we could come to was that, maybe, he was going in for one of those symbolic items or "correspondences" to which he gave intellectual and psychical allegiance. Still there must have been someone in the company besides myself who thought it was pure cussedness and who sympathized with the downcast looks of the ladies who had arranged the party. The symbolic "correspondences," whether they were active on this occasion or not, he followed as Hitler was said to have followed astrological predictions. One of the "correspondences" that he developed with great interest was concerned with James Stephens.

We were anxious for the two to know each other, though Stephens at this time was not strong for the meeting. We arranged a dinner, but as luck would have it, James Stephens had to go to London; his wife, Cynthia, came with a number of our other friends, and she made the link between her husband and Joyce, inviting him round to their apartment. How ever Joyce with his blind eyes managed to struggle up the dark stairs to the Stephenses' little *pied-à-terre*—for their home at this time was in London—was always a mystery to me, but he did, and managed to carry up with him six bottles of Swiss wine as a present. He and James Stephens became fast friends, and nobody could be more of an amusing and heartening companion than Stephens. The "correspondences" that Joyce worked out in this case were very puzzling to me, who, I think, am more literal-minded and logical than any of the males I know and dread self-bamboozlement as a bird dreads a snake. Joyce decided that both Stephens and he had the same birthday, February 2, which I was sure was a fact, but that they were the same age, or born in the same year, I have the gravest doubts; indeed I have a dismal suspicion that these two, or at least one of them, made some concealment of their age, which men do at least as often as women. The next "correspondence" was in the fact that Stephens's first name was the same as his own, and that his second name, except for the final s, the same as that of the hero of *Portrait of the Artist* and *Ulysses*. Then both had two children, a boy and a girl. Joyce explained all this with the utmost gravity, reciting Baudelaire's poem, "*Correspondances*" as a sort of corroboration.

However, I noticed that for old-time Dublin friends like my husband, he did not seem to need any "correspondence." With me the "correspondence" was of a superficial order and lay in the fact that we both had been educated in the same way, had studied the same languages, the same grammars and texts in these languages, had the same university degree in modern languages and literature, and that neither of us had concerned ourselves with gaining academic distinctions, but with the general literary movements of the time. He would be satirical about those who had got all the prizes, and even in the years after he left Dublin he would peruse the examination results with cynical curiosity. Still the difference in the way that similar education had affected us was so great that it almost blew to pieces the "correspondences." I had only the slightest interest in the beginning of languages, in the development of linguistics, or grammars of the early periods of languages. To all these Joyce attached himself with intensity of interest: he knew off by heart paragraphs or pages of early Anglo-Saxon, of the Italian that preceded Dante, of pre-Luther German, and the *Serments de Strasbourg*. At some of his parties, when he was not singing, he delighted in going into competition with me in repeating the rhymes we both had learned out of grammars, doggerel that helped our memories of rules, declensions, and genders. Why repeating lines such as "with *nemo* never let me see *neminis* or *nemine*," or:

> Common are to either sex
> Artifex and opifex,
> Conviva, vates, advena,
> Testis, civics, incola [etc.]

gave him such hilarious delight would certainly be of more interest to diligent interpreters of his work than it was to me. Apropos of all this, I should remark that he was *not* educated for the priesthood, as has been stated both in print and over the radio in America. He received the usual secondary education of the middle and professional classes in Ireland, the university course being provided for, I think, by a godfather. And what has often been dwelt upon as Joyce's great learning was mostly what he held in his prodigious memory of what we learned in school and college. In my own case, I think I held more of it in my mind than most, but it was nothing in comparison with what Joyce held in his and in minute detail and ready availability. At the same time I cannot help believing that these minutiae of scholarship got in the way of the course of *Finnegans Wake*, which, I think, even the most extreme Joyce devotees would admit is overelaborated.

More even than the lentil-eating episode, another piece of cussedness reaching the limits of a practical joke, was exasperating to me. As most of his readers know, Joyce was profoundly interested in the discoveries of the psychoanalysts: the stream of consciousness, the theory of association—in fact, everything that the new psychologists were opening up. Living in Austria before the first World War, when Freud was flourishing, and, during the war, in Zurich, the headquarters of Dr. C. G. Jung, he learned a great deal about psychoanalysis long before many in the outside world knew much about it, and, with that marvelous mind of his, so acquisitive as well as creative, there were few details of the new psychology that escaped him. Then Mrs. McCormick, of Chicago, who had backed Dr. Jung, backed Joyce for some of the time he was writing *Ulysses*. He applied his knowledge in *Portrait of the Artist*, to a far greater degree in *Ulysses*, and to a degree still greater in *Finnegans Wake*. Mrs. Bloom's monologue in the last chapter of *Ulysses* is simply the application of the technique of an actual psychoanalysis, with Mrs. Bloom lying in bed, letting her mind run on and on without any imposition of logical direction. But when Joyce was badgered by interviewers and other seekers of information and questioned as to how he had discovered what is such an important mechanism in *Ulysses* and *Finnegans Wake*, the interior monologue, the sardonic, prankish part of his mind set to work and evolved something that regaled him. He fished up an old French novelist, Edouard Dujardin, whom we had all heard of in Dublin because George Moore used to talk about him and who had monologues of some kind in a novel called *Les Lauriers sont coupés*, and in an interview Joyce informed a credulous reading public that he got the whole idea of the interior monologue from him. The more people he was able to bamboozle with this bit of information, the more details he added, the more it became a real creation equal to a section of *Ulysses*. Dujardin himself was made extremely happy: the author of the great modern literary creation had acknowledged indebtedness to him who had not been heard of for a generation. Publishers brought out a new edition of *Les Lauriers sont coupés*, and Dujardin, informing Joyce that he had restored him to life, inscribed the book to him with the sentence, "You have said to me, 'Lazarus, arise!'" The old gentleman blossomed like a rose and, when in Joyce's presence, would gaze at him in rapture.

To some extent I enjoyed the episode myself. Then once, after a lecture to which Joyce had brought me, by the Abbé Jousse, the experimenter in the origin and development of languages, we were followed from the hall to a café by a young American who hesitatingly asked if he could sit with us for a few minutes. He turned out to be a college instructor who was anxious to talk to Joyce about technical inventions in *Ulysses*. Again Joyce handed out details of the Dujardin influence; this time, after a few potations, he made it so luxuriant that the young man drew out a notebook into which he scribbled furiously what he had just been told. I saw visions of his solemnly handing it all out to his students and began to get perturbed. When the young man left I said, "Haven't you had enough fun with this? Haven't you pulled enough people's legs? And, anyway, why deny your indebtedness to Freud and

Jung? Isn't it better to be indebted to great originators like that than to——" He stopped me. A slow fury mounted to his face, and he moved irritatedly in his chair. "I hate women who know anything," he said. "No, Joyce, you don't," said I. "You like them, and I am going to contradict you about this in print when I get the chance." After a few seconds of silent anger, a whimsical smile came on his face, and the rest of the afternoon with him was pleasant. And I don't think he put forward the Dujardin legend again.

A little later he wrote some verses on his women friends and their interference with him which he read to me with great gusto. The piece was brief, but I do not think I remember all of it; the numerous Joyce fans will be interested in what I can give:

> As I was going to Joyce Saint James'
> I met with seven extravagant dames;
> Every dame had a bee in her bonnet,
> With bats from the belfry roosting upon it.
> And Ah, I said, poor Joyce Saint James,
> What can he do with these terrible dames?
> Poor Saint James Joyce.

He was happy enough at this period, but some months after the birth of his grandson there fell on him one of those blows of fate that sometimes come without warning. In this case there was some warning, though it was not apparent to him or his wife. They were starting out to spend the summer in England, 1932, as they had done on the previous year, but as they were about to board the train at Paris, their young daughter, Lucia, suddenly gave way to an outbreak of what seemed hysterics and refused to go; she said she would not go to England or anywhere else. They hastily got their baggage off the train and went to a hotel in complete bewilderment. That was the moment to get a psychiatrist, but nobody thought of it, not even I, who had made some study of mental ailments, even attending sessions at the asylum of Sainte Anne in Paris. A complication of matters had worked up to Lucia's illness: she had fallen in love with a young man who seemed to be unaware of it; she had become engaged to another, and so her life suffered from both interior and exterior confusions. Then the demands of Joyce's literary life, intensified by his partial blindness,

were such that he hardly noticed his children's need for a life of
their own. His son married, but no companionship with young
people was provided for his daughter: indeed in Paris, in a non-
French household, it was difficult to provide such companionship.
At the same time a part of Joyce's mind that was not taken up
with his own work became absorbed in the career of a singer, John
Sullivan, who was at the Paris Opera. The singer that was in Joyce
seemed to identify himself with this Irish tenor who also was in
exile from his country. Joyce put on a campaign on Sullivan's behalf that took up a good deal of his mind; he wanted to get him
an engagement in Covent Garden and even in the Metropolitan
Opera House. Sullivan, he believed, had been slighted by opera
directors, and for a while he thought of little else except remedy-
ing this state of affairs. He hardly noticed what was happening in
his daughter's life until the breakdown came.

When I suggested that he provide Lucia with a dowry and devote himself to getting her married in the customary French way,
he thought the suggestion proper and made some arrangements
along that line. She became engaged, but actually she did not recover her stability. For a while she stayed with some friends; then,
getting one of those uncontrollable outbreaks that are the mark
of coming trouble, she left their house and told Joyce she wished
to stay with myself and my husband. As it happened we had plenty
of room at the time, but even if we had not, when I saw Joyce's
desperate, unhappy face as he came in and sat on the sofa with
her, neither I nor any other human being could have refused aid.
His face brightened as we welcomed her, but as I was due to go to
the hospital in a week or two for a serious operation, I knew her
stay with us could not be long.

As nothing could induce Lucia to go to a doctor's office, Joyce
got a psychiatrist to come every morning to our apartment. She
listened to him only because she thought he was my doctor and
she had to help me in some way. We both sat together every morning on the sofa, the psychiatrist hurling questions at us which
sometimes I answered, sometimes she did, she explaining what she
considered my symptoms—tiredness, anemia, and so on—and I
injecting an explanation of hers. At intervals, on some excuse, I
left them alone, and the conversations went on and on. Frankly

I had not much faith in the proceedings, but I realized as they went on that Lucia was worse than any of us had thought; her emotions were all in disorder, and to get them in order would take a long and very careful treatment by that sort of therapy which we have in America, but which I do not think existed in France. If an operation had not been hanging over me and I could have kept her with me, I thought I could have managed to bring her back to normal. I believed she could get well only in new surroundings that had an atmosphere of affection and interest, and she herself believed we were giving that to her.

As with her brother I accompanied her to the sanitarium, deceiving her as to where we were going, I never felt so mean in my life—to deceive anyone who so trusted me shook me very greatly. But I was obeying the doctor's orders and did not know what else to do. As we entered the office of the director of the sanitarium and he began to talk to me, she threw a startled, appealing look at me that I can never forget. Later he sent both of us upstairs to a room where she was received by a pleasant nurse of her own age for whom she took an immediate liking, for she had had but little chance of making girl friends. The young nurse made her feel at ease, told Lucia she would be with her all the time, and pointed to two beds in the room. This meeting made the good-by I dreaded pass off easily enough.

For Joyce, coming at a time when the death of his father, a few months previously, had left him very lonely, all this was an intense tragedy. Oddly enough as it seemed to me when thinking of that hopeless parent, Simon Daedalus of *Portrait of the Artist* and *Ulysses*, Joyce had a great affection for his father and believed he owed a lot to him. He often remarked that many of the characters in *Ulysses* had been friends of his father whom he had a good chance of studying closely and whose conversation he noted. These two events, I think, greatly changed his life, and they occurred around his fiftieth birthday.

Between Lucia's going to the sanitarium and my going to a little French hospital for an operation, Joyce, restless and, I think, remorseful for not having seen her state of mind earlier, came round to our apartment every day. It was one he was thoroughly familiar with as well as with its grand piano, for we had rented it from his

friends, the Eugene Jolases. When anything hit him hard, Joyce
had relief in singing, and all his songs were sad. Previously we
had heard him sing only at parties where Sullivan or Maria Jolas
would also perform. But at this period, almost at the moment he
came in, he would sit at the piano and begin to sing as if he were
alone in the room and nobody were listening to him. He had no
such large voice as John McCormack, who had been the winner of
the competition they both had entered. But for emotional ex-
pressiveness Joyce was the most effective singer I have ever heard:
the fact that the knowledge of so many arts, so much human
drama, had gone into the making of his voice made it more impressive than all the grand-opera tenors I ever listened to. He sang
songs in many languages, mostly love songs, and this was strange,
for he had a sinister way of commenting on that emotion called
romantic love. "What they call love," he would say argumenta-
tively, "is merely a temptation of nature in one's youth." When,
sitting on the sofa, I would hear him turn from the Italian or
French songs he was singing to the "Ballad of the Brown and the
Yellow Ale," I thought I had never listened to a more mysterious
voice:

> Oh, the brown and the yellow ale.
> I met a man who was no right man,
> And he said to me, "Will you lend me your love
> For a year and a day, for a year and a day?"
> Oh, the brown and the yellow ale,
> The brown and the yellow ale!

And when he would sing, in his own setting, Yeats's:

> Who will go drive with Fergus now,
> And pierce the dim wood's woven shade?
>
> .   .   .   .
>
> And no more turn aside and brood
> Upon love's bitter mystery,
> For Fergus rules the brazen cars,
> And rules the shadows in the wood,
> And the white breast of the dim sea,
> And all dishevelled, wandering stars.

his voice would be so charged with emotion, so full of overtones of yearning for a life he could never have, a life he never told of in his books, that one saw there were whole regions of his mind that could only be expressed in music and that would have been expressed if he had become a musician rather than a writer. Then he would turn from the piano and talk about his daughter, with whose future he was now perpetually concerned.

For a while Lucia came out of the sanitarium, and we saw her the following winter in Nice with her nurse. Later, however, she had to go back: during all the war years she was in a sanitarium in that part of France that was occupied by the Germans. We managed to get some news of her from time to time. Lucia had a real artistic gift: she did the lettering for Chaucer's poem to the Blessed Virgin so exquisitely that it attracted a good deal of notice, including one written by the editor of the *Nouvelle revue française*, who compared it to the lettering of the *Book of Kells*.

⮞ CHAPTER 34

Guggenheim Fellowship

DURING ALL these troubles of our friends we were acquiring a few of our own: these included the fact that the depression that had hit the publishers also hit the authors; my husband's monthly income was at first stopped and then partly restored, though very much reduced. I remember once being so overwhelmed with my own and everybody's troubles, all increased by my physical condition, that, sitting in a little park near where we lived, I seriously contemplated a plunge into the Seine as a solution of all that was pressing in on me.

But I think that doctors are the nearest approach to saints on earth; they devote themselves so wholeheartedly and disinterestedly to their patients. My doctor, Dr. Thérèse Fontaine, who was also Joyce's and Hemingway's doctor, pulled me together, and the surgeon she sent me to, Dr. Bergeret as well as some French friends were so wonderful, that I will forever after believe that if one has to be seriously ill, it is better to be ill in France than elsewhere, for in an emergency there are no people so helpful as the French.

But before all these worries befell me, I had worked hard on my Guggenheim Fellowship, not so much in writing as in plain reading and research. I was quite aware that there was a lot I should learn if I was to be a real literary critic and do the sort of book I was mulling over in my mind. Frankly I think the publishers who signed me up would have been quite satisfied with one of those books of literary essays that pass as criticism or even with a sort of history of modern literature. But as I worked day after day in the Bibliothèque Nationale as well as at home, I evolved a conception of my own: it was not only difficult to bring to completion, but to get the whole into easy, readable English would be a feat, I knew; but I really did not feel that anything less was worth doing—all the other things had been done by distinguished and undistinguished people. Though, maybe, as I often remarked jocosely to some writers I knew, I was going into competition with Aristotle, Taine, Dryden, and Coleridge, I had chosen my way and was going to keep on it. When a friend of mine told Virginia Woolf what I projected, she said cynically, "Tell her she will be compared to a dog walking on its hind legs." "Not in America," I said, when I was told this: "I'll just be called arrogant or something of the kind."

I had really enjoyed working in the Bibliothèque Nationale, though it had the worst-arranged and most complicated catalogue of all libraries I had ever been in. I never knew where to look for a book, and the *ancien combattant*, one-armed and apparently analphabetic, who was mounted on a chair at the counter, would splutter furiously whenever I inquired the whereabouts of a German book. Once when I tried to discover where Herder's *Philosophy of History* could be found, the submerged fury in him became an outbreak, and a man who was standing near came to my rescue and showed me how to struggle with the catalogues that were the last word in obsolescence.

I struck up quite a friendship with my informant, who was pleasantly mocking about himself. He told me he was a German historian so celebrated that he could not reveal his real name or he would be mobbed by the savants in Paris and annoyed by newspaper interviewers. Whenever I entered the library I would find him always in the same seat, and he would stand up when he saw me, raising his arm in salute. Occasionally we stopped work at the same time and went to one of those dreary cafés near the library for an *amer picon* or some such item, and when he inquired what sort of book I was engaged on and I told him, he raised his eyebrows and asked with male condescension, "Why should a charming woman like you want to write a book like that? Besides, you could never do it in literature as well as I have done it in history. I have written the only work of that kind." When I told all this to my husband, he advised, "Why don't you ask him if he is Oswald Spengler?" Whoever he was, he had one of the sharpest, most brilliant and disillusioned minds I have ever encountered. He helped me in a lot of ways; he showed me how to look up references I needed in large tomes without reading the whole of them; he had quite a remarkable system. The last meeting I had arranged with him in the library, this time to inform him of something, I could not attend: there were Lucia and my operation, and between them I never saw him again.

At the British Museum, where the catalogues were efficient, I also worked now and again, when my husband went over to see his London publishers or to the British Broadcasting Company, visits that gave us a chance to see our friends. Two happenings in London stand out in my mind, though perhaps in themselves they were of little importance. Before leaving Paris for London I had been talking to Paul Valéry after a lecture he had given on poetry, a lecture at which his own verse had been read by Helene Vacaresco, who, like Madame de Noailles, was a Rumanian. French was at least as native to her as Rumanian; she was one of the members of the Committee of Intellectual Co-operation in the League of Nations. On this occasion she read Valéry's very difficult poetry in a striking way, not exactly well, but in such a manner that the meaning and rhythm became clearer than if one had read it oneself. Later a number of the company retreated to a café, and I was brought along. Valéry asked me amiably if, as I seemed to know his work, I could explain why, on the rare occasions he was written about in America, all the information was so inaccurate, and why those who wrote of him did not seem to know enough French to under-

stand his work. Now, because two of my men friends in America
had written condescendingly about him, I felt a little on the de-
fensive and said, "It is not exactly a question of knowing French;
it is a question of knowing how to approach that sort of poetry."
One of those present whom I had previously met with Abel Chevalley said sharply, "*Allons donc, madame, it is* a question of knowing
French, of knowing French literature. Anyone who knows Baudelaire, Mallarmé"—and a number of other names he tossed off—
"can understand Paul's poetry. Americans do not know French
poetry at all."

And now in London, at a reception, I found myself beside an
oldish man whose face was marked by many experiences. A young
man present at a center table read a poem about an eel that recalled
something in Valéry's "Serpent," and the man beside me surprised
me by remarking the resemblance and by asking diffidently if I
knew the poem. I did, and rattled on, telling him of Valéry's lecture
and of the remarks that had passed between us. He speculated as to
what were Valéry's chances for the Nobel Prize, and his comments
were so informed and brilliant that I wondered who he was, but
forbore asking him, as this is not so readily done in London as
in New York. Who could he be? There seemed to be nothing in
modern poetry that this strange man had not considered.

After about half an hour, Lady Ottoline Morrell, who knew
everybody, approached us and said, "You two are so engrossed in
each other that I should like to know what you are talking about."
"Poetry," he said. "But we don't know each other," said I. She
presented him: "Lord Alfred Douglas." The sudden announcement
of that name that had so many affiliations staggered me. As a young
girl I had read diligently the review he had edited, the *Academy;*
I knew his poems and those of his wife, Olive Custance; later I
read all about his relation with Oscar Wilde and the connection
of his father, the Marquis of Queensberry, with Wilde's arrest and
trial. Then there were all sorts of other connections: his mother
had been a supporter of Arthur Griffith and his paper, *Sinn Fein,*
and the whole history of the Douglases, the black and the red
Douglases, was one of the most romantic in British history: they
had been one of the great Scots families, but had gone in with the
English. But that this was the Alfred Douglas of the historic

scandal, one of the characters of Frank Harris's life of Oscar Wilde—the shock of this must have shown itself staringly in my face. He held out his hand, then withdrew it, stuck it in his coat, and looked at me with confused, harassed eyes. We who had been so gay and friendly, and so amusing with each other that I had made him laugh heartily, now endured a sudden estrangement. Lady Ottoline, seeing the confusion, drew me away, but Alfred Douglas's expression at my so obvious reaction to his name gave me a sort of remorse that was sufficiently intensive to make me hold it in mind ever since.

The next incident was in its own way even more dramatic: I had a correspondence with an English writer, and during a visit to London I wrote and invited him to dinner with my husband and myself and James Stephens in a restaurant. My would-be guest wrote inquiring if he could also bring the doctor with whom he was staying; I telegraphed a reply, and as the five of us sat down to dinner, I asked the doctor, who did not look English but of some foreign descent, in what I thought was a humorous vein, if he was one of those Freudian doctors who would take some formidable meanings out of our innocent dinner conversation. "But I am," he said solemnly. "I call myself a medical psychologist." Though he did not look as if he could psychologize anything or anybody, his answer put a little constraint on us, more, I think, because he seemed to have such a strong influence on our other guest and because he seemed to want to dominate the conversation. After a few minutes' talk about himself, he got round to his American patients, none of whom we knew. Just as I was getting perplexed as to why Americans, who have such good psychiatrists and psychoanalysts at home, should want to cross the Atlantic to consult a young man who did not seem exactly to have taken the oath of Hippocrates, he brought up the name of a friend whom we knew quite well, but whose inner and family conflicts, naturally, we knew little about. Our doctor guest gave us a sort of psychoanalysis of our friend, whom, apparently, he had been analyzing for months; he gave us details of the letters his patient's wife had written him, giving him information about all her husband's friends. In spite of ourselves, we were interested to hear of another side to the life and character of one we knew or thought we knew, and to learn of attitudes of his that we had never guessed. Our guest, seeing our interest, handed us more and more information, and did not stop even after my husband told him we knew his patient well. The doctor was trying to convince us that his skill had cured him, but later we learned that this was far from being the case, for he had returned to America several degrees worse than when he had left and remained ill for years. Very easily it might have happened that the revelations of our medical psychologist might have done a great deal of harm to his patient.

I am inclined to believe that very few people, men or women, have the character, the sympathy, or the knowledge of human nature necessary to become a psychoanalyst or a psychiatrist: some of them seem to swallow anything the patient tells them. And this was not the only time I had been informed by a psychoanalyst of a patient's revelations; in the other cases, however, it was a warning, necessary, they thought, against the intentions and accusations of paranoiac patients. In fact the things people say about their friends in psychoanalytic sessions add a new shudder to life. One whom I knew charged that though she was my intellectual superior she got a frightful inferiority complex every time she talked to me, and she had a hallucination that I was a "projection" of a relative of hers who was in an asylum, imagining herself a monkey. She thought that I might give her some similar notion and was concerned about ridding herself of me. The psychoanalyst persuaded her that the proper method of removal was not to see me any more, or else I might by now have been murdered.

Like many people, I came in contact with mental cases in early life without knowing what they were, and was completely bewildered at their complaints, accusations, and deceptions. Mentally ill people have caused me considerable trouble and difficulties, though nothing like those some of my friends have had to endure. Some insane, or partly insane, people are sweet and kind and heartbreakingly pathetic, and, no matter how upsetting, are not really destructive in their intentions. Others can and do bring ruin to everyone who comes in contact with them. The worst of this kind in my experience were women paranoiacs, who not only seemed normal most of the time but who were intelligent and could hold down a job for long periods until some outbreak betrayed their condition.

The wrecking instinct was so strong that they seemed not to be able to live at all without attempting to destroy the happiness, the reputation, of some of their nearest relations or associates, sometimes by their actions, sometimes by unfounded accusations. They seemed to have no real emotion, only instincts and biological urges which, with their delusions of importance, could get any man of their acquaintance into a position of difficulty. A well-known actor, a paranoaic, who seemed merely eccentric to his acquaintances, could not brook the slightest competition of any kind, so that sometimes a walk-on actor, with only a speech or two to deliver, could arouse the most disruptive jealousy. But he could continue to act wonderfully except at intervals when his lack of control brought on some happening that obliged his devoted wife to isolate him in the country for a stretch. If only insanity could be partly eliminated, and if whatever leads to insanity could be tackled in early life and rendered innocuous, one great source of unhappiness could be spared the human race. I feel this very strongly, for of all the unhappy people I have ever known, the most unhappy were those associated with insane relatives or friends; maybe insanity accounts for criminality as well.

ε CHAPTER 35

Life on the Riviera: Return to America

To RECOVER from my operation we went to Nice in the fall of 1932. We left Paris in the evening in cold, dark, drizzly weather on the Blue Train going south, and as we rose in the morning we looked out on sunshine, flowers, orange trees, olive trees. I had often gone on journeys twice as long in America and at the end arrived at the same sort of place, but this was a different world, the Mediterranean world, with its traces of the Roman empire.

The Joyces were there already, the whole family, including Lucia and her nurse. It was they who found us a hotel near them, but later, when they had gone back to Paris, we got a furnished apartment on a hill, a few minutes' walk from the Promenade des Anglais, for the sum of about forty dollars a month. It had two terraces, an olive garden where nightingales sang, and a view over the Mediterranean. It took me a long time to recover my strength—years, I think—and at this time I could not write or even read anything except the headlines of newspapers without getting completely exhausted. I have often wondered at the stories of people who wrote big books as they were convalescing from an illness. My Nice doctor finally told me to attempt nothing at all for a while, and so I got to spending days basking in the Mediterranean sun when it was warm enough, which was not always.

The worst of a severe illness is that it gets one too concerned with one's self, almost immersed in one's self, a state of mind I don't care about. But the sun and the surroundings that had so much interest and so much poetry gradually brought back some strength, though not sufficient to tackle once more the very difficult critical book I had projected. Besides, the publishers had shown almost no interest in it; I knew they would bring it out when it was ready, for I had a contract and an advance. However, I did write and sell a couple of short stories; I found fiction far easier to write in poor physical condition than criticism, and indeed easier to write in any situation, because it does not make such demand on the conscious mind, the reasoning mind, or the faculty of using what one has learned about literature and philosophy. Then, in addition, for criticism, one has to use a sort of distilled experience of life, whereas raw experience, with some choice, can go into fiction. However, my publishers turned down cold the idea of a novel: I was a critic and that was that. And their firm notion that the critical mind and what they conceive to be the creative mind were two totally different things could not be shaken. And as, from my earliest days, I could never write anything on speculation without assurance of publication, I was frustrated.

I think nowhere in the world could life be pleasanter, easier, and cheaper than on the Riviera at the time. Owing to the crash and the near failure of many publishing houses, our income had been reduced by something like seventy per cent, yet we lived almost as well on the reduced monthly sum his publishers paid my husband, though we had little to spare for clothes or extras. My husband never got so much work done. After work, recreation was easy to find, food was about as cheap in restaurants as we could get it at home; we had a part-time maid for the morning hours for a sum corresponding to three dollars a week, and I could breakfast in bed on coffee and fresh rolls and a new-laid egg while gazing out of the large window of my room at the Bay of Angels with its blue, blue waters and sailing craft of all kinds. The fresh eggs we got from a neighbor, a marquis of old Norman descent, who helped run a boardinghouse and a little chicken farm; he sold us the best he had quite cheaply, delivering them himself. He was a character, the marquis. When living in Paris I had got to know some Royalists —there were far more of them in France than Americans ever imagined and represented, I should judge, really a large minority. Though the important Royalists were, I suppose, the aristocrats of the Faubourg St. Germain, the bulk of them belonged to the *petite bourgeoisie*. I was in the first instance brought to some of their meetings by a young French girl who herself marched every year in the Joan of Arc procession when the Royalists turned out in force. Their great organization was, of course, the Action Française, with Léon Daudet and Charles Maurras the leading figures.

Now, in Nice, my slight acquaintance with the movement stood me in good stead with my neighbor the marquis and helped to make my relationship with him and the friend he worked with pleasant. He had in his room large reproductions of the Duc and Duchesse de Guise, the Bourbon claimants to the throne of France, whom he always referred to as "our king and queen." He believed in the tenets of the Action Française, the organization that supported the return of the Bourbons as communists believe in communism or fascists in fascism: it was a sort of religion with him, as I am sure it was with the bulk of its members. And when Pope Benedict denounced the Action Française, which professed Catholic philosophy and Catholic morality and principles and claimed to uphold the whole Catholic tradition, a lot of the membership stuck by the Action Française as against the Church. My neighbor, the marquis, would say solemnly to me, "If there is a truth revealed by heaven, it is the Action Française . . . one can be a very good Catholic without going to Mass." I reminded him once of the commandments of the Church, the very first of which is that

Catholics have to attend Mass on Sundays and holidays of obliga-
tion. But he had a ready answer: "That, madame, is not a commandment of God; it is a commandment of the Church; the
Church can change it at any time and does change it in some places;
it is just a remnant of the age of martyrs."

When Léon Daudet came to Nice to lecture on Rabelais, the
local members of the Action showed up in force; I accompanied
the marquis, who informed me that Daudet, whose face I thought
rather plebeian myself, was very like the portraits of Louis Quatorze.
His remark led me to tell him of a reception we were brought to
in Paris which had been given by the Duchesse de Guise to introduce the young princess who was to marry her son, the Comte de
Paris. The policemen who marshaled the crowd entering the old
house on the quays, being Republicans, were good-naturedly mocking of the whole affair and smiled at the Royalist emblems displayed. I asked one of the policemen if he was not impressed by the
loyalty to their old kings that the crowd showed. He shrugged his
shoulders and said:

"Ah, if it were a Bonaparte, madame——" Then he stopped.

Now what impressed me, as I told the marquis, was that those
at the reception looked for all the world like a meeting of the
D.A.R. in America, though they were not so well dressed nor so
well groomed, and that what passed for the aristocratic countenance
was just as frequent in the American assemblies as it appeared
to be in these descendants of an ancient noblesse. The marquis
was shocked, and the only thing that brought me back to his good
graces was the thought that I had gazed on the faces of the Duchesse
de Guise and the royal fiancée. I had seen none of the men claimants to the throne, for they were never allowed to enter France and
lived, I think, mostly in Belgium or North Africa. The marquis
pretended to think that I was an aristocrat myself. "We owe it to
each other to be truthful on these matters," he would say, and talk
feelingly about the inroads the proletariat were making in high
places. But he knew this state of things could not last: God and
the Action Française would not permit it.

I read diligently the weekly paper of the movement, the *Action
Française*. It must have been amongst the very best written weeklies
in Europe; it certainly had the best literary criticism I ever read in

any periodical; often the critical articles were written by Daudet or Maurras. The crowd that attended the Action Française lectures in Nice took in a varied group which included not only whatever comtes, comtesses, marquis and marquises in the neighborhood, but also American professors on sabbatical leave, foreign journalists who came to improve their minds or their French. As I have the greatest interest in any expression of human longings, emotions, and allegiances, I was considerably stirred by the Action Française meetings, much more than by the couple of communist meetings I attended, meetings which had more indignation but nothing of a like fanaticism of faith. Besides, they had not the attraction of a lost cause: communism seemed to be going ahead. Meanwhile we had good news of Lucia: Joyce wrote us that the doctors were of the opinion she was getting better.

In spite of my illness, I think the fifteen or sixteen months in Nice were almost the happiest in my life. Like most writers and artists, we know somebody everywhere, and a number of our acquaintances were either living in Nice or came there for the winter —Nellie Harris, Frank Harris's widow, Sholom Asch and his wife, Ludwig and Thelma Lewisohn, Sisley Huddleston, Raymond and Dorothy Weaver, and several non-literary English and Americans who preferred life in France to that of their own countries. A group of us met nearly every afternoon in a café on the Promenade for coffee and liqueurs. Somerset Maugham, who later became a great friend and one to whom I am strongly attached for his real warmth of heart and fundamental simplicity, lived near, but at the time we did not know him. H. G. Wells, whom my husband knew slightly, lived up in the mountains in Grasse, but we never got round to calling on him. We seemed to have endless time on our hands, time for work, time for idleness, and time for recreation: the looking back on it makes me almost believe what Stephen Vincent Benét said to me about France—that time goes further there and the days are three times as long as in America. But Nice had passed the heyday that was marked by the beautiful villas on the hills and the palatial hotels on the Promenade des Anglais. The Russian princes and the American millionaires for whom they were built were driving taxicabs in Paris or keeping boardinghouses or living on reduced incomes. It was pitiful to look into the splendid dining room of the Negresco and see six waiters for a table that had four guests, the only table that had any at all.

Every Sunday and on an occasional weekday we made an excursion on a bus to a neighboring town or village, occasionally going over the border into Italy: Italy was not too far away, but immediately on entering we felt a completely different civilization, one we could almost feel the minute we crossed the frontier, even before the handsome, opera-like official in a flowing cape had stamped our passports. At this time a good deal of France and most of the people of Nice seemed to be strong for Mussolini, but then he had made no preparations for war; he had done all sorts of things that appealed to the Italians, giving employment to everyone, sending opera companies to remote villages, planting flower beds along the roads, draining marshes, and so on, and, what impressed foreigners, running the trains on time. In fact, at this time, before the invasion of Ethiopia, Mussolini had a great many supporters in all countries.

When taking a bus from Nice we had to keep our passports always on us, for one never knew when the bus would make a sudden detour into Italy; even walking from the hill towns we sometimes found ourselves inadvertently over the border and accosted for our passports. The coast towns, Cannes, Saint Raphaël, Menton, Monte Carlo, and all the others were a continual source of delight and within easy reach for a few francs. Then there were the Mediterranean islands, and we never tired of the Iles de Lérins, with the old monastery and the fortress where so many famous prisoners had been held. There were endless stories of Napoleon, who, in the escape from Elba, had landed somewhere near; the local people who told them seemed to feel as romantically about Napoleon as our friend the marquis did about the Bourbons. Places were pointed out to us—"on this rock Napoleon stopped to have a meal. There he was met by a group of his devoted followers and presented with a flask and some chickens for his journey." The hill town of Vince was the most favored by Americans, but to us the most enchanting was the town of St. Martin Vésubie, high in the Alpes-Maritimes, with its medieval streets and houses and a stream down the middle to carry away the garbage. The ancient and decrepit houses had a little square hole cut in their doors to let the cats and smaller dogs go in and out as they pleased in the nighttime. St. Martin had a town crier who at fixed times came round blowing a bugle and telling us the news of the world in French and Provençal. I never met anyone there who read a newspaper or one who cared much about the outside world except, of course, the summer tourists. The Catholicism of the town was full of imagination: I think the only physician for soul or body was the curé who concocted wonderful medicines from herbs he gathered in the early morning when the dew was still on them. There were lovely religious processions in which the whole town walked carrying statues and religious banners, with some of the people playing musical instruments. The housewives would hang out of the windows their best linen sheets inlaid with lace they had made themselves, and they would fasten on the sheets little bouquets of flowers, pictures of saints, and heavy rosary beads.

Some of those who walked in the processions had aged before their time; men and women of forty were stooped and old and were looking forward to rest and perpetual joy in the heaven their curé told them of. They lived laborious lives and had their little farms that were often miles away from where they lived, sometimes over the frontier into Italy, and if one wakened early one could see them starting off at dawn, husband with his implements, wife with baby in her arms, and in summer, when school was closed, the older children following, all carrying their luncheons with bottles of the good *vin rosé* of the Alpes-Maritimes. Life was hard for them, but while it lasted they were happy, I am sure, and in the evenings those who had vigor and a few francs sat around in the village stand, listening to a little orchestra and drinking beer or wine, the young people dancing. These gatherings were frequented by the town watch mender, whom we got to know, a dwarf who drank cognac when it was given to him and who told us that the young men who had left the hill towns in the last war never came back to this monotonous life: the ambitious ones wanted something else—careers, or variety, or, sometimes, learning. It was here that I heard once again the remark that had so exasperated me when I heard it first in a post office in the Rue de Vaugirard, that America had a subconscious desire to destroy Europe.

But of course this Mediterranean life could not last all our lives, and we knew it. When, after one of these visits to the hill town, we returned to our apartment in Nice, there was a pile of letters, and it came on us we must return to America soon. My husband had done a great deal of work—in fact he had never accomplished so much before; but now he had to go back to see his publishers. One of the letters for me was from Henry Goddard Leach, editor of the *Forum*; he wanted me to do some articles on current books and asked for some suggestions. What I proposed was a literary article each month around the most important books that were being published. And the long and the short of it was that he suggested as a start that I do a series of six articles to see how they would go. I did the first and second in Nice, and then he sent me a check to return to America to continue.

One sunny day in November we bought our tickets for one of the new Italian liners, the *Conte di Savoia*, boarded it later at Villefranche, seen off by our friends, Raymond and Dorothy Weaver, Mrs. Sholom Asch, and Nellie Harris. It was the most beautiful ship I ever was on, and for a hundred and fifty dollars each we had a cabin that, because so few people were traveling in them, had been taken over from the first-class. The passengers were mainly Italian-American grocers, restaurateurs, waiters, and a few musicians who played humble instruments in an orchestra. Unlike our experience on the Atlantic liners, we knew nobody except a New York speakeasy owner in whose place, downtown, writers congregated. The food and wine—the wine, as part of the meal, free—were wonderful; there were white and red chianti on week-days, with, on Sundays, an Italian champagne to accompany the dessert. This was the time when Mussolini and some of his associates had organized the *dopo lavoro* clubs and cultural amusements for the people: the crew gave an entertainment for the passengers; it was by a long way the best entertainment I had ever been at on board a ship, with well-trained singing voices and excellent acting. One could not help feeling that if notions of war had not seized Signor Mussolini and the Fascists, they could have made Italy such a great country. The Italians on board were by no means all for him, but at the same time there was appreciation, even enthusiasm, for the constructive work he was doing. The French whom we met on the liner, however, were strong for him, as indeed we had found them in Nice, perhaps on account of that disgust with the Third Republic that was so widespread in France and which gave me the impression that even representative governments do not represent the bulk of the people any more than other kinds of governments. People vote out of the interest or prejudice of the moment, and sometimes later change their minds.

As I got off the liner I was met by my new editor and his secretary with that courtesy that was always characteristic of him. Some time later he gave a party for us to meet all our friends and literary and publishing New York. After three years' absence I was happy to meet everybody.

I continued doing that monthly article for the *Forum* until, about seven years later, it met the fate of so many fine and well-known American magazines—the *Century, Scribner's, Lippincott's, Everybody's*—and ceased publication. I was happy in the job; I had a free hand, and the editor never tried to direct me in any way; I could write what I liked and had responsive readers. It was an enviable job, and, as Ernest Boyd said, it gave me a platform. The letters I received showed that I was really catering to a section of the public that, in our day, American editors pay little attention to, a great number of whom, as the correspondents told me, subscribed to the literary supplement of the London *Times* for want of enough American literary articles. Their minds were above the bulk of the book reviewing that appeared in the weeklies. I did my level best; I never underestimated the intelligence of my readers, which, I think, is a great fault with editors. I assumed that nothing I could write was over their heads if indeed it reached up to them. The editor was satisfied, I was satisfied, the readers seemed to be. The best American literary public is away ahead of anything that is written for them. I really believe that in the end it is impossible for a good book, good poetry, good criticism to escape readers in America, though sometimes they may escape the attention of reviewers. The reviewers, maybe, cannot help this, for too many books are turned out by publishers.

II

I worked hard; in addition to my monthly article, which kept me on my mettle—for my discerning public would have noticed any falling off—my husband and I taught in the winters in Miami University in Florida. I gave some lectures, tried to keep writing on my book now and again. But for this I had little time except in the summer, when the Forum allowed me three months off. Looking back now, I wonder how I got through all the work, for a multiplicity of jobs is more tiring than any one laborious one. Then, in addition to everything else, I had another severe illness which demanded surgical intervention. However, we lived in a hotel which eased me from housekeeping, and we spent the summer months in Connecticut near Norwalk and did not see as many people as we had been in the habit of seeing.

Occasionally we managed to take a day or two off to visit friends, and this was always a good vacation from work. The most interesting of these visits, I remember, was to Mrs. John D. Ryan in Manhasset who was giving a dinner party for Cardinal Pacelli in the summer of 1936, and who invited us to be her house guests at the time. Actually, the cardinal was staying with Mrs. Nicholas Brady, the sister and sister-in-law of two great friends of ours, Agnes and John Cavanagh, who lived near us in Norwalk. With them we started for Mrs. Ryan's in the early afternoon of the party and drove along roads in Long Island with secret service men stopping us at intervals, more, actually, I think, than used to protect the rare visits of British royalty to Ireland. Our hostess, with an amusing mixture of assumed primness and real humor, was a charming, hospitable person, with that great American gift for liking her friends for what they are rather than for what they have: she succeeded in making what might have been a formidable occasion not only memorable but enjoyable.

As in all such affairs, there was a comic side to it, and I can still have my risible faculties stirred by a memory of some of the incidents. Except that extreme décolleté was supposed to be avoided at a dinner or reception for a prince of the Church, most of the female side of the company set out to be very gorgeous, wearing tiaras, pearls, diamonds, emeralds that might have adorned a maharajah. A hairdresser had come from New York early in the day to do the coiffures of the ladies of Long Island and anchor the tiaras thereon. As she had to do so many, she started early in the day, going from one house to another, and when we reached the home of our hostess in the middle of the afternoon she was presiding at the tea table in a negligee with a glittering tiara fastened to her elaborately coifed head. She endured the banter of her guests with great good humor, and then was suddenly stricken almost to tears by the belated announcement that a guest was laid low with influenza and could not come. She worked up the notion of dressing the coiffeuse and having her sit as a guest to balance the table and bore our united laughter tolerantly. It might have been a situation in a comedy where a total stranger is drafted to fill a place with startling results, but in the end it was conventionally resolved. The cardinal, as a prince of the Church, was not supposed to arrive until all the guests had assembled, when Mrs. Brady, whose house was near, was to be notified by telephone.

Then a new situation developed as soon as the guests began to arrive. Some of the women came in such a state of décolleté that a maid had to be sent rummaging drawers for scarves to cover their bosoms. We were given only one cocktail each so that our wits would not seem bamboozled in the presence of the cardinal, who, it was whispered, would certainly be Pope. However, unknown to our hostess, some of the men retired to a washroom and imbibed a few more to brace up their spirits. They were to emerge startledly when Mrs. Brady and the cardinal were abruptly announced, actually before the appearance of the last guest, who, for lack of the right identification, had been delayed along the road.

Cardinal Pacelli, standing in the drawing room as the guests were presented to him, was a marvelous figure, so tall that he dominated the men in the room, who, in comparison with his ascetic leanness, his spiritual expression, his wonderful red robes, looked drab, fat, even plebeian. Nothing can give such an aristocratic appearance as height joined with intellect and spirituality: the cardinal had them all. And there was something touching about him: his smile was almost that of a child. He was the most withdrawn man I had ever encountered, withdrawn because he seemed constantly to be considering some matter remote from the people round him. He was grave, concerned, perhaps sad, and the dark eyes behind the glasses reminded me of Yeats's deep ruminating eyes. But he seemed to me a far simpler man, whose training had given him, not only the responsibility of a statesman, but concern for everybody, affection for everybody.

Our little hostess had warned us women in advance to have our curtsies well practiced, so that none of us would run a leg too far backwards and have to grasp the cardinal's ringed hand to keep from falling. I had none of the jewels of the other ladies present, but I believed myself complete mistress of that curtsy and ring-kissing ceremony; I had practiced so often in convent schools, I had kissed so many bishops' and cardinals' rings, that I felt I could acquit myself better than anybody else present, especially those who had not been brought up in the ceremonies of the Church. However, the guest who outdid us all, not only in beauty and attire —attire which, though it was for the hostess frighteningly décolleté, managed with its floating white tulle to give the impression that its wearer was adequately covered—was Mrs. Clarence Mackay, who had been Anna Case, the opera singer. She executed a curtsy so graceful, so perfect, so stylized, and fluttered such a graceful kiss on the cardinal's ring, that I had perforce to tell her how wonderful her performance was. To be sure, it was a performance, for she had done curtsies on stages before great audiences many times, and the rest of us were just amateurs.

In the background the comedy part was still continuing. The last guest had not arrived, and the company had to go in to dinner after the presentation; my husband was sent to wait for her in the entrance hall and bring her to her place. As he loitered in the hall, filled with busts of Roman emperors, men in brown derby hats sprang at him to ask that he give an account of himself—they were the secret service men who were still trailing the cardinal. My husband had some difficulty in explaining his casual appearance among the busts, but he was saved by the arrival of the late guest, Mrs. Murray Crane, who had been held up at intervals along the road by similar brown-hatted gentlemen. However, they both reached their places at the table safely and not too late.

At dinner I was placed between Bishop Spellman and Mr. James

W. Gerard, who had been ambassador to Germany. The talk at the table was subdued, and my partners and I had few topics of conversation. The bishop told me that Joseph Kennedy, the husband of a girl I had known for a brief space at a German school, was a genius, and I ruminated on what sort of a genius. At the other side of me, Mr. Gerard strained his diplomatic accomplishments in an effort to discover who the jewel-less female who had been placed beside him was. Outside this, his conversation was limited to the pronouncement that I had a Scotch accent—not too wide of the mark, because it is an Ulster accent. Then he proceeded to discourse on the Scotch-Irish, a race of people I never encountered in Ireland. I had seen his excellency only once before, when he was playing himself in a propaganda movie called *The Kaiser, the Beast of Berlin*—no doubt he thought it his patriotic duty to appear in it.

After dinner in the drawing room he was more entertaining; he gave me some advice as to what to write to gain the interest of the American public. "You should," he told me, "write about the everyday life of the Irish people. What, for instance, do they have for breakfast?" "Bacon and eggs," I answered truthfully. "No orange juice. They don't grow oranges, but they grow pigs and hens." Then he inquired, "What sort of clothes do they wear? What kind of underwear? An Irishman I know," he said encouragingly, "tells me he never wore any underwear until he came to America." "I'll take that up," I said thoughtfully, "but up to the present I've had slim opportunities to become versed in male underwear." We were seated not far from the cardinal, who was again standing, speaking to the guests who came up to him in ones and twos. As I looked up I met his glance over the head of the man he was speaking to, and at the back of those grave eyes there appeared for a moment what seemed to be a twinkle. When a few minutes later I stood with another guest speaking to him, the twinkle was repeated, and I had an embarrassing thought that the remark to Mr. Gerard had not escaped him. He spoke several languages, but, outside Italian, the only one he seemed to have much command of was French. I never listened to such diversity of French accents and pronunciations as were turned on him, but he was equal to all of them. Still, like royalties, he was left alone a little; he did not mingle with the guests; they approached him respectfully in ones and twos, leaving him somewhat like a priest on the altar.

He attended few parties and, I think, went only to houses of those whom he knew already. Mrs. Brady, later, gave a big reception for him, but all the guests could do was to gaze at him for a second. She had from time to time so many high ecclesiastics visiting her that the grand suite in her house was always called the Cardinal's Suite. Once she gave it to my husband and myself for a week end, but I found the bed so hard that I could not sleep. The previous occupant, a cardinal, had got a board inserted somewhere, perhaps as a discipline like a hair shirt, or maybe he just had sacroiliac trouble.

ଛ~ CHAPTER 36

Publication through Difficulties

I WAS within a couple of weeks of finishing my book; indeed, some part of it had actually been set up and I had received galley proofs, when the jinx that had pursued me for years caught up with me again. My husband and I were crossing a street in Norwalk to take a turn after working all day, when out of a side street a car tore at great speed; my husband stood still, and the car swerved round him, but I must have automatically jumped to avoid it; I was run down, with the result that I got a series of broken bones and a concussion of the brain. I was picked up immediately by another car and taken to the hospital, which was near. The correct procedure, I believe, would have been to leave me lying on the ground for fear of spinal trouble until an ambulance with trained attendants came and picked me up.

I remember lying in a hospital room in terrific pain, which, because of the concussion, I could be given nothing to relieve. I remember when still partly unconscious receiving a letter from my publisher demanding the return of the galleys. My bewildered, concussed brain could not take it in, and I kept repeating to the nurse, "Galleys and triremes—where are the galleys and triremes?" But one morning I heard a terrible racket of dishes being washed loudly or else being broken. I spoke to my nurse about it: she said, "That noise has been there all the time; you are now completely conscious—that is why you hear it now." I was removed then to the pleasantest hospital room I have ever been in—I have been in many, and in several countries. That room in the Norwalk Hospital was as much a help to recovery as all the medical treatments. My brain began to get into stride again and back to the book.

Still I had to lie helpless for many weeks, but with the help of a brilliant and devoted friend, Mary Van Buren, who took down dictation from penciled pages and typed the manuscript for me, I finished the book.

It was hard going, and one chapter I projected had to be omitted; still the book was published, in 1937, with the title *From These Roots*, a title which had been given me by Frances Phillips, the editor of Morrow's, publishers. The good was mitigated, however: working at it while my head wound was not yet healed gave me a headache that became almost perpetual and delayed the complete recovery of my memory. For a long time afterwards, even when I was able to walk, I would fall suddenly, the aftereffect of the concussion and of making active use of my brain too soon.

The reviews came slowly, and what astonished me was how few of the first reviewers understood what the book was about, or its plan or direction—in fact the general readers knew more about it than the reviewers. I intended the book to be a breakaway from old ideas of writing about literature or literary history. I had, of course, to deal with some difficult ideas and with literature in many languages, though I think the writing was as clear as hard work could make it, and for anybody who read it as it was intended to be read, continuously from beginning to end, it should not have been difficult to understand. But a lot of the reviewers had a preconceived notion of what books of criticism should be about and did not bother to discover what I had intended to do. The *New Yorker*, for some reason, announced that it was a series of thirty-two essays (sic) by a distinguished conservative critic. Now I never was conservative in literature, and the word must have had some political connotation. Other reviewers had a notion that it was a history of criticism and took me to task for not including this or that critic. The *New Republic* reviewer wondered why I did not include R. P. Blackmuir and thought I was writing according to the Mallarméan formula of suggestion and evocation. The *Nation* reviewer seemed to think the book was an attack on some form of left-wing politics and lectured me accordingly. But the crowning ineptitude was perpetrated by Howard Mumford Jones in the *Saturday Review of Literature.* He actually, openly, and before my eyes, did what Virginia Woolf prophesied, and trotted out the dog walking on its hind legs. Virginia had tracked that dog back to Shakespeare's time when somebody said that a woman acting put him in mind of a dog dancing; Dr. Johnson repeated the phrase two hundred years later of a woman preaching—but I quote Mrs. Woolf:

And here . . . we have the very words used again in the year of grace 1928 of women who try to write music: "Of Mdlle Germaine Tailleferre one can only repeat Dr. Johnson's dictum concerning a woman preaching translated into terms of music: 'Sir, a woman's composing is like a dog walking on its hind legs; it is not done well, but you are surprised that it is done at all.' "

"So accurately does history repeat itself," commented Virginia Woolf. And behold, in the year of grace 1937, there it was again repeated. But of course, I have to say that after the first reviews, the others revealed insight and knowledge, and, if anything, gave me too high praise. But I remember my relief when the first reviews came out by writers who knew what the book was about, the very first being by Henry Canby, followed by Carl Van Doren on the first page of the *Tribune* and Donald Adams in the New York *Times.*

In London I got what is called a "large press." The London *Times* not only published a page review, but in the same issue an editorial dealing with the ideas of the book. The best reviews were by poets and the most appreciative. But, as in America, a few of the reviewers did not know what the book was about, and spluttered and spluttered. In the London *Mercury,* Sean O'Faolain somehow dragged in a comparison with Mrs. Eddy and, failing to get the idea of the book, wound up in helpless indignation: "This book could only have come out of America." The *Criterion's* review had a childlike naïveté and seemed to be written by a very young person who demanded why I had not included the younger poets. Among the many letters asking me why I did not feature the works of Marx, Professor Babbitt, and Upton Sinclair, there came one from Robert Graves demanding why I did not include Laura Riding.

When a new edition of the book was brought out recently, it was reviewed all over again, and this time the most understanding review was by Joseph Freeman, who had the high integrity to make an apology for his first review in which he had not got the point of the book at all. Some other reviewers made similar amends, but Howard Mumford Jones did not lead that dog back to the dog-house.

In the end I got quite a bit out of the book in praise, congratulations, awards, and, above all, in the satisfaction of having produced a work on the Guggenheim Fellowship. Now, as a result of the book, I got a second Guggenheim Award; later I received an award in criticism from the American Academy, and a few other items, such as the offer of an honorary degree which I was unable to accept, but the offer of which I thoroughly appreciated.

With my new Fellowship we went back to Europe in the spring of 1938; if we had not gone then, we would never again have seen some of our old friends, for the next year, 1939, war broke out, and though we had our tickets for Europe once again, we were advised by someone who knew what was happening not to leave America. As it was, people we were looking forward to seeing as we left New York were not living when we got over. In London, Lady Ottoline Morrell had died shortly before we got there, and the present I had brought her had to lie in my trunk. We saw her husband, Philip, living alone in their house, brooding on their life together, startled a little, I think, by the memoirs she had left behind, looking back with resentment at some of their exploiteering guests in Garsington Hall. The ones we saw most of in London were our old Dublin friends, James and Cynthia Stephens, and Arnold Bax. Arnold, now with a title, laden with honors as a leading English composer, had grown portly and was somehow changed from the old Arnold of our young married days in Dublin when he frequented Irish-speaking districts and wrote plays that out-Synged Synge and Irish poems and stories. London was different from the London we had known: some of the old publications like the *Nation* had ceased to exist, and the old-line publications like the *Spectator* had acquired sprightly new young editors; the *Criterion* and the *Mercury* had come to be looked down on: I think they also had new editors. And the poets we met were all complaining that there was now no audience for poetry, and that poetry reviewing was ignorant and filthy. One heard everywhere that this was not a literary age in Europe; some frankly said that they believed the future of literature in English was with America, but others declared that America was destroying the English language, there were so many writers of foreign descent, without an inherent knowledge of its rhythm, using it. As we walked the streets a lot of those we met looked poorly fed, with the bad teeth common in England and Ireland. As the war correspondent, William Shirer, said, the English had not looked after the health of their young men, and they did not compare in physique with the Germans. But I have no doubt they surpassed them in some imponderables that cannot be reckoned in any estimate or by any figures. The pure Anglo-Saxon type seemed to be disappearing—that tall, lean, fair-haired man who, maybe, was really Norman, and who used to be commonly encountered, seemed now to be largely confined to the aristocracy or to army officers.

In Dublin, my writing uncle, John Gunning, had died the very day I arrived, and so a link, the strongest link with my childhood, was broken. Others had gone before: Dr. Sigerson, Horace Plunkett, A.E., his wife Violet, and his friend and helper, Susan Mitchell—the three last had died of cancer. I do not think that in the end A.E. was entirely at home in the new Ireland; he had left it and gone to live in London, finally dying there, though his body was brought back. George Moore had been dead for a while, and his ashes scattered over his own Mayo. But Sarah Purser, now nearly ninety, was still going strong, and we went to a reception in her beautiful and well-remembered house. Douglas Hyde was still living and full of honors: we attended his inauguration as President of Eire in Dublin Castle. But the only members left of what had been called the Irish Literary Renaissance in Ireland were Yeats, Seumas O'Sullivan, and Lord Dunsany: Stephens was living in London, Joyce in France, my husband in America.

Now more faces were missing than during our last visit: the younger writers had been infants when we left, and some of them were the children of our friends of our young days. It was then twenty-four years since we had first left, and the change of atmosphere was very great. We were not staying long, as we had to go to Paris. Yeats asked us to dinner, but his sister Lolly warned us that it might excite him unnecessarily, for he would be sure to talk late, and that would be too much for his strength, as he was now seventy-three. So we asked if we might see him at tea in the afternoon instead.

As we sat for a minute or two in the library of his lovely little eighteenth-century house in Rathfarnham waiting for him to come downstairs, we wondered if he was much changed. But then we heard his step coming towards us in the old swift, eager way, and when he spoke, it was in his well-remembered, eager voice. As he entered we saw that one eye was covered with a black patch; he examined me as I stepped up to him. "We are both changed," he said to me, and he repeated his old remark. "You were once my ideal of a youthful nihilist." Now I knew I was no longer a slim girl; my gilt locks were approaching the color of a mist or a London fog, and the swift feet that could dance jigs and reels had to be supported by a cane—at least for a while and on account of my accident the year before.

But because the transition from teens to middle age is greater than from the thirties or forties to old age, I am certain I looked more changed to him than he did to me: in some ways he was almost entirely the same, except that his once raven hair was white; the old excitement was in his talk; the old reverence before intellectual achievement of any kind; then his humility as he talked of young men he knew, statesmen and writers, was strangely impressive in such a proud and arrogant spirit. He talked with lively interest of American poetry, especially of the poetry of Elinor Wylie and Edna Millay, about whose lives he had heard considerable gossip: he was not averse to a little gossip, and his humor could be very penetrating. I never saw any wit in him but he had that different thing, humor, though the two sometimes go together. I remember that he talked a good deal about Archibald MacLeish, but the poet he seemed most interested in was Stefan George. At first I was puzzled by this interest, but I discovered that someone had told him that George was responsible for some German political ideals and ideas. The old idea of the writer as leader and prophet was still with him; he always had thought that poets should influence their country, the life of their people and the state, whether they were politicians themselves or not. I do not think he knew much in detail about fascism, nazism, or communism, but his attitude towards all of them was one of eager curiosity. He certainly was no democrat: he always believed in a sort of elite who would serve their country; he had an idea not very different from one expressed by Dr. Carrel in *Man the Unknown*, that there should be a few trained and superior men who would devote their lives to the service of others.

"Never have I danced for joy," he wrote. Yet I am sure that he had not only a lucky but a happy life as far as one who feels strongly can be happy. At this time, of course, he was one of the famous men of Europe, surrounded with admiration: he had a devoted wife and devoted friends. Now for the first time I saw him in the role of a parent concerned with the future of his children: his daughter was present, and he talked about her work as a stage decorator with a father's interest. But as he conversed eagerly of many things, I saw he was tiring himself; the great psychic and physical energy that once had been his was no longer there or came only in flashes. Mindful of his sister's warning not to stay too long, I got up a little abruptly to take leave, but this seemed to sadden him, and he turned on us a slightly reproachful look: we promised that when we came back in the fall we would come to dinner and have a long talk once more. As we went away, he sank back tired and sad on his chair. I believe he thought he had not interested us, and he did not want us to go like that.

We never saw him again; he died in a few months, and the threat of war in France prevented our returning to Dublin. I never knew a greater mind or a greater man, one with such all-round endowments, such a variety of intellectual interests, or more generosity about another's gifts. He was always overpraising his friends; some of his swans were certainly geese, but, at the same time, if anybody injured or hurt him or someone close to him, he never forgot or forgave it. He was the most all-round Irish of all the Irish poets, not so much for the material he used, but for his expression of all sorts of innate emotions, attitudes, psychic qualities, racial ideas, Celtic chivalries. Of course his descent was not completely Irish, but it was Celtic, very different from the Anglo-Saxon, and consequently, in spite of devoted English friends, he was far less at home in England than almost any other Irish person I have ever known, less than A.E., less than Stephens. He was made by Ireland. "I am of Ireland," he wrote, "and the land of Ireland. Come dance with me in Ireland."

I do not recall a time when I did not know of him, or when I did not know his poetry, having learnt his more simple verses when I was a child. He was the first poet, the first famous person, I ever met. Then, in my early teens at boarding school, I was awakened by his poetry and plays from the half sleep, the almost wholly dream that is childhood. We had some few of those "correspondences" that Joyce gave such attention to: we both spent an impressionable childhood in the same section of Ireland and had childhood memories of the same places, the same legends, and some of the same people. I had once been cured of the scars of a bad burn by a relative of his who had inherited a mystic formula, "the cure of the burn." Then we had been born on the same date, June 13, I nearly a quarter of a century later, and he had a great belief in astrology and the influence of stars, planets, and the connection between people born under the same stars and planets and zodiacal signs. Of course, as I once informed him, Queen Victoria was likewise born on June 13, but he turned his head away at the information. In a manner, I do believe there is something in astrological influences; I know there are some faint likenesses between his interests and mine, something that makes me able to get inside everything, even the things that seem so esoteric to others, that he has written. In what must be a distant way, and as far as my intellect goes, I think I have, as he had, an interest in every manifestation of the human mind, but that may be because I came under his influence so early, at the most impressionable time of my life. From 1914 until his death I saw him only at rare intervals, perhaps a dozen times in all, yet he is for me still a reality such as were only one or two persons in my life.

ॐ CHAPTER 37

Uneasy Europe

We took an American liner which stopped at Cobh to discharge its Irish passengers and take on those for the Continent, and it was homelike to meet in the dining room and lounge Americans —teachers, professors on sabbatical leave—French hairdressers and waiters, Polish families and German families, all that diversity of nationalities that reside in America and save up to go to Europe once or twice in their lifetimes, either to imbibe culture, transact business, see relatives, or show American-born children to old-country grandparents. They had come from all parts of America, and the distance some of them had already traveled was immense —from California, Alaska, and one even from Hawaii. At Cherbourg it was pleasant to hear French voices once more and to be accosted by that peculiar Norman-French type of porter or railway official, the porters who are so bellicose and shout so loudly and demand such preposterous fees from Americans for carrying a suitcase, fees that one gives them to prevent one's ears from being stunned by their protests.

And it was pleasant to arrive in Paris and to go to a hotel where the employés remembered us, and to telephone the Joyces and other friends. Lucia Joyce was in a sanitarium outside Paris, but her father and mother promised we should see her. In a few days we settled down for the summer in an *appartement meublé* near the Etoile, an apartment of seven rooms, for the chief luxury I want in life is space, and maybe in the modern world that is the dearest luxury of all. As Paris, to my mind, is a collection of villages with palaces and houses of nobles and historic buildings joining them, we soon got to know our neighbors—the grocers, bakers, the café and drugstore owners, the shoe menders who are nearly always Italian, and the tailors and pressers who are nearly always Russian-Jewish. We thought we were settling down for the summer to that comfortable, easily lived life that was European, with plenty of service, and recreation always handy. But it had been nearly five years since we left France and six since we had been in Paris, and we soon saw that the change in France was greater than the change in Britain or Ireland. Restlessness and irresponsibility were in the air. The generation born during the last war, or not long before it, were now very much in evidence, and the old French virtues were conspicuously lacking in them. The middle-aged working people, the professional people, and the shopkeepers were the same hard-working, thrifty, polite people, but the younger generation seemed not to want to do anything except amuse themselves. Their childhood had been during the war years, and it was said that some of them had never been to school and had run wild in villages; they were unfamiliar with the old French discipline, the old French habit of orderliness and work; it was impossible to get a maid who could cook or who really wanted to do anything, and who did not mind walking out without notice if it suited her.

Then there was a sort of irresponsible radicalism everywhere: the waiters in the expensive hotels, a friend told us, were rude and inefficient, and insolent to Americans, and did not seem to care whether they were fired or not. Morale had visibly deteriorated. Our own experience showed an example of this: workmen from a warehouse who brought us a couple of trunks and tables that we had left in storage since 1932 spent the whole day delivering what American workmen would have accomplished in less than an hour; they took off two hours for luncheon and potations; then, before leaving, broke the elevator as an act of sabotage, intimidating the concierge so that he was afraid to complain. It was hard to get anything mended, and for days we had to walk up and down the seven flights to our apartment; there were numerous strikes; the banks and stores closed for a long week end; every sort of holiday was an excuse for closing for a day; idleness and a passion for amusement seemed to have seized the country. For all this there was a tendency to blame the Blum ministry which had brought in the forty-hour week: actually it all went back to the last war and to the fact that so many of the flower of young France had fallen in battle, so many out of a generation had been destroyed at Verdun that, as was said, one could feel the smell of corpses for years. What so many of the next generation had remembered was mostly disintegration—their fathers dead, their mothers unable to cope with life, their families' savings gone. Government officials went on making speeches—"France must get to work—all this idleness must stop." The standard of commercial honesty, never as high as in Anglo-Saxon countries, had lowered; in small shops and country busses one was frequently short-changed, and if any attention was drawn to this, an outburst of fury was the only result. Something was happening to that appealing French civilization, even to that old French patriotism and devotion to family life; the limitation of families had gone to an extreme; one saw very few children, and these seemed pale and unhealthy.

Paris was crowded with foreigners of all kinds and degrees; the most pathetic were old Orthodox Jews with beards, caftans, and skullcaps who, having rushed across the frontier, sat on seats in the boulevards, eating dry bread and sausages out of paper bags. The more fashionable restaurants were so crowded that one had to wait one's turn for a table, a common enough experience in New York, but rare in Paris in the old days. We did not go to them except as somebody else's guests; for ourselves, we liked those little restaurants that the moderate-income French go to and eat their little familiar dishes and salads and vin ordinaire, and where one can get a table without any waiting.

Since the illness of his daughter, I think Joyce liked to dine in places where there were lively crowds, and now went regularly to Fouquet's in the Champs Elysées, the haunt of celebrities of all kinds—high-class cocottes as well as stage and movie stars from all over the world. Though he could not with his poor eyes see many of the diners, he liked to be told who they were. Once when waiting for a table we were ushered to a bench, and I sat beside a tired-looking woman in a black suit without any make-up who looked so familiar that I began to ruminate on where I had seen her. Nora Joyce informed me, "You have seen her in the cinema; she's Marlene Dietrich." I am of an impulsive temperament, and before the reserved Joyce could intervene I had asked her, "Are you Madame Dietrich?" "Yes," she answered pleasantly, "and who, madame, are you?" I responded that I did a little writing. "Oh, then," she said eagerly, "you will like to meet M. Remarque," and she introduced the tweed-clad man with her. In return I introduced the man at my side, "M. James Joyce." The effect was electrical. I had not known that such a writer would be of interest to movie stars, but both she and, more naturally, Remarque were excited at the encounter and loath to leave when their table was announced. As the observant waiter gave us the table next them, we joined from time to time in the conversation. "I saw you," said Joyce as if he were speaking of something in history, "in *L'Ange bleu*." "Then, monsieur," she said, "you saw the best of me." Joyce was amused. "I thought the years when I was a lion were over," he said with his whimsical smile. A sort of melancholy had settled on him; he was on the last lap of *Finnegans Wake*, and, as was usual with him, was mobilizing helpers. But we did not see so much of him this time, as he and his family did not stay in Paris in the summer except for short intervals.

We saw some more of our old friends, particularly Charles du Bos. He now had an apartment somewhere near the Hôtel de Ville, and, astonishingly enough, a house in the Middle West of America, in Indiana. For, more remarkable than anything Time had done to any of the characters in Proust's *La Recherche du temps perdu* was what had happened to Charles du Bos. He had become a professor in the University of Notre Dame, and one can hardly imagine anything stranger than for this Proustian *gentilhomme* to be teaching young baseball players the subtilties of literature. There he was, talking pleasantly enough of his life in the Middle West, his wife and daughter and a couple of secretaries present, for he did not know how to live any way else except on a scale of lavishness. I wondered how long he could survive this new life; his leaving France for America, I felt, was something of a portent; it showed that a representative European intellectual was without prospect in his own country. A later visit to him before his departure for America was the last we ever saw of him, for he did not live long after that.

It was summer in Paris, and ordinarily Parisians leave the city in droves during the hot months, closing up their apartments, for subrenting was never a custom in Paris. Now more people than usual were staying; the streets were being decorated, hotels and palaces were being renovated, for the King and Queen of England were coming on a state visit, and neither money nor trouble was being spared to make their visit memorable. Fêtes such as must have surpassed any in the court of Versailles were being organized—land fêtes and water fêtes; dressmakers were working night and day to fill the orders for clothes; the troops got new uniforms; bands were rehearsing all the time. In the streets and cafés people said that all this was a sign of approaching war and showed that France was being cajoled to fight for England; others said, equally determinedly, that it meant that the Anglo-Saxon world was to fight for France and see that she was not overrun by Germans. The Queen, whose toilettes, by an inspiration of her dressmaker, were all in white, and the King, less gorgeous, drove through the city among cheering crowds. There were bands and marching men, speeches and banquets, and the Queen made no secret of her delight in every spectacle and was photographed with a look of girlish interest in all that was provided for her. But everybody was not equally delighted: there were vague rumors and suggestions in some of the newspapers that maybe the whole business did more to provoke Hitler and his entourage than it did to intimidate them with the grandeur and power of their neighbors. It must not be forgotten that there were many French—how many, I do not know—who were more in favor of Continental alliances, even with Germany and Italy, than with the island empire. This group seemed to be strongest south of Vichy. Somerset Maugham has in a book expressed his belief that the French really liked the Germans better than they liked the English, but then the Germans, and especially Hitler, liked the English better than they liked the French, better indeed, I think, than they liked any other people. Likes or dislikes seem to have nothing to do with wars.

At this time in Paris nobody seemed to know what was happening in Germany; it seemed odd that, about a country touching the frontiers of France as one American state touches another, the public and even the press seemed to have such little information. As we knew it might be a long time before we would be in Europe again, we decided to go into the Third Reich and see what it was like. But the resolve was easier than the putting into execution of it: it was difficult to get our passports visaed; the German passport office in Paris looked on us with suspicion; we were placed in a little room, and as our passports said we were writers, we were put through our paces as to what we proposed to write about Germany. Actually we were going to satisfy our curiosity and had no intention of writing anything. After some delay we got our visas and bought our "travel marks." The people at the Paris bank advised us to buy more than we first asked, as they told us we could not buy such in Germany. But this was only another example of the ignorance in Paris of Germany and its ways, for actually, on production of a passport and payment for what must have been an imaginary telegram to Antwerp to discover the travel mark's valuation on some exchange, we found we could get all the travel marks we wanted at any Deutscher Bank.

We started off, broke the journey at Strasbourg, which is German enough by race not to have made the change to Germany too abrupt, yet with a suddenness that was startling, as we crossed the Rhine we were cast into another civilization. The German crew who took the train over exuded another atmosphere and made it into a different train; they were taller, more confident, more vigorous, more efficient, and, oddly enough, they seemed rather more well disposed. We arrived at a little hotel in Baden-Baden so pleasant, so perfectly kept, and with a cooking that turned the rather meager German diet of the time into fancy meals, that later I did not wonder that some American soldiers in the second World War were more pleasantly impressed by Germany than by any other country. One young soldier I knew later came to his own conclusions, and I think as he revealed them they are worth repeating: "The Germans are awful in groups, but individually and in families, very likable, and more like Americans than other Europeans. The French are charming in groups, but individually are disagreeable, and sometimes even hostile." The manager of the Baden hotel was very far from being nazi in his politics and was outspoken in his criticism. "They are heading us for war," he told us in his American-acquired English: he had been years in the United States and wanted to get back. At Baden-Baden the regime was not very obvious, but there were a few unpleasant notices: "Die Juden sind nicht erwünscht." However, it was not followed very carefully,

I think, and I took pleasure in writing my name down as "Cohen" in a massage establishment, and even before the proprietor had gazed at my very Northern European countenance I got an appointment. Also I encountered in many places people whom I should have taken to be Jewish.

In Munich we arrived late at night and went to the first hotel which could take us in, as they were all crowded on account of the coming Nazi convention in Nuremberg. We never encountered a more disagreeable hostelry. The clerk at the desk examined our countenances with a slow, all-embracing gaze, and though we wrote our names down correctly in the register, it did really look as if the name might be Cohen. The next morning no amount of telephoning to the dining room would induce them to send us up our breakfast, that usual custom in Continental hotels; apparently our names in the register did not look as if we were all right according to the Nuremberg race laws. We got out as soon as we could get a room in another hotel, which we finally did in the fashionable Regina Palast. It was nothing but an attic room, but comfortable enough and reasonably priced. Here everybody was all courtesy and good breeding, with all the employees on such a footing of equality from the manager down, and all ready to do any old chore, that as far as a leveling process and the doing away with class distinctions were concerned, one might imagine oneself in a perfect democracy.

The swastika was not too prevalent, and I was positively startled the first time I heard "Heil Hitler!" In Baden we had not heard it at all. When I went into a little store in Munich to buy something, I was greeted by the fair-haired, rosy-cheeked girl behind the counter in the old way I remembered, "*Gruss Gott!*" Then, realizing she was confronting a foreigner, she pulled herself up and said slowly and impressively, raising her arm slightly, "Heil Hitler!" Like Paris, Munich seemed to be crowded with foreigners, especially young Americans, though once, when, having lost my way somewhere, I asked for direction from a stately young gentleman in a uniform that I thought might be that of an Elite Guard or something, I was answered with dignity. "*Ich bin nicht deutsch. Ich bin italienisch.*" I saw the Italian insignia on his uniform and apologized. But evidently there was a delegation from Italy for the Nuremberg Conference; afterwards I saw quite a few in that same uniform. A few days later there were more and more uniforms and in greater variety as men in regimental formation marched along the streets with bands, wonderfully trained and playing great music.

Outside Munich, we saw a labor battalion marching with spades on their shoulders and saluting an official who was reviewing them. It was an impressive sight; it made one feel for a moment that maybe the spade was on a level with the sword and the machine gun. But over it all there was a touch of the theatrical, as if everything was being staged for some effect. Then the figures in black uniforms and dramatic capes, leaning over in an attitude of woe, guarding the tomb of the sixteen men who had fallen at the famous Beer Hall *Putsch*, looked like a stage tableau. The lines of the tomb, the men guarding it, and the buildings that had been recently put up had a rigidity that was deathlike and quite at variance, quite counter to, the rest of Munich. But in the streets the young people looked gay and happy and well dressed, and, what was stranger, with the limited diet fixed by the government, well fed; their calories were probably scientifically fixed; they were taller, stronger-looking than the young people in the streets of London. Every night, the hotel was filled with smartly dressed young men and women who came to dance. In the country outside Munich there seemed to be dancing and singing everywhere, young people in the lovely costumes everybody in Bavaria seemed to wear. There must have been a good deal of hard work, but there seemed to be plenty of recreation, and the "Health through Joy" campaign there did not seem to be the foolish slogan that was mocked at in France and in America. There seemed to be a personal devotion to "*Unser Führer*," and when I once baldly referred to him as "Hitler" I was gently corrected: "*Der Führer, gnädige Fräulein.*" No more than in Paris, even less, did the average man in the streets and cafés think there was going to be a war. The churches were more filled than in France, but the theater offerings, outside music, were rather infantile. At a vaudeville theater a performance by young Americans was billed which, for pure meaninglessness, could hardly be beaten. What must have happened was that a resourceful group of American students, to get funds to take them someplace, had sold themselves to the theater in a piece they seemed to have concocted themselves and never properly rehearsed.

II

We got back to an even more restless Paris than we had left: that Nuremberg Conference was worrying everybody; Hitler was demanding that the Sudetenland be made part of Germany; war began to look as if it was a good way nearer. One early morning, after a sleepless night, disturbed by the rumbling of vehicles, I looked out of the window of my room and saw a number of delivery vans marked "Galeries Lafayette," "Printemps," and the names of other stores, with furniture vans, tearing along; the vans were covered, but I beheld the legs of uniformed soldiers hanging down at the back. Mobilization was on; the troops were being rushed to the Maginot Line. In other countries, too, mobilization was starting; there were complicated negotiations. One Sunday, coming back from a visit to friends in the country, we found the lights in Paris so dim that it was difficult to drive through the streets. Evacuation trains loaded with people were leaving for remote parts of France. Everybody was urged to leave who was at liberty to leave; those of us who stayed got instructions about air-raid shelters and what to take to them, and about gas masks. But I doubt if there were enough gas masks to go round one boulevard of Paris. A helpless-looking pile of sand was placed in front of our apartment house, for the extinction of bombs, I presumed. The inhabitants of the house were mostly Spaniards, refugees from the Spanish Civil War, and some of them had seen enough of airplane raids and bombings to have a fear of them in their souls. The concierge tried to encourage them to stay by telling them that in the case of a sudden raid they would have plenty of time to get to the shelter, as we on the top floor would be hit first. One calm and self-possessed señorita came up to ask me what we proposed to do, as the French people in all the houses around were leaving Paris, some headed for neutral countries—Switzerland, Holland, Ireland. I told her that we proposed to stay exactly where we were, war or no war. She was reassured, but I do not think I felt as confident as I sounded.

All the ships going to America were crowded, but our return tickets were on a North German Lloyd steamer, and the line had

stopped running. Some of the people in the avenues near behaved
with a curious demoralization; they fired ancient servitors and
made a rush for the non-warring countries; those who had ordered
clothes from the *grands couturiers* at the August openings canceled their orders. But I declined to cancel my little order at
Lelong's for a few of their cheaper garments; then, one day or
night, I forget which, we were notified by press, radio, telephone,
that the danger of war was over. M. Chamberlain and M. Daladier
had fixed up a peace with Hitler, and everybody went almost crazy
with relief. There was dancing in the streets, and champagne
poured in the cafés. The few inexpensive garments I had ordered
at Lelong's were turned out for me with a handsomeness of design
and material beyond original specifications, and they sent a tailor
and a fitter to my apartment to try them on. They were expressing
appreciation that I had been among those who had not canceled
orders.

But nevertheless there was uneasiness everywhere; one heard the
remark, "If they go on like this, they'll have to give him all Europe."
There was a general impression that the danger of war was not
over, but a breathing space had been gained.

The mobilized soldiers began to return; in the cafés they were
welcomed back, and some of them seemed harassed and ashamed
at what had happened; some believed Hitler was only bluffing
about a war, some said that within a year they would have to go
through the same mobilization again. It was a restless summer,
and I did not succeed in doing much on my Guggenheim Fellowship. As soon as the liners started again we prepared to return to
America; we could not pay a parting visit to Ireland as we had
promised, for lecture dates were summoning my husband back to
America. I left some of my Guggenheim money behind in a Paris
bank, so that I could return the next summer, 1939, to work in
tranquillity. I have seen neither France nor my money since; the
Germans annexed the latter. Many we knew congratulated us on
being able to return to America, leaving that insecure, tousled
Europe. Bidding good-by to some of our friends, as we went to
spend the night at the Hotel Terminus so as to catch the early
train at Gare St. Lazare for the boat at Cherbourg, I had an ominous feeling, but still I could not believe that men would be so

insane as to start another war. Early as the hour was, some friends came to see us off, and as we mounted the train I saw, away down the platform, Joyce stumbling along with his blind eyes, accompanied by Nora. As they reached our carriage he seemed sad and very lonely. "We don't want you to go," he said, "but anyhow you will be safe in America." As the train steamed out, we waved to him, calling "Au revoir." We never saw him again.

Back in America, we found people bewildered about what had happened in Europe, not understanding the compromise, perhaps at the time a necessary compromise, made by England and France. There is always a difficulty about America understanding Europe; it is too far away, and only a few Americans have ever read its history, its complex history, or laid eyes on its shores. In the hinterland the bulk of Americans don't want to be bothered about Europe at all, any more than Europe wants to be bothered about America. All they knew now was that a cowardly submission had been made to Hitler.

III

Great preparations were on foot for the New York World's Fair, which was to be the finest and grandest ever held; invitations were issued to crowned heads, princes and potentates, and important personages of every kind. The international organization of writers, the P.E.N., asked over the outstanding European writers; Joyce sent us the letter of invitation he had received; he was pleased to get it, but could not come; for one thing, he did not want to take his mind off *Finnegans Wake*, and for another he was no ocean-crosser. Yeats was invited, too, but before we knew whether he intended coming or not, we heard over the radio that he had died at Menton. Then, later, we knew that he had asked that his body be buried in the hill above Menton and then dug up after a year and transported to Ireland. Perhaps he expected that the Irish Government might pay their great poet the homage of officially bringing back his body, for writers always hope that their country will make some acknowledgment.

With Yeats's death the Ireland whose development had been accompanied by his plays and poems came to an end; another Ireland had taken its place. A little bit of one dies with the death of each of one's friends, but now, I think, quite a large bit of me went into dissolution. Joyce sent me a water color of that grave on the hill above Menton that some artist had sent him, remarking that there did not seem to be any wreaths on the grave except his, Joyce's, own, and one other. All the happenings of the year left me a little stunned, and I hardly remember the passing of the winter months. Then came the repetition in New York of a happening that the summer before had seemed a little ominous to some Parisians—the city was being prepared for the visit of the King and Queen of England, suites were being decorated in the White House and in Hyde Park; again one heard the same remarks in restaurants and cocktail bars, "A war is coming—these big men in Washington want a war," and then again, "We are not going to war; we do not want a war."

The fair and the hospitality to visiting guests was on a grand scale; there were dinners and receptions for all the notables and the visiting writers. As a matter of fact, to these affairs, which entailed overseas traveling, not so many important writers came; usually the organization was represented by minor members or a member whose vitality was not easily drained: the bulk of the important writers stayed at home, and a great number of the delegates seemed to be exiles of one kind or another who had already taken refuge in America. As the crowning social event, every member of the P.E.N. who was a delegate or a speaker at the fair was invited to luncheon at the White House. Everybody invited was pleased to go, native as well as foreign, for we were to meet the head of the state, one of the outstanding figures of our time. Early in the morning we got on the train with its special cars for the P.E.N., a little gadget with our names on it and ribbons floating from it, and "P.E.N." stamped in gold, fastened to our coats or our dresses.

"What is this?" asked a train conductor, gazing on our marks of identification. "It's sort of mixed, some of you folks don't speak English." "It's a real-estate convention," someone answered snappily, but the secretary of the P.E.N. took the conductor in hand and explained that we were all headed for the White House as luncheon guests, and he looked at us, duly impressed.

 క CHAPTER 38

A Luncheon at the White House

THE WHITE HOUSE itself is a beautiful building in beautiful grounds, but any moderately wealthy squire's house in Ireland would have exuded a more pretentious air once inside; the furnishings, particularly the bedroom furnishings, were of the sort that would have been in such houses—large, solid beds of Victorian vintage, armchairs with their coverings worn, books placed higgledy-piggledy in shelves, with their blurb jackets still on. But the sort of formality that pervaded any little middle-class household in the islands that used to be called the British was absent, including the formality of welcome. A cold chill blew on us as we entered; we were surrounded by an array of Negro retainers who took our hats and coats but who prevented us from going to the washroom or powdering our noses. When remonstrated with, one of the lackeys said that he was confused between the luncheon guests and the usual run of callers who merely came to view the White House, and that he had to take care that casual visitors did not enter the lavatories. The Polish delegate was armed with a notebook in which he diligently described every sight and every happening.

"On m'a dit toujours," said he to me as he scribbled away, "que les nègres sont opprimés aux Etats Unis, mais c'est tout le contraire, tous les laquais sont nègres; le président doit avoir une grande confiance en eux."

Indeed they all seemed to have an impassioned desire to preserve the President's life from some imaginary attacks, and they seemed to be afraid that, if admitted to a lavatory, some of us would place a bomb there. They herded us into a room where we all waited standing like people waiting before a barrier for a train. There was a constrained pause; the foreigners were bewildered; a good many of them in their own countries had been accustomed to official luncheons and dinners and to being wined and dined by state dignitaries; the French especially were used to it, and an uneasy chill fell on us in this small room without being able to sit down or even to talk much as we awaited the presence. At any such luncheon before that I had been part of, we had been warmly welcomed by a carefully dressed hostess in a friendly drawing room after repairing our looks in powder rooms, and had been served with sherry or cocktails before lunch. Of course this was a large luncheon, over sixty people, and so not easy for a hostess to cope with. After some minutes, huddled in the antechamber, we saw Mrs. Roosevelt enter, dressed in a plain shirtwaist frock.

"You will all go over first," she said, "to the President's office to shake hands with the President." She made a few more remarks which I forget, but which caused Harry Hansen to remark in a pleased tone, "She is putting us at our ease."

"But we are at our ease," said Nathalie Colby, who was beside me. We were not, as a matter of fact. Most of us by this time had got the impression that the mistress of the White House had asked us to luncheon as part of a duty she had to go through with as best she could, and her attitude was one of complete lack of interest, though she went through a routine politeness gracefully enough. But we might just as well have been the graduating students of the Sauk Center High School. Except from a few of the higher circles in New York and large cities generally, I have always received the unmistakable impression that in most places in America writers were really disapproved of or were regarded as a sort of romantic vagabonds who never did any work.

In the White House, certainly, the International Congress of the P.E.N. did not seem to cut much ice, and it must have been a trifle humbling for some of the beribboned foreign delegates who were great figures in their own countries and whose entrance into a room in Paris would have been received with delight by a flattered hostess. But then literature is very important in Paris, as important, or even more, than baseball here.

We crossed a lawn from the White House, entered the President's office, and were introduced to him one by one. The President shook hands with each of us as our names were pronounced. I was presented by Mrs. Henry Goddard Leach as "Mollie Colum."

"*Je le trouve un petit peu trop démocratique,*" somebody, a South American, I think, breathed in my ear.

The President was very handsome, very distinguished-looking, and very powerful; he did not look a man of iron or anything theatrical like that, but a man of extreme sources of psychic strength. I have seen hard-featured, iron-jawed men who looked as strong as lions but who could be reduced by some unexpected happening, but I have never seen anyone as strong-looking as this man—strong in mind, in body, in intelligence. Yet he lacked something that the men around us, particularly the foreigners, had: it was not temperament exactly, but he seemed to be all vigor and intelligence and lacking in emotional power as I understood it—a power of feeling for people as individuals. The same impression of strong intelligence, unimpassioned intelligence, that one finds common in America pervaded the White House. Still, as I watched the smiling eyes, the face that seemed incapable of betraying anything but a pleasant graciousness, somewhere behind there was an untried intensity that sometimes colored his actions and the language of his speeches. It was a generous face, the face of one with an aristocratic mind and an aristocratic lack of prejudices, but at the same time it was not an open face; one would have difficulty in guessing what was really going on in his mind, as one often has with New Englanders. One might be fooled by that ingratiating smile, but at the same time all his public actions would be as just as he could make them. He had no prejudices of race, religion, class, or sex; he was, in his administration, purposeful in his consideration of minorities. Though his name was an old New York Dutch one, both he and his wife seemed to me thorough New Englanders, and that means, among other things, that they had a power of concealing their feelings, a power of not revealing anything in their faces but a conventional graciousness. I have seen royalties look intensely bored, statesmen blaze with rage, aristocrats express their feelings with the frankness of people who were always sure of themselves, but a well-bred New Englander can keep a look of serenity, of patient graciousness, through any situation.

We all passed, one by one, by that inscrutable smiling figure as he remained seated in his chair, for his physical condition was such that he could not stand, but no signs of the paralysis that affected him were visible in that strong face. All trace of the extreme sensitivity shown in his early portraits, a sensitivity that some of his political enemies mistook for weakness, was gone from his eyes and the lineaments of his countenance. He had made strange conquests and fought strange battles, and the result was, as is sometimes the case in such conquests, an untroubled face, a smiling, almost carefree face—very carefree for the head of a great state. He had achieved an indifference to the slings and arrows of fortune; he had somehow achieved, too, perfect health in spite of the fact that he could not stand without being supported.

But something about him changed suddenly in me the old, nebulous, idealistic notions of democracy that had been the legacy from the fighting poets and teachers I had known in my youth. The face was totally different from a European face, different not only because European faces so often show an emotional fire, or the ashes of what had been emotional fire, but because of the amazing smile that was a combination of so many kinds of smile, and none of them evoked by any of the people he was addressing. All the smiles were a habiliment of state, a public decoration like orders on an ambassador or a star on a statesman. I had an uneasy conviction that I looked into the eyes of a dictator, different from other dictators the world has known, because no emotional lapses, no human passions, would divert him from his goal. And yet he was similar to the European dictators of this century in that he hardly regarded men as individuals no matter how much he was for the collective masses.

Pondering on the dictators, I could not help feeling that this was the master of them all—the master because of his lack of those confused personal emotions that dominate the men of Europe, but also because the past in America had a far less unbreakable mold. He might even make the past fit into his own scheme of things, he might even be able to overthrow a few forces out of that past, out of the tradition, by a suitable combination of smiles, a suitable arrangement of words, and a suitable service to various freedoms that the world associated with American ideals. The smile somehow showed that he did not believe that the past, or even the present, would ever rise and break him; no matter what happened there would be no tragedy for him; tragedy only pursues those who feel strongly, and in this it pursues the good and the evil man alike.

Pondering on him, I had wandered away from the rest of the group, and as with another loiterer I made an attempt to rejoin them, we were, in aggressive tones, ordered back by a commanding young man who seemed to be a private detective of some sort. He, too, regarded us, not as a collection of individuals, some few of whom were world-famous, but as a mass of humanity that had to be bent to his will. If one tried to go towards a table he put up a barricading arm and ordered us elsewhere. His performance took away the last illusion that we were guests. "This way, please," the young man would order in aggrieved tones, with a firm set face. Why, instead of that vigilant young man with his constant surveillance, were there not a few hostesses to help the mistress of the White House make these foreign visitors feel welcomed and at ease?

We sat down to lunch, I beside two diligently scribbling foreign delegates, in the state dining room beneath a portrait of Lincoln with his melancholy eyes fixed on us. Down all this went in the notebooks. The luncheon was at groups of little tables set with cheap crockery and silver; doubtless guests were in the habit of carrying away table utensils as souvenirs, and it was well that the burden of this should not weigh too heavily on the taxpayers. A large cup was at the right of each place, the use of which I did not grasp for some time. Soon it was cleared up: as the colored lackey first of all placed before us a cup of cold jellied soup, another came along and poured coffee into the cups. A cream pitcher and sugar bowl were on the table. Then I saw that, as the average American is supposed to drink coffee simultaneously with the main dish of any meal, the custom was being observed at the White House. The delegate to my right was intensely puzzled and did not at first realize that the hot brown liquid was coffee, but he had already noted down that the first course was consommé gelé, and on my explanation that the liquid poured into the cup was coffee, he wrote down that the second course was café crème. As we finished the soup a lackey handed us a plate with a slice of cold ham on a leaf of lettuce and another jellied substance of thicker consistency than the soup. The scribbling gentleman at my side wrote down, "*Hors d'œuvres—jambon.*" Evidently disappointed that nothing else followed except some ice cream, he wrote. "Après les hors d'œuvres, rien. Au déjeuner à Washington on ne mange rien sauf les hors d'œuvres." We had saved the coffee for the last, but it had become coldish and it but increased the feeling of chilliness that invaded us.

At the end of the luncheon Mrs. Roosevelt came in from her table on the terrace and announced that she would now show us the house. She explained the uses of the various rooms, but they all gave the sense of belonging to a deserted house, a little like those empty French or German castles that tourists visit, but without their age and stateliness. Even the homely Victorian walnut of the sitting room, the old-fashioned beds, the bright, gay Washington sunshine without, did not really give the impression that anybody lived there. Informality and democracy pervaded everything, but no warmth or hospitality. Both the President and Mrs. Roosevelt gave the sense that they regarded everybody as their equals and nobody as their inferiors or superiors; they were completely free from all snobberies. But for myself, I would not mind at all being looked down on by people if they would only regard me with some slight interest or make me feel pleased to be there. Again I heard that remark, this time in the undoubted French of Paris, and not of Warsaw or Buenos Aires, "un peu trop démocratique."

There was a complete lack of state, not anything like the formality that there used to be at the Viceregal Lodge under the Irish governor general, and nothing like the warmth. Mrs. Roosevelt was not one of those hostesses who learned everything about her guests beforehand from her secretaries, as the wives of certain heads of other states did and then discoursed fluently to them about their works or their interests, as I have known to happen many times. She showed, as far as I could see, no interest of any kind, feigned or otherwise; she was entirely without pretenses and, unlike New England women of her type, she was not only natural but genuinely simple, which perfectly natural people seldom are, for naturalness and unaffectedness are generally the result of both complex emotional and intellectual gifts and also of great experience. In Mrs. Roosevelt's case the naturalness was the result of experience: she had seen too much of the world and of people to think any pose worth while.

We left the White House marshaled once more by the detective-looking young man assisted by the secretary of the P.E.N. I saw a look of profound irritation on the face of one of the beribboned French delegates, a look of amused patience on another. We would have been allowed to hop into taxis in France in any order of our own, but I think the sense of all the freedoms is stronger there than anywhere else. Other countries in some matters may have a higher level of freedom, but there are more freedoms in France.

Before going on to a cocktail party we went to a hotel to eat a sandwich, for the White House fare left us hungry, and to powder our noses. The cocktail hostess was delightfully hospitable, and her house exuded a warmth that made us feel happy. It was delightful, as are all those houses where the hostess makes an art of living and of entertaining, and has the wealth to do it with beauty and lavishness.

৪ CHAPTER 39

Prelude to War

COMING BACK in the train from Washington, I encountered among the delegates some European writers I already knew. I sat near Ernst Toller, who looked sad and bewildered, and we listened to some of the others discuss the President tactfully and remotely, very differently from the frank criticism and disagreement that were voiced on the seats behind, where the delegates were all Americans of differing political convictions. We had certainly seen a great man, and maybe a great woman, both of a type that, on my part, I was not really equipped to appreciate. I have somewhat of a prejudice against persons with great political power or authority, and I have a notion that democracies will sometime find a way out of delegating such vast power to a few individuals, leaving the rest of us docilely following whatever programmes they arrange for us. There was some talk of approaching war which made poor Ernst Toller more bewildered and more sad, but the writers soon got back to things connected with their own jobs—writing, lecturing, publishing. The bulk of the delegates had, I think, not written anything of earth-shaking importance, for at such congresses too few important writers are apt to be present; they are likely to stay at their desks. There were too many novelists, and of these several were of the simple fictioneering class; there were no outstanding English writers, and too few Americans, so that the Europeans kept asking, "Why have we not met Hemingway? Willa Cather? Sinclair Lewis? Frost? And why were they nowhere to be seen?" For some reason American writers take less readily to anything co-operative than Europeans, and this is a pity, because, for one thing, it detracts from their influence on public affairs. There were a couple of English writers who had been fighting in Spain—Spain at the time was all the rage—but I do not think they knew exactly why; there were others who had helped Spain by staging auctions of their manuscripts, but what sort of aid this was I could not estimate. However, from the way a couple talked of the prices their manuscripts had gone for, they seemed to be more interested in their manuscripts than the cause.

In the dining car later I was approached by a heavy-faced man who had saluted me in the distance in the White House and whose Slavic face seemed vaguely familiar. As he took the chair beside me at the table he assumed that I knew him, and as he was obviously of some Central European nationality I guessed I had met him somewhere abroad, but not being able to place where, I asked him point-blank where we had last met. "Well, the very last time was in a box at that wild Trocadero meeting which ended that Disarmament Congress."

Then my memory cleared up: we had indeed, this man and myself, met every day for a week at the end of 1931 in the sessions of the International Congress for Disarmament at the Palais Royale in Paris, to which we had both been delegates. I remembered certain happenings with a sharp clarity, for of all the groups I had ever met to further a cause, the delegates at that congress seemed to have the least capability, or even zeal, to push towards the ostensible ends. Yet it had been attended by persons from all over the world and by world-famous statesmen—Lord Robert Cecil,

Herriot, Paul Painlevé, Paul Boncour—representatives of the League of Nations, well-known pacifists from every country, idealistic leaders from pre-Hitlerian Germany. The man who now took the seat beside me, whose name I could never spell or even pronounce, whom I shall call "Mr. X," and myself had not been important delegates—in fact I have a notion that we belonged to the most futile group of all, representatives from university organizations, some of whom, particularly a number of the American delegation, did not understand French. As all the speeches in no matter what languages were immediately after delivery turned into French by the astonishing League of Nations interpreter on the platform, it so happened that some of our colleagues, ignorant of the language, were frequently in the dark as to what was being discussed or what the discussion was leading up to. Mr. X and myself had found ourselves on one of the subcommittees that held meetings in an anteroom for a short period every day for the purpose of concocting resolutions and rules for the prevention of war and the reduction of arms and armaments. The goings on of the delegates were supposed to produce some notable effect on the League of Nations Disarmament Congress, which was to take place in Geneva soon after. Mr. X was in some way connected with the Committee of Intellectual Co-operation of the League of Nations and was to write an account of the proceedings at the Palais Royale for some Geneva publication. I was to write an account for the *New Republic* of New York, and before the end of the week we had both been rebuked for our pessimism and cynicism by a couple of the hard-working women who had labored to get the congress together. They were worried about what he would say in Geneva and what I might write for the American publication, though I assured them it would not make much difference what I wrote, as what the American newspaper people present cabled would have a thousand times more influence.

Mr. X, now taking his dinner beside me in the dining car, really did know a good deal about high European politics—imperialisms, colonies, armaments, and such things. What I knew of arms or armaments would have fitted in the eye of a needle, and as for the classification of battleships and the strength of navies that came up in the discussion, I did not know the difference between a corvette, a cruiser, and a first-class battleship, and was really astounded at how few big ships the navies contained, especially the British, as I had thought battleships ran into the tens of thousands, and not just into a few first-class fighting ships and so on. However, our subcommittee soon got off ships and concentrated on peace and disarmament proposals. My companion remembered more of what I had said than I remembered of what he had said, for the reason that he thought I was unpractical, perhaps entertainingly so, and that a resolution I had wanted to put forward, to the effect that incitement to war be made an offense punishable like murder, burglary, or sedition, naïve and unworkable. Personally I did not see that mine was as naïve as some of the other proposals, and something similar to mine, it turned out, had been presented by another subcommittee. However, I was willing to admit that I was that person I despise in literary or artistic affairs, the amateur.

I was not the only amateur: too many of the delegates were, as I said to him then, of a kind who would have gone to any other congress, say a nudist congress, a temperance congress, or an antivivisection congress, with the same interest. And here, as if to prove what I had said, were myself and Mr. X delegates to the P.E.N. congress. My especial contribution to the present one was to make a speech at a conference in a hall at the World's Fair grounds explaining that literature could not be propaganda for opinions—an idea which always annoyed those whose stock in trade was Marxist literary criticism, a form of intellectual gymnastics it would be difficult to associate with Marx, who knew a great deal about literature, as his writings and correspondence reveal. My especial feat in that subcommittee, years before, was to announce that there was too much propaganda, too many prejudices among the delegates, that too many national axes were being ground, and there I had aroused antagonism, too. A Polish delegate to the Paris conference, apparently a well-known person, had declared from the platform that he could not abandon the love of his country for the love of mankind. There were others who would not abandon more selfish attachments for the love of mankind or the love of peace or reduction of armaments.

The diversity of prejudices, of opposed interests, had been alarming; there was a distinct prejudice among the rank-and-file delegates in favor of the big battalions, of the big three or the big four, or some such numeration. One encountered every sort of anti—anti-Semitic, anti-Catholic, anti-Oriental, anti-capitalist, and some stout anti-democrats. But the strong currents of anti-Russianism and anti-Germanism were, as far as the success of the congress was concerned, the most fatal antis of all. Too many people wanted to keep somebody else or something else out. Strange as it all was, I should not be at all surprised if the whole thing did not have a make-up similar to those more grandiose shows staged by history from time to time for settling the affairs of the world—the Congress of Vienna, the Conference of Versailles, and our own U.N., and that is why, in this last chapter, my mind keeps running on my one and only venture into high political discussions; in that one week I learnt more about people's national biases and the way countries rule themselves than in a lifetime spent among artists and intellectuals.

Of the higher order of delegates, statesmen and men who run their countries' affairs, each seemed to be too much tied up with the special interest of his own country or even of his own political party, or with imperialism—"we'll keep what we have"—to be of much real use in a congress of this kind. Then there were blocs who blocked matters; there was a section of the British-American bloc anxious to see that Germany got no chance of rising again; at the time nobody paid much, if any, attention to what Russia might do in the future, and I do not think there was a single Russian delegate present. There was a sort of British-German bloc who seemed to be the most serious of all about keeping the peace as the French seemed to be the least: the French watched all of them with a suspicious eye. The delegates from the small Continental nations—Belgium, Holland, Greece—seemed to contain the only representatives of that personage who used to figure in liberal periodicals—the good European—and they were the most open-minded and had the most human wisdom of all.

As Mr. X and I recalled our experiences, the others at the table occasionally interjected a remark, and somebody hesitatingly ventured an interrogation: "Do you think the next war will be soon?"

My companion's answer was prompt: "Yes, I do think so—in a couple of months." "This country will not go into another European war," said somebody else, for by this time our conversation had attracted the attention of neighboring tables. "France will not go into another war, either," I said blandly; "the relief over Munich last year was too great." "All this may be true," said Mr. X. "Still there's going to be a war. Too many stupidities have occurred." "But who is going to fight whom?" "In the beginning, perhaps Germany and Russia," answered Mr. X. This recalled to me that at that congress there seemed to be a stronger undercurrent of anti-Russian sentiment among the German delegation than among the others. One of the German delegation, Baron von Rheinbaben, had created a sensation by declaring off the platform that a certain country that had war reserves of four and a half million returned as its official figures twelve thousand. We figured out that on the basis of the population that he must have meant Russia. Then an angry man on the platform turned on him and accused Germany of having arranged her factories and industries in such a way that they could be speedily turned into instruments for making arms and ammunition. When Dr. Schreiber, of the German Center party, read a carefully thought out paper, he was interrupted and mocked at by the audience, though it was obvious that no man could be more anxious to keep the peace of Europe. All this was a year before Hitler, and pre-Hitlerian Germany was not getting much of a chance from anybody, so that, maybe, it was no wonder that all that was left for it was the Nazi party.

The end of the whole congress proceedings was the public meeting at the Trocadero which my companion had recalled as he sat beside me. There the platform had been well staged for a real plea for peace and disarmament; M. Herriot took the chair, the English ambassador sat beside the German ambassador, the ministers from the smaller states were well in evidence, the roster of speakers included distinguished men from all countries—Alanson Houghton from America, Lord Robert Cecil, M. Painlevé, M. de Juvenal, Madariaga from Spain, Scialoja from Italy, one or two well-known German pacifists. But except for a few remarks from Lord Robert Cecil there was no hearing for anybody. Unexpectedly the audience got into an angry uproar, and we could not help but see there was a prearranged attempt to disrupt the proceedings. The members of the Action Française, that organization headed by Daudet and Maurras, and the Croix de Feu, headed by Colonel de la Roque, stamped, booed, sang the Marseillaise, waved flags, and successfully prevented the meeting from getting anywhere. The French audience, it seemed, wanted no demonstration for peace, and what started as a Congress for Disarmament wound up with a demonstration that looked in favor of war. I never before was in the midst of such a melee. It was the kind that in an Anglo-Saxon country would have ended up with dead and wounded. But nobody hit or killed anybody.

The man now beside me, Mr. X, was seated in the same box as I with other delegates, and I remember saying something to him to the effect that if incitement to war had been made a penal offense, Daudet, Maurras, and De la Roque could have been gaoled that very evening. Maurras, as it happens, is, as I write this, in gaol as a *collaborateur*, as well as some of those who made the demonstration against peace in the Trocadero.

At Pennsylvania Station Mr. X bade me good-by in almost the same words he had used eight years previously, "There is a craze for war in the world." It happened that, a short time before, my husband had engaged our passage for Europe, and we had planned to sail in a week or two, I to use up what remained of my Guggenheim Award which lay in a Paris bank to work on a book, my husband to work on a play. Now when I got back from Washington at midnight he was waiting up for me, and I told him of Mr. X's warning about the coming war. The previous summer in France had been too disrupting to face another similar one, and we talked about canceling our tickets and staying at home. In the morning a telephone message from Mr. X, whom I have never seen since, decided us. "I would advise you not to leave America. Peace is a vain hope." We canceled our passages sadly enough. Then I spent ten dollars in sending telegrams to some few people who I thought might have influence, begging them to use whatever powers they had to stop the approaching war. How could anybody who knew Europe contemplate the effects of another war? Not only materially, not only in the dead and maimed and separated, but in the terrible psychic effects that were bound to follow—the frustrated rage and vengeance of the defeated turned against the helpless because they could not be turned against the strong. In 1933, and again in 1938, I had, like many others, spent sleepless nights after seeing the hopeless faces of the persecuted who crossed the border into France; the richer ones could take their possessions and sail for America, but the poor ones had to use their feet to make their way to the nearest friendly country and live as best they could. I was sure that whatever country was defeated in the coming war would also become a persecutor.

We took a small bungalow in Connecticut for the summer; it seemed as if every time we turned on the radio we heard some dispiriting news—the suicide of Ernst Toller, the death of Charles du Bos, accounts that we could not then believe of the cruelties of concentration camps. Then suddenly, ominously, came the news of a German-Russian agreement. Not long after—how long, I don't remember—we turned on the radio and heard a vigorous German voice talking of the offers, or to demands on Poland. Then came the invasion of Poland from both sides and England's declaration of war with Chamberlain's sad speech. He could have no heart for war, and it was no surprise when he later resigned as Prime Minister in favor of Churchill. A war was on, to be unimaginably more awful than the last. Europe was out to destroy itself!

When France fell less than a year later I think I wept for a week: later the newspaper pictures of five hundred bombed bodies buried in a common grave in Coventry made friends of mine sob over the telephone as we spoke of it. Soon things got to be such that neither our emotions nor our imaginations could take them in, as one form of destruction piled on another. . . .

I had not heard from the Joyces for some time, and the second World War was on. Then, in reply to a letter of mine, I received from Joyce what was to be the last communication we had from him. He wrote: "It is plain that you know nothing of the second calamity that has befallen my family. X's catastrophic collapses have spread around her ruin moral and material which seems to me irreparable." This letter came from Vichy, to which he had retreated from Paris when the war started. It was so full of sorrow that I did not see what armor was left him with which to fight fate. He died shortly afterward in Switzerland as the result of an operation. But what will to live could a man have who had endured so much?

II

The great facts of the world of my mature years have been wars and destruction—they have crushed everything else out of sight. Before 1914 the most important thing in the world I knew was literature—I suppose we lived in an ivory tower. When a famous writer died the newspapers were bordered with mourning and pages were given over to his life and works. Now, if a column or half a column is given to an artist or any intellectual, it is the most. People who have grown up since 1914 cannot comprehend the tranquillity, the happiness, and the possibilities that were before youth in Europe at the beginning of this century. As one who has lived through the two most destructive wars that the world has seen, and as a member of a number of futile organizations that tried to prevent the last war, I, like many others, have pondered on what is wrong with a world in which such disasters can happen and why scientists have given their genius to the forwarding of destruction and why intellectuals have allowed themselves to be fitted into this destructive pattern. If my conclusions seem naïve, they are not, I think, the conclusions of one who is inexperienced or unintelligent, and if they appear platitudinous, they are not, I think, the conclusions of one who has lived platitudinously or inertly.

I think the most dangerous things in the world and the ones that have caused continual turbulence are the inequalities, the senseless, man-made inequalities that could be done away with—social inequality, economic inequality, race inequality, sex inequality—they mean not only unhappiness, but terrible waste. It may be suggested that after these inequalities are abolished, the real inequalities begin, and with that I agree. But the others are inherent inequalities which have always benefited the race—inequality of mind, of emotional powers, of strength, or of beauty. In our time it looks as if economic equality is the one we are first headed towards abolishing. But I believe, of all the inequalities, sex inequality may have caused the most waste. The spectacle of a number of males, mostly white in color, seated around a table, deciding the future of the world with not only some races left out, but the whole of one sex, makes our democracy farcical. Where world affairs are concerned, even in those matters which have always been considered as belonging to a woman's sphere, like food supplies in army and navy commissariats, women were given no responsibility, and as our returned service men tell us, food was squandered hopelessly and spoiled recklessly.

I think there is no superior race or superior sex; there are only superior or inferior individuals. While I believe a prejudice such as anti-Semitism is a communicable psychic disease like war incitements, and consequently could be stamped out if tackled properly as physical diseases are tackled, sex bias, like color bias, is a habit based on the fact that the occupations of women, as of the colored races, have been too largely of the servile kind. Sex bias has existed everywhere, in every country, in every age, and among all races. But there have been countries unacquainted with anti-Semitism. I do not think men are spiritually stronger than women, or more courageous, or more intelligent. But they have been physically stronger and, at least in the past, have had greater endurance, though the difference in physical endurance may grow less and less. Then, if as much energy had been turned on trying to find out, in a rough way at least, what makes people happy as has been turned on inventing weapons of destruction, there would be less inhumanity. There are imponderables, of course, that could not be coped with, but some more general distribution of the means to happiness could be undertaken. Then the craze for conformity, for uniformity, the passion to make people all have the same religious or political principles, the same social habits, has always been a great cause of trouble. There never have been so many books before telling us how to act the same, think the same, look the same. There have been religious wars in the past; now we have political wars, wars of one collectivity against another. When Germany was persecuting and banishing the Jews, her own citizens, we did little but pass resolutions; but when it looked as if some political ideology different from ours was making headway, we went to war. I have not enough respect for the reasons for which men make war, any war. A leavening of women in high places might make things very different. I think if countries want to be democratic, communist, or fascist in their governments, it is their affair, but they ought to leave other countries alone, and if they persecute whole sections of their people, some aggregation of states should have power to stop it. These may not be any startling truths to have arrived at, but they are those to which I give strong allegiance.

Index